REAL ESTATE
and the FEDERAL
INCOME TAX

ALAN R. CERF, Ph. D., C. P. A.
UNIVERSITY OF CALIFORNIA AT BERKELEY

PRENTICE-HALL, INC. Englewood Cliffs, New Jersey

PRENTICE-HALL SERIES IN REAL ESTATE

To my wife

Lila

and to

*Robert
Douglas
Jeffrey
Richard
Nancy*

PRENTICE-HALL INTERNATIONAL, INC., *London*
PRENTICE-HALL OF AUSTRALIA, PTY., *Sydney*
PRENTICE-HALL OF CANADA, LTD., *Toronto*
PRENTICE-HALL OF INDIA (PRIVATE) LTD., *New Delhi*
PRENTICE-HALL OF JAPAN, INC., *Tokyo*

Library of Congress Catalog Card No.: 65–25226

Printed in the United States of America
76267-C

Preface

A prime objective of this book is to explain a complex subject comprehensively and in simple terms—to give the reader the understanding he needs to project the tax implications of his real estate decisions and to sharpen his judgment concerning the equity aspects of the law.

The essentials of the tax law are the foundation for the book. From this basic foundation, the book proceeds to special areas of interest such as shopping centers, subdivisions, cooperatives, and condominiums. The problem areas of depreciation recapture, of dealer status, and of personal holding companies are covered.

Each subject is unfolded carefully and is developed in depth. No previous background is assumed. Because it is particularly important to consider the tax implications of a decision before the decision is made, special stress is placed on the tax-planning aspects of real estate transactions. The law is put into a decision-making context and is related to decisions. Numerous examples are provided to illustrate appropriate points of law. Exercises and problems are included so that the reader may test and clarify his understanding of primary areas.

Besides its expected use by the student of real estate, the real estate broker, and the casual investor, this book should prove useful to the practicing attorney and to the practicing accountant who does not specialize—but is sometimes involved—in real estate transactions. The complexity and dynamic nature of the subject make this book an especially valuable reference for the nonspecialist.

I wish to thank my colleague, John Denton, for helping to stimulate my original interest in the subject. I am similarly indebted to Professor Paul Wendt, Director of the Center of Real Estate and Urban Land Economics at the University of California.

For their review of the manuscript and for their valuable comments, I am indebted to Karl F. Venter of the University of California Extension; Maurice C. Iddings, Attorney and Realtor; and Daniel Lempres and Marvin T. Levin, Attorneys.

I am grateful to Stuart Gould, a Ph.D. candidate, and to John Ellingsen and James Singleton, graduate students, for help in preparing the problem material. My thanks to Ann Kauth and her staff for aid in preparing the manuscript.

ALAN R. CERF

iii

Contents

is given; "Boot" is received; Gain recognized on receipt of "boot"; *No loss recognized on receipt of "boot";* Basis of the property when "boot" is received; *Potential gain—"boot" received in form of money; Potential gain—"boot" received in money, trade for more than one piece of property; Potential loss—"boot" received; "Boot" received—loss not recognized, allocation required; Potential gain—"boot" received, allocation required.* BASIS OF PROPERTY WHEN LOSS IS RECOGNIZED. EXCHANGE OF PART BUSINESS, PART PERSONAL ASSET. MORTGAGES AND TAX-FREE EXCHANGES: Mortgage on property transferred only; Mortgage on both parcels of property; Basis of property when both parcels in exchange are mortgaged; Brief review. TRANSFERS TO CONTROLLED CORPORATION. MULTIPLE EXCHANGES. INVOLUNTARY CONVERSIONS: Examples of involuntary conversions; Condemnation and threat of condemnation; Not considered involuntary conversions. DETERMINATION OF GAIN OR LOSS: Direct conversion; Making an election; Time limit on replacement. STANDARDS FOR REPLACEMENT PROPERTY. REQUIREMENTS OF REPLACEMENT PROPERTY: Similar or related in service or use; Special rule for condemnation of real property. LEASEHOLDS. CALCULATION OF GAIN AND LOSS: Meaning of proceeds; Identical proceeds; No taxable gain on direct conversion; Gain partially recognized; Elect to have entire gain taxed; Loss recognized; No gain recognized. BASIS OF PROPERTY ACQUIRED BY INVOLUNTARY CONVERSION: No gain recognized because of direct conversion; Basis of new property when loss is recognized; Basis of new property—gain recognized; Allocation of basis; No gain recognized—cost of replacement greater than proceeds. USE AND OCCUPANCY INSURANCE PROCEEDS. SPECIAL ASSESSMENTS AND SEVERANCE DAMAGES IN CONDEMNATIONS: Special-benefit assessment; Severance damages; Consequential damages. EASEMENTS: Involuntary conversion of residence.

native tax. SECTION 1231 TRANSACTIONS: Property used in trade or business; Additional Section 1231 transactions; Brief look at depreciation recapture; Basic treatment of 1231 assets on tax return; Example of Section 1231 calculations; Clarification of Section 1231 categories; *Items subject to involuntary conversion; Not covered by insurance; Property condemned for public use; Timber; Disposal of timber under a contract; Livestock; Unharvested crops; Coal.*

tages of accelerated depreciation methods. OTHER METHODS OF DEPRECIA-
TION: Unit-of-production method. ADDITIONAL FIRST-YEAR DEPRECIATION
ALLOWANCE: Qualifying property. USEFUL LIFE OF DEPRECIABLE PROPERTY:
Depreciation guidelines; Guideline lives and real estate; Useful lives of
vehicles; Land improvements; Agricultural lives; Buildings; Contract con-
struction; Recreation, amusement, and services; Reserve-ratio test. AGREE-
MENTS ON USEFUL LIFE. INCREASED USE OF PROPERTY. OBSOLESCENCE. IN-
VESTMENT CREDIT.

IMPROVEMENTS BY LESSEE—EFFECT ON LESSOR: Improvements a substitute for rent; Opportunity for planning. CANCELLATION OF LEASE: Bonus to lessor; Bonus to lessee; Bonus from landlord for cancellation—capital gain to tenant; Opportunities for planning. ASSIGNMENT OF LEASE AND SUBLETTING: Assignment of lease; Subletting; Cost of acquisition to purchaser; Purchase lease—part of cost for improvements; Abandonment of leasehold improvements; Assignment or sublet—planning considerations. LEASE WITH OPTION TO BUY: Possible advantages; Manipulation of terms; Possible disallowance; Conditions generally resulting in sale rather than a lease; Transfer of title not essential; Lease classified as a purchase—can still get accelerated depreciation; Planning in leases with options to buy; Planning— evaluation of risk. LEASING LAND ONLY.

of individual form; Corporate election to have income taxed directly to shareholders; Dummy corporation; Variety of noncorporate ownership. TITLE TO REAL ESTATE FOR INDIVIDUALS: Income tax—joint tenants; Income tax—tenants in common; Not a partnership for tax purposes; Joint tenancy—estate tax; Community property—estate tax; Tenancy in common—estate tax; Gift tax considerations. PARTNERSHIPS IN GENERAL. TAXABILITY OF GROUP ENTERPRISES: Associations; Syndicates and pools; Limited partnerships; Tenants in common; Partnership associations. TAXABILITY OF PARTNERSHIP INCOME: Deductions not allowed to a partnership; Items not figured in determining taxable income; Salaries and interest paid to partners; Comparison of book income and taxable income; *Income statement; Segregation; Tax return.* PARTNERSHIP ITEMS INCLUDED IN PARTNER'S INDIVIDUAL RETURNS.

property to corporation; Effect of services rendered; Disproportionate transfers; Effect of assumption of a liability; Liability in excess of basis; Gains from depreciable property; Problem of depreciated property mortgaged in excess of basis; Taxable incorporation. DIVIDENDS: Constructive dividends; Stock dividends; *Taxability; Effect of stock dividend on basis;* Corporate transactions in own stock; Property dividends; *Special rules;* Effect on corporation of property dividend; *Property dividends resulting in tax to corporation; Property subject to a liability; Section 1245 property.* REDEMPTION OF STOCK: Exchange or dividend; Redemptions that are dividends; Distributions to pay death taxes and expenses.

CAPITAL GAINS TAXATION FOR CORPORATIONS: No deductions for net capital loss; THIN INCORPORATION: Example of thin incorporation. COLLAPSIBLE CORPORATIONS: Meaning of a "collapsible corporation." ACCUMULATED EARNINGS TAX: Penalty surtax; Purpose to avoid income tax on shareholders; *Reasonable anticipated needs; Burden of proof;* Action to avoid the accumulated-earnings tax. PERSONAL HOLDING COMPANY PENALTY TAX: Rates of tax; Definition of a personal holding company; *Stock-ownership requirement; Personal holding company income; Inclusions in PHC income; Dividends, interest, royalties, and annuities; Gains from capital assets and Section 1231 assets; Taxable income from estates and trusts; Personal-service contracts; Certain payments for use of corporate property; Rents under the old law; Rents under the new law; Example of change in handling rents; Mineral, oil, and gas royalties;* Base for imposition of tax; Opportunity to liquidate. DUMMY REAL ESTATE CORPORATIONS. AFFILIATED AND RELATED CORPORATIONS: Reasons for filing a consolidated return; Inclusions in an affiliated group; Election is binding. MULTIPLE CORPORATIONS: Disallowance of surtax exemption; *Rule tightened; Meaning of control for individual transferee;* Allocation of income, etc., by Revenue Service; Acquisition of corporation to avoid tax; Tax alternatives for multiple corporations; *Corporations included; December 31 the crucial date; Dividing a surtax exemption;* Six per cent penalty tax; Dividends-received deduction of 100 per cent; *Consequences of election.* LIQUIDATION OR SALE OF STOCK: Sale of stock; Liquidations; *Partial liquidation;* Liquidating dividends—taxability; *Shareholder's gain or loss; Possibility of ordinary income; Gain or loss to liquidating corporation;* Twelve-month liquidation; *Depreciation recapture; Inventory property;* Liquidate and distribute property to shareholders; One-month (Section 333) liquidation; *Strict requirements; Qualified stockholders; Some gain is taxed; Basis to stockholders; Depreciation recapture makes liquidation dangerous;* CURRENT INFORMATION AND COMPETENT ADVICE.

Federal Income Tax
and Real Estate Decisions

If you are a homeowner or aspire sometime to be a homeowner, you are affected significantly by the federal income tax.
When you read Chapter 9, you will see the tax advantages which
the homeowner has as opposed to the renter of a home.

Those who have excess funds remaining when their con-
sumption needs have been met have the alternative of investing in
real estate as one choice among many as a deposit for their savings.
The purchase of a house or of shares in a cooperative apartment is
an investment. Small investors may join together with others in
various kinds of syndicates to invest in real estate. Some will invest in small limited partnerships, others will buy shares of public
real estate corporations, and still others will purchase shares of
beneficial interest in real estate investment trusts.

Some investors will purchase raw land with the anticipation
that it will increase in value. Others will build or purchase rental
units, which may be single-family residences, duplexes, or four-
plexes--all the way up to the high-rise apartment house. Some of
these investors will hold title to their property as tenancy in common
or in joint tenancy. In other cases, partnerships will be involved,
or the corporate form will be used. Where rents are not an important source of income, the form of ownership may be the corporate form with an election to avoid the corporate tax.

These investors in making their investments will be moti-
vated by a variety of factors. Some will attempt to maximize their
over-all rate of return on their investment in the long run. Others
will be concerned primarily with current spendable income. Various people in different circumstances will be willing to take dissimilar amounts of risks.

It is difficult to conceive of a real estate investment that is
not influenced in some manner by federal income taxes. The purchase of a home means that a taxpayer is able to deduct mortgage

interest and real estate taxes in arriving at taxable income. He may postpone tax on any gain on the sale of the residence by reinvesting the proceeds according to certain requirements. If he is over 65 years of age and the sale proceeds are within certain limits, there will be no tax on the gain on sale of a house.

TAX CONSIDERATIONS

The tax advantages of real estate investments have been praised by many. Many a professional man at his peak earning period of life who is attempting to plan for security at his retirement has invested in real estate so that the combination of current depreciation deductions and leveraged financing would give him some current tax-sheltered income and also the prospect that on retirement he would be the owner of appreciated property that could be sold at a capital gain.

An investor has certain alternatives in the use of his funds. Although he will be influenced by a variety of considerations, depending on his particular circumstances, the return on his investment will most certainly be important to him. The crucial fact is that the federal income tax is not neutral in investment decisions. The before-tax consequences and the after-tax consequences of a decision are not the same. The rational investor, therefore, must do his best to consider the after-tax consequences rather than the before-tax consequences of his investments. Surely in certain cases the law is such that he will not be able exactly to project these consequences. In a number of instances, we shall point out where different courts have come to dissimilar decisions on the same point of law. Of course, the basic difficulty of making any income projections in the future makes it difficult to project consequences even if there is no question about the law. Nevertheless, many a dollar would be saved if an attempt were made to project tax consequences of decisions before the decisions are made, rather than at the time when an Internal Revenue Agent is examining the records of the taxpayer.

In the United States we have a voluntary self-assessment system of taxation. Under this system of taxation each taxpayer has rights, and he also has obligations. Just as a builder will take great pains to ensure that his building has a sound structural foundation, so should the investor also exert the same effort to determine the tax implications of his projects. Just as the purchaser of a rental unit will attempt to survey the rental demand for his units, so should he exert similar effort in projecting the tax consequences of his actions. At the other extreme, the less cautious investor must be careful that he is not so carried away with the highly praised tax advantages of depreciation and capital gains that he makes an unsound investment.

Tax Factor Only One Factor

The real estate investor must be sure that the tax factor is placed in its proper perspective. Certainly there are important tax consequences from any real estate investment. The investor must not give too much weight to the tax factors. He must ask whether the after-tax consequences of this investment are commensurate with his objectives, and that the risk he is willing to take yields the best of all his alternatives.

"Leverage" relates to the relative amount of capital supplied by the owner as compared with the amount supplied by creditors. A highly leveraged investment would be one where there is a relatively small amount of capital supplied by the owner compared with that supplied by the creditors. A highly leveraged investment yielding large amounts of depreciation deductions is not of much use to the investor who is holding an apartment house with such a large number of vacancies that he cannot meet the upkeep costs and the principal and interest requirements of the mortgage.

Warning

It is not sufficient to understand the material at hand. It is necessary to be sure that the information is the most current relating to the specific problem. Considering the relevant facts and circumstances, the particular problem at hand should be researched by competent counsel.

Ordinary Tax Rates

We have made the point that it is hard to find a real estate investment that is not affected by the federal income tax. It has also been indicated that the tax law is not neutral in respect to decisions. As we shall see when we explore the different areas of real estate transactions, operations, and organizations, certain kinds of income are treated differently. Some give rise to an ordinary income tax rate, whereas others are taxed at a preferable capital gains tax rate. Some losses may be deducted in full against taxable income and give rise to operating loss carrybacks and carryforwards. Other losses are designated capital losses and are subject to limitations in their deductibility against ordinary income.

In some cases, such as the sale of a residence or the exchange of investment property or property used in the production of income, taxable gain may be postponed. If a taxpayer keeps his appreciated property until he passes away, the federal income tax on this appreciation may be avoided entirely. It will, however, be subject to an estate tax.

Significance

The best way to appreciate the significance of the income tax rates is to look at the tax rates. To emphasize the significance of these rates, individual tax rates for taxable years beginning in 1965 are presented in the following tables at the top of pages 5, 6, and 7. These will also be useful in solving certain of the problem materials in the text.

Note the tax advantage that a married person has over a single taxpayer. The reader is asked to look at the percentage rates he is paying on his current taxable income and what he will pay on his maximum expectation of taxable income. The rates are, of course, progressive, and the rate in a particular bracket is a marginal rate and is not paid on the entire taxable income.

For example, if a taxpayer has taxable income of $10,000 and is a single taxpayer, he pays 28 per cent on the excess over $8,000. He does not pay 28 per cent on his entire income. He pays 14 per cent on the first $500, 15 per cent on the next $500, and so on.

Corporate Tax Rates

Corporations are a separate taxable entity and are subject to a corporation income tax. Corporate tax rates for taxable years beginning in 1965 and later are 22 per cent on the first $25,000 and 48 per cent on the balance. As an example of getting up-to-date information, it may be advisable to check these rates, as Congress may change them.

If a corporation has taxable income, it will be taxed at 22 per cent of the first $25,000 and 48 per cent of the balance. When and if the corporation distributes its income in the form of dividends to its shareholders, the shareholders include this income in their personal tax returns and pay ordinary income tax on these dividends, subject to the dividend exclusion.

1965 Tax Rate Schedule

INDIVIDUALS
(Other Than Head of Household or Surviving Spouse)
Taxable Years Beginning After December 31, 1964

Taxable Income	Tax
Not over $500	14% of the taxable income
$ 500 to $ 1,000 .... $	70 plus 15% of excess over $ 500
1,000 to 1,500	145 plus 16% of excess over 1,000
1,500 to 2,000	225 plus 17% of excess over 1,500
2,000 to 4,000	310 plus 19% of excess over 2,000
4,000 to 6,000	690 plus 22% of excess over 4,000
6,000 to 8,000	1,130 plus 25% of excess over 6,000
8,000 to 10,000	1,630 plus 28% of excess over 8,000
10,000 to 12,000	2,190 plus 32% of excess over 10,000
12,000 to 14,000	2,830 plus 36% of excess over 12,000
14,000 to 16,000	3,550 plus 39% of excess over 14,000
16,000 to 18,000	4,330 plus 42% of excess over 16,000
18,000 to 20,000	5,170 plus 45% of excess over 18,000
20,000 to 22,000	6,070 plus 48% of excess over 20,000
22,000 to 26,000	7,030 plus 50% of excess over 22,000
26,000 to 32,000	9,030 plus 53% of excess over 26,000
32,000 to 38,000	12,210 plus 55% of excess over 32,000
38,000 to 44,000	15,510 plus 58% of excess over 38,000
44,000 to 50,000	18,990 plus 60% of excess over 44,000
50,000 to 60,000	22,590 plus 62% of excess over 50,000
60,000 to 70,000	28,790 plus 64% of excess over 60,000
70,000 to 80,000	35,190 plus 66% of excess over 70,000
80,000 to 90,000	41,790 plus 68% of excess over 80,000
90,000 to 100,000	48,590 plus 69% of excess over 90,000
Over $100,000	55,490 plus 70% of excess over 100,000

Capital Gains

As we shall see in the chapter on capital gains, a taxpayer
receives a deduction of 50 per cent of the excess of the long-term
capital gains over short-term capital losses. Generally, the sale
or exchange of capital assets held over six months yields a long-
term capital gain. The general effect of this is that, if there are
only long-term capital gains, then only one-half of the gain is added
to other taxable income and taxed at ordinary rates. There is also
a maximum tax in that special calculations implement the rule that
the maximum tax on the excess of long-term capital gains over
short-term capital losses is 25 per cent.

1965 Tax Rate Schedule

MARRIED TAXPAYERS FILING JOINT RETURNS,
AND CERTAIN WIDOWS AND WIDOWERS
Taxable Years Beginning After December 31, 1964

Taxable Income	Tax
Not over $1,000	14% of the taxable income
$ 1,000 to $ 2,000 .... $	140 plus 15% of excess over $ 1,000
2,000 to 3,000	290 plus 16% of excess over 2,000
3,000 to 4,000	450 plus 17% of excess over 3,000
4,000 to 8,000	620 plus 19% of excess over 4,000
8,000 to 12,000	1,380 plus 22% of excess over 8,000
12,000 to 16,000	2,260 plus 25% of excess over 12,000
16,000 to 20,000	3,260 plus 28% of excess over 16,000
20,000 to 24,000	4,380 plus 32% of excess over 20,000
24,000 to 28,000	5,660 plus 36% of excess over 24,000
28,000 to 32,000	7,100 plus 39% of excess over 28,000
32,000 to 36,000	8,660 plus 42% of excess over 32,000
36,000 to 40,000	10,340 plus 45% of excess over 36,000
40,000 to 44,000	12,140 plus 48% of excess over 40,000
44,000 to 52,000	14,060 plus 50% of excess over 44,000
52,000 to 64,000	18,060 plus 53% of excess over 52,000
64,000 to 76,000	24,420 plus 55% of excess over 64,000
76,000 to 88,000	31,020 plus 58% of excess over 76,000
88,000 to 100,000	37,980 plus 60% of excess over 88,000
100,000 to 120,000	45,180 plus 62% of excess over 100,000
120,000 to 140,000	57,580 plus 64% of excess over 120,000
140,000 to 160,000	70,380 plus 66% of excess over 140,000
160,000 to 180,000	83,580 plus 68% of excess over 160,000
180,000 to 200,000	97,180 plus 69% of excess over 180,000
Over $200,000	110,980 plus 70% of excess over 200,000

Search for Capital Gains

Considering the capital gains rates described on the preceding page, and considering the ordinary income tax rates, it should not take much study to see why people attempt to plan their transactions so that gain is taxed at capital gain rates rather than ordinary income tax rates.

The fact that a corporation pays an income tax and then the shareholders pay a second tax on dividends has led to the motivation to attempt to get earnings out of corporations in a manner other than by dividends--and, where possible, at capital gain rates. Methods have taken a variety of forms, including: (1) retaining the earnings and then liquidating a corporation, (2) retaining earnings and selling the stock of the corporation with the idea that the value of the stock would reflect the retained earnings, and (3) retaining earnings and leaving the stock to the owner's heirs. Other approaches have been

1965 Tax Rate Schedule

HEADS OF HOUSEHOLDS
Taxable Years Beginning After December 31, 1964

Taxable Income	Tax
Not over $1,000	14% of the taxable income
$ 1,000 to $ 2,000 .... $	140 plus 16% of excess over $ 1,000
2,000 to 4,000	300 plus 18% of excess over 2,000
4,000 to 6,000	660 plus 20% of excess over 4,000
6,000 to 8,000	1,060 plus 22% of excess over 6,000
8,000 to 10,000	1,500 plus 25% of excess over 8,000
10,000 to 12,000	2,000 plus 27% of excess over 10,000
12,000 to 14,000	2,540 plus 31% of excess over 12,000
14,000 to 16,000	3,160 plus 32% of excess over 14,000
16,000 to 18,000	3,800 plus 35% of excess over 16,000
18,000 to 20,000	4,500 plus 36% of excess over 18,000
20,000 to 22,000	5,220 plus 40% of excess over 20,000
22,000 to 24,000	6,020 plus 41% of excess over 22,000
24,000 to 26,000	6,840 plus 43% of excess over 24,000
26,000 to 28,000	7,700 plus 45% of excess over 26,000
28,000 to 32,000	8,600 plus 46% of excess over 28,000
32,000 to 36,000	10,440 plus 48% of excess over 32,000
36,000 to 38,000	12,360 plus 50% of excess over 36,000
38,000 to 40,000	13,360 plus 52% of excess over 38,000
40,000 to 44,000	14,400 plus 53% of excess over 40,000
44,000 to 50,000	16,520 plus 55% of excess over 44,000
50,000 to 52,000	19,820 plus 56% of excess over 50,000
52,000 to 64,000	20,940 plus 58% of excess over 52,000
64,000 to 70,000	27,900 plus 59% of excess over 64,000
70,000 to 76,000	31,440 plus 61% of excess over 70,000
76,000 to 80,000	35,100 plus 62% of excess over 76,000
80,000 to 88,000	37,580 plus 63% of excess over 80,000
88,000 to 100,000	42,620 plus 64% of excess over 88,000
100,000 to 120,000	50,300 plus 66% of excess over 100,000
120,000 to 140,000	63,500 plus 67% of excess over 120,000
140,000 to 160,000	76,900 plus 68% of excess over 140,000
160,000 to 180,000	90,500 plus 69% of excess over 160,000
Over $180,000	104,300 plus 70% of excess over 180,000

the payment of excess salaries and the conversion of equity capital to debt obligations. Interest on debt obligations is deductible in arriving at taxable income, whereas dividends, of course, are not.

There has been a variety of reactions to these attempts. A particularly far-reaching and relatively recent development has been the depreciation-recapture rules relative to personal property in the 1962 Revenue Law and the modified depreciation-recapture rules relative to buildings and leaseholds in the Revenue Law of 1964. We shall discuss these rules in detail in Chapter 5, but the basic result is to convert gain which was formerly taxed at capital gain tax rates to ordinary income taxable at ordinary tax rates.

Oftentimes, because of a variety of reasons, including inflation, property does not depreciate in value in an amount equal to the allowable depreciation deductions. Thus, when an asset is sold, it yields a taxable gain. Formerly, depreciation deductions were deductions against ordinary income, whereas the gain on sale was usually a capital gain.

Thus, if a taxpayer bought equipment that cost $10,000 and depreciated it down to zero and he was in a 50 per cent tax bracket, his deductions saved him $5,000. Assume that he sold the asset for $10,000; he would have a $10,000 gain which would be taxed at a maximum rate of 25 per cent. The net result is that he is $2,500 better off. The $10,000 deduction saved him $5,000, and the $10,000 gain cost him $2,500 in taxes.

This can no longer be done for tangible personal property to the extent of depreciation taken since 1961. For buildings, the depreciation-recapture rules are not so extreme. For sales after the first year, a portion of the excess of accelerated depreciation over straight-line depreciation is recovered, depending on the time the asset has been held. If the building is held over ten years, there is no depreciation recapture. Here the depreciation considered is the amount after December 31, 1963.

Formerly, a desirable technique was to retain earnings and then liquidate the corporation at capital-gain rates. Here, as we shall see in the chapter on corporation, the depreciation-recapture rules make these liquidations very dangerous.

Penalty Tax

The ability to retain earnings in a corporation to avoid the tax on dividends is hampered by the accumulated-earnings tax, which is a penalty tax imposed on unreasonable accumulations of earnings. The personal holding company tax is another and a severe tax on corporations whose income consists mainly of passive sources, such as interest, dividends, rents, and personal service-contract income. Important changes have been made in these rules in the 1964 Revenue Law with respect to rentals. Prior to this law, the general effect was that there was not a personal holding company if gross rentals amounted to over 50 per cent. Since the 1964 Revenue Law, this has been changed, subject to a variety of technicalities, to net rentals. Any real estate venture that is incorporated and whose income consists primarily of interest, dividends, and rentals should investigate the consequences of the change in this law.

The Internal Revenue Service may cause certain payments

by corporations that are not designated as dividends to be treated as dividends and taxable as such. Here are a few examples. If there is a belief that there is excess compensation, then there will be a comparison with compensation for similar services. If the compensation seems excessive, there may be an attempt to tax the excess amount as dividends rather than salary. Salary, of course, is a deductible item in arriving at corporate taxable income and, therefore, is not subject to a "double tax."

In cases of "thin-incorporation," where the relationship of the amount of capital supplied by the owners and designated as capital is small relative to the capital supplied by the owners and designated as creditor's equity, there may also be attack by the Revenue Service. Here the attack is that the payments on the "loans" are dividends rather than deductible interest.

Advantages

The deduction for depreciation is still an important tax advantage if the real estate investment is sound. The combination of depreciation and leverage is particularly important. "Leverage" refers to the use of a large proportion of creditor's equity relative to the amount contributed by the owner.

Assume that a taxpayer puts in $200,000 and borrows $800,000 and builds an apartment house. Let us say that the non-depreciable land cost is $250,000 and the building cost is $750,000. The taxpayer's depreciation deduction is based on the $750,000 and not on the $200,000 he put in.

Certain accelerated depreciation methods, such as the double-declining-balance method and the sum-of-the-years'-digits methods, may be used to depreciate improvements on property. The general effect of these methods is to allow more depreciation in the earlier years of the life of the improvement and less in the later years than is allowed by the straight-line depreciation method.

Because depreciation is a deduction for tax purposes which does not cause cash to flow out of the operation, it is often possible to set up a real estate venture so that in the early years there is cash flow, whereas there is very little or no taxable income. As demonstrated with examples at the beginning of the chapter on depreciation, this is a result of the combination of (1) accelerated depreciation, (2) depreciation computed on the total of the basis of the improvements, and (3) depreciation not causing funds to flow out of the business.

Capital gains are not completely destroyed by the depreciation-recapture rules in the case of buildings. If a building is held ten years or more, there is no depreciation recapture. Thus, if a building is purchased and its value does not depreciate as much as the allowable depreciation deductions, there still will be an advantage of ordinary income deductions while the building is held and of capital gains when it is sold.

POSTPONEMENT OF TAX

We shall study many areas where tax on gain may be deferred. The homeowner who sells his residence at a gain and reinvests the proceeds in another residence may postpone gain. The investor in real estate may exchange rather than sell his property and pay no immediate tax. As his equity increases, he may use this equity in an exchange for a larger piece of property without any current tax. The owner of property used in a trade or business may trade his property rather than sell it and defer any gain on the property. There may be successive exchanges. The taxpayer who holds appreciated property that is subject to a casualty may invest his insurance proceeds according to certain rules and defer any gain. Similarly, a taxpayer who has his property condemned is subject to similar rules. Also, it is important that, if appreciated property is refinanced, there is no tax.

Tax consequences are always with the real estate investor or operator. He cannot demolish a building without considering what the tax consequences are. Whether it is a small residence or a skyscraper, there are important tax consequences. If he entertains a customer at a "quiet business meal," he must record this in his diary.

Chapter 2

Taxable Sales and Exchanges

Property may be sold for money or exchanged for property or for a combination of both money and property. Usually there is a difference between the taxpayer's investment in the property and the value of the assets received for the property on disposition. At first glance, it would seem that the determination of gain or loss on sale or exchange would be just a matter of arithmetic. However, for income tax purposes, all gains are not taxable and all losses are not deductible in the year the property is disposed of. For example, there are certain nontaxable transactions in which gain is postponed until the property acquired in the exchange is sold or otherwise disposed of in a taxable transaction.

Depending on the nature of the property, a gain or loss may be an ordinary gain or loss or it may be a capital gain or loss. If it is an ordinary gain or loss, it will directly enter the taxpayer's computation of taxable income which is taxed at ordinary rates. On the other hand, if disposition gives rise to capital gain or loss, then special rules and special tax rates will apply.

Taxable sales and exchanges are discussed in this chapter. Problems involved with nontaxable exchanges and involuntary conversions are treated in Chapter 3. The rules governing whether gains or losses are capital or ordinary are treated in Chapter 4.

SALES AND EXCHANGES

It is important to distinguish a sale from an exchange because a sale results in recognition of gain or loss whereas an exchange may not. A sale is a transfer of property for money only. An exchange is a transfer of property for other property. A gain on the sale of a factory has been held taxable even though the seller agreed to use the proceeds to build a new factory. The fact that a taxpayer might give cash in addition to giving up property does not prevent the transaction from being treated as an exchange.

If you transfer property to satisfy a debt, the transaction is a taxable exchange. However, a charitable contribution of property to an organization is not a taxable exchange; this assumes, of course, that the contributions are deductible.

A transaction is not an exchange generally when you voluntarily sell property for cash and immediately purchase similar property to replace it. These are considered to be two separate transactions. However, where there are circumstances which indicate that the sale and the purchase are reciprocal and mutually dependent transactions, the Internal Revenue Service may treat the transaction as an exchange rather than a sale. This is of importance because, whereas sales are taxable transactions, exchanges may not be.

GENERAL RULES FOR DETERMINING WHEN GAIN OR LOSS IS RECOGNIZED

Most often a sale or exchange results in the recognition of gain or loss. But special rules apply in the case of some exchanges, and in the case of involuntary conversions, sales of residences, and some other situations.

Nontaxable Exchanges

Under the special rule for nontaxable exchanges, either no gain or loss is recognized or in some situations gain (but not loss) is partially recognized. There are two main kinds of nontaxable exchanges. The commonly thought of nontaxable exchanges are generally based on circumstances that indicate that the new property is basically a continuation of the old investment. Here would fall the cases of an exchange of investment property and also the trade of depreciable assets used in trade or business. There is another class of nontaxable exchanges which basically depend on statutory reorganizations of a corporation which we will not discuss.

Involuntary Conversions

Property may be destroyed, stolen, seized, or condemned. In these situations, the taxpayer may receive insurance or other compensation which is greater than his adjusted basis for the property, so that he has a gain. This gain, however, may not be recognized if the taxpayer replaces the property with similar property within a certain time and also elects not to recognize the gain.

Sale of Residence

The sale of a residence falls under special rules for recognition of gain. If the owner of a residence buys or builds a residence and occupies it within a certain time limit, the gain on the sale of the old residence may not be recognized.

Postponement, Not Forgiveness

It is important to realize that the fact that no gain or loss is recognized on certain exchanges does not mean the gain is never to be taxed. Rather, it means that the property received is considered to be taking the place of the old property given up; gain or loss is merely postponed until a later date when the property received in exchange is sold or otherwise disposed of in a taxable transaction. Note, also, that there may be more than one nontaxable exchange. For example, a real estate investor may trade one apartment house for another and later repeat the process without giving rise to a taxable transaction.

Sometimes Gain Recognized But Not Loss

In certain cases, a gain on the sale of certain property may be recognized. Nevertheless, a loss on exactly the same property may not be deductible.

For example, broker Maxwell has two automobiles. One is used entirely by his wife and therefore has no business use. If he sells this automobile for a gain, he has a taxable gain. However, if he sells this same automobile for a loss, he does not have a deductible loss. However, the loss on his automobile which he uses entirely in his brokerage business would be deductible as a loss incurred in business. Losses are only deductible if incurred: (1) in a trade or business, (2) in a transaction entered into for profit, or (3) through a casualty loss.

DETERMINATION OF AMOUNT OF GAIN OR LOSS

"Basis" is an important factor in the determination of the amount of gain or loss. The methods of acquiring property will control the tax basis. For example, generally basis may be the cost of property to the taxpayer. However, sometimes basis is fair market value of the property, or it may be a basis determined by reference to the basis of someone else. Property may be acquired in a variety of ways other than by purchase. For example, it may be acquired by inheritance, as a gift, as a dividend, through a corporate liquidation, or as compensation for services or in satisfaction of a debt.

Adjusted Basis

"Adjusted basis" is basis plus additions less reductions. The original basis of the property in the owner's hands must be adjusted when changes affect the property. Thus, depreciation deductions reduce the basis. If the owner makes capital improvements on his property, basis is increased by the amount of the improvements. Deductible losses and recoveries of investment in the property decrease the taxable basis. There are special rules governing additions to basis for circulation expenditures, taxes, and carrying charges which will be discussed later.

To illustrate this, take the example of Winters, who bought a building for $5,000 on January 2, 1964. On July 1, 1964 he paid $1,000 for an addition to it. In 1965, he sold the property for $7,000. Assume also that Winters took $500 depreciation on the improvements to the date of sale. Winters' adjusted basis is $5,500; this is the $5,000 cost plus the $1,000 improvements less the $500 depreciation. His gain is $1,500 ($7,000 - $5,500).

Amount Realized

The amount realized is the consideration the taxpayer receives for disposition of the property. The amount realized includes the fair market value of property received as well as money. A taxpayer who sells mortgaged property realizes an amount equal to the cash received plus the mortgage debt he is relieved of paying. Real estate taxes assumed by the buyer are included in the amount realized. Selling expenses are deducted from the amount realized.

If property is exchanged for other property in a taxable exchange, the amount realized is the fair market value of the property received in exchange. When both money and property are _received_ in a fully taxable transaction, the amount realized is the sum of the money plus the fair market value of the property received. When both money and property are _given_ in exchange for property, the amount realized is the fair market value of the property received less the money given.

To illustrate this, assume that you purchased rental units for $35,000. At various times since the purchase, you have made improvements at a cost of $10,000. Depreciation has been allowed in the amount of $5,000.

The rental units are sold for $50,000 cash and other property; the other property has a fair market value of $10,000. The buyer assumes the current real estate taxes of $1,500. At the time of the sale, the mortgage amounts to $8,500. Selling expenses were $2,000. The gain is computed as follows:

Amount realized:		
Cash	$50,000	
Other property (fair market value)	10,000	
Real estate taxes (assumed by buyer)	1,500	
Mortgage	8,500	
Total	$70,000	
Less: Selling expenses	2,000	$68,000
Adjusted basis:		
Cost of rental units	$35,000	
Improvements	10,000	
Total	$45,000	
Less: Depreciation allowed	5,000	40,000
Gain		$28,000

Note that fair market value generally represents the amount which an owner who is not under a necessity of selling is willing to take and which another person who is not under a necessity of buying is willing to pay. If gain is taxable or if loss is deductible, it may be either a capital gain or loss or ordinary income or loss. The rules for determination of capital gains or losses are discussed in Chapter 4 and Chapter 5.

EASEMENTS

A sale of an easement in land is considered to be a sale of an interest in the land. Therefore, the amount received for granting an easement in land ordinarily is used to reduce the basis of the entire property, provided that a beneficial interest is retained. If the amount received for an easement is greater than the basis for the entire property, a gain results in the amount of the excess which is includible in the taxpayer's income.

If, however, a perpetual easement is granted and the taxpayer gives up all or substantially all beneficial use of that part of the property upon which the easement has been granted, the transaction is treated as a sale of such part. Thus, gain or loss is recognized. In the situation where the taxpayer retains a beneficial interest, the amount received reduces his basis in the property and does not result in immediate recognition of gain or loss unless the amount received was greater than the basis of the entire property. Whether the gain, if any, from granting an easement is considered capital or ordinary depends upon the purpose for which the land is held.

Cost As Basis

Cost is used as the basis of a taxpayer's property acquired on or after March 1, 1913 provided that it was purchased or acquired in a taxable exchange. Cost is the amount of cash paid or the fair market value of the property given in exchange.

Real estate taxes. When the purchaser of real property agrees to pay taxes on the property which were obligations of the seller, the amount of the taxes are included as part of the basis of the property; they may not be deducted as taxes paid. However, if the purchaser pays amounts to the seller which represent taxes imposed upon the purchaser, these taxes, ordinarily, are deductible by the purchaser and therefore are not included in the basis of the property acquired. Under certain circumstances, taxes imposed may be capitalized. This is discussed in the next section.

Settlement fees. The costs of purchase commissions, legal and recording fees, and so forth, are included in the basis of the property for the purchaser.

Compensation to employees. Amounts paid to employees for services in connection with construction of property have to be included in the cost basis of the property. The taxpayer is not allowed to deduct such compensation as a current business expense.

Assumption of mortgage. It is important that when property is acquired subject to an existing debt, the basis of the property is the amount paid for the property plus the unpaid amount of the debt assumed by the purchaser.

For example, Sampson acquires an apartment house for $20,000 cash and assumes a mortgage of $80,000. Sampson's basis is $100,000.

ADDITIONS TO BASIS FOR TAXES AND CARRYING CHARGES

Carrying charges, interest, and certain taxes which are otherwise deductible with respect to certain real and personal property may be capitalized if the taxpayer so elects. Obviously, they cannot be both capitalized and deducted. The taxpayer may make a separate election for each project and for each type of expenditure for a project. These items include real property taxes, mortgage interest, and fire insurance premiums as well as other items discussed below.

Unimproved and Unproductive Real Property

A new election to capitalize annual taxes, mortgage interest, and deductible carrying charges on unimproved and unproductive

real property may be made each year. However, the election cannot be made once the property is improved or becomes productive
of income.

For example, Graham paid $5,000 for an unimproved and
unproductive lot with the idea of turning it into a parking lot at a
later date. Each year he made an election to capitalize rather than
deduct the property taxes; these taxes amounted to $1,500. Graham's
basis is thus $6,500 ($5,000 cost plus $1,500 taxes capitalized).
However, once this land produces income as a parking lot, Graham
must deduct his taxes and cannot capitalize them.

How to Make an Election

The election to capitalize taxes and other carrying charges
is made by filing a statement with the tax return showing what
charges have been capitalized.

What May Be Capitalized

Taxes, interest on mortgages, and other carrying charges
on unimproved and unproductive real property may be capitalized.
A taxpayer engaged in the development of real estate or in the construction of an improvement to real estate may elect to capitalize
interest on a loan, carrying charges, and taxes incurred in connection therewith which are otherwise deductible. Note that this is
an election and is not mandatory.

The taxes that the election relates to must be imposed on the
taxpayer. These taxes include State and Federal Unemployment Act
taxes and Federal Insurance Contributions Act taxes (Social Security
taxes) on the wages of the taxpayer's employees engaged in the
development or construction work. The election also applies to
state and local sales taxes.

Interest on a loan to finance the purchase, transportation,
or installation of machinery or other fixed assets may be capitalized.
State and local taxes imposed in connection therewith, such as sales
or use taxes on the purchase, may also be capitalized. Also, taxes
on the wages of the employees engaged in the transportation or
installation of the asset may be capitalized. The election applies
to insurance premiums paid in connection with a construction loan
for business improvements.

Sometimes the buyer of real estate may agree to pay all the
back taxes on the property. In this case, the amount of the taxes
must be included in the basis for the property; they cannot be deducted as taxes.

What May Not Be Capitalized

The following items may not be capitalized because they are
not considered to be carrying charges: (1) advertising expenses
with respect to the property, (2) rent of office necessary to do
business, and salaries of bookkeepers to maintain records, and
(3) real estate taxes and mortgage interest paid on property while
it is being used as taxpayer's own residence.

The election also would not apply to the costs of maintenance
and upkeep. This would include salaries of a manager, wages of
laborers for minor repairs, and wages for supervision of properties.

Special Rules for Charges on Improvements

The items listed in the previous section may be capitalized
whether the real estate is improved or unimproved and productive
or unproductive. However, capitalization may be made only for
such expenses paid or incurred only up to the time that development
or construction work is completed. In the case of machinery, the
election to capitalize is until the machinery is installed or placed
into use, whichever is later.

It is possible to allocate charges. Thus, for an example,
Carpenter Smythe spends one-third of his time on the construction
of a new factory, and two-thirds of his time working on the Contractor's office. One-third of his Social Security tax may be capitalized.

Construction work may be for a personal residence as well
as for a productive asset, such as a factory. Also note that charges
may be for additions to an improvement. Thus, for example, an
election may be made in the case of a construction of another floor
in a factory or in the case of the installation of insulation in a
building.

When several charges of the same type are incurred on a
single project and election is made for one, then all others of the
same type must be capitalized. But if the charges are not of the
same type, one or more may be capitalized without the other being
capitalized. Also, if the same type of charges are incurred on
different projects, the charges may be capitalized on one project
and not the other.

BASIS OF PROPERTY ACQUIRED PRIOR TO MARCH 1, 1913

We have seen that property purchased or acquired in a taxable
exchange has a basis of cost. Bases other than cost are used in a

variety of situations. The basis for determining gain or loss on the
sale or exchange of property acquired before March 1, 1913 depends
on whether the property is disposed of at a gain or a loss. The
reason for this is that the increase in value prior to 1913 is not
taxable.

The basis for determining gain from the sale or other disposition of property acquired before March 1, 1913 is the cost or
the fair market value as of March 1, 1913, whichever is greater.
The purpose of this rule is to prevent the taxation of any gain prior
to March 1, 1913. The basis for determination of loss on property
acquired before March 1, 1913 is cost. Interestingly, we can have
neither taxable gain nor a deductible loss when the selling price is
greater than cost but is less than the March 1, 1913 value.

Improved Real Estate

For improved real estate and other depreciable property,
the cost must be adjusted to March 1, 1913. Also, the basis must
be adjusted for additions and reductions for the period after February
28, 1913. This is illustrated by the following: In 1908, Carter
bought an apartment building for $100,000. Assume that the March
1, 1913 value was $94,000; that there had been no additions or im-
provements; that the sustained depreciation before March 1, 1913
was $10,000; and that the depreciation after that date was $43,240.

The basis for determining gain is the March 1, 1913 value
($94,000) because that is greater than cost, adjusted to March 1, 1913
($100,000 - $10,000). The March 1, 1913 value will be adjusted by
the depreciation since that date ($94,000 - $43,240), and the adjusted basis for determining gain will be $50,760.

The basis for determining loss is cost. The cost ($100,000)
will be adjusted by the depreciation sustained before March 1, 1913
($10,000) and the depreciation after that date ($43,240); the adjusted
basis for determining loss will be $46,760 ($100,000 - $10,000 -
$43,240).

BASIS OF PROPERTY ACQUIRED FROM A DECEDENT

The basis of property acquired by inheritance, bequest, or
devise is its fair market value at the date of the decedent's death.
However, the executor may elect to value the property for estate
tax purposes at its value one year after death or, alternatively, at
the date of distribution, if the property is distributed within one
year after death. Under these alternative elections, the basis becomes the value on the date of election. For example, Mullen died

on January 15, 1964, leaving land to his son, Aaron. The land had been purchased by Mullen in 1947 for $6,000. Carrying charges capitalized amounted to $2,000. When Mullen died, the land was worth $10,000. The land was not actually distributed to Aaron until July 15, 1965, a year and one-half later, when it was worth $10,500. The basis of the land to Aaron is $10,000. If the executor had elected for estate-tax purposes to value the land at its value one year after Mullen's death, that value would then be the basis to Aaron.

If the estate is exempt from federal estate tax, as in the case of a small estate (under $60,000), then there is no option and the only available basis is date of death.

Determination of Fair Market Value

Fair market value for property acquired from a decedent is the value for the federal estate tax. If the estate is not subject to such tax, as when it is valued at less than $60,000, the value for State inheritance or transmission tax is generally used. A higher value may be used if a taxpayer can prove it. A higher value may be desirable because a larger basis would mean more depreciation deductions in the case of depreciable property; a larger basis would also mean a smaller gain or larger loss on subsequent disposition by the heir.

Mortgage on Inherited Property

There is no reduction in fair market value for a mortgage debt on inherited property. This is true even though the devisee does not assume the mortgage.

Transfers in Contemplation of Death

Property transferred to a taxpayer by a decedent without consideration within three years of a decedent's death is presumed to have been transferred in contemplation of death, unless the executor can prove the contrary. The value of property transferred in contemplation of death is included in the decedent's estate, and such property is considered to be acquired from the decedent. The basis of this property to the taxpayer is market value on date of death or alternative valuation date if that is chosen by the executor. However, if the taxpayer: (1) sells the property before decedent's death, or (2) the executor proves the transfer was not in contemplation of death, then the above rules do not apply and the rules relating to gifts discussed later apply.

The basis of property received as a transfer in contemplation

of death must be reduced by depreciation taken on the property by
the taxpayer prior to the decedent's death.

For example: Blumenthal acquired an apartment house by
gift on January 1, 1963. The property had a fair market value of
$50,000 on the date of the donor's death, January 1, 1965, and was
included in his gross estate at that amount for estate-tax purposes
as a transfer in contemplation of death. Blumenthal took depreciation
of $500 for each of the years 1963 and 1964. The adjusted basis of
the property as of the date of the decedent's death is $49,000
($50,000 fair market value at decedent's death, less $1,000 depreciation).

Property Received in Settlement of Cash Legacy

Fair market value on the date of receipt is the basis of
property received in settlement of a cash legacy. Such property is
considered not to be acquired from the decedent. Rather, it is
received in a transaction treated as a sale or other disposition by
the executor.

For example: Zim died on January 5, 1964 and left $2,000
cash to his nephew Elmer. The executor settled the legacy on
September 23, 1964 by distributing to Elmer stock having a market
value of $2,000 on that date. This stock, which was part of Zim's
estate, had a market value of $1,600 on January 5, 1964, the date
Zim died. The basis of the stock to Elmer is $2,000, its value
when he received it.

Property Subject to a Long-Term Lease

Consider the situation in which a landlord passes away and
leaves property subject to a long-term lease to his heir. Assume
the tenant has made substantial improvements on this land. The value
of the tenant's improvements are not taxable to the landlord when they
are built by the tenant, nor when they revert to the landlord on the
termination of the lease. However, on the death of the landlord, the
property must be valued as of that date. This valuation reflects the
value of the improvements for estate-tax purposes and thereby es-
tablishes a basis for future depreciation by the landlord's heir.

BASIS OF PROPERTY TO SURVIVING SPOUSE

The basis of property received by a surviving spouse depends
partially on whether the property is held as community property or
in joint tenancy.

Community Property

In community-property states, such as California, husband and wife are generally considered as each owning half of the estate; this, of course, excepts separate property. If death occurred after December 31, 1947, the fair market value of the community property at the date of death becomes the basis of both halves of the estate, provided that at least half of the whole of the community interest is includible in the decedent's gross estate. This rule applies whether or not the estate is required to file a return. Thus, for example, if the fair market value of the community interest is $100,000, the basis of the surviving spouse's half of the property is $50,000 and the basis of the other half to the decedent's heirs is also $50,000.

It is interesting to note that the basis of the survivor's interest for state tax purposes may not be the same as the basis for federal tax purposes. For example, as of September 15, 1961, in California the basis of community property in the hands of the surviving spouse is not fair market value at date of death of the deceased spouse as for federal tax purposes. For California tax purposes, the basis of community property received from a deceased spouse will be cost as to the survivor's interest and market value as to the deceased spouse's interest. Property passing to the surviving spouse is no longer included in the decedent's estate for state inheritance tax purposes.

For example, John and Mary Dillinger bought a $30,000 home in 1958 as community property. John passed away in 1963 and the home was appraised at $36,000; John left his one-half interest to Mary. John's interest was subject to both federal estate and California inheritance taxes. Mary's one-half interest was not subject to either federal estate tax or California inheritance tax, because she always owned her one-half and did not receive it by "bequest, devise, or inheritance."

The basis to Mary for her one-half interest is $18,000 (fair market value of one-half) for federal income tax purposes and $15,000 (one-half of cost) for California income tax purposes. Her basis for both federal and state for the half interest received from her husband is $18,000 (fair market value).

Thus, Mary has a total basis for federal income tax purposes of $36,000 (fair market value) and of $33,000 ($18,000 plus $15,000) for state income tax purposes. These figures are important because any gain or loss on disposition of the property will be measured by the difference between the basis and the amount realized.

Joint Tenancy and Tenancies by the Entirety

When two persons own property together with the right of survivorship, they are joint tenants. If one passes away, his interest passes to the survivor. Such property owned by a husband and wife is known as a "tenancy by the entirety."

The value of the entire property is included in the estate of the one who dies, unless the survivor can prove that he contributed to the acquisition of the property. In that case, the portion that represents the survivor's contribution is excluded from the estate. The part of the property that is included in the decedent's estate is considered as acquired from the decedent by the survivor. The basis to the survivor of the part of the property included in the decedent's estate is the value at which it was included in the estate. This value is fair market value on date of decedent's death or on the alternative date if the executor elects. The basis of the portion not included in the decedent's estate remains the same as prior to death.

For example, Mr. and Mrs. Randolph purchased real estate as tenants by the entirety for $10,000. Mr. Randolph paid 60 per cent of the price ($6,000) and Mrs. Randolph paid the other 40 per cent ($4,000). When Mr. Randolph died, the fair market value of the property was $15,000. Mr. Randolph's interest was included in his estate at $9,000 (60 per cent of $15,000).

Mrs. Randolph's basis for the property after her husband's death is $13,000. This is calculated as follows:

Cost of Mrs. Randolph's portion (not included in estate)	$ 4,000
Value of portion included in estate	9,000
Total basis	$13,000

Thus, if Mrs. Randolph sells the property for $13,000, she will have no gain or loss for federal income tax purposes.

Thus, property acquired by a surviving joint tenant takes a basis in the hands of the survivor equal to its value on the date of the death of the deceased joint tenant to the extent that the property was includible in the decedent's estate for estate tax purposes. If only one-half of the property is included in the estate, only one-half would take a basis equal to value on death. However, if the total was included, the entire property takes a basis equal to fair market value on death. Property held in the name of both spouses as joint tenants may actually be community property in community-property states if it was the intent of the spouses to hold the property as community property. The surviving joint tenant would, however, have to overcome the presumption of joint tenancy.

Effect of Depreciation on Basis of Joint-Tenancy Property

The basis of joint-tenancy property must be reduced by depreciation on the property taken by the survivor <u>before</u> the other died. If property was owned by husband and wife and joint returns were filed, a part of the depreciation taken on these returns must be allocated to the surviving spouse.

The portion of the depreciation taken prior to death is calculated by the following formula:

$$\frac{\text{Surviving spouse's share of income}}{\text{Total property income}} \times \text{Total depreciation taken}$$

Each spouse's income is determined according to state law.

The following example illustrates this rule: On January 1, 1959 Martin Guggenheim bought for $30,000 an apartment house, which he conveyed to himself and his wife as tenants by the entirety. Under state law, each spouse was entitled to one-half of the income from the property. Mr. Guggenheim died on January 1, 1962 when the fair market value of the apartment was $40,000. The entire value of the apartment house was included in his estate. Mr. and Mrs. Guggenheim filed joint returns for 1959, 1960, and 1961 and took $1,000 depreciation each year.

The adjusted basis of the property in Mrs. Guggenheim's hands on January 1, 1962 is $38,500 ($40,000 value on the date of Mr. Guggenheim's death, less $1,500 depreciation allocated to the widow). One-half ($1,500) of the total $3,000 depreciation was allocated to the widow because she was entitled to one-half the income. If under state law all of the income from the property was allocable to Mr. Guggenheim, no adjustment for depreciation would be required. The widow's basis would be $40,000.

Tenants in Common

If property had been held as tenants in common rather than as tenants in the entirety, only one-half of the value of the property would be included in the deceased's estate. Therefore, only one-half of the property would receive an adjustment of basis equal to its value at the date of death.

To summarize, we should note that an adjustment of basis

to fair market value at date of death is particularly important if there has been an increase in the value of the property over its adjusted basis. For example, assume that husband and wife purchased a property for $50,000 and that it is worth $100,000 at date of the husband's death. If the property gets a "stepped up" basis to fair market value at date of death and the wife sells the property for $100,000, there will be no taxable gain.

In the case of community property, the entire property takes a basis of fair market value at date of death of either spouse. If the couple holds the property as tenants in common, one-half of the property takes a basis of fair market value at date of death. For property held in joint tenancy, the portion that is includible in the estate is valued at fair market value at date of death. We should note also that the creation of a tenancy in common or the transfer into community property, when one spouse had acquired the property entirely with his own funds, is treated as a taxable gift of one-half of the property. The tax incidence at the time of the gift may be lessened by the availability of the marital deduction.

To illustrate the results of the different methods of holding property, let us take the following example: Barton and Millicent Blackwell purchased an apartment house for $200,000. Millicent does not contribute to the purchase price; the apartment was bought entirely from the separate funds of Barton. Ten years later Barton dies. During the ten-year period, $30,000 depreciation was taken on the apartment. On Barton's death the property is appraised at $190,000. The property is left to Millicent.

The amounts included in Barton's estate are as follows, according to how title is held:

Barton's Name Only	Tenants in Common	Joint Tenancy	Community Property
$190,000	$95,000	$190,000	$95,000

Under joint tenancy, the entire fair market value at date of death, $190,000, is included in Barton's estate, because Millicent did not make any contribution. Note that, on purchase of the property, the transfer into tenancy in common or into community property would give rise to a gift on purchase of $100,000 (one-half of cost), because the property was purchased entirely from the funds of one spouse. The availability of the marital deduction may lessen the effect of the gift tax. However, the transfer of real property into the names of the husband and wife as joint tenants will escape gift-tax liability under the following conditions: (1) tenancy is created in real property; (2) tenancy is between husband and wife; (3) right of survivorship is given the surviving spouse; and (4) creation of the tenancy is not reported as a taxable gift. If the above rules are satisfied, the donor spouse has the election to decide whether or not he wishes to treat the creation of the tenancy as a taxable gift.

Millicent's basis for Barton's share after his death is as follows:

Barton's Name Only	Tenants in Common	Joint Tenancy	Community Property
$190,000	$95,000	$190,000	$95,000

In each case, the husband's share is included in the estate, and his share in each case receives a basis of fair market value at date of death. In the case of holding title in his name only and in the case of joint tenancy, his share is the entire property.

Millicent's basis for the total property after Barton's death is as follows:

Barton's Name Only	Tenants in Common	Joint Tenancy	Community Property
$190,000	$180,000	$175,000	$190,000

In the case of the property being held in Barton's name only, the wife had no share and the property takes the fair market value at date of death, $190,000. The basis of $180,000 under tenancy in common is the $95,000 share of Barton's plus $85,000 for the other half. Millicent's basis for her own share under tenancy in common is $100,000 (one-half of the cost of the apartment); this amount is reduced by one-half of the depreciation taken on the apartment ($15,000).

Recall that Millicent did not contribute to the joint tenancy. Therefore, the apartment was included at fair market value of $190,000. However, Millicent must reduce this amount by one-half of the depreciation taken, or $15,000, to arrive at the new basis for the total property, $175,000. The reduction for depreciation assumes that Millicent had been entitled to one-half the income under the law of the state. The community-property basis is $190,000, because both shares receive a basis of fair market value at date of death.

LIFE ESTATES AND REMAINDERS

Oftentimes a life estate in property is left to one person and someone else is a remainderman. A life estate may be created by a gift as well as by a will. The one who has the life estate is called a "life tenant"; his basis, if he sells his interest, is a function of his age at the time of sale.

For example: David Jones had improved realty with a fair market value of $20,000 when he died on January 1, 1960. He devised this property to his brother George for life, with the remainder over to George's son William. On January 1, 1964 George sells his life interest for $12,500. During each of the years 1960 - 1963, inclusive, George was allowed a deduction of $300 for depreciation. Thus, the adjusted uniform basis of the property is $18,800 ($20,000 minus $1,200 depreciation). At the time of the sale, George was 39 years of age. The life factor to be used is .63898 (taken from a "Table of Factors" in the regulations). The part of the basis allocated to George's life interest is $12,012.82 (.63898 X $18,800). George's gain on the sale is $487.18 ($12,500 less $12,012.82).

The basis of the life tenant's interest is the part of the "uniform basis" adjusted for depreciation and other reductions and additions to time of sale that is allocable to the interest sold. The "uniform basis" is the unadjusted basis of the entire property at the date of the decedent's death. The part allocable to the interest sold is found by multiplying the uniform basis by a percentage derived from the mortality tables. If the remainderman sold his interest, he would also use the mortality tables. When both the remainderman and the life tenant sell their interests at the same time, the basis must be apportioned between them.

BASIS OF PROPERTY ACQUIRED BY GIFT

When property is acquired by gift, it is necessary to know the adjusted basis to the donor, the fair market value at the time of the gift, and the amount of gift tax paid.

Gifts Made Prior to January 1, 1921

If property was received as a gift prior to January 1, 1921, its basis for gain or loss is the fair market value of the property when the gift was made. The basis of these gifts is subject to a gift tax adjustment just as are gifts made later. See the discussion following.

Gifts Made After January 1, 1921

The basis of property acquired by gift after December 31, 1920 depends on whether a gain or loss is realized on the sale of the property. Thus, it is possible to have one basis for gain and another basis for loss. The rules are as follows:

(1) If subsequent disposition by <u>donee</u> results in a loss, the basis is either: (a) the same as in the hands of the donor or the last preceding owner by whom it was <u>not</u> acquired by gift, or (b) the fair market value of the property at the time of the gift, whichever is lower.

(2) For determining gain, the basis is the same as in the hands of the donor or the last preceding owner by whom it was <u>not</u> acquired by gift.

Note that it is possible to apply the basis for determining gain and compute a loss, and then apply the basis for determining a loss and get a gain. In this case, there is neither gain nor loss.

These rules are illustrated by the following example: On April 11, 1956 Zawacki bought a country lot for $1,000. On June 11, 1964 Zawacki gave the lot to Thompson when it had a fair market value of $800. No gift tax was payable on this gift. The basis of the lot to Thompson is as follows:

For determining gain (same as in hands of donor)	$1,000
For determining loss (fair market value on date of gift, since that is less than basis in hands of donor)	$ 800

If Thompson sold the lot for $1,200, his gain would be $200 ($1,200 - $1,000).

If Thompson sold the lot for $700, his loss would be $100 ($800 - $700).

If Thompson sold the lot for any amount between $800 and $1,000 (for example, $925), there would be neither gain nor loss.

Adjustment of Basis Required

Property which has a basis determined by reference to someone else's basis must have its basis adjusted for the period that it was held by the present owner.

On January 2, 1962, Gerald Oxford bought an apartment building having an estimated useful life of 30 years. The purchase price for the building was $30,000. On January 2, 1964, Oxford gave the building to his daughter Evelyn. (Assume that no gift tax was paid on the transfer.) On January 2, 1965, Evelyn sold the building for $35,000. The recognized gain on the sale (assuming no figures other than those mentioned) would be $8,000. The basis would be adjusted for depreciation while in the hands of both the donor (2 years) and the donee (1 year). Because the rate of depreciation is $1,000 a year (straight-line depreciation is used), the adjusted basis would be $27,000 and the recognized gain on the sale $8,000.

Adjustment for Gift Tax

If property was acquired by gift after 1921 and its fair market value at the time of the gift was greater than the donor's adjusted basis prior to the gift, the donee's basis is the donor's adjusted basis at the time of the gift plus any gift tax paid. However, such increase is limited to the amount by which the fair market value of the property at the time of the gift exceeds the donor's adjusted basis at that time.

The following illustrates this: John McGuire gives his daughter Barbara a home in 1962. At the time of the gift, the home had a fair market value of $21,000, and its adjusted basis to McGuire was $20,000. John paid a gift tax of $500 on the gift. Barbara's basis for gain or loss is $20,500. This would also be Barbara's basis if she decided to rent out the house.

If we change the situation and assume that John had previously made sufficient gifts so that his gift tax on the residence was $1,500, then Barbara's basis would be $21,000. The adjusted basis to John of $20,000 plus the gift tax of $1,500 comes to $21,500, but this exceeds the limit of market value of $21,000, so the fair market value is used.

For purposes of computation of depreciation, depletion, or amortization, an increase in basis by reason of the gift tax paid is effective on September 2, 1958 or the date of the gift, whichever is later.

For example: James Franklin gives his son Paul a gift of a small rental unit on June 1, 1958. The property had a fair market value of $21,000 at the time of the gift; its adjusted basis to James Franklin just prior to the gift to his son was $20,000. James Franklin paid a tax of $500 on the gift. Assuming that the rental unit had a 20-year life with no salvage value, the adjusted basis for depreciation, assuming straight-line depreciation, would be increased to $20,250 on September 2, 1958, as follows:

Basis for depreciation, June 1, 1958	$20,000
Depreciation for three months at 5 per cent per year	250
Adjusted basis, September 1, 1958	$19,750
Add gift tax	500
Adjusted basis for depreciation, September 2, 1958	$20,250

ALLOCATION OF BASIS

Sometimes a lump-sum price is paid for property consisting of several units. In such a case, the cost must be allocated among the several units if each unit is sold separately. Gain or loss will have to be calculated when each separate unit is sold. The allocation is usually based on the relative value of each unit to the value of the whole property. When allocation is impractical, no gain or loss will be realized until the entire cost is recovered. Students of real estate will be interested in the following two situations requiring allocation of basis: (1) allocation between depreciable and nondepreciable property acquired together; (2) allocation in the case of subdivided real estate.

Allocation Between Depreciable and Nondepreciable Property

When a parcel of improved real estate is bought for a lump sum, the purchase price has to be allocated between the nondepreciable land and the depreciable building. The basic rule requires allocation in proportion to relative fair market values at date of purchase. The big problem, of course, is the determination of fair market values. This subject is discussed in detail in the chapter on depreciation.

Subdivided Real Estate

Real estate development companies often purchase a tract of land to be subdivided into lots. Significant expenditures are required for development of roads, installation of sewage, and surveying. These costs must be equitably apportioned to the separate lots.

The sale of each lot will be a separate transaction, and a gain or loss will be figured separately on each; the development company cannot wait until it has recovered its capital investment in the tract before determining if there is a gain or loss.

In order to determine gain or loss on sale of lots, the development company then has to allocate the cost of the land plus the cost of the improvements to the lots. A variety of procedures have been used; among these are: (1) foot frontage; (2) tentative sales prices; (3) assessed valuations; and (4) released prices. The tentative sales price method of allocation is illustrated in the table on page 31.

The cost of the land, including the improvements, was $25,000, and the development company expects to sell the lots for $100,000. The cost of any one lot is 25 per cent of the sale price

at which it was offered for sale to the public on the day the tract
was first opened.

Lot Number	Number of Lots	Tentative Sales Price Each	Total	Estimated Cost Price Each	Total
1-10	10	$5,500	$55,000	$1,375	$13,750
11-20	10	3,000	30,000	750	7,500
21-25	5	2,000	10,000	500	2,500
26-30	5	1,000	5,000	250	1,250

There are many other important tax problems involved in
subdivisions. For example, there is the problem of determining
whether gain or loss is ordinary or capital. This is discussed in
Chapter 5.

BASIS OF PROPERTY CONVERTED TO BUSINESS USE

When property is converted from personal use to business
use, a different basis must be used for determination of gain from
that used for determination of loss. These rules are as follows:
(1) The basis for gain is the cost or other basis of such property at
the time it was acquired, adjusted for depreciation, and so forth,
to the date of sale. (2) The basis for loss is either: (a) the basis
of such property at the time of conversion; or (b) the fair market
value at date of conversion, whichever is lower, with, of course,
adjustments to the date of sale. The reason for this rule is that a
taxpayer might otherwise take an asset whose fair market value is
considerably below its adjusted basis and convert it to business use
so that he could take a deductible loss. Sales of personal automobiles and personal residences at a loss do not give rise to a deductible loss. However, the sale of an automobile used in business
or of a rented house does give rise to a deductible loss.
Martin Maxwell, formerly an insurance broker, decided to
go into the real estate business. After studying and receiving his
license, he opens a real estate office on January 1, 1963. He has
personal office furniture, which he has never before used for business purposes, which he converts now to business use. This furniture cost him $4,000 on January 1, 1961. He has never taken any
depreciation on this furniture, because it was always used for
personal use. At the time of conversion, the fair market value of
the furniture is $3,000. On January 1, 1964 he has had such a good
year that he sells this furniture and buys some new furniture. His
basis for depreciation on January 1, 1963, when he converted the
asset to business use, was $3,000. The basis for depreciation on

assets converted to business use is the adjusted basis or fair market value, whichever is lower, at date of conversion. He has taken $300 depreciation (10-year life--straight-line method) in 1963.

If Martin is a good salesman and sells his furniture for $4,200, his gain is $500 ($4,000 less $300 depreciation equals $3,700 cost, adjusted to date of sale, subtracted from amount realized of $4,200).

Alternatively, assume that Martin can get only $2,000 for his furniture. His loss would be $700 (fair market value at date of conversion of $3,000 less $300 depreciation equals $2,700; because it was sold for $2,000, there is a loss of $700).

PROPERTY PARTIALLY USED FOR BUSINESS

In the previous section we discussed how basis is determined when personal property was converted to business use and later was sold. This section deals with the situation in which property is used both for business and for pleasure. Thus, for example, a real estate broker or salesman may use his automobile for business part of the time and for pleasure part of the time, or an individual may rent out a room in his residence.

The basis of property used partially for business and partially for pleasure must be allocated. A sale of the asset will give rise to two separate gains and losses: (a) personal portion; (b) business portion. A gain on the sale of the personal portion will be taxable. A loss, however, on the personal portion will not be deductible. On the business portion, the gain will be taxable and the loss will be deductible.

For example: Basil Smith purchases a home with four bedrooms, a bath, and a kitchen for $20,000 on January 1, 1955. The estimated life is 40 years and the straight-line depreciation method is to be used. Basil rents out three bedrooms and keeps one for himself. Assume that other facilities in the house are used proportionately. Ten years later, Basil sells the home for $24,000. Basil is able to deduct $375 depreciation each year ($20,000 cost divided by 40 years equals $500; the production-of-income portion of 3/4 equals $375).

Gain is computed as shown in the table at the top of page 33.

Basil in this case will have a $1,000 capital gain for the personal portion. He will have a gain on an asset used in the production of income of $6,750 which will be treated as a capital gain.

	Personal (1/4)		Production of Income (3/4)
Sales price allocation:	$6,000		$18,000
Adjusted basis:			
Cost allocation	5,000	$15,000	
Depreciation allowed		3,750	11,250
Gain	$1,000		$ 6,750

See the discussion of "Section 1231" assets in Chapter 4 for a further discussion of capital-gain treatment of the sale of assets used in a trade or business. Note, however, that if Basil's calculation would have resulted in a loss on the personal portion, the loss would not be deductible. A loss on the business portion would be deductible.

EXERCISE OF OPTION FOR PURCHASE

If property is purchased through the exercise of an option, the cost of the option is treated as part of the cost of the property. Consider the situation in which a purchaser of property buys the buildings and at the same time purchases an option on the land. However, he does not exercise the option until a later period. In this case he must add the entire cost of the option to the basis for the land and cannot add any to the basis for the building.

Options will be encountered in a variety of other real estate situations. For example, the problems of taxation of gains or losses on sale of options are taken up in the chapter on capital gains and losses. An option may be useful, for example, in postponing passing of title and, therefore, recognition of gain; this would be advantageous, for example, to extend the holding period of property in order to get capital gains. Options for the renewal of a lease are important in determining the useful lives of depreciable assets, as is discussed in the chapter on leasing.

PROPERTY ACQUIRED AS COMPENSATION

If a taxpayer received property as compensation for services, he is taxed according to the fair market value of the property The fair market value of the property then becomes his basis for computing gain or loss on sale.

PROPERTY RECEIVED AS CORPORATE DISTRIBUTIONS

Property may be received from corporations as dividends and on liquidations of corporations.

Property Received as a Dividend

If a stockholder received property rather than cash as a dividend, his basis for the property acquired is fair market value at the time of receipt of the dividend.

Property Received on Liquidations

Some corporate liquidations are taxable and some are not taxable. If property is received by an individual shareholder on a taxable liquidation of a corporation, the basis of the property will be its fair market value at the time of distribution.

In the case of the liquidation of a subsidiary corporation and the case of a one-month liquidation of a corporation, the fair-market-value rule does not apply. If a corporation, other than a collapsible corporation, is completely liquidated within one calender month, special rules under Section 333 I.R.C. apply. If gain is limited under these rules, the shareholder's basis for the property received is the basis of the stock canceled or redeemed in the liquidation minus the amount of any money received and plus the amount of any gain recognized to him. There are many complex problems in the liquidation of corporations; these are discussed in the chapter on corporations.

ABANDONMENTS

In certain situations, it may be advisable to abandon real estate as worthless. When real estate is abandoned, a loss deduction is allowed in the amount of the difference between the adjusted basis of the real estate and any salvage value.

Ordinary Loss

An abandonment gives rise to an ordinary loss rather than a capital loss. This follows because an abandonment is not considered to be a sale or exchange of property. If the asset is used in trade or business and has been held over six months, then it might be advisable to sell such an asset for salvage value. This loss, as we shall see in the discussion of Section 1231 assets in the chapter on capital gain and loss, is deductible in full. The advantage would be that it would not be necessary to prove the abandonment loss.

Time of Deduction

The deduction for the loss on abandonment of business assets is claimed in the tax year in which the loss of usefulness is actually sustained. This is true even though actual disposition does not occur until a later year.

Evidence

Real estate must be abandoned by some clear and unmistakable affirmative act. It must be shown that the real estate is actually worthless; it is not sufficient to show that a shrinkage in value has occurred.

The Sixth Circuit Court has held the following factors sufficient to constitute identifiable events to indicate the worthlessness of real estate:
(1) Taxes in arrears exceeded the value of the real estate and the owner surrendered the realty to the taxing authorities;
(2) charges against the land, such as mortgages, exceeded the value of the real estate; (3) efforts to sell had failed after real estate was rendered worthless as a result of a hurricane.

Abandonment may be indicated by some of the following acts:
(1) mortgagor offers conveyance to the mortgagee; (2) possession of the real estate is completely relinquished; (3) default in payment of principal and interest on a mortgage; (4) charging off the value of the real estate on books of account; (5) cancellation of insurance; (6) refusal to make repairs and to keep real estate in good condition; (7) nonpayment of taxes, water, rents, and other charges; (8) cancellation of all public utility contracts. Note that just one of the above may not be sufficient to prove abandonment for tax purposes.

Buildings

If a building used in a taxpayer's business is demolished to make room for other improvements, the abandonment loss is the undepreciated basis of the building increased by the net cost of demolition or decreased by the net proceeds from demolition. Demolition of a building will prove intent to abandon; however, if other satisfactory proof is available, it is not necessary to demolish it in the same tax year for which a deduction is claimed.

If buildings are permanently devoted to a radically different use, a loss deduction will be allowed. For example, a loss is allowed when a building especially designed for one purpose is reconstructed for another purpose which is radically different from its original use.

Demolish Building to Get Lease--No Immediate Deduction

In order to get a favorable tenant, a landlord may be required to demolish a building. If there is a requirement to demolish a building by terms of a lease, or by an agreement resulting in a lease, no deduction is allowed to the landlord for the demolition. The cost of the lease includes the adjusted basis of the demolished buildings plus the cost of demolition less any proceeds from demolition; this cost may be amortized over the term of the lease.

Demolish Building to Sell Land

No abandonment loss is allowable if a building is demolished as a condition to a contract to sell land on which the building is situated. This rule holds even though it was the intent of the seller to raze the building at a future date to make way for other improvements. The net costs or net proceeds resulting from the demolition must be shown as an adjustment to basis in computing gain or loss from the sale.

IMPROVEMENTS TO BE DEMOLISHED

If a taxpayer intends to demolish a building when he buys both land and buildings, no cost may be allocated to the building. This is true even though the new building is not erected for a period of time.

Allocation of Basis

The entire basis of the property is allocated to the land. This basis is increased by the net cost of demolition and is decreased by any proceeds from demolition.

For example, Barton Brown buys property in a redevelopment area; his intent is to demolish the old building on the land so that he can use the underlying land for a new building. He paid $25,000 for the lot and building and in addition had to pay $3,000 to the Rapid Wrecking Company to demolish the building. Barton Brown sold the salvage from the old building for $5,000. His adjusted basis is $23,000; this is the sum of the cost of $25,000 plus the demolition charge of $3,000 less the salvage of $5,000.

Note that the proceeds from the sale of salvage is not income, and that the cost of demolishing the building is not deductible. Barton Brown could not allocate any of his $25,000 cost to the building. If a taxpayer is going to remove the improvements to another location rather than demolish them, a portion of the cost may be allocated to the building.

However, if improved property is purchased with the intent to demolish the building after using it for a brief period of time either in business or for production of income, a taxpayer may allocate a part of the total cost of the land and building to the building and depreciate that amount over the period of such use. The portion of the basis that can be allocated to the building may not exceed the present value of the right to receive rentals from the building over the period of its intended use. The present value of this right is determined at the time the building is first used in trade or business or first held for production of income.

Thus, in order to allocate part of the cost to a building, a taxpayer must indicate that the property was purchased with the intent of using the building and that the decision to demolish came later. Intent to demolish would be indicated by such things as a short period between date of purchase and date of demolishing, or by obvious indications that the building was unsuitable for the production of income.

Alternatively, indication that the decision to demolish came after purchase would be supported by such things as the prolonged use of the building for production of income or by the adding of improvements to the building after purchase. Substantial decline in value after the purchase caused by changes in business conditions or by a decline in the taxpayer's business or by substantial damage to the building would be support for a decision to demolish after purchase.

Demolition and Loss Deductions

If a taxpayer decides to demolish after property is acquired, a loss is allowed to the extent of the adjusted basis of the building plus the cost of demolition less any salvage received on demolition.

Chapter 3

Nontaxable Exchanges
and Involuntary Conversions

In the previous chapter we noted that certain questions need to be answered in determining gain or loss on the sale or disposition of property: (1) Is the transaction taxable, nontaxable, or partially taxable? (2) What is the amount of the gain or loss? (3) Is there an ordinary gain or loss, or is there a capital gain or loss? In the last chapter we considered the general principles which determine the time of recognition and the amount of gain or loss on fully taxable transactions. In this chapter we shall consider when gain or loss is recognized and how much gain or loss is recognized in nontaxable exchanges and involuntary conversions.

In certain exchanges no gain or loss is recognized, and in others gain (but not loss) is partially recognized. Certain strict rules must be observed to meet the qualifications of these so-called nontaxable exchanges. Special rules for recognition of gain or loss are also found in the case of property destroyed, stolen, seized, or condemned that is replaced by similar property. This is the subject of involuntary conversions.

In studying these subjects, particular attention should be given to the following principles: (1) the fact that an exchange is currently nontaxable does not mean that gain o loss is forgiven; rather, it is postponed until such time as the property is disposed of in a taxable transaction; (2) in some situations, a gain on the sale of property may be recognized but nevertheless a loss on the sale of the same property may not be deductible. The primary example of this situation is the sale of a personal asset at a gain.

NONTAXABLE EXCHANGES

The exchange of certain property does not result in the recognition of gain or loss at the time of the exchange. This means that the gain is not taxed or the loss is not deductible at the time of the exchange. This rule is based on the principle that the new property is substantially a continuation of the old investment. In the case of corporate reorganizations, the idea is that the new enterprise or the new corporate structure is substantially a continuation of the old corporation. The result is to postpone the taxation of the gain or the deduction of the loss on qualified exchanges until such time as the property received is disposed of in a taxable exchange. There may be a continuation of nontaxable exchanges, starting with one parcel of property.

For example, the owner of Apartment A may trade it for Apartment B, and at a subsequent date trade Apartment B for Apartment C in a nontaxable transaction. If the requisite rules are met, this process may be continued. A so-called nontaxable exchange may be partially taxable. Receipt of other property or money in addition to the property received in an otherwise nontaxable exchange may result in a partial recognition of gain. Also, the assumption of liabilities in connection with certain otherwise nontaxable exchanges may also result in partial recognition of gain. Some property may be exchanged tax-free while other properties may not.

Kinds of Nontaxable Exchanges

These are the nontaxable exchanges which we shall discuss in this chapter. They basically involve exchange of property for like property. There are also nontaxable exchanges which involve the exchange of stock and property in connection with corporate reorganizations.

The following exchanges are considered to be nontaxable: (1) common stock in a corporation exchanged solely for common stock in the same corporation; (2) preferred stock in a corporation exchanged solely for preferred stock in the same corporation; (3) transfer of property to a corporation controlled by the transferor under certain conditions; (4) exchanges of certain insurance policies; (5) exchanges of certain United States bonds, such as the exchange of E and J bonds, and F bonds issued after 1947 for H bonds, if exchanged not later than six months after maturity; (6) property held for productive use or investment exchanged solely for property of a like kind. Note that stock in trade, shares of stock, bonds, notes, and so forth, are not productive-use or investment property within the meaning of the statute. A person interested in real estate is primarily interested in the last category. However, as a businessman he will be interested in the other types of nontaxable exchanges.

Property Held for Productive Use or Investment

This is the most common type of nontaxable exchange. Here property is exchanged for like property. The property traded as well as the property received must be held for business or investment purposes. Property used for personal purposes, such as a personal automobile, would not qualify. Property held for productive use in trade or business may be exchanged for property held for investment. Also, property held for investment may be exchanged for property held for productive use in trade or business.

The term "like kind" refers to the nature or character of the property rather than the grade or quality of the property. For example, it would not matter whether real estate was improved or unimproved; such is considered to be related to the grade or quality of the property.

Property Held for Productive Use in Trade or Business

The nontaxable-exchange rule does not apply when the property exchanged is stock in trade or property held primarily for sale. Machinery, buildings, land, trucks, and rented houses are examples of property to which the "productive use in trade or business" rule applies. The rule does not extend to inventories, raw materials, or accounts receivable, or to real estate held for sale to customers by dealers.

An exchange of property used in your trade or business or for investment for property to be used for personal use, or vice versa, does not qualify for the nonrecognition of gain. If property is used for both business and personal purposes, the nontaxable-exchange rule applies only to the business part.

For example, an exchange of an automobile used by a realty salesman partly for business purposes for a new car results in a nontaxable exchange of the business part and a taxable exchange of the personal part. An exchange of an automobile used entirely for pleasure purposes for a new car is a taxable exchange. And in a taxable exchange of personal-use property, a gain is recognized but a loss is not deductible. An exchange by an automobile dealer of a new car in his stock for an old one is a taxable exchange.

Property Held for Investment

The category "property held for investment" does not apply to exchanges of stocks, bonds, notes, choses in action, certificates of trust or beneficial interest, or other securities or evidences of indebtedness or interest. Conversion of United States currency into foreign currency and reconversion to United States currency are taxable transactions; this is not considered property held for investment. However, the exchange of securities in one corporation for stock or securities in another corporation may be tax-free in a corporate reorganization.

Included in the nontaxable category would be the following exchanges. The exchange of real estate for real estate and the exchange of personal property for personal property are exchanges of like property. The trade of an apartment house for a store building qualifies. The exchange of investment real property for a lease with 30 years or more to run in investment property is an exchange of property for like property. Exchange of city investment property for farm investment property and improved investment property for unimproved investment property also qualifies. On the other hand, an exchange of personal property for real property does not qualify.

Example of Nontaxable Exchange

To note the effect of the above rules, assume that a building-maintenance firm trades an old truck for a new one. The new truck costs $5,800. The firm is allowed a trade-in of $2,000 for the old truck and pays $3,800 cash. There is no taxable gain or deductible loss on the transaction regardless of the adjusted basis of the old truck. Recall that the adjusted basis is the original basis (for example, the cost of the truck) plus additions less reductions (for example, depreciation). Note, however, that if the building-maintenance company sold the old truck to a third party for $2,000 and then purchased the new truck, they would have a recognized gain or loss measured by the difference between the amount realized and the adjusted basis of the old truck.

"BOOT" IN NONTAXABLE EXCHANGES

It would certainly be difficult to find properties of exactly the same value to exchange. The usual case is that one party to the exchange will contribute cash or other property in addition to the like property which can be exchanged tax-free. This cash or other property (sometimes referred to as "unlike property") is called "boot." The "boot" in the transaction may make the transaction partially taxable. As we shall see, it is important to distinguish between the party of the exchange who is giving "boot" from the other party who is receiving the "boot."

No "Boot" Given or Received

When no money or property in addition to the property that can be exchanged tax-free is involved (no "boot" is involved), the basis of the property acquired is the same as the basis of the property transferred. The basis of the property transferred, of course, is adjusted to the date of transfer for additions and reductions. Recall that additions are for improvements and reductions are for such things as depreciation, casualty losses, and recovery of capital.

For example, Farrell exchanges his farm having an adjusted basis of $30,000 for an apartment house. The basis of the apartment house to Farrell is $30,000, regardless of its fair market value.

"Boot" is Given

For the party giving the "boot," the basis of the property acquired is the same as the basis of the property transferred plus the amount of the "boot" given. The giving of the "boot" does not cause the transaction to be taxable for the giver of the "boot." We shall see below that the receipt of "boot" does make the transaction taxable.

For example, realty salesman Smith is allowed $1,000 on his old car (used entirely for business) in acquiring a new business car listed at $1,500. The transaction is nontaxable, even though salesman Smith was required to pay $500 cash in addition to giving the old car.

The adjusted basis of the old car is $900 (cost less depreciation taken to date of exchange). Smith's basis of his new car will be $1,400 regardless of its actual or fair market value.

Basis of new car:	
Adjusted basis of old car	$ 900
"Boot" given	500
Basis of new car	$1,400

"Boot" is Received

If cash or other property is received in addition to the property that can be exchanged tax-free, the transaction may become partially taxable to the party receiving the "boot." Any taxable gain will be limited to the cash plus fair market value of the "unlike property" received. The receipt of "boot," however, does not cause a loss to be recognized.

Gain Recognized on Receipt of "Boot"

Assume that Siegel exchanges real estate held for investment for other real estate to be held for investment. The real estate given up has an adjusted basis of $36,000 and a fair market value of $42,000. Assume that the real estate received has a fair market value of $40,000. Siegel receives an additional $2,000 in cash.

The gain realized in the transaction is computed as follows. Note that this is not the gain recognized for tax purposes.

Received:		
Fair market value of property	$40,000	
Cash	2,000	$42,000
Given:		
Adjusted basis of property traded		36,000
Potential gain		$ 6,000

Siegel, however, is not taxed on the $6,000 gain, his gain in a nontaxable exchange is limited to the amount of "boot" received.

Gain taxed (limited to "boot" received)	$2,000

In summary: (1) the receipt of "boot" can cause an otherwise nontaxable exchange to become partially taxable; (2) taxable gain when "boot" is received is limited to the amount of "boot" received. However, if Siegel were a dealer in real estate rather than an investor, he would be taxed on the entire $6,000 gain.

No loss recognized on receipt of "boot." The receipt of "boot" does not result in the recognition of a loss. For example, assume that Fox exchanges a lathe having an adjusted basis of $5,000 and a fair market value of $4,400 for a similar lathe having a fair market value of $4,000. Fox also receives $400 in cash in the transaction. Fox's potential loss is as follows:

Received:		
New lathe (fair market value)	$4,000	
Cash	400	$4,400
Given:		
Old lathe (adjusted basis)		5,000
Potential loss		$ 600

The fact that Fox has received $400 "boot" does not cause the loss to be recognized. In this case it might have been more desirable for Fox to sell his old lathe and then purchase a new one.

In this case the loss would then be recognized. A transaction is not considered an exchange, ordinarily, when property is voluntarily sold for cash and then similar property is immediately purchased to replace it. Such a sale and purchase are considered two separate transactions. If, however, there are circumstances which indicated that the sale and the purchase are reciprocal and mutually dependent transactions, the transactions may be treated by the Internal Revenue Service as an exchange.

Basis of the Property When "Boot" is Received

In the previous sections, we discussed the fact that the receipt of "boot" may make an otherwise nontaxable exchange partially taxable. The question we shall face in this section is, what is the basis of the property received for depreciation and for gain or loss on disposition? This basis will be affected by the amount of gain recognized as well as the amount of "boot" received. Carefully distinguish between the gain recognized for tax purposes and the potential gain as measured by the amount realized less the adjusted basis of the property given up. We shall now consider the amount of gain recognized and the basis of the property received in a variety of situations.

Potential gain--"boot" received in form of money. In the situation in which a taxpayer has a potential gain and receives "boot" in the form of money, the basis of the property received is computed as follows.

Basis of acquired property equals adjusted basis of old property less amount of money received plus any gain recognized on the exchange. This is illustrated in the following example.

Contractor Smythe exchanges a machine having an adjusted basis of $1,000 for a similar machine having a fair market value of $900, and also receives $300 in cash. His gain is $200, all of which is recognized (because it does not exceed the amount of cash received). The basis of the new machine is figured as follows:

Adjusted basis of old machine	$1,000
Less: Amount of money received	300
	$ 700
Plus: Gain recognized on exchange	200
Basis of new machine	$ 900

The logic of the computation of the basis of the property becomes clear if we assume that Smythe sells the new electric saw immediately after the exchange for its basis of $900. Contractor

Smythe originally had an electric saw with an adjusted basis of $1,000. He now has $1,200 cash; this is the $300 received on the exchange plus the $900 received on the sale. Thus, Smythe has made a profit of $200 ($1,200 total cash received less adjusted basis of old machine of $1,000), and this is the amount on which he must pay tax.

Potential gain--"boot" received in money, trade for more than one piece of property. Assume that MacPherson holds a lot held for investment purposes with an adjusted basis of $5,000. He exchanges this lot for another lot to be held for investment purposes, a truck, and $1,000 in cash. The fair market value of the lot received at the time of the exchange is $2,500 and that of the truck is $1,800. There is a recognized gain on the transaction computed as follows:

Amount realized:		
Lot received (fair market value)	$2,500	
Truck received (fair market value)	1,800	
Cash received	1,000	$5,300
Given:		
Lot traded (adjusted basis)		5,000
Potential gain and realized gain		$ 300

Because the amount of "boot" received (cash of $1,000) is greater than the $300 potential gain, the $300 is the amount recognized.

The total basis of the new properties, the new lot and the truck, is computed as follows:

Real estate transferred (adjusted basis)	$5,000
Less cash received	1,000
	$4,000
Plus: Gain recognized	300
Basis of new lot and truck to be allocated	$4,300

The basis of $4,300 is allocated between the truck and the real estate. The basis of the truck is its fair market value of $1,800; the basis of the real estate is $2,500.

Potential loss--"boot" received. The fact that a taxpayer receives "boot" does not cause a loss to be recognized. In this case, the basis of the new property is determined as follows.

The basis of acquired property equals the adjusted basis of the old property less the amount of money received.

For example, Builder Wright exchanges a truck having an adjusted basis of $1,000 for a similar truck having a fair market value of $700. He also receives $100 in cash. His potential loss, which is not recognized, is computed as follows:

Received:		
Truck (fair market value)	$700	
Cash	100	$ 800
Given:		
Truck (adjusted basis)		1,000
Unrecognized loss		$ 200

The basis of his new truck is calculated as follows:

Adjusted basis of old truck	$1,000
Less: Cash received	100
Basis of new truck	$ 900

Again we can see the logic of this if we consider what Wright's loss would be if the truck were immediately destroyed in an accident. His loss would be $900; this is the adjusted basis of the old truck, $1,000, less the $100 cash which he received on the exchange.

"Boot" received--loss not recognized, allocation required. An exchange may be made in which a loss is not recognized, even though unlike property is received. In the previous section, we noted that the basis of the acquired property equals the adjusted basis of the old property less the amount of money received. If both like and "unlike" property are received, an amount of the basis equivalent to the fair market value of the unlike property at the date of the exchange must be assigned to the "unlike" property.

For example, Harbor Developers, Inc. exchange a boat used in their business for another boat to be used in their business, a cabin (nonbusiness), and $500 cash. The boat they traded had an adjusted basis of $8,000. The respective fair market values of the properties received are as follows: boat, $5,000; cabin, $1,500. There is a nonrecognized loss of $1,000 on the transaction, computed as follows:

Received:		
Boat (fair market value)	$5,000	
Cabin	1,500	
Cash	500	$7,000
Given:		
Boat (adjusted basis)		8,000
Unrecognized loss		$1,000

The basis to be allocated is the adjusted basis of the boat given up, $8,000, less the cash received, $500. The basis of $7,500 is allocated, to the cabin received, at its fair market value of $1,500, and the remainder, of $6,000, to the boat.

Potential gain--"boot" received, allocation required. Assume that O'Hara exchanges a lot having an adjusted basis of $8,000 for another lot having a fair market value of $8,500, and also receives $1,500 in cash and the note of the purchaser having a fair market value of $1,000. O'Hara's gain is $3,000, of which $2,500 is recognized (the cash plus the fair market value of the note). The combined bases of the new lot and the note is figured as follows:

Adjusted basis of old lot	$8,000
Less: Amount of money received	1,500
	$6,500
Plus: Gain recognized on exchange	2,500
Combined bases of new lot and note	$9,000
Basis of note (its fair market value)	1,000
Basis of new lot	$8,000

The reason for this computation is clear if it is assumed that the note and the new lot are sold immediately for $9,000 (their bases). O'Hara originally had a lot with an adjusted basis of $8,000. He now has $10,500 cash ($1,500 received on the exchange and $9,000 on the sale). His profit is $2,500, and that is the amount recognized.

BASIS OF PROPERTY WHEN LOSS IS RECOGNIZED

In the previous sections, we noted that the receipt of "boot" could make an exchange partially taxable, but that the receipt of "boot" did not cause a loss to be recognized for tax purposes. Now we shall consider a one-transaction situation in which a taxpayer transfers property that may be exchanged tax-free plus other property that may not be transferred tax-free and receives in exchange property that may be exchanged tax-free. Loss is recognized to the extent that the adjusted basis of the property that may not be exchanged tax-free exceeds its fair market value at the time of the exchange. This is illustrated in the following example:

Mandeville exchanges an apartment building with an adjusted basis of $100,000 and a fair market value of $150,000 plus shares of stock with a basis of $60,000 and a value of $50,000 for an apartment building worth $200,000. Because the exchange of the stock in part consideration for the apartment building does not fall within the nontaxable-exchange provisions, Mandeville will be able to recognize a loss: the recognized loss is $10,000; this is the $60,000 basis of the "unlike" property (stock) less its fair market value of $50,000.

The basis of the new apartment building is computed as follows:

Adjusted basis of old apartment building	$100,000
Basis of stock surrendered	60,000
	$160,000
Less: Loss recognized on the exchange	10,000
Basis of new apartment building	$150,000

EXCHANGE OF PART BUSINESS, PART PERSONAL ASSET

A taxpayer may have an asset used in trade or business or for production of income that is used partly for business and partly for personal use. For example, a real estate broker may use an automobile for both personal and business purposes, or the owner of rental property may live in a portion of the property. The following example illustrates an exchange of an automobile that was used partly for business and partly for pleasure and was traded in for another automobile.

Broker Twist kept careful records and determined that he drove his automobile two-thirds for business use and one-third for personal use. His automobile cost him $3,600 and he had taken $1,350 depreciation on it prior to trading it in for a new automobile. The automobile dealer sold him a car for $4,000 and allowed him a trade-in allowance of $1,200. Broker Twist expects to drive the new automobile two-thirds for business use.

The business portion (the portion he will be able to depreciate) is computed as shown in the table on page 49.

If there was an unrecognized gain applicable to the business portion of the old car, it would be subtracted rather than added in arriving at the depreciable basis of the new car. Note that the personal portion is eliminated in the above example. If there had been a gain on the personal portion, it would be recognized as a taxable gain; a loss on the personal portion would not be deductible. In the table at the top of the next page there is a nondeductible loss of $800. This is the difference between the $400 portion of the trade-in allowance (one-third of $1,200) and the personal portion of the original basis of the old car, $1,200 (one-third of $3,600).

1. Cost of old car allocable to business use --
   2/3 of $3,600 $2,400
2. Less:
   (a) Trade-in allowance applicable to
       business portion -- 2/3 of $1,200 $ 800
   (b) Total depreciation allowed on old car   1,350
                                                                    $2,150
3. Unrecognized loss applicable to business portion   ($ 250)
4. Purchase price of new car $4,000
5. Less: Salvage value   400
                                                                    $3,600
6. Portion of cost of new car allocable to business
   use -- 2/3 of $3,600 $2,400
7. Plus: Unrecognized loss on trade-in (from line 3)   250
8. Depreciable portion of basis of new car $2,650

MORTGAGES AND TAX-FREE EXCHANGES

Mortgages on property affect the amount of gain realized and the basis of the property acquired in otherwise tax-free exchanges. We shall examine a variety of situations involving mortgages on one or more of the properties involved in an exchange.

Mortgage on Property Transferred Only

Otherwise tax-free exchanges of property of "like kind" may involve property encumbered by a mortgage. The mortgage is treated the same as cash in determining recognized gain if the person getting the property assumes the mortgage or takes the property subject to the mortgage.

Investor Dollar owns a ranch which has an adjusted basis in his hands of $50,000. The ranch is subject to a mortgage of $10,000. He exchanged the ranch for an office building worth $65,000, the transferee assuming the mortgage. Dollar realized a gain of $25,000 on the exchange, figured as follows:

Value of property received	$65,000
Mortgage on property exchanged -- assumed by transferee	10,000
Total consideration received	$75,000
Less: Adjusted basis of property transferred	50,000
Gain realized	$25,000

Note that Dollar has realized a gain of $25,000 measured by the amount received (including the value of the mortgage) less the adjusted basis of the property transferred. His gain is recognized

for tax purposes only up to the amount of the mortgage ($10,000);
thus, the mortgage is treated like "boot" received in determining
recognized gain.

If property subject to a mortgage is exchanged for unen-
cumbered property, as in the table at the bottom of page 49, the
amount of the mortgage debt is treated as the equivalent of "boot"
received on the transaction. The owner who transfers his mortgaged
property must reduce the carry-over basis to be allocated to the new
property by the amount of the outstanding mortgage debt. He may increase the carry-over basis by the amount of the taxable gain. The
same rules apply to other liabilities attaching to land obtained in an
exchange and assumed by the recipient. The basis of the property
received in the preceding example (page 49) is determined as follows:

```
Basis of new property:
    Adjusted basis of property transferred       $50,000
    Less:  Mortgage assumed by transferee          10,000
                                                  $40,000
    Plus:  Recognized gain                         10,000
                                                  $50,000
```

From the standpoint of the former owner of the office building
who traded for the ranch, the assumption of another's liabilities
(the mortgage debt) is treated in the same manner as the giving of
"boot," and, as we studied before, the giving of "boot" does not
make the exchange taxable. The basis of the ranch to its new
owner is the same as the carry-over basis of the office building
plus the mortgage assumed.

Mortgage on Both Parcels of Property

If both properties in an exchange are subject to mortgages,
the respective mortgage debts are offset and only the net debt is
treated as the receipt or payment of "boot."

To illustrate this situation, let us take the facts of the above
situation, where Dollar traded his ranch for an office building, except to assume that the office building was encumbered by a mortgage
of $6,000, which Dollar assumed. The figures are shown in the
table at the top of page 51. Here Dollar realizes a gain of $19,000,
which is taxable to the extent of $4,000. The recognized gain
(taxable amount) is the difference between the mortgage assumed
by the transferee ($10,000) less the mortgage assumed by the
transferor, Dollar ($6,000).

From the standpoint of the other party to the transaction, the
former owner of the office building, he has assumed a debt of $10,000
and has been relieved of a debt of $6,000. Thus, he is treated as
giving "boot" of $4,000, and the exchange is tax-free to him.

Value of property received		$65,000
Mortgage on property exchanged --		
assumed by transferee		10,000
Total consideration received		$75,000
Less: Adjusted basis of property		
transferred	$50,000	
Mortgage on property received --		
assumed by transferor (Dollar)	6,000	56,000
Gain realized		$19,000
Gain taxed		$ 4,000

Basis of Property When Both Parcels in Exchange Are Mortgaged

If both parcels of property to an exchange are mortgaged, then the basis of the property received is equal to the adjusted basis of the property given up plus the mortgage assumed on the new property less the mortgage on the property given up plus any gain recognized on the exchange.

Recall the facts of investor Dollar's exchange. Dollar had a farm with an adjusted basis of $50,000 which was encumbered by a $10,000 mortgage. He traded this property for an office building with a value of $65,000 which was encumbered by a $6,000 mortgage. Dollar's basis for his office building is computed as follows:

Adjusted basis of farm	$50,000	
Add: Mortgage on office building	6,000	$56,000
Less: Mortgage on farm		10,000
		$46,000
Plus: Gain recognized on exchange		4,000
Basis of new property		$50,000

The basis of the farm to the old owner of the office building is computed as follows (assume that the office building had an adjusted basis of $55,000 at the time of exchange):

Adjusted basis of office building	$55,000	
Add: Mortgage on farm assumed	10,000	$65,000
Less: Mortgage on office building		
transferred		6,000
Basis of farm		$59,000

There was no gain realized by the old owner of the office building when he exchanged it for the farm, because he assumed a larger mortgage ($10,000) than the one he was relieved of ($6,000).

In the examples above involving mortgages on both properties, there was no cash involved. It may be that cash is needed to balance an exchange. Let us assume that Dollar had to give $2,000 cash in the foregoing example to balance the exchange. In determining the amount of "boot" received, which helps determine the amount of gain taxed, the cash given is an offset to the consideration received. For example:

Amount of "boot" received:		
Liability against farm transferred		$10,000
Less "boot" given:		
Liability on office building	$6,000	
Cash paid	2,000	8,000
"Boot" received		$ 2,000

Thus, Dollar's taxable gain on the exchange will be limited to the "boot" received of $2,000.

From the standpoint of the old owner of the office building, cash <u>received</u> on an exchange is not offset against the consideration given in the form of the assumption of the liability against the farm. For example:

Amount of "boot" received:	
Cash received	$2,000
Excess of liability on office building transferred (6,000) over debt on farm acquired (10,000)	None
"Boot" received	$2,000

The old owner of the office building had a potential gain on exchange computed as follows (assume that Dollar's farm was worth $67,000):

Amount realized:		
Value of farm	$67,000	
Mortgage on office building transferred	6,000	
Cash received	2,000	$75,000
Amount given:		
Adjusted basis of office building	$55,000	
Mortgage on farm assumed	10,000	65,000
Potential gain		$10,000

Thus, the old owner of the office building has a potential gain of $10,000. This is now taxable to the extent of $2,000, the amount of the "boot" received. The receipt of cash by the office building owner makes the exchange taxable to him even though he assumed a larger mortgage than the mortgage he was relieved of.

Brief Review

Considering that we have examined some fairly complex examples, it may be worth while to review the following basic points:

(1) "Boot" received in an exchange may be taxed only to the extent of gain realized on the exchange.

(2) The gain realized on an exchange is taxed only to the extent of the "boot" received.

(3) The receipt of "boot" will cause the exchange to become partially taxable to the party receiving the "boot," provided he has a realized gain.

(4) The giving of "boot" does not make the exchange taxable to the giver of "boot."

(5) The assumption of a mortgage is treated as giving of "boot."

(6) If a party is relieved of a mortgage, he is treated as receiving "boot."

(7) When both parcels are subject to mortgages, the respective mortgages are offset and the net debt is treated as the receipt or payment of "boot."

TRANSFERS TO CONTROLLED CORPORATION

Nontaxable exchange rules apply to transfers to controlled corporations. These are discussed in detail in the chapter on corporations. No gain or loss is recognized if a party transfers property to a corporation solely in exchange for its stock or securities and immediately after the exchange such person or persons are in control of the corporation. In a transfer to a controlled corporation, a mortgage is not considered "boot" received by the transferor in determining his recognized gain.

MULTIPLE EXCHANGES

In the previous discussions of nontaxable exchanges, we have always assumed that there were only two parties to an exchange. It is entirely possible, however, to have more than two parties to the exchange and still enjoy the benefits of the tax-free exchange provision of the law.

For example, assume the following situation involving property held for investment. Anderson owns a lot near Lake Margaret. He would like to acquire a lot in Ski-Valley from Spitzer, but he does not wish to liquidate any of his investments and, thus, does not want to pay cash for it. Thus, he offers to exchange his lake lot for the Ski-Valley lot. Spitzer does not want the lake lot, but he is desirous of selling his Ski-Valley lot. Broker Rivard learns that Martin wants to buy the lake lot. Rivard suggests to Martin that he buy the Ski-Valley lot from Spitzer and then exchange it for Anderson's lake lot. If the tax-free exchange requirements are met, Anderson would be entitled to treat this transaction as a tax-free exchange of his lake lot for the Ski-Valley lot.

Assume that, instead of cash, Martin had a lot he wished to trade in Feather Mountains. The exchange of the three lots could be handled as a tax-free exchange.

INVOLUNTARY CONVERSIONS

An involuntary conversion occurs when property is destroyed, stolen, requisitioned, or condemned and other property or money is received in payment. The form of the property or money received is usually insurance or a condemnation award. The insurance or condemnation proceeds may amount to more than the adjusted basis of the property destroyed or seized and the property owner will have a realized gain. However, if the property owner purchases new property to replace the old property within a specified period of time, part or all of the gain may not be recognized. Recall that we can have a realized gain measured by the difference between the amount realized and the adjusted basis of the property given up but still not have a recognized gain for tax purposes under certain situations.

In the case of an involuntary conversion, there may be either a recognized, nonrecognized, or partially recognized gain, depending on the specific circumstances and on the taxpayer's election in each case. There may also be a deductible or a nondeductible loss.

Examples of Involuntary Conversions

Some typical examples are the destruction of business property by disease, casualty, drought, hurricane, flood, and so forth, and the receipt of insurance proceeds for the loss. Casualty includes fire, storm, and theft. Condemnation by the government is also an involuntary conversion. The destruction of livestock by disease, or their sale or exchange because of disease, is treated as an involuntary conversion. Sale or other disposition of property in an irrigation project to conform to the acreage-limitation provision of federal reclamation laws is treated as an involuntary conversion.

Condemnation and Threat of Condemnation

An involuntary conversion may occur whether property is transferred under a threat or imminence of condemnation or after the condemnation actually occurs. "Condemnation" means taking private property for public use without consent of the owner but upon award and payment of just compensation.

The threat of condemnation occurs when a city authority or other public body indicates by a public resolution or public act that specific property will be condemned. It occurs if the condemning authority advises the taxpayer orally or in writing that the property is to be condemned for public use. However, note that any oral notification may necessitate confirmation in writing upon request of a District Director of Internal Revenue.

The same rule applies if a taxpayer obtains information as to a decision to acquire his property for public use through a report in a newspaper or other news medium. However, he has to obtain confirmation from a representative of the governmental body or public official involved as to the correctness of the published report and have reasonable grounds to believe that the necessary steps to condemn will be instituted if he does not voluntarily sell.

At one time the Revenue Service challenged cases unless the owner learned that official action to condemn had started. Now it seems to be enough if a taxpayer can reasonably infer that the threat can or will be carried out. It is advisable to have proof in form of a written notice from the condemning authority.

Not Considered Involuntary Conversions

Some examples of situations not considered involuntary conversions follow: The sale of a building because the Health Department declared it to be unfit for human use; The sale of a fertilizing plant because of being offensive to residents; The sale of property to avoid meeting the requirements of a housing ordinance. Property may be sold because of threats from people not having the power to condemn property. This does not cause the property to qualify for the involuntary-conversion benefits. However, sale of property adjacent to that involuntarily converted when continued operation of the business on adjacent property was impractical seems to qualify.

DETERMINATION OF GAIN OR LOSS

The following are the general rules for determination of gain or loss in the case in which there is an involuntary conversion and the taxpayer replaces the original property by buying other property that is similar or related in service or use to the original property.

(1) If the amount realized on the involuntary conversion equals or is less than the cost of the replacement property, no gain is recognized.

(2) If the amount realized is greater than the cost of replacement, gain is recognized to the extent of the excess amount.

For the above rules to apply, the replacement must be made within a certain period of time, as discussed below. Also, the replacement must be in kind and the taxpayer must elect to have the rules apply.

(3) If a loss results from an involuntary conversion, it will be recognized.

Direct Conversion

No gain nor loss is recognized if property is converted directly into other property similar or related in service or use to the original property. This rule does not apply if the taxpayer receives insurance and then used proceeds to buy new property.

Assume, for example, that a taxpayer owns a parking lot for his customers which is condemned for public use by the state. The adjusted basis of the property is $5,000. The state offers and the taxpayer accepts a similar tract of land having a fair market value of $7,500 to be used for the same purpose. No part of the gain measured by the difference between the fair market value of the land received and the $5,000 adjusted basis of the old parking lot is taxable.

Making an Election

We noted above that, for the rules on nonrecognition of gain to apply, a taxpayer must make an election. He makes this election on his return by including gain in gross income only to the extent recognized under the above rules. He must make an amended return and recompute his gain if the requirements are not met. The requirements may not be met for the following reasons: (1) the converted property is not replaced within the time limit; (2) a decision is made not to replace the property; (3) replacement is made at a lower cost than was anticipated. If a taxpayer does not make the election when he files his return but desires to do so later, he may file a claim for refund if he is within the time limit.

All details in connection with an involuntary conversion of property at a gain must be reported in the tax return for the tax year in which the gain is realized. If the gain is to be included in income only to the extent of the excess of the proceeds over the cost of replacement, such election should be indicated. If replacement property is acquired before the return is filed and election is made, the following information should be included: (1) computation of gain; (2) amount realized; and (3) amount of gain, if any, to be reported. If there are excess proceeds which are not to be spent for replacement, these should be included in gross income.

If replacement property is acquired after the return is filed, the taxpayer may still elect not to report gain from involuntary conversion. The following information should be provided: (a) facts relating to involuntary conversion; (b) computation of gain; (c) statement of intention to replace within required time limit. When replacement property is finally acquired, a second detailed statement should be attached to the return which contains detailed information with respect to the replacement property.

Time Limit on Replacement

If a taxpayer decides not to report a gain on involuntary conversion, the replacement property must be acquired within certain time limits. It must be acquired on or after the date on which the old property was damaged or stolen. In the case in which the old property was condemned or requisitioned by the government, or if condemnation was threatened or iminent, the replacement period begins on the date of threat or imminence of requisition or condemnation.

The replacement period ends one year after the close of the first tax year in which any part of the gain on involuntary conversion is realized. This period may be extended by a request to the District Director which shows reasonable cause for not being able to make the replacement within the regular period of time. If delay was for a reasonable cause, an application for extension made after the period may still be considered. Note that, if replacement property is not completed prior to the end of the replacement period, then an advance payment to a contractor for construction of the replacement property is not a timely purchase and does not satisfy the time limits.

To illustrate the operation of the time limits, assume the situation of Bob Martin, a calendar-year taxpayer, who is notified by the state on March 1, 1964 of its intention to acquire his property by negotiation if possible, or by condemnation if necessary. On June 12, 1965, at which time the property had an adjusted basis of $40,000 to Martin, the state converted the property to its use and posted an award of $50,000 with the court. On July 1, 1965 the court released $45,000 of the award to Martin and the $5,000 balance was paid on April 1, 1966. The replacement period starts on March 1, 1964, when Martin was notified. Because part of the $10,000 gain was realized in 1965, when $45,000 of the award was released to Martin, the replacement period ends on December 31, 1966, the last day of the following tax year. By replacing the property within the time limit, Martin may postpone the recognition of the $10,000 gain.

There is no time limit when property is converted directly into other property similar or related in service or use to the original property. A "direct conversion" is where property is received for the property involuntarily converted; this is to be contrasted with the more usual situation in which insurance or condemnation proceeds in the form of money is received and then this money is reinvested into property.

Replacement property may be acquired before the conversion and still meet the time-limit requirements. The property must be acquired after the threat or imminence of condemnation, and the replacement property must be held at the time of the condemnation.

STANDARDS FOR REPLACEMENT PROPERTY

Replacement property may be acquired in the following manner: (a) by direct conversion; (b) by purchase; or (c) by acquiring control of a corporation that owns similar property. Control involves ownership of 80 per cent or more of the voting stock and 80 per cent of the nonvoting stock of the corporation.

For example, assume that Viandi's land was condemned by the state for a freeway. Rather than give Viandi money, the state gave him similar land to replace the condemned land; this is a direct replacement.

Simmons' warehouse was destroyed by a fire. Within the proper time period, Simmons bought another warehouse. This is replacement by a purchase. Simmons could have replaced the warehouse by securing control of a corporation that owned a warehouse.

REQUIREMENTS OF REPLACEMENT PROPERTY

Replacement property must meet certain qualifications for the benefits of the involuntary-conversion rules to apply. These rules are as follows:

(1) Replacement property must be similar or related in service or use to the property that was involuntarily converted;

(2) Replacement property must be held on the date of destruction, seizure, and so forth, of the old property, if the new

property was acquired before the date of condemnation or threat or imminence of condemnation.

(3) The acquisition of the replacement property must be for the purpose of replacing the old property.

(4) The replacement property must not be acquired by gift; rather, it must have a cost basis to the taxpayer. If the replacement method was by acquisition of the control of a corporation owning similar property, then the stock of the corporation must have a cost basis to the taxpayer.

Similar or Related in Service or Use

It is essential that the new property be similar or related in service or use to the converted property. There is a special rule in the case of condemnations that we shall discuss below. However, for other involuntary conversions, such as the result of fire, careful attention has to be given to the "related in service or use" test. For example, it is not sufficient that the old and new properties were used for rental purposes. Also, unimproved real estate is not considered similar to improved real estate.

The Internal Revenue Service and the Tax Court have taken the position that the new tenant must put the property to a functional use similar to that of the old.

Other courts have taken a more moderate approach and compare (1) the extent and nature of the landlord's management activity, (2) the amount and kind of services he renders to the tenant, and (3) the nature of his business risks.

There was no current tax when an office building was replaced with apartments. The controlling factor was that there was no substantial difference in the management activities and the type and amount of services rendered to tenants. As to risk, it was considered that both buildings were in good areas of New York City with similar financing and insurance coverage available. In another case, tax was postponed when an award was given for old property leased to a shoe manufacturer and the amount was reinvested in property rented as a grocery warehouse.

However, in another case, gain was recognized on replacement of a commercial office building with a hotel. The reason was the difference in the landlord's relationship to the properties. Professional management was needed for the hotel, and there were about 140 employees in the hotel but only two in the old office building.

Special Rule for Condemnation of Real Property

If real property is used in a taxpayer's trade or business or is held for investment, and this real property is condemned, seized, requisitioned, or disposed of under threat or imminence of condemnation, a special rule applies. The replacement property may not be similar or related in service or use to the property converted, but if it is replaced within the replacement period by other real estate used either in the taxpayer's trade or business or held for investment, the gain may be postponed.

Thus, under this special rule for real property, property of a like kind has the same meaning as it had in the rule for nontaxable exchanges of property held for productive use or investment previously discussed. Thus, unimproved real estate would be considered similar to improved real estate, provided that the involuntary conversion is a result of a condemnation, requisition, or seizure or threat of such action. This special rule, however, does not apply when the replacement property is acquired by purchasing control of a corporation. It does not apply to involuntary conversions by fire, storm, or other casualty.

The following examples illustrate the operation of the special rule.

Butler and Brown, Inc. owns real property used for the production of income. The firm owned unimproved real property on which it planned to build warehouses, which was condemned before the warehouses were built. Butler and Brown, Inc. reinvested the condemnation proceeds in improved real property on which there was a garage, service station, and automobile salesrooms. Note that the replacement property is not similar or related in service or use to the unimproved property which was condemned. Nevertheless, under the special rule it is considered property of a like kind, and the tax on any gain could be postponed to the extent provided by the involuntary-conversion rules.

Consider the following situation, in which gain could not be postponed under the special rule.

Rawlings and Twist, Inc. owned a commercial office building and leased offices to various firms. The firm sold the office building to the city under threat of condemnation. A gain was realized on the transaction, and Rawlings and Twist immediately used the entire proceeds to purchase more than 80 per cent of the stock of a corporation owning the Midtown Hotel.

In this situation, Rawlings and Twist could not postpone the reporting of the gain on the sale of the office building. Consider the following: (1) Real estate held for the production of income was replaced by real estate held for the production of income. (2) The two properties are not similar or related in service or use even though the Midtown Hotel might rent various storerooms, meeting rooms, and living rooms to daily, weekly, and monthly tenants. (3) The special rule which would allow the otherwise dissimilar properties to qualify for the involuntary-conversion benefits could not be used because the stock of the corporation owning the hotel was purchased rather than the hotel itself. If the hotel and not the stock had been purchased by Rawlings and Twist, then the gain could have been postponed.

LEASEHOLDS

A lease may be given up in a condemnation or under a threat of condemnation. If an award is received in consideration of the lease given up, and if replacement property is purchased within the required replacement period, a taxpayer may elect to postpone tax on realized gain. A taxpayer will be considered to have purchased replacement property if a leasehold similar or related in service or use to the lease given up is purchased.

In order to qualify, there should be an actual purchase of a leasehold, as contrasted with just entering into a lease. In some cases, the construction of new buildings on land owned by the taxpayer or acquired after the condemnation will qualify as replacement property. It is necessary that these be used to carry on the same business as that for which the old leasehold was used.

For example, consider Flynn Furniture Manufacturing, Inc. Flynn Furniture leases improved real property which is used in its manufacturing operations. The property is condemned for public use, and Flynn, Inc. is awarded $100,000 as damages for the loss of its lease. Flynn, Inc. is unable to locate other improved real property suitable for its manufacturing operations, and thus it purchases unimproved land and constructs a new building on it at a total cost of $100,000. These buildings are to be used for the same business of manufacturing furniture. In this situation, the new land and buildings qualify as replacement property. However, if Flynn Furniture had invested part of the proceeds from the condemnation in furniture machinery, the machinery would not qualify as replacement property.

CALCULATION OF GAIN AND LOSS

In the case of an involuntary conversion, a taxpayer may realize a gain or loss as measured by the difference between the proceeds from the involuntary conversion and the adjusted basis of the asset involuntarily converted. In this section we shall discuss the taxability of this realized gain or loss.

Meaning of Proceeds

"Proceeds" means money plus the value of dissimilar property received less the expenses incurred in obtaining the dissimilar property. The amount of the proceeds received is not reduced if part is used to pay off a mortgage or other lien on the old property.

For example, Williams owned property with a basis of $100,000 which was condemned by the state. An award of $200,000 was made to Williams with $150,000 paid directly to him and $50,000 paid to the holder of a mortgage on the property on which Williams was not personally liable. Williams met the time limits for replacement and purchased similar property for $175,000. Williams had a $100,000 gain ($200,000 proceeds less $100,000 adjusted basis), and he is taxable on $25,000 of this gain. (Amount not reinvested.) Note that the $50,000 paid on the mortgage is considered a part of the award received by Williams even though it was not paid directly to Williams and even though the mortgage was not the personal liability of Williams, but instead was attached to the converted property.

Identical Proceeds

In order to qualify for the involuntary-conversion benefits, it is not necessary for the taxpayer to use the identical proceeds from the old property to acquire the new property.

No Taxable Gain on Direct Conversion

If there is a direct conversion, as discussed previously, there is no taxable gain. A taxpayer may not elect to report a gain even though the fair market value of the awarded property exceeds the adjusted basis of the converted property.

Gain Partially Recognized

If the proceeds exceed the cost of replacing the converted property a gain will be partially recognized for tax purposes. The gain will be taxable to the extent that the proceeds exceed the cost of replacement. The taxable gain, of course, cannot be larger than the realized gain as measured by the difference between the amount received and the adjusted basis of the property. Also, the taxpayer has to elect not to have the balance of the recognized gain recognized.

For example, Great Western Realty had an office used in their realty business with an adjusted basis of $9,000 which was totally destroyed by fire in 1965. During 1965 Great Western Realty received $11,000 in insurance proceeds and immediately spent $9,500 to replace their offices. A gain of $2,000 is realized ($11,000 proceeds less $9,000 adjusted basis). However, because Great Western did not spend $1,500 of the insurance proceeds for the replacement of their old offices, they are taxable on $1,500. They may elect not to report the balance of the gain ($500).

If the proceeds that are not reinvested exceed the amount of the realized gain, then there is a tax on the entire realized gain. For example, if Great Western spent only $8,500 on their new offices, they would be taxed on their entire gain of $2,000. The unexpended portion of the insurance proceeds, $2,500 ($11,000 - $8,500), is greater than their realized gain of $2,000 ($11,000 - $9,000).

Elect to Have Entire Gain Taxed

A taxpayer may elect to have the entire gain taxed even though all the requirements for postponement are satisfied. He may also decide not to replace the property, and then his gain would be entirely taxable.

Loss Recognized

If the adjusted basis of the property involuntarily converted exceeds the insurance or other proceeds, a loss is realized and this loss is recognized for tax purposes.

For example, River Realty had offices with an adjusted basis of $20,000 which were rendered completely useless by flood damage. The insurance proceeds amounted to only $15,000, and therefore River Realty had a $5,000 realized loss ($20,000 adjusted basis less $15,000 proceeds) which is recognized for tax purposes.

There are statutory provisions which govern loss deductions, which are discussed in a later chapter. A loss on involuntary conversion, like any other loss, is deductible to the extent allowed by these statutory provisions. For example, losses are deductible only if incurred in trade or business, in a transaction entered into for profit, or if arising from fire, storm, or other casualty.

A loss from fire or storm would be deductible as a casualty loss. Condemnation, however, is not considered a casualty. A loss from involuntary conversion due to condemnation proceedings is not deductible unless incurred in trade or business or in a transaction entered into for profit.

For example, a loss incurred on the involuntary conversion of Karman's personal residence due to condemnation proceedings (no business use) is not deductible. However, a similar loss on Karman's office would be deductible. A loss on the destruction of Karman's personal residence by fire would be deductible as a casualty loss.

No Gain Recognized

If the proceeds exceed the adjusted basis of the converted property and there is a replacement, no gain is recognized when the cost of replacement is greater than the amount received and the taxpayer elects not to have the gain taxed.

For example, Fireside Motel was destroyed by fire. The adjusted basis was $30,000 and the insurance proceeds were $37,000. A new Fireside Motel was purchased within the required time limit for $40,000. Thus, there was a realized gain of $7,000 (proceeds of $37,000 less adjusted basis of $30,000). However, none of this gain is taxable, because the cost of replacement was greater than the amount received.

Note that Fireside Motel would have been taxed on the $7,000 gain if they did not replace. Also note that the $3,000 excess of cost of replacement ($40,000) over insurance proceeds ($37,000) cannot be taken as a loss. It must be added to the basis of the motel as a capital expenditure.

BASIS OF PROPERTY ACQUIRED
BY INVOLUNTARY CONVERSION

In the previous sections we discussed the calculation of gain or loss on involuntary conversions as well as the requirements which must be met in order to postpone gain. The next problem to be discussed is how the basis of the replacement property is determined. This basis, of course, is important for the determination of depreciation in the case of depreciable property, as well as for determination of gain or loss on subsequent disposition of the newly acquired property.

No Gain Recognized Because of Direct Conversion

When property is converted directly into other property similar or related in service or use, the basis of the new asset is the same as that of the old asset adjusted to the date of conversion.

Thus, if Fitzgerald has land with an adjusted basis of $15,000 which is condemned by the city and Fitzgerald receives similar land from the city as a direct replacement, the basis of the new land is $15,000. Note that the basis of the old land carries over regardless of the market value of the new land.

Basis of New Property When Loss is Recognized

A loss is recognized in the case of involuntary conversions, as was explained previously. The basis of the replacement property is the cost of the replacement property.

For example, the factory building of Missles, Inc. was destroyed by explosion. The factory had an adjusted basis of $30,000 but the insurance proceeds were only $25,000. Missles, Inc. purchased a new plant for $33,000. A loss of $5,000 is recognized for tax purposes ($30,000 adjusted basis less $25,000 proceeds). The basis of the new plant is its cost of $33,000.

Basis of New Property--Gain Recognized

Gain is taxable when there is a realized gain and when the amount received on an involuntary conversion of property exceeds the cost of replacement. Gain is taxed to the extent of the excess of the amount of the proceeds over the cost of replacement.

A warehouse owned by Koontz and having an adjusted basis of $14,000 was condemned by the state. Koontz received $20,000 from the state. He bought a new warehouse for $18,000. The realized gain was $6,000, but that gain is recognized only to the extent of $2,000 (excess of condemnation proceeds over cost of new property). The basis of the new warehouse is $14,000, figured as follows:

Realized gain	$ 6,000
Recognized gain	2,000
Gain not recognized	$ 4,000
Cost of new warehouse	$18,000
Less: Gain not recognized	4,000
Basis of new warehouse	$14,000

Allocation of Basis

If two properties replace one property, the cost of the new properties less the gain not recognized on the conversion of the old property must be allocated to the two new properties. This is illustrated by the following example.

A farm owned by Farrell, and having an adjusted basis of $14,000, was condemned by the state. Farrell received $20,000 from the state. As a replacement, Farrell bought two adjoining farms totaling about the same acreage as the condemned land. He paid $10,800 for farm No. 1 and $7,200 for farm No. 2. Although the realized gain was $6,000, this is recognized only to the extent of the excess of the condemnation proceeds over the total cost of the new properties--$2,000. The basis of each of the new properties is: farm No. 1--$8,400, farm No. 2--$5,600, figured as follows:

Realized gain	$ 6,000
Recognized gain	2,000
Gain not recognized	$ 4,000
Cost of new property (both farms)	$18,000
Less: Gain not recognized	4,000
Basis of new property (both farms)	$14,000

Basis of farm #1--10,800/18,000 X $14,000 = $8,400
Basis of farm #2-- 7,200/18,000 X $14,000 = $5,600

No Gain Recognized--Cost of Replacement Greater Than Proceeds

No gain is recognized when the cost of replacing involuntarily converted property exceeds the amount received. The basis of the new property is the cost of the new property less the amount of gain not recognized. If more than one parcel of property is purchased, then the basis is allocated to the new properties in proportion to their respective costs.

Dunn's manufacturing plant, having an adjusted basis of $30,000, was destroyed by fire. The insurance proceeds were $37,000. Dunn bought a new plant for $40,000. No gain is recognized, and the basis of the new plant is figured as follows:

Realized gain	$ 7,000
Recognized gain	0
Gain not recognized	$ 7,000
Cost of new plant	40,000
Less: Gain not recognized	7,000
Basis of new plant	$33,000

Assume the same facts as in the table at the bottom of page 66, except that Dunn bought two new plants: (1) at cost of $10,000, (2) at cost of $30,000. Basis of the two new plants is figured as follows:

Basis of plant #1--10,000/40,000 X $33,000 = $ 8,250
Basis of plant #2--30,000/40,000 X $33,000 = $24,750

USE AND OCCUPANCY INSURANCE PROCEEDS

Use and occupancy and business interruption insurance proceeds are not considered proceeds from an involuntary conversion insofar as they are reimbursement of actual net profits in a taxpayer's business. Thus, they are considered taxable income. Insofar as the proceeds are compensation for loss of profits, taxation cannot be deferred by investing the proceeds in replacement property.

If, however, the taxpayer receives payments for loss of use and occupancy based on a flat per-diem or weekly rate, the payments may be treated as involuntary-conversion proceeds. These proceeds then will not be taxed if reinvested in replacement property.

SPECIAL ASSESSMENTS AND SEVERANCE DAMAGES IN CONDEMNATIONS

Only part of a taxpayer's property may be condemned. The taxpayer may receive a condemnation award for the part condemned. For the part not condemned, the taxpayer may receive severance damages, or alternatively, if he is benefited by the condemnation, a special-benefit assessment may be levied against the property he has retained.

Special-Benefit Assessment

A special-benefit assessment against the part of the taxpayer's property that is not condemned is not deductible by the taxpayer against his income. The treatment is as follows: (1) reduce the severance damages; (2) reduce the condemnation award; (3) add any amount left over to the basis of the property that is retained by the taxpayer.

Severance Damages

Severance damages are not considered to be taxable income. Severance damages are applied against expenses in the following order: (1) against the proportionate share of expense of securing the condemnation award; (2) against the full amount of any special assessment levied for benefits to the remaining real estate; (3) against the expenses of restoring the retained property to its former use. If there is still a balance of the severance damages left, this balance will reduce the basis of the retained property. Any balance still remaining after the above offsets and after reducing the basis of the retained property to zero will be taxable as income.

The Internal Revenue Service maintains that severance damages have to be separately stated in the contract with the condemning authority or the entire amount will be treated as a condemnation award. However, the Tax Court has held that these damages need not be separately stated. If a taxpayer received interest which is added to the condemnation award, this interest is taxable as ordinary income.

It is important for the owner of condemned property who also receives severance damages to have these severance damages separately stated.

Consider Sterling's cherry orchard: The state condemned part of Sterling's land to build a freeway. The total amount to cover severance damages and condemnation was $120,000. The adjusted basis of the land that was to be used for the freeway was $40,000 and the basis of the retained land was $150,000. Assuming that there was no allocation in the award, Sterling's gain would be as follows:

Amount received	$120,000
Basis of land condemned	40,000
	$ 80,000

However, assume that Sterling had the award stated separately, with $70,000 being the condemnation award and $50,000 being severance damages. The gain is now only $30,000. The balance reduces the basis of the remaining land to $100,000, as shown below:

Amount received allocated to condemned land	$70,000	Old basis of remaining land	$150,000
Basis of condemned land	40,000	Severance damages	50,000
Gain	$30,000	New basis	$100,000

Thus, Sterling pays tax on $30,000 instead of $80,000. However, his basis for the remaining land is now $100,000 instead of $150,000, a fact which will be of importance for future disposition of the property.

Consequential Damages

A taxpayer may receive compensation because of damages caused by improvements made by a state, city, or other public body when there is no actual taking of the taxpayer's property. These damages are paid, for example, for impairment of access, flooding, or erosion of property. They are treated for tax purposes in the same manner as severance damages.

EASEMENTS

In the previous chapter we discussed the fact that a sale of an easement in land is considered a sale of an interest in the land. The amount received for granting the easement was used to reduce the basis of the entire property, and if the amount received exceeded the basis of the entire property, then there was a taxable gain. An easement acquired in condemnation or under the threat or imminence of condemnation is an involuntary conversion subject to the involuntary-conversion rules.

Involuntary Conversion of Residence

In a later chapter on home ownership we shall discuss the rules in respect to the determination of gain or loss on the involuntary conversion of a residence. A taxpayer may elect to defer gain if there is an involuntary conversion of his residence through seizure, requisition, or condemnation. He may also postpone recognition of gain if there is a sale or exchange under threat or imminence of such an involuntary conversion. However, note that the special rule for nonrecognition of gain does not apply to an involuntary conversion of a personal residence by theft or destruction.

Chapter 4

Capital Gains and Losses

When gain or loss is recognized on the sale, exchange, or other disposition of an asset, this gain or loss may be either ordinary or capital gain or loss. Whether it is ordinary or capital gain or loss is important to the taxpayer. The maximum tax that can be paid on the excess of long-term capital gain over net short-term capital loss is 25 per cent and it may be less. Ordinary tax rates in 1965 and subsequently go to a high of 70 per cent. In earlier years the tax rates went even higher; for example, in 1964 the high was 77 per cent and in 1963 the high was 91 per cent. The spread between the ordinary tax rate and the tax on long-term capital gains is such that a great deal of tax planning is concerned with how to obtain capital gains.

We have a variety of problems to study in the next two chapters on capital gains. The sale or exchange of a capital asset yields capital gain. Thus, we have to carefully study the meaning of the term "capital asset." In addition, we find capital gain arising in other situations, such as in the case of involuntary conversions, liquidating dividends, and so forth. In real estate we have a particular problem in distinguishing between an investor and a dealer. In one case we have capital gains or loss; in the other we have ordinary income or loss. How long an asset is held is often important, because short-term capital transactions are distinguished from long-term capital transactions. Short-term gain or loss results when the asset is held for six months or less. There are special calculations that we shall study which implement the rule that the maximum tax on the excess of long-term capital gains over short-term capital losses is 25 per cent. Note that this is a maximum tax and, depending upon the taxpayer's position on the scale of progressive tax rates, it might be less. Then we have the so-called Section 1231 assets. These assets mainly consist of depreciable property and real property used in a trade or business, and they are treated as capital assets if they are held for more than six months and if recognized gains on their sale or exchange exceed recognized losses.

As we noted before, it is desirable to have a long-term capital gain rather than ordinary income. Thus, taxpayers would depreciate assets as much as allowable. This depreciation would be a deduction against revenues in arriving at ordinary income. Often, because of inflation or for some other reason, the assets would eventually be sold at a capital gain. This was advantageous to the taxpayer, because the depreciation deduction offset revenue taxed at ordinary income rates, and the gain was taxed at a maximum capital gain rate of 25 per cent. To counteract this, depreciation recapture rules were established for depreciable personal property in 1962. Buildings and livestock were not included in the recapture rules in the 1962 law. However, in the Revenue Act of 1964, a modified version of depreciation recapture was applied to buildings and leaseholds of buildings and land. The effect of the recapture provisions is to make a portion of gain ordinary gain rather than capital gain.

The next problem we shall examine consists of the tax problems arising in the subdivision of property. This is included here because we again have the issue of whether gain on sale is ordinary gain or capital gain.

CAPITAL GAINS AND LOSSES

Basically, the sale or exchange of a capital asset yields capital gain or loss. Thus, it is important to know what is included under capital assets. There are other transactions which yield capital gain or loss which we shall discuss later. The law defines a "capital asset" by exception. Instead of saying what is included in the term "capital asset," the law indicates what is not included.

Not a Capital Asset

A capital asset is everything owned by a taxpayer except the following: (1) stock in trade; (2) real or personal property includible in inventory; (3) real or personal property held for sale to customers; (4) accounts or notes receivable that are acquired in the ordinary course of a trade or business for services rendered and receivables from the sale of any of the properties described above, or for services rendered as an employee; (5) depreciable property used in a trade or business; (6) real property used in a trade or business; (7) a copyright, or a literary, musical, or artistic composition, or similar property if they were created by personal efforts. These are also included if they were acquired from the creator under circumstances entitling the recipient to the basis of the creator; (8) federal, state, and municipal obligations issued on or after March 1, 1941 on a discount basis and payable without interest at a fixed maturity date not over one year from the date of issue.

The above must be handled with care. For example, later in this chapter we shall consider how gains from depreciable property and real property used in a trade or business are treated as capital gains if held over six months and if gains exceed losses. This is a Section 1231 transaction. Note also that we have the phrase "in a trade or business" in several of the above categories. Here we have the sometimes ticklish problem of establishing whether something is a trade or business or whether it is just an investment.

Securities

Unless they fall into one of the categories described in the previous section, securities such as stock, bonds, and notes are capital assets. An example of an exception would be shares of stock that are owned by a dealer in securities and which are held for sale to customers. There are even exceptions to this rule when a dealer in securities identifies his securities as being held for investment. As we discuss in the chapter on corporations, stock in a collapsible corporation is not a capital asset under certain circumstances. Stock in a small business investment company or in a small business stock is not a capital asset if it is sold at a loss under certain conditions.

REAL PROPERTY

Real property used in a trade or business is not a capital asset, as we noted in the description of items excluded from the category of a capital asset. Conversely, real property not used in a trade or business is a capital asset. Thus, we have the problem of when real property is used in a trade or business. Real property may be inventory in the hands of a dealer. The factor of classification of real estate is particularly important in determining whether the sale or exchange of real estate will give rise to capital gain or loss or to ordinary income or loss. First, we shall consider whether each classification gives rise to capital gain or loss or to ordinary gain or loss. Then we shall consider the problem of placing properties in the right classification.

Real Estate Held for Investment

If property is held for the production of income, it is a capital asset. To be a capital asset, however, it cannot be used in the trade or business of the taxpayer or be held primarily for sale to customers. In the discussion below, carefully note the following three categories: (1) real estate held for investment; (2) real estate used in the trade or business of the taxpayer; and (3) real estate held primarily for sale to customers.

Included in this category would be unimproved real estate or vacant improved property. Also included would be property held for production of income but not used in the trade or business. When rental property is held for the production of income and when it is used in a trade or business is not entirely clear, as we shall discuss below. The sale or exchange of property held for investment or for production of income results in a capital gain or capital loss. The depreciation recapture rules of the 1964 Revenue Act may cause some of the gain to be ordinary gain.

Personal Residence

A personal residence of a taxpayer is a capital asset. If the residence is sold at a gain, the result is a capital gain. This gain, however, can be deferred if certain requirements are met as to the investment of the proceeds in a new residence, as explained in a later chapter. A loss on the sale of a personal residence is not deductible in any manner. Problems arise with personal residences when they are used either at the same time or at a different time for the production of income as well as for the home of the taxpayer.

Used in Trade or Business

If real estate is used in a trade or business, it is not a capital asset. Sale or exchange of property used in a trade or business is a Section 1231 transaction and as such is treated in a special manner. If the property is held for more than six months and if recognized gains on sales of Section 1231 assets are larger than the recognized losses, the net gain is considered to be a gain from the sale or exchange of capital assets and is reported with other capital gains and losses. The end result of all this is a long-term capital gain. If, however, the property used in the trade or business is sold at a loss and the loss is larger than the recognized gains from Section 1231 transactions, then the net loss is an ordinary loss. There are other Section 1231 assets besides real property or depreciable property used in a trade or business, as we shall discuss later, when we shall also demonstrate the handling of the mechanics of Section 1231 transactions. Note also that, in the case of gains, a certain amount of the gains may be changed into ordinary gain by the recapture rules of the Revenue Act of 1964.

An ordinary loss arising from a Section 1231 asset has the advantage of being able to be carried back and forward as a net operating loss. A capital loss, on the other hand, is subject to certain limitations and may be carried forward only under the capital loss-carryover provisions. Since the 1964 Revenue Act, there is no limit in time for the capital loss carryover. Prior to this time there was a five-year limit.

Property Held for Sale to Customers

Property held for sale to customers is considered to be inventory. The sale of inventory gives rise to ordinary income and ordinary loss. Many of the problems discussed below relate to the problem of "dealer or investor." Generally the dealer has ordinary income and the investor has capital gain. The result obviously is that everyone wants to be an investor and not a dealer, and that there are many court cases on this controversy.

PROBLEM OF TRADE OR BUSINESS
OR PRODUCTION OF INCOME

First, we shall not be concerned with the dealer problem but shall just consider the distinction between trade or business on the one hand and production of income or investment on the other hand. Ignoring the depreciation recapture rules for now, the investor has capital gain or loss. The taxpayer using property in a trade or business has a Section 1231 transaction when he sells the property. Thus, he has capital gain on sale subject to other Section 1231 transactions or he has an ordinary loss. The advantage of the latter status, then, is that losses may be deductible in full.

To illustrate the difference, let us take the situation of Dr. Schmidt, who holds an apartment as an investment and just receives a check from the property managers monthly, and compare it to that of apartment house operator Rose Armstrong, who owns, operates, and manages her apartment house. We shall assume that there is no controversy about the fact that Dr. Schmidt is an investor and that Rose Armstrong is in a trade or business.

Dr. Schmidt has an adjusted basis of $50,000 for his apartment and he sells it for $70,000. In addition, this year he sold some medical equipment that he used in his medical practice at a loss of $3,000. As he is using the medical equipment in his profession, this is a Section 1231 loss. As a result of the above transactions, Dr. Schmidt has a capital gain of $20,000 on his building, on which he pays a maximum tax of 25 per cent. He also has an ordinary loss of $3,000 from the sale of his medical equipment.

Rose Armstrong also has an apartment with an adjusted basis of $50,000 which she sells for $70,000. In addition, this year she sold some appliances at a loss of $3,000. Because Rose is engaged in a trade or business, she has a Section 1231 gain of $20,000 and a Section 1231 loss of $3,000. These are offset, and the result is a $17,000 Section 1231 gain, which is treated as a capital gain. Obviously, Dr. Schmidt is in a better position because he gets his $3,000 loss as a deduction from other income.

When real estate is classified as used in a trade or business, it is desirable to attempt to have all the gains in one taxable year and all the losses in another taxable year. Thus, if in the example above Rose sold the appliances in a different year, when there were no other Section 1231 transactions, she would have had a fully deductible loss. The entire $20,000 gain on the apartment in a different year (with no other capital transactions) would be treated as a capital gain. If, in the above example, Dr. Schmidt holding the property for investment sold the property at a loss, he would have a capital loss which could be applied against capital gains and $1,000 per year written off against ordinary income. Rose Armstrong, holding the property in a trade or business, would have a Section 1231 loss which (assuming there are no Section 1231 gains) is fully deductible.

To summarize, it is more important to have the property classified as used in a trade or business if it sold at a loss. If the property is sold at a gain and has been held for more than six months, it does not make much difference unless there have been other Section 1231 transactions.

Determination of Classification

The important factor for determining whether or not there is a trade or business use seems to be a question of the taxpayer's activities in connection with the project. If the taxpayer spends a great deal of his time in the operation and management of rental property, he probably would be considered to be engaged in a trade or business.

Residences for Rent

There is a difference of opinion as to whether the rental of one unit constitutes a trade or business. The Second Circuit Court has ruled that the rental of a single piece of property is not a trade or business. The result of this is that a loss is a capital loss. However, the Tax Court in similar situations has ruled that the rental of one building constituted a trade or business and the loss was deductible in full. In the case in the Second Circuit Court, the taxpayer was renting an inherited house until it could be sold.

Conversion to rental use. If a personal residence is converted to rental use, there is a special rule for the determination of basis for future gain or loss. The basis for loss is the lower of the following: (1) fair market value and (2) adjusted basis on date of conversion to rental use. For gain, the basis is adjusted basis on date of conversion.

PROPERTY HELD FOR SALE TO CUSTOMERS

The area of greatest controversy is whether property is held for investment or for sale to customers. This is important because the sale of investment property gives rise to capital gain or Section 1231 gain, whereas the sale of inventory gives rise to ordinary gain. A dealer is unable to use the tax-free exchange rules that we discussed in the last chapter, which an investor is able to do. A dealer can deduct his expenses of making a sale according to his accounting method, whereas an investor offsets his expenses against the selling price. An investor will have a Section 1231 loss if it is property used in a trade or business. He will have a capital loss otherwise, whereas the dealer has an ordinary loss.

Not Just Brokers

Many taxpayers are in the business of selling real estate. Real estate is their inventory and they realize ordinary gain or loss when they sell it. It is important, however, that others involved in real estate investments may be classified as a dealer even though this is not their only or main business. A person can be considered to be in the real estate business in one year and not in it in the next year. Whether a person is considered a dealer or investor depends on the facts in the particular situation. There is no one test used for determination. Below we shall discuss factors that are considered in both directions.

Factors Indicating that Taxpayer Is a Dealer

If sales are frequent and continuous, there is an indication that the taxpayer is a dealer. Active participation in sales and promotion by the taxpayer or agents of the taxpayer is another factor. Another indication is if a taxpayer obtains a license to deal in real estate or gives indication that his main business is real estate. The intention to resell at a profit at time of acquisition, as well as quick turnover of property, is obviously more indicative of a dealer than an investor.

In the following situation, Walter Miller would be considered to have ordinary income on the sale of his apartments. These are considered to be property held primarily for sale to customers in the ordinary course of his business. In the first year Walter, who is in the business of building and selling houses, purchased six lots, resold one, and built apartments on five. The next year, after the apartments were finished, he started a vigorous selling campaign related to these properties. The selling of the apartments was handled in the same way as the house sales and by the very same sales outlet. It took a while to sell some of the apartments, so Walter rented them during that year and the following year before he sold them. Nevertheless, Walter's apartments are considered to be inventory property and not property used in a trade or business, and the result is ordinary income.

Factors Indicating that Taxpayer Is Not a Dealer

If the taxpayer is not a real estate dealer, this is in his favor. Also, if his records show that the intent of holding the property is for investment rather than sale, and if on acquisition he had no plans of selling, he is more likely to be classified as an investor. An investor is more likely to make only a few sales of real estate over a long period of time. Where there is no sign, no advertising, and no sales office, and when the purchaser seeks the seller, there is an indication that there is an investor and not a dealer. Other favorable factors are when the real estate is rented before sale and when there is no subdivision of the real estate into lots. We shall discuss the problem of subdivisions in the next chapter. There are special rules in the case of subdivision of real estate which, if met, allow the subdivider to achieve capital gain.

Number of Sales

Frequent and continuous sales of realty were indicated earlier as a factor indicating that the taxpayer was a dealer. It is important to note, however, that it is not just number of sales that is the criteria.

For example, in one case, an attorney had acquired realty through foreclosure of bonds and tax deeds which he had purchased in the early 1930's. He sold a total of 134 parcels of land in the three years about which he was questioned and had had an average of 40 sales per year in the pervious years. The Ninth Circuit Court ruled that he was an investor because: (1) he principally practiced law; (2) he did not advertise or solicit offers; (3) he did not improve the real estate; and (4) he held the property on an average of ten years before selling.

A similar decision was reached in the case of another lawyer who bought a number of unimproved lots intending to hold them until they increased in value. During four years he purchased 32 lots and he had sold 31 two years later. The court, in indicating that he was an investor, considered that he did not advertise or improve the property and indicated that the number of sales alone did not make him a dealer.

A similar result was reached where the taxpayer had other regular businesses, did not advertise or solicit offers, did not improve lots, and held them for a long period of time. Thus, other factors besides sheer number of sales may be most important.

DEALERS GETTING CAPITAL GAIN

Usually the sale of property by a real estate dealer gives ordinary income. The very fact that he is in the real estate business is against him. It is possible, however, for real estate dealers to get capital gain on the sale of certain properties held for investment. The property must have been purchased for investment purposes and not for resale; it should be segregated from his properties held for resale.

In one situation, a company acquired a 65-acre tract to be subdivided into small residential lots and sold to builders. Two of the parcels (of 11 and 13 acres) were unacceptable to both the builders and the bankers. The company set up investment accounts for these two parcels and allocated cost to them. They were sold to unsolicited buyers. The court ruled that they yielded capital gain as land held for investment. Reasons given were that the parcels were not commensurate with the business operations of the company and that the company did not solicit sales.

In another situation, the taxpayer owned 50 per cent or more stock in about a dozen corporations. These companies developed and sold residential tract homes. In two situations, he purchased land and resold it to the companies for subdivision, development, and resale. The Court pointed out the separateness of the taxpayer's business and the business of the corporation he controlled. The result was the allowance of capital gain on the sale of land to the corporations. The taxpayer had made two isolated transactions and there was not enough frequency to establish a selling pattern. The Court considered it immaterial that the companies were dealers who would develop the land and sell it to customers.

Subject to the hazards we shall discuss shortly, there is an additional advantage in a situation like this in that the taxpayer can sell the property at a gain which is capital gain. The corporation then gets this higher market value as its basis, so that the company has less ordinary income when it subdivides and sells.

The dangers are as follows: (1) Under Section 351 of the Internal Revenue Code, no gain or loss is recognized if property is transferred to a controlled corporation by one or more persons solely in exchange for stock or securities. The transaction then would be tax-free and there would be no capital gain and no stepped-up basis for the corporation. We discuss tax-free transfers to controlled corporations in the chapter on corporations. (2) Another danger is that, if the corporation is too thinly capitalized, the Internal Revenue may claim that even short-term notes are really stock. A thinly capitalized corporation is one in which there is a small amount of equity capital in relation to debt obligations. (3) In the case of depreciable property, gain on sale between an individual and a corporation more than 80 per cent owned by the individual or certain related parties yields ordinary income rather than capital gain.

CAPITAL GAIN OR LOSS IN OTHER SITUATIONS

We have seen that the sale or exchange of a capital asset results in capital gain or loss. In addition, subject to other Section 1231 transactions, sale or exchange of property used in a trade or business if sold at a gain and if held over six months gets capital-gain treatment. Now we shall consider other transactions which result in a capital gain or loss.

Options

A taxpayer may have recognized gain from the sale or exchange of an option to buy or sell property. Such gain or loss is handled in the same manner as gain or loss from the sale or exchange of the property subject to the option. When a taxpayer has a loss because he did not exercise an option, the assumed date of sale is the day the option expires.

Thus, if a taxpayer has an option on a capital asset, he has capital gain or loss from the sale or exchange of the option. Conversely, an option to buy or sell property which is not a capital asset in the taxpayer's hands yields ordinary gain or loss. An option on Section 1231 property would be treated the same as Section 1231 property.

For example, an architect owned and rented several parcels of real estate. He purchased an option on vacant land for $4,000. His intent was to build a store on this vacant land when he located a suitable tenant. Because he was unable to find a tenant, he did not exercise the option.

The architect's loss is an ordinary loss. The loss was on Section 1231 property, and thus it is treated as a Section 1231 loss, which, as you recall, is an ordinary loss. The Court ruled that the architect was in the business of operating real estate for rent, and that the land on which he purchased the option was to be used in this business.

Granting options. In the above discussion, we have considered the situation of the taxpayer that bought the option. The party that grants the option realizes ordinary income in the amount he receives if the option is not exercised. This is true even though the option was on a capital asset. When the option is exercised, the amount of the option is added to the other sales proceeds to determine gain or loss on sale. The total gain or loss on sale then depends on the nature of the property that is sold.

Dealers in options. A dealer in options that has an option as inventory does not get capital-asset treatment.

Tax Planning with Options

We shall see below that, in order for a long-term capital gain to result, property must be held more than six months. The holding period for property acquired under an option to purchase starts on the day after the property was acquired. It does not start on the day after the option was acquired.

Selling an option. A person who has an option on property

may either exercise it or sell it. As described above, if he sells
the option, he has capital or ordinary gain or loss, depending on the
nature of the property that it represents.

Assume that investor Bertha felt that certain property on the
outskirts of Westchester would be developed as business property.
As a result, he purchased an option on this property. Bertha's
calculations were correct, and at a later date (after he had held the
option for over six months) plans were announced for development
of the area. The value of the property increased accordingly, and
so did the value of the option. Bertha wisely sells the option and
gets long-term capital-gain treatment.

If he exercised the option and then sold the property, his
gain would be short-term capital gain, because it would be considered an immediate sale of the land. If he gave an option to the
developer of the area to purchase the property, he would also have
a short-term capital gain. The giving of the second option is considered to indicate a sale of the land rather than a sale of the option.

A seller might use the option as a way of extending the holding
period of the property past six months in order to achieve long-term
rather than short-term capital-gain treatment. If the option does
not really give the purchaser an opportunity for exercising the option
or letting it expire, the transaction may be challenged. A seller
also may use an option to get income in one year rather than another. Again he has to be careful, because, if the amount of the
option is quite large as compared to the selling price, it may be
attacked as a down payment on the property.

For example, investor Barton Wilkins purchased property
for $40,000 and three months later had an offer of $60,000 for it.
Wilkins wished to accept the offer, but he was not anxious to have
a $20,000 short-term capital gain this year. However, he was in
need of some cash, so he was in a quandary as to what to do.

Wilkins went to lawyer Caulins, and the result was an option
contract. The option contract called for a $5,000 payment for a
six-months' option to purchase. The purchaser had complete rights
of exercising the option or forfeiting it. As a result, Wilkins had
$5,000 cash on which he did not have to pay any tax until the option
was either exercised or forfeited. In addition, he was likely to have
a long-term capital gain rather than a short-term capital gain, as
the option would not be exercised until after the six-months' holding
period on the property was past. Note that Wilkins definitely gave
an option under which the purchaser had full rights. If the option
was merely a disguised sales contract, the transaction could well
be challenged.

Cancellation Payment on a Lease

The taxability of these payments depends on whether the landlord or the tenant is receiving the cancellation payment.

Tenant receiving payments. If the tenant receives the cancellation payment, he is considered to have gain or loss from the sale or exchange of the lease. How this gain or loss is treated depends on the nature of the property. If the property is used in the tenant's trade or business, he has a gain on the sale of a Section 1231 asset, which is usually a capital gain. If it is his home, a gain would be a capital gain but a loss would not be deductible.

In the case of a sublease, where the tenant transfers the property to another tenant and the new tenant takes over the lease payment obligations and pays the original tenant an additional amount for giving him use of the property, the payments are ordinary income. A sublease is not considered the sale or exchange of a leasehold subject to capital-gain or loss treatment.

Landlord receives payment. If a landlord receives a payment from the tenant for cancellation of a lease, he has ordinary income and not capital gain.

Sale of a Partnership Interest

The sale of a partnership interest is considered to be the sale of a capital asset with certain important exceptions. The exceptions relate to the part of the gain or loss that is attributable to unrealized receivables or to inventory items which have appreciated substantially in value. The latter amounts are taxed as ordinary gain or loss.

Sale of a Sole Proprietorship

The sale of an unincorporated business is considered to be a sale of all the individual assets which comprise the business. To decide how much of the gain or loss is ordinary in nature and how much is capital in nature, it is necessary to classify the assets according to their nature. This classification would include: (1) capital assets; (2) real property and depreciable property used in the trade or business and held for more than six months (Section 1231 assets); and (3) other property.

Classification of assets. Inventory and real property and depreciable property used in a trade or business held six months or less are considered other property. Accounts and notes receivable acquired for services rendered or for the sale of inventory are included here and are not capital assets. Installment notes and installment receivables resulting from the sale of inventory are also classified as other property.

Land and leaseholds used in trade or business are not capital assets. If held over six months they are put in classification (2) on page 82. Buildings, machinery, furniture and fixtures also fit in this category.

Good will and covenants not to compete. Good will is a capital asset. Thus, the sale of good will yields capital gain or loss. However, there are problems as to what is good will. A covenant not to compete is considered to be nonseverable from good will if it accompanies the transfer of good will in the sale of a going concern and its primary function is the assurance of the beneficial enjoyment of the good will that is acquired. Conversely, a covenant not to compete that is for a fixed number of years and is not in effect the sale of good will is classed as other payments. The burden is upon the taxpayer to prove whether he sold good will or a covenant not to compete.

Professional skills. The determination of whether good will is sold or not depends upon the facts of the particular case. If a seller retains the right to fees collected after the sale for services performed before the sale, this is attributed to services performed and results in ordinary income. Similarly, the right to amounts for services performed after the sale results in ordinary income. If a seller, a member of a professional firm continues to be a member of the firm and still has his name in the firm, he cannot allocate a portion of the sale price to good will.

Allocation. The selling price for the business must be allocated amongst the various assets according to the value of each individual asset relative to the total value. If the business that is sold depends solely on the professional skill of the seller, no portion of the selling price can be allocated to good will. This is true whether or not the exclusive use of the firm name is also transferred to the purchaser.

Determination of gain or loss. Once the assets are all classified into the three categories and the sale price is allocated, then gain or loss is computed for each asset. Capital assets yield capital gain or loss. Real or depreciable property held for over six months yields capital gain or ordinary loss subject to the offset rules we shall discuss in the section of this chapter on Section 1231 assets, and other property gives ordinary income or loss.

SALE TO RELATED PARTY

When depreciable property is sold or exchanged directly or indirectly between certain related parties, ordinary gain results. Losses are not allowed between related parties. Related parties here include: (1) husband and wife; and (2) an individual and his controlled corporation. A controlled corporation is one in which the individual, his spouse, his minor children, and his minor grandchildren own together over 80 per cent in value of its outstanding stock.

PATENTS AND COPYRIGHTS

Patents and copyrights may be depreciable property used in a trade or business. If they are held more than six months, they are classified with other Section 1231 assets. There are two important exceptions. A copyright which was created through the personal effort of the taxpayer, even though it is used in a trade or business, is considered as other property and gives rise to ordinary income. This is true also if the taxpayer derived his basis from the person whose efforts created the property.

Patents

Under certain circumstances a patent is a capital asset. An individual inventor receives capital-gains treatment on transfer of a patent provided that the transfer is not to certain related parties. An individual backer of an inventor who received his interest by advancing money prior to the completion of the invention may also be entitled to capital-gains treatment. Again the sale must not be to certain related parties.

TRANSACTIONS TREATED AS SALES OR EXCHANGES

Generally, to achieve capital gain or loss, there should be a sale or exchange. However, some transactions which do not come under the usual connotation of sale or exchange are treated as such. Among these are the following items of interest to real estate: (1) involuntary conversion of business property; (2) cutting of timber; (3) liquidating dividends of corporations; (4) securities that become worthless during the tax year; (5) nonbusiness debts that become worthless in the tax year; (5) repossession and foreclosures of mortgaged property. A discussion of these items is found in appropriate sections.

HOLDING PERIODS

The period during which the capital asset was held determines whether a gain or loss from the sale or exchange of a capital asset is short-term or long-term. Short-term results come from capital assets held not more than six months. Long-term gain or loss is the result of holding capital assets more than six months. As we shall discuss in more detail shortly, an individual taxpayer is allowed a deduction from gross income of 50 per cent of the excess of net long-term capital gain over net short-term capital loss. Thus, it is important to distinguish between short- and long-term items.

Calculating the Period Held

The taxpayer who miscalculates his sale by one day and as a result has ordinary income on a short-term capital gain rather than a long-term capital gain may be sadly disappointed. The date that the property is acquired is not included, but the date it is disposed of is included. The same date in each succeeding month is considered the beginning of a new month, regardless of the number of days there are in the preceding month.

For example: Bernie Smith purchases property on March 4, so that his holding period begins on March 5. The 5th of each succeeding month is considered the beginning of a new month. If Bernie sells the property on September 4, his holding period is not more than six months and he has a short-term capital gain. However, if he sells it on September 5, his holding period is more than six months and he has a long-term capital gain.

Real Property

The holding period of real property begins on (1) the day after the day on which title passes or (2) on the day after the day on which delivery or possession is made and the burdens and privileges of ownership are assumed by the buyer, whichever happens first. The delivery or possession of real property is without significance under an option agreement until a contract of sale comes into being through the exercise of the option. Thus, the holding period of a seller does not end prior to the date the option is exercised.

New Buildings

Part of a building can be considered as being finished prior to the entire building. In this case the holding period for each part starts at the time of its completion.

Community Property

The holding period for a surviving spouse's share of community property generally begins on the date the property was acquired by the spouses. The share that is inherited from the deceased spouse has a holding period which begins on the date of the decedent's death.

Gifts after December 31, 1920

For gifts after December 31, 1920, the holding period of property starts with the date the property was acquired by the donor, with the following exception. If the property has a value lower than cost at the date of the gift, and the sale results in a loss, the holding period starts on the date of the gift. Recall from Chapter 2 that, if property is acquired by gift, the basis for determination of gain is the donor's basis, but the basis for determination of loss is the lower of cost or fair market value at date of gift. This holding-period rule is consistent with the determination of basis.

For example, George Brown purchased a lot in Palatial Acres for $1,000 on April 1, 1960. The subdivision did not develop as expected, so that the lot had a fair market value of only $600 on December 25, 1964, when George gave it to his sister Darlene. Darlene held it for a short time and sold it on March 5, 1965 for $300. Darlene has a short-term capital loss, because she sold it at a loss, and her holding period starts on December 25, 1964, the date of the gift. She has a loss of $300, which is the difference between the sales price of $300 and her basis of $600. Her basis is the lower of cost ($1,000) and fair market value at date of gift ($600).

Now let us change the situation and assume that Darlene sold the lot for $1,200. Then she has a long-term capital gain of $200. Her holding period goes back to the date of purchase by brother George, and her gain is measured by the difference between sales price and her basis, which is the same as George's ($1,000).

Securities

The date of trade and not the date of settlement is used as the date of acquisition or disposition for securities bought and sold through stock exchanges. There are a variety of rules which relate to identification of securities when securities are purchased at different times, and also rules relating to short sales, which we shall not discuss in this text.

Property Transmitted at Death

The date of death is the beginning of the holding period when property is transmitted at death.

Amos Thompson passed away on March 15, 1965 of a coronary and left two lots to his son, Samuel. The lots had been purchased by Amos in 1953 for $5,000, but their fair market value on date of death was $10,000. The lots were distributed to Sam on June 15, 1965. Sam sold the lots for $11,000 on August 15, 1965. The result is that Sam has a short-term capital gain of $1,000. His gain is measured by the difference between the sales price ($11,000) and his basis, which is fair market value at date of death ($10,000). He has a short-term capital gain measured by the holding period March 15, 1965 to August 15, 1965. Sam should have waited and held the property for six months after his father passed away, and then he would have had a long-term capital gain.

Sale of Partnership Interest

The date when the individual acquired the interest in a partnership determines the beginning of his holding period. If the operation of the business continues, the death of one of the partners does not change the holding period of the other partners.

Old Residence Replaced by New One

When we discuss home ownership in a later chapter, we will note how gain on sale of a residence may be postponed by investing the proceeds in a new residence. In this case, the holding period of the new residence includes the time that the old residence was held.

Acquisition in a Nontaxable Exchange

In the previous chapter we discussed nontaxable exchanges where the new property took the basis of the old property subject to adjustments for "boot," and so forth. The property that is received in a nontaxable exchange has the same date basis as the property for which it was exchanged, provided that the property exchanged was either a capital asset or depreciable property used in taxpayer's trade or business.

For example, on January 4, 1962 James Swenson purchased a lot, which he exchanged for another lot on March 4, 1964. James, who purchased these lots for investment purposes, paid $10,000 for the first lot. Because the value of the first lot went up to $12,000, he did not have to add any money in order to exchange it for the second lot, which was worth $12,000.   Under the tax-free exchange provisions of the Internal Revenue Code, he did not have to pay any tax on the exchange.   James sold the second lot four months after he acquired it.   Nevertheless, he has a long-term capital gain because the date basis is January 5, 1962; this is the day after the first lot was acquired.

PLANNING TIMING FOR PASSING OF TITLE

There are a number of situations where timing is important. For example, there may be Section 1231 gains in the taxable year and there may be another Section 1231 asset to be sold at a loss.   It thus may be desirable to postpone the loss until the following year so that it will be an ordinary loss rather than have it offset against the Section 1231 gains.   Another situation would be the case of an asset which is not a capital asset and where it would be better for a gain to occur in a subsequent year when other income is smaller than in the current year.   Still another possibility is when losses are anticipated for the following year and there is an asset to be sold that will yield a gain.

Timing of taxability of transactions may be handled by postponing the passage of title in certain cases and the postponement of receipt of payments in others.   Recall that we noted above that the holding period of real property begins on the day after that on which title passes, or on the day after that on which delivery of possession is made and the burdens and privileges of ownership are assumed by the buyer, whichever occurs first.   Thus, if the passage of title is postponed in order to defer a sale, then possession and the burdens and privileges of ownership cannot be delivered first, or the purpose of postponement will be defeated.

The giving of an option to purchase is useful in this case. We gave an example of this in our earlier discussion of options. Note that the purchaser must have a real choice between exercising the option and letting it expire, or the transaction may well be challenged.

Escrow

The escrow may be used as a method of timing a sale.   An escrow might be established with the purchase price being held by a third party in escrow until certain conditions are met.   Funds would not be distributed from the escrow until these conditions are met.

Installment Sales

If a sale is made on an installment basis, as we discuss in the chapter on methods of deferring income, the taxation of the profit occurs as payment is received in subsequent years. Also, in this chapter we discuss deferred-payment sales, where a taxpayer receives nonnegotiable notes which are considered to have no fair market value and in which case all payments are recovered tax-free until the basis of the property is recovered.

A contract to sell made in one year with the buyer closing in the following year and taking possession in the following would result in taxation in the year of the closing. Title or possession must not pass, however, until the second year.

If property is held in escrow pending certain conditions but title is passed in year one, then gain or loss occurs in year one. Title will also pass in year one when the deed and possession are delivered in year one even though the price may not be determined until year two.

CALCULATING CAPITAL GAIN AND CAPITAL LOSS

Knowing what items constitute capital assets and knowing the determination of holding periods, we can now classify capital gains or losses into long-term and short-term capital gains and losses. Certain procedures are used in reporting these gains and losses, which we shall now consider.

Short Term

Short-term capital gains and short-term capital losses are merged to obtain the net short-term capital gain or the net short-term capital loss.

For example, W. W. Taylor, investor, purchased a lot on January 5 for $6,000 which he sold on March 19 of the same year for $7,000. In addition, a lot he purchased for $7,000 on October 5 was sold on December 28 of the same year for $5,000. W. W. has a net short-term capital loss of $1,000; this is the $1,000 gain on the first transaction and a $2,000 loss on the second. We have assumed that there were no other short-term capital transactions.

Long Term

Long-term capital gains and losses are next merged with each other to obtain the net long-term capital gain or net long-term capital loss.

W. W. Taylor sold an apartment with an adjusted basis of $30,000 for $40,000 this year. In addition, this year he sold a lot for $14,000 which he had purchased for $18,000. The apartment was purchased ten years earlier and the lot three years earlier. His net long-term capital gain is $6,000; this is $10,000 gain on the apartment less $4,000 loss on the lot.

Total Net Gain or Loss

The next step is to merge the short-term and long-term results. In our above example, Taylor had a net short-term capital loss of $1,000 and a net long-term capital gain of $6,000. His net capital gain is obviously $5,000.

LONG-TERM CAPITAL-GAIN DEDUCTION

If the net long-term capital gain is more than the net short-term capital loss, then the net gain is reduced by 50 per cent of the excess of the net long-term capital gain over the net short-term capital loss. The net gain from sale of capital assets included in income is the net gain after being reduced by the long-term capital-gain deduction. On the tax return, the long-term capital-gain deduction is used in calculating net gain from sale or exchange of capital assets. This net gain or loss is then a determinant of adjusted gross income. Examples of different possibilities will be shown later. As explained in the chapter on corporations, a corporation does not get a long-term capital-gain deduction. Capital-loss carryovers also are not the same.

NET LOSS FROM CAPITAL-ASSET TRANSACTIONS

If there is a net loss from capital-asset transactions, all or a portion of it may be deducted from other income in calculating taxable income. The amount that may be deducted depends on the amount of taxable income calculated without deductions for exemptions and without regard to capital gains and losses. If taxable income from other sources is over $1,000, the net loss can be deducted up to a $1,000 limit. Any balance of loss is not deductible for the current tax year but may be carried over to later years, as is to be explained. However, if the taxable income (without deductions for exemptions) from other sources is less than $1,000, the net loss may be deducted up to the amount of this income. If there is a balance, it may be carried over to subsequent years.

EXAMPLES OF POSSIBLE RESULTS

The following will illustrate the handling of the various possible combinations of long- and short-term capital gains and losses. For simplification, we shall use the following abbreviations:

Net loss   = net loss from merged capital asset transactions
Net gain   = net gain from merged capital asset transactions
L. T. C. G. D. = long-term capital-gain deduction
N. L. T. C. G. = net long-term capital gain
N. L. T. C. L. = net long-term capital loss
N. S. T. C. G. = net short-term capital gain
N. S. T. C. L. = net short-term capital loss

The following examples illustrate various combinations of net gains:

(a) Net Long-Term Capital Gain and Net Short-Term Capital Loss:

Salary		$20,000
Capital transactions:		
N. L. T. C. G.	$4,000G	
N. S. T. C. L.	3,000L	
Net gain	$1,000G	
(-)L. T. C. G. D.	500	500
Adjusted gross income		$20,500

(b) Net Long-Term Capital Gain––No Net Short-Term Capital Gain or Loss:

Salary		$20,000
Capital transactions:		
N. L. T. C. G.	$4,000G	
N. S. T. C. L. or G	--	
Net gain	$4,000G	
(-)L. T. C. G. D.	2,000	2,000
Adjusted gross income		$22,000

(c) Net Long-Term Capital Gain - Net Short-Term Capital Gain:

Salary		$20,000
Capital transactions:		
N. L. T. C. G.	$4,000G	
N. S. T. C. G.	3,000G	
Net gain	$7,000G	
(-)L. T. C. G. D.	2,000	5,000
		$25,000

(d) Net Long-Term Capital Loss and Net Short-Term Capital Gain:

Salary		$20,000
N.L.T.C.L.	$1,000L	
N.S.T.C.G.	3,000G	
Net gain	$2,000G	
L.T.C.G.D.	--	2,000
		$22,000

(e) Net Short-Term Capital Gain and No Net Long-Term Capital Loss:

Salary		$20,000
N.L.T.C.G. or L.	$ none	
N.S.T.C.G.	3,000	
Net gain	$3,000	
(-)L.T.C.G.D.	none	$ 3,000
Adjusted gross income		$23,000

In summary, the net long-term capital gain deduction is equal to one-half of the excess of net long-term capital gain over net short-term capital loss. The net gain less the capital gain deduction then is added to other income in the computation of adjusted gross income. This gives rise to the common statement that long-term capital gains are taxed at one-half the taxpayer's marginal tax-rate, assuming that there are no other capital transactions.

For example, R. N. Watkins (married) in 1966 has taxable income of $4,000 (after deductions and exemptions), not counting an $8,000 long-term capital gain. This $8,000 long-term capital gain less the long-term capital gain deduction of $4,000 adds $4,000 to taxable income.

Tax without capital gain	$ 620
Tax with capital gain	1,380
Difference	$ 760

Now let us consider what percentage the $760 additional tax is on the $8,000. This is nine and one-half per cent, which is just one-half the 19 per cent tax rate on income from $4,000 to $8,000 for a married taxpayer.

CAPITAL-LOSS CARRYOVER

We noted before that if, after all the capital gains and losses were merged, there was a capital loss left over, then up to $1,000 could be deducted against taxable income. If taxable income without exemptions was less than $1,000, then the net capital loss could be deducted to the extent of the taxable income. As a result of the Revenue Act of 1964, a capital loss may be carried over for an unlimited number of years. This applies to capital losses arising prior to January 1, 1964 as well. However, there is a difference in the character of the capital loss, depending on when it was sustained in taxable years beginning in 1964 or earlier. Also note that corporations are still limited to a five-year carryover.

Example of Carryover

George Fitzgerald had a $5,000 short-term capital loss in 1964 and no other capital transactions. He offset $1,000 against ordinary income in 1964, so that he had a carryover of $4,000. In 1965 he had a short-term capital gain of $2,000 but no other capital transactions. The effect of this is as follows:

Salary		$20,000
N.S.T.C.G.	$2,000	
Carryover	4,000	
Deductible against ordinary income		1,000
Adjusted gross income		$19,000
Carryover to 1966	$1,000	

Note that the carryover first offsets the net capital gain of the year; then $1,000 was deducted from ordinary income and the balance is available for succeeding years.

Character of Loss

The importance of the character of the carryover loss (short-term or long-term) derives from the long-term capital-gain deduction of 50 per cent of the excess of net long-term capital gain over net short-term capital loss. Here we must distinguish between losses arising in taxable years beginning before 1964 and those beginning after. Capital losses sustained in taxable years beginning prior to 1964 are carried over as short-term capital losses. This is true whether they were short-term or long-term in nature when they were sustained. As such they are first used to offset short-term capital gains. For capital losses sustained in taxable years beginning in 1964, the capital loss retains its original character. Thus, if there is a long-term capital loss, it is carried over as a long-term capital loss and thus is first used to offset long-term capital gains. The basic result of the change in the law is to increase the amount of gains that are treated as short-term capital gains and to decrease the amount that are subject to long-term capital-gain treatment.

For example, in the calendar year 1965 Terrence Smith has a carryover still left over from 1963 of $20,000. This loss arose as a long-term capital loss. In 1965 Terrence has $20,000 of net long-term capital gains and $20,000 of net short-term capital gains. The $20,000 carryover sustained in 1963, even though it arose as a long-term loss, is carried over as a short-term loss and wipes out the short-term capital gain. The result is that Terrence has a net long-term capital gain of $20,000 which will be offset by a 50 per cent long-term capital-gain deduction and is taxed at a maximum rate of 25 per cent.

Compare the situation with that of Barbara Brown, who had a $20,000 long-term capital-loss carryover from the calendar year 1964 and a $20,000 long-term capital gain and a $20,000 short-term capital gain in 1965. As a result of the 1964 law, the carryover retains its original character as a long-term capital loss. This long-term capital loss of $20,000 is offset against the long-term capital gain of $20,000 in 1965, and Barbara is left with a $20,000 short-term capital gain which is taxed at ordinary income tax rates of up to 70 per cent.

Unlimited Carryover

Net capital losses sustained in taxable years beginning in 1964 may be carried over indefinitely. Corporations are still limited to five years as in prior law. Net capital losses still existing from prior years also may be carried over indefinitely.

For example, Samuel Wilkins sold some acreage he acquired in Lakeview Vista, 30 miles from Lake Tehama, for $20,000 in 1963. He had paid $40,000 for the acreage in 1962. Assume that Mr. Wilkins decides not to have any more capital transactions after this debacle. Under prior law, he could deduct $1,000 in 1963 against his other income and $1,000 in each year, 1964 to 1968 inclusive. His total benefit from the loss, assuming there were no other capital transactions, was $6,000. As a result of the 1964 law, he can carryover this loss indefinitely, first applying it against capital transactions of succeeding years and then deducting $1,000 against taxable income.

Both Short- and Long-Term Losses

For losses sustained in taxable years beginning in 1964 and thereafter, capital losses are carried over separately as long-term capital losses or short-term capital losses. Whether they are short-term or long-term depends on the nature of the losses in the year

sustained. As is shown in the example below, the short-term carryover loss is used first to offset ordinary income.

Wilbur Wilkins has a $6,000 net short-term capital loss and
an $8,000 net long-term capital loss in the calendar year 1964. His
carryover to 1965 is a $5,000 short-term capital loss and an $8,000
long-term capital loss. He used $1,000 of the short-term loss a-
gainst taxable income in 1964. If he has no capital transactions in
1965, he will use $1,000 of the short-term loss against taxable in-
come in 1965 and have a carryover of $4,000 short-term and $8,000
long-term.

Carryover Loss and Capital Loss in Current Year

A taxpayer may have a carryover loss and also sustain a
net capital loss in the current year. The current year's capital
losses are deducted to the extent allowable before a capital-loss
carryover is deducted.

Samuel Wilkins has a long-term capital-loss carryover
from 1964 of $5,000. In 1966 he has net short-term capital losses
of $3,000. In computing his tax liability for 1966, Wilkins subtracts
$1,000 of the 1966 short-term capital loss from taxable income and
is left with a carryover of a $2,000 short-term capital loss from
1966 and a $5,000 long-term capital loss from 1964.

Joint and Separate Returns

If a taxpayer and his spouse file a joint return, they may
deduct up to a total of $1,000 capital loss. However, if they file
separate returns and if they both have capital losses, they can deduct up to $1,000 on each separate return. This sometimes made
it advantageous to file separate returns when there was a five-year
limit on capital-loss carryovers. This will not be so important
now that there is an indefinite carryover. However, there still
will be a present-value effect of an earlier deduction, and in addition there may be some advantage in the case of fluctuating in-
comes to file separate returns and get a total $2,000 deduction in
one year.

Capital-loss carryovers from separate returns have to be
combined if a joint return is filed for the current year. Only a
person who actually sustained a loss can use a carryover from a
joint return on a separate return.

Manfred and Millicent Grange have a capital loss of $5,000
in 1966 and file joint returns. Thus, they can use $1,000 of the
capital loss in 1966 and have $4,000 as a carryover to 1967. In

1967 there are no capital transactions and they file separate returns. If the 1966 loss was from community property or from property jointly owned by Manfred and Millicent, they may each use one-half the carryover on their separate returns for 1967. However, if we change the situation and assume that the 1966 capital loss was entirely from separate property that Millicent inherited, then only Millicent can use the capital loss on her separate return and Manfred cannot use any.

ALTERNATIVE TAX

The alternative tax on a net long-term capital gain cannot exceed an amount which is equal to 50 per cent of the capital-gain deduction. The capital-gain deduction is 50 per cent of the excess of the net long-term capital gain over net short-term capital loss. Because the tax cannot be greater than 50 per cent of the capital-gain deduction, it cannot be greater than 25 per cent of the excess of the net long-term capital gain over the net short-term capital loss. When the taxpayer's marginal tax rate approaches 50 per cent, the tax should be computed according to the regular and alternative method, and the lower result should obviously be used.

Example of Alternative Tax

The calculation of the alternative tax will be illustrated by the situation of an executive, V. R. Rich. Rich has income from other than capital transactions of $80,000. His capital transactions gave the following results: L. T. C. G., $10,800; L. T. C. L., $3,500; S. T. C. G., $5,200; S. T. C. L., $7,580. Rich is married and files a joint return with his wife Emily. They do not have any other dependents. His itemized deductions for contributions, taxes, interest, and so forth, amounted to $5,260.

Calculation of Regular Tax

First we shall compute the Rich's tax under the regular method. The tax is determined from the tax table for married taxpayers filing joint returns for taxable years beginning after December 31, 1964.

Salary, dividends (after exclusion) etc.			$80,000
Capital transactions:			
L.T.C.G.	$10,800		
L.T.C.L.	3,500	$7,300G	
S.T.C.G.	$ 5,200		
S.T.C.L.	7,580	2,380L	
Excess of net long-term capital gain over net short-term capital loss		4,920	
Capital-gain deduction (50 per cent of excess of N.L.T.C.G. over N.S.T.C.L.)		2,460	2,460
Adjusted gross income			$82,460
Exemptions	$ 1,200		
Itemized deductions	5,260		6,460
Taxable income			$76,000

Tax on $76,000 = $31,020

Calculation of Alternative Tax

Now we shall compute the alternative tax to see if it yields a lower tax. Recall that the taxable income from the preceding case is $76,000; this is the starting point. The 50 per cent of the excess of the N.L.T.C.G. over N.S.T.C.L. is subtracted from taxable income and a partial tax is calculated. To the partial tax is added 25 per cent of the excess of N.L.T.C.G. over N.S.T.C.L. This procedure computes a tax on taxable income exclusive of the capital transactions and then adds 25 per cent of the excess of N.L.T.C.G. over N.S.T.C.L.

Taxable income	$76,000	
Less: 50 per cent of the excess of N.L.T.C.G. over N.S.T.C.L.	2,460	
Balance subject to partial tax	$73,540	
Partial tax ($24,420 on $64,000 taxable income plus $5,247 on $9,540 balance at 55 per cent		$29,667
Add 25 per cent of excess of N.L.T.C.G. over N.S.T.C.L. (25 per cent of $4,920)		1,230
Alternative tax		$30,897

The regular tax computation yielded a tax of $31,020 as compared with $30,897 under the alternative method. Thus, the alternative tax method is used by V. R.

SECTION 1231 TRANSACTIONS

In our discussion of what constitutes capital assets we indicated that certain assets which are not capital assets are treated as capital assets under certain circumstances. These are so-called Section 1231 transactions. Now we shall consider handling these transactions in detail. Note particularly how, even though under certain circumstances these assets when sold or exchanged will yield capital gain, some of this capital gain may be converted into ordinary income by the depreciation-recapture rules.

Property Used in Trade or Business

Probably the most important category to us includes depreciable property and real property used in a trade or business. These assets are treated as capital assets if they are held more than six months and if the recognized gains on their sale or exchange exceed recognized losses. Property held for sale to customers is not included.

For example, a car that a real estate dealer uses 100 per cent for business is a depreciable asset used in trade or business. However, a car that is in the stock of a car dealer is an inventory item.

John Jenks is in the business of renting single-family residences. He has 12 houses he rents. These houses are depreciable properties used in a trade or business.

George Sweeney builds a dozen houses a year and sells them. These houses are inventory to George and are not depreciable property used in a trade or business.

Additional Section 1231 Transactions

In addition to real property and depreciable property used in a trade or business, the following are grouped to determine whether the Section 1231 gains exceed the Section 1231 losses. These are: (1) nonbusiness property subjected to a casualty or theft, if held for more than six months; (2) business property subjected to a casualty or theft, if held for more than six months and covered by insurance in any amount; (3) property held for the production of rents or royalties subjected to a casualty or theft, if held for more than six months and covered by insurance in any amount; (4) notes, bonds, and other investment property subjected to a casualty or theft, if held for more than six months and covered by insurance in any amount; (5) sales or exchanges of leaseholds used in the trade or business and held for more than six months;

(6) property condemned for public use, if such property was held for more than six months; (7) an unharvested crop, sold with land, where the land was held for more than six months; (8) livestock (excluding poultry) held for draft, breeding, or dairy purposes and held for 12 months or more; (9) timber or coal under certain circumstances.

Brief Look at Depreciation Recapture

When depreciable property (except livestock or buildings and their structural components) is sold or exchanged in a tax year starting after 1962, any gain is ordinary income to the extent of depreciation taken after 1961. Dispositions other than sales or exchanges are included. For dispositions other than sale or exchange, the gain is determined as the excess of the fair market value of the property over its adjusted basis at the time of disposition. Depreciation recapture on the above assets is referred to as Section 1245 potential or income.

The 1964 law added a modified version of depreciation recapture for buildings and for leaseholds of buildings or land. In respect to dispositions of depreciable real estate after December 31, 1963, the excess of depreciation taken after December 31, 1963 over that allowable under the straight-line method for the post-1963 period generally will be partially treated as ordinary income to the extent of gain on such disposition. All depreciation is ordinary income if the property is held less than a year. The amount goes down after the property has been held over 20 months, and after 10 years there is no depreciation recapture on these assets. We shall have to come back to the many details on depreciation recapture in the next chapter.

In our discussion of Section 1231 transactions in calculating gain on the sale of a Section 1231 asset, the amount that is ordinary income because of depreciation recapture is excluded in determining the amount to be considered in determining the Section 1231 results.

Basic Treatment of 1231 Assets on Tax Return

Before we go into the definition of all items included, such as the cutting of timber, and so forth, we shall indicate the basic handling of these items on the return. If gains exceed the losses from Section 1231 transactions, then all are treated as long-term capital gains and losses, and they are reported in the same manner as other long-term capital gains and losses, including the use of the capital-gain deduction. However, if losses exceed the gains, all are treated as ordinary gains and losses.

Example of Section 1231 Calculations

Daniel Lampson is an attorney and a calendar-year taxpayer. During the year he had the following transactions: Professional fees amounted to $40,000. A sale of securities held for nine months yielded a $4,000 gain. Royalties from an investment in coal lands he has owned for five years amounted to $6,000. During the year he sold a vacant lot that he had held for only three months as an investment. He made $2,000 on that transaction. The sale of an office machine that was unsatisfactory resulted in a $400 loss. This machine was only held two and one-half months. Lampson sold a car that was used solely in his practice for $5,400. He had driven the car for only one year, and the car had an adjusted basis of $4,400. He had taken $800 depreciation on the car (all since 1961). The stove was left on in his home, and as a result there was a loss of $1,000 after insurance proceeds.

The determination of Mr. Lampson's adjusted gross income is shown below:

Professional fees	$40,000	
Other business income	800	
Loss on office machine	(400)	$40,400
Capital transactions:		
N.L.T.C.G.	$ 9,200	
N.S.T.C.G.	2,000	
	$11,200	
Less: Long-term capital gain deduction	4,600	6,600
		$47,000

The net long-term capital-gain deduction above is 50 per cent of the net long-term capital gain. The sale of the car yielded a gain of $1,000, which is $800 ordinary income and $200 Section 1231 gain. The gain, to the extent of depreciation taken after 1961, is ordinary income.

The total Section 1231 gains and losses are as follows: car, $200 gain; coal investment, $6,000 gain; involuntary-conversion loss on residence, $1,000. This is a net of $5,200. Because a gain resulted, these items are all considered as long-term capital gains and long-term capital losses.

To summarize: There are long-term capital gains as follows: Car, $200; coal, $6,000; stock, $4,000. This is a total of $10,200.

Long-term capital losses include only the $1,000 involuntary-conversion loss on the residence of $1,000. Thus, there is a net long-term capital gain of $9,200.

Short-term capital gains included only the $2,000 sale of

the vacant lot held less than six months. There were no other short-term capital transactions, so that there is a net short-term capital gain of $2,000.

When the Section 1231 gains and losses were segregated and totaled, the result was a gain. Thus, they were all treated as long-term capital items. However, if the result was a loss, they all would have been treated as ordinary gains and losses.

Because the office machine was held less than six months, it gives rise to an ordinary loss and does not enter into the Section 1231 calculation. It is a depreciable asset used in trade or business. The missing requirement for the sale of the office machine to be a Section 1231 transaction is that it was not held six months. The vacant lot and the securities are capital assets to start with; therefore, gain or loss on their sale is a capital gain or loss.

Clarification of Section 1231 Categories

Some of the Section 1231 categories require a little more elaboration.

Items subject to involuntary conversion. When we noted the categories which give rise to Section 1231 transactions, we noted business property, nonbusiness property, property held for the production of rents or royalties, and notes, bonds, and other investment property if, and in all cases, they were held more than six months or subjected to a casualty or theft and covered by insurance in any amount.

Not covered by insurance. If there are uninsured casualty and theft losses to property used in the taxpayer's trade or business or capital assets held for the production of income, they are not included in the grouping. The factor that there is no insurance causes their exclusion. Property that is "self-insured" is considered uninsured for this purpose.

There seems to be a difference of opinion on uninsured non-business property losses.

For example, Smith has $18,900 Section 1231 gain and in addition has a casualty loss to his residence of $5,000 which is not covered by insurance. Smith deducted the casualty loss in full rather than netting the loss against the gain. The Commissioner claimed that the loss should be netted against the Section 1231 gain. Some courts, however, follow the taxpayer's approach and allow the full deduction of the casualty loss under Section 165(c) of the Internal Revenue Code and do not offset it against the Section 1231 gain.

Property condemned for public use. If business property

or capital assets such as investment property are condemned for public use, it is included in the Section 1231 groupings. Losses from condemnation of property held for personal use are not deductible and are not included in this grouping.

Timber. "Timber" includes evergreen trees over six years old when cut down and trees sold for ornamental purposes such as Christmas trees. Cutting of timber is treated in the same manner as a sale under the following circumstances: (1) the taxpayer owned the timber or contract right to cut it for more than six months before the beginning of the tax year in which it was cut; (2) the timber was cut for sale or use in the taxpayer's trade or business; (3) an election was made on the taxpayer's return.

The selling price is the fair market value of the timber as of the first day of the tax year. The cost basis is the adjusted basis for depletion. The gain or loss is included in the Section 1231 transactions.

Disposal of timber under a contract. The disposal of timber under a contract in which the taxpayer retains an economic interest in the timber may be considered a sale provided that the taxpayer has owned the timber for more than six months before the disposal. The gain or loss is the difference between the amounts received for the timber in the tax year and the adjusted basis for depletion of the timber.

Livestock. Section 1231 applies to livestock held for draft, breeding, or dairy purposes. The holding period in this case is 12 months and starts from the day of acquisition rather than the time when the animal was put to use for draft, breeding, or dairy purposes. Cattle, hogs, horses, mules, donkeys, sheep, goats, fur-bearing animals, and other mammals are included. Not included are chickens, turkeys, pigeons, geese, other birds, fish, frogs, reptiles, and so forth. The facts of the particular case determine whether the livestock is held for draft, breeding, or dairy purposes.

Unharvested crops. In order for an unharvested crop to fall under Section 1231, the following conditions must exist: (1) the crop is on land used in trade or business and is held for more than six months; (2) the crop and land are sold, exchanged, or involuntarily converted to the same person at the same time; (3) no right or option is kept by the taxpayer at the time of sale, exchange, or conversion to acquire the land, directly or indirectly. An estate for years or leasehold is not considered land. It is the time that the land is held and not the crop that is important in determining whether it is held for six months.

No deductions for production of the crop are allowed when gain is treated as capital gain under Section 1231. The disallowed deductions are added to the basis of the crop.

  Coal. If a taxpayer disposes of coal which he owns but keeps an economic interest in it, and if he had held the coal for more than six months, the disposal may be considered a sale. The date when the coal is mined is considered the date of disposal. Gain or loss is the difference between the amounts received for the coal and the adjusted basis for depletion.

  For example, a George Swank owns a coal mine which he has held for six months. His adjusted basis for depletion is five cents a ton. Mr. Swank enters into a contract with The Coal Company of North America to mine the coal. The company has the right to mine the coal for 25 cents per ton. The result is that Mr. Swank has a Section 1231 gain of 20 cents per ton on the coal mined. Expenditures attributable to the making and administering of the contract and to the preservation of the economic interest retained under the contract are not deductible but rather are added to the adjusted basis of the coal. The taxpayer is not allowed depletion.

Chapter 5

Depreciation Recapture
and Subdivisions

The desirability of a taxpayer's receiving capital-gain treatment on a gain does not need further elaboration. In the case of losses, an ordinary loss is superior to a capital loss because an ordinary loss is deductible against other income and gives rise to an operating-loss carryback or carryforward. A capital loss can only offset $1,000 of ordinary income and the balance must be carried forward.

Depreciation recapture under Section 1245 and Section 1250 causes a certain amount of gain which formerly was capital gain to be treated as ordinary gain. Buildings and leaseholds of land and buildings are not treated so severely as personal property, as we shall see.

When land is subdivided to be sold, there is the question of whether the subdivision is done by an investor who should receive capital gain or by a dealer who receives ordinary income. There are special rules which, if met, yield capital-gain treatment. In other areas, the situation depends on the facts of the particular case. These are the problems that we shall discuss in this chapter.

DEPRECIATION RECAPTURE

As illustrated in the example following, a tax advantage is achieved by deducting depreciation which is deductible against ordinary income at the cost of a larger capital gain on sale or exchange. We shall discuss three important developments which to a large degree eliminate this possibility for personal property and limit it for real property. These are: (1) Section 1245 depreciation recapture in the Revenue Law of 1962; (2) Section 1250 depreciation recapture in the Revenue Law of 1964; and (3) the imposition of the so-called Cohn rule by the Internal Revenue Service.

Conversion of Ordinary Income to Capital Gain

Let us first take an example and see what these developments are attacking. The basic idea of converting ordinary income into capital gain is to depreciate an asset below its market value. Because depreciation is deducted from ordinary income and capital gain is taxed at a lower rate than ordinary income, a taxpayer benefits through a reduction in taxes.

For example, contractor O'Hara has depreciated an electric saw costing $20,000 down to zero under the allowable depreciation rules. The $20,000 depreciation deductions from ordinary income have saved O'Hara, who is in the 60 per cent bracket, $12,000 in taxes. Now O'Hara sells the saw, which he has taken very good care of, for $20,000. He has a gain of $20,000, because the adjusted basis of the saw is zero. This $20,000 gain, however, prior to the depreciation-recapture rules, was taxable as a Section 1231 gain, because it is derived from depreciable property used in trade or business. The maximum tax on the profit, assuming that there are no other Section 1231 transactions, is only $5,000 (25 per cent of the $20,000 gain). Thus, O'Hara has saved $7,000; this is the $12,000 benefit of the depreciation deductions less the $5,000 capital-gain tax.

For sales in years beginning after 1962, this is stopped for depreciable personal property as explained below. For sales of buildings, and leaseholds on buildings or land, a modified version of depreciation recapture applies.

SECTION 1245 DEPRECIATION RECAPTURE

The 1962 Revenue Law introduced depreciation recapture for the sale or exchange of depreciable property except livestock and buildings and their structural components. If such property is sold or exchanged in a tax year beginning after 1962, any gain will be ordinary income to the extent of depreciation taken after 1961. Depreciation, for this purpose, includes additional first-year depreciation and amortization of emergency facilities in addition to normal depreciation. For property received in a tax-free exchange, it includes depreciation taken on the property exchanged. Note that this rule also applies to most dispositions and not just sales or exchanges. In such dispositions, gain is the excess of the fair market value of the property over its adjusted basis at the time of disposition.

"Property" for this purpose includes all depreciable personal property other than livestock. It also includes all other property (except buildings and their structural components), but only if such property is or has been an integral part of certain business activities or was a research or storage facility used in connection with such activities. These activities are: manufacturing, production, extraction, or furnishing transportation, communications, or certain other public utility services.

Example of Section 1245 Depreciation Recapture

Any gain up to "recomputed basis" is ordinary income under Section 1245 of the Internal Revenue Code. "Recomputed basis" is the adjusted basis of the property plus depreciation or amortization deductions taken after 1961. Any gain above recomputed basis is Section 1231 gain. However, if the sale or exchange is for less than the recomputed basis, the amount of gain is limited to the actual gain.

For example, George Lincoln, contractor, sold a lathe for $3,000 on January 2, 1965. This lathe had an adjusted basis of $2,500; this is cost less depreciation to date. There was $300 depreciation taken since 1961. Thus, the recomputed basis at the date of sale is $2,800 ($2,500 adjusted basis plus $300 depreciation taken since 1961).

The nature of the gain realized by Lincoln is as follows:

Gain on sale: $3,000 less $2,500 = $500
Excess of recomputed basis ($2,800) over adjusted basis ($2,500) = $300
Nature of gain: Ordinary income, $300; Section 1231 gain, $200

If we change the situation and assume that Lincoln sold the lathe for $2,700, his gain would have been only $200 ($2,700 proceeds less $2,500 adjusted basis), and this gain would have been entirely ordinary income, because it is less than the $300 depreciation taken since 1961.

From these rules it can be seen that, as time passes, there will not be much capital gain realized from the sale or exchange of depreciable property other than buildings and their structural components or livestock.

Dispositions Other Than Sale or Exchange

The recapture rules described above apply to most dispositions of depreciable property. Certain transactions which normally do not give rise to taxable income may do so because of the depreciation-recapture rules. These are as follows: (1) depreciable property distributed by a corporation as a dividend in kind or in a partial or complete liquidation; (2) depreciable property that is sold by a corporation in a 12-month liquidation. These are explained in the chapters on corporations; (3) involuntary conversions and exchanges of like kind to the extent that depreciable personal property is not involved, as is explained below; (4) sales of partnership interests are taxed to the partners to the extent of the underlying depreciable property as if the depreciable property had been sold directly; the same treatment applies to distributions to partners.

Tax-Free Exchanges

If a tax-free exchange is made, a taxpayer generally has ordinary income which is limited to the "boot" received. Additional gain may be recognized because of depreciation recapture. For example, contractor O'Hara owns a bulldozer which has an adjusted basis of $20,000, and a market value of $60,000. Depreciation since 1961 amounts to $30,000. O'Hara trades this bulldozer for a smaller bulldozer which has a market value of $35,000 and receives $7,000 cash and a boat worth $18,000 to balance the exchange.

O'Hara has a recognized gain of $25,000, which is ordinary income, because it is less than the $30,000 depreciation taken since 1961. His realized gain is $40,000 (total received of $60,000 less adjusted basis of $20,000), which is recognized to the extent of the $25,000 "boot" received.

Involuntary Conversion

In the case of an involuntary conversion, a taxpayer's ordinary income resulting from the recapture rules is limited to the amount not reinvested. However, if the reinvestment is not in depreciable property, then he may have additional ordinary income.

Rose Minton owned an apartment building which she rented. On April 16, 1965 a fire destroyed all of Rose's furniture. The adjusted basis of the furniture at the time of the fire was $5,000 and there had been $800 depreciation taken on the furniture since 1961. The insurance company paid $6,000 for the fire damage on the furniture, and Rose reinvested $5,400 in new furniture. The result is a $600 recognized gain. There is a $1,000 gain ($6,000 proceeds less $5,000 adjusted basis), which is recognized to the extent of the amount not reinvested ($600). This $600 is ordinary income because it is less than the $800 depreciation taken since 1961.

Ordinary income may result in an involuntary conversion

because of the depreciation-recapture rules in an amount greater than the proceeds not reinvested. If proceeds from an involuntary conversion are used to purchase nondepreciable property, ordinary income is the smaller of the following: (a) gain from disposition of the property; (2) depreciation since 1961 on the property; (3) any recognized gain on the transaction plus the fair market value of any nondepreciable property acquired in the transaction.

Contractor Sweeney owned a roadscraper, which was destroyed by a rockslide. Sweeney collected $60,000 on his insurance and purchased a smaller landscraper for $35,000. He used another $20,000 to acquire a controlling interest in a corporation that manufactures roadscrapers. Sweeney had taken $30,000 depreciation since 1961 on the old scraper, which had an adjusted basis at the time of the casualty of $20,000.

Before the depreciation-recapture rules, Sweeney would have had a gain of $5,000, which is the amount that was not reinvested under the involuntary-conversion rules. Recall that a purchase of a controlling interest in a corporation manufacturing similar equipment qualifies for the replacement rules. However, as a result of Section 1245, I.R.C., Mr. Sweeney has ordinary income on the transaction of $25,000. This is the $5,000 cash and the $20,000 stock.

EXCEPTIONS TO DEPRECIATION RECAPTURE

Certain dispositions of depreciable property are excepted from the recapture rules. Excepted are (1) gifts; (2) charitable contributions; (3) transfers at death.

Gifts

A person receiving a gift receives the Section 1245 potential with the gift. The donor does not receive income on the gift. The donee on sale of the property has to take into account the donor's depreciation deductions since 1961.

For example, on January 2, 1965 Walter Winston gave furniture used in his rental apartments to his son, Walter, Jr. The furniture had a fair market value at date of gift of $30,000 and an adjusted basis of $25,000. Walter, Sr. paid a gift tax of $2,250 on the transaction.

Walter, Jr. in turn sold the furniture on December 31, 1965 for $30,000 without taking any depreciation. The father had deducted $4,000 in depreciation since 1961. Walter, Jr. has ordinary income on the sale of the furniture in the amount of $2,750. This is the sale price of $30,000 less the adjusted basis of $27,250 (father's basis of $25,000 plus gift tax of $2,250). The entire amount of the gain is ordinary income, because the gain is less than the recomputed basis minus the adjusted basis. The recomputed basis in this case is $31,250 (adjusted basis of $27,250 plus depreciation since 1961 of $4,000).

Charitable Contributions

No income is realized when depreciable property is given to a charity. However, the deductible charitable contribution must be reduced by the amount of Section 1245 income that would have resulted had the property been sold for its market value.

Transfers at Death

The Section 1245 potential is not taxed to a decedent. Neither is it taxed to the heirs.

ELEVATORS AND ESCALATORS INCLUDED

The depreciation-recapture provisions of Section 1245 apply to elevators and escalators if they are acquired or if construction is completed after June 30, 1963. Ordinary income may result if there is a gain on disposition. The amount of ordinary income is limited to the amount of depreciation allowed or allowable after June 30, 1963. This provision was added by the 1964 Revenue Law, as elevators and escalators had not been included in the original depreciation-recapture rules.

RECAPTURE ON REAL ESTATE

The 1964 Revenue Law extended a modified version of depreciation recapture to buildings and leaseholds of buildings or land. Under Section 1245, as was discussed above, depreciation recapture can apply to all depreciation taken since 1961. However, for the depreciation recapture under Section 1250 on buildings, the amount recaptured after the first year is limited to the excess of accelerated depreciation taken over straight-line depreciation. And as the time passes, the amount of recapture is reduced.

Basic Computation

The key terms are "applicable percentage" and "additional depreciation." The applicable percentage is the percentage used to determine the amount recaptured and depends on the time that

the property has been held. The additional depreciation is the a-
mount of depreciation taken after 1963 in excess of straight-line
depreciation. The amount recaptured is the applicable percentage
times the lower of the following: (1) gain; (2) additional depreciation.

For example, Blevel owns an apartment, and he has held it
for a period of time such that the applicable percentage is 75 per
cent. The property is sold for $100,000, and Blevel has an adjusted
basis of $50,000 and, therefore, a $50,000 gain. Depreciation taken
since 1963 in excess of straight-line depreciation (the additional depreciation) is $20,000. Thus, Blevel has $15,000 ordinary income
(75 per cent of $20,000) on the transaction and $35,000 Section 1231
gain.

If we change the situation and assume that Blevel received
only $60,000 for the apartment, the ordinary income would be 75
per cent of $10,000, or $7,500, because the gain of $10,000 is less
than the additional depreciation.

First-Year Dispositions

All depreciation after 1963 may be recovered in the case of
dispositions in the first year. The applicable percentage is 100 per
cent, and the additional depreciation is all depreciation after 1963.

For example, on January 1, 1965 Quick purchases an apartment which he sells on December 1, 1965 after taking $15,000 de-
preciation. Assuming that the gain is at least $15,000, Quick would
have ordinary income of $15,000, which is equal to the total depre-
ciation taken after 1963. After the first year, all of the post-1963
depreciation is not converted to ordinary income.

Dispositions Within the 13th to the 20th Month Inclusive

After the first year, there is no recapture if straight-line
depreciation has been employed. However, if accelerated depreciation is used, the additional depreciation is the excess of accelerated depreciation over straight-line depreciation taken since
1963, and the applicable percentage is 100 per cent.

Mattern owns a building, which he sells 19 months after
purchase. Mattern has an adjusted basis of $40,000 for the building
and sells the building for $55,000, thus realizing a gain of $15,000.
He has used the double-declining-balance depreciation method and
has taken $15,000 depreciation on the property since 1963. Straight-
line depreciation since 1963 would have been $7,500. Mattern has
ordinary income of $7,500 ($15,000 accelerated depreciation less
$7,500 straight-line depreciation).

Dispositions Within the 21st to the 120th Month Inclusive

After the 20th month, the applicable percentage decreases. After 20 full months, the applicable percentage declines one per cent per month. And when the property has been held 120 months or more, there is no more depreciation recapture.

Stedry buys an apartment on December 31, 1963 for $100,000 and sells it on January 1, 1967 after 36 months of ownership. A total of $14,262.50 depreciation deductions had been taken using the double-declining-balance method and a life of 40 years. Straight-line depreciation based on a 40-year life, no salvage, and the passage of three years amounts to $7,500 (2.5 per cent per year). Stedry sold the building for $95,737.50, which gave him a gain of $10,000 (adjusted basis is $85,737.50).

Stedry has ordinary income of $5,680.50 and Section 1231 gain of $4,319.50. The amount of ordinary income is the applicable percentage of 84 per cent times the additional depreciation of $6,762.50. The additional depreciation is the $14,262.50 declining-balance depreciation minus the $7,500 straight-line depreciation. The applicable percentage of 84 per cent is 100 per cent minus the months held over 20 (36 - 20).

AMORTIZATION OF LEASEHOLDS

Amortization of leaseholds of land and land improvements are also affected by these recapture rules. Sales of land are not affected, because land is not subject to an allowance for depreciation. There is, of course, a necessity of allocating both the basis and the proceeds when land and buildings are sold in one transaction.

Recapture on Leasehold

In determination of recapture in the case of leaseholds, renewal periods are counted within a certain limit. The following example illustrates recapture in the case of leaseholds.

Gong pays $100,000 for a lease with 25 years remaining in the original lease and a 15-year option. Gong adds improvements in the form of a building at a cost of $2,400,000. The building is to be depreciated on a 40-year life. After five years, $20,000 of the leasehold payment has been deducted; that is the $100,000 divided by 25 years times five years gone. The building has been depreciated $480,000 ($2,400,000 divided by 25 years times 5).

The potential recapture is calculated as follows: There is a $7,500 potential on the lease. This is the $20,000 actual deduction less $12,500, which is the amount of deduction on a 40-year basis. Recall that the total remaining life of the lease, with the 15-year option, is 40 years. There is a $180,000 potential on the building. This is the actual deduction of $480,000 less $300,000. This latter figure is depreciation based on a 40-year life.

The write-off period cannot be extended beyond two-thirds of the original term. For example, on a 25-year lease with a 25-year renewal period, the straight-line write-off would be based on 41 2/3 years. This is 25 plus 2/3 of 25.

EFFECT OF SUBSTANTIAL IMPROVEMENTS

We observed how the amount of depreciation recapture on real estate declined as the holding period lengthened after 20 months, and that after 10 years there was no recapture. Substantial improvements may also be subject to recapture even though the property that they relate to has been held over 10 years.

For example, Mr. and Mrs. Schmick purchased Pleasant Pines Tavern for $200,000 and have held it for 20 years. During the last two years, the Schmicks improved the tavern at a cost of $200,000 and have used the 200 per cent declining-balance depreciation method, as suggested by their accountant. If the Schmicks decide to sell in this situation, there would be no problem with the property owned for 20 years. However, the improvements that have been held for only two years would be subject to depreciation recapture.

Meaning of Substantial Improvements

There is a test which is used to determine whether improvements are substantial or not and, thus, whether they are subject to recapture. Improvements within a 36-month period are considered substantial if the total of capital additions within the 36 months is greater than each of the following three figures: (1) 25 per cent of the adjusted basis at the beginning of the period; (2) 10 per cent of the unadjusted basis at the beginning of the period; and (3) $5,000. To determine the 36-month period, the taxpayer starts with the last day of the tax year and counts back 36 months. The unadjusted basis in (2) above is the adjusted basis plus all prior depreciation and amortization write-offs, including those before and after 1963. There is another test that the substantial improvements also have to meet to be subject to recapture which will be discussed shortly.

William LeBlanc owns the Fondulac Apartments, which on January 1, 1962 had an adjusted basis of $700,000 and on the same date, an unadjusted basis of $1,000,000. LeBlanc sells the apartment on January 1, 1966. We shall determine which of the following improvements are considered substantial improvements under the 36-month test: (1) In 1962 a new roof was added at the cost of $100,000; (2) in 1963 a new boiler was added at a cost of $70,000; (3) in 1964 alterations in the amount of $25,000 were made; (4) in 1965 alterations in the amount of $25,000 were made.

The $25,000 alterations in 1965 are not substantial improvements under the 36-month rule. The improvements for the years 1963, 1964, and 1965 amount to $120,000. This is less than 25 per cent of the January 1, 1963 adjusted basis, which we shall assume to be $770,000 after depreciation and capital improvements. As a result, the $25,000 improvements in 1965 are not subject to the depreciation-recapture rules.

However, the balance of the improvements--the roof, boiler, and the 1964 alterations--are substantial improvements under the 36-month rule. These total $195,000, which is larger than 25 per cent of the $700,000 adjusted basis at the beginning of the 36-month period counting back from the end of 1964, and is also larger than 10 per cent of the unadjusted basis of $1,000,000. Thus, the 36-month test for these improvements is met and they are subject to depreciation recapture if the one-year test is met.

One-Year Test

In addition to the 36-month test explained above, there is a one-year test. Improvements will not be counted for the 36-month test if, in the tax year in which the improvement occurs, the sum total of capital-account additions is less than each of the following two amounts: (1) one per cent of the adjusted basis at the beginning of the year; (2) $2,000.

For example, let us assume that the 1964 additions to the Fondulac Apartments in the example above amounted to $10,000. This is less than one per cent of the unadjusted basis at the beginning of 1964, which was $1,170,000. (This is the original $1,000,000 plus improvements of $100,000 in 1962 and $70,000 in 1963.)

Because the one-year test is not met by the $10,000 improvements, LeBlanc does not have to consider them in the 36-month test. And, as a result, the sum of the 1962 and 1963 improvements of $170,000 do not satisfy the 36-month test any more, and, as a result, none of the improvements would be considered substantial. Twenty-five per cent of the $700,000 adjusted basis on January 1, 1962 is $175,000, which is larger than the 36-month total for 1962, 1963, and 1964 of $170,000.

SPECIAL TREATMENT FOR UNITS

Each separately opened unit receives separate Section 1250 treatment. This is true whether the units are considered substantial or not. The 36-month and one-year tests described on page 113 apply only to substantial improvements and not to units.

For example, the Mountainside Motel has had 25 cabins in occupation since 1945. There is no problem with depreciation recapture on these units, because they have been held for over ten years. However, assume that the Mountainside Motel adds some new units in 1964. These new units will get separate Section 1250 treatment from the old cabins. They are considered separate property for this purpose and have their own holding period.

CALCULATION OF DEPRECIATION RECAPTURE WITH SUBSTANTIAL IMPROVEMENTS

When property is sold which includes substantial improvements, the total sales price must be allocated between the various elements in order to determine the amount of the ordinary income involved.

The determination involves the following steps, which will be illustrated by an example: (1) a holding period, applicable percentage, and additional depreciation are figured for each of the elements making up the whole; (2) the lower of gain on sale of the entire property and the additional depreciation on the entire property is determined; (3) a pro-rata portion of the lower of gain on sale and additional depreciation determined in step (2) is multiplied by the applicable percentage for each element of the property.

Example of Calculation

We shall assume that an apartment building was opened January 1, 1963 and that a substantial improvement was made on September 1, 1964. Declining-balance depreciation at twice the straight-line rate was used. The apartment was sold on January 1, 1967.

Step I. The first step is to determine the holding period, applicable percentage, and additional depreciation for both the original apartment building and the substantial improvement.

For the original apartment building, the holding period is 48 months (January 1, 1963 to January 1, 1967), and therefore the applicable percentage is 72 per cent. Recall that the applicable percentage is decreased by one per cent per month after 20 months.

We shall assume that there has been $60,000 additional depreciation on the apartment. This is the excess of declining-balance over straight-line depreciation since 1963.

The substantial improvement has a holding period of 28 months (September 1, 1964 to January 1, 1967), and therefore the applicable percentage is 92 per cent. Assume that $30,000 additional depreciation has been taken on the substantial improvement since 1963.

Step II. The second step is to determine the lower of the gain and the additional depreciation for the entire property. For purposes of our example, we shall assume that the adjusted basis at the date of sale is $1,350,000 and that the building sold for $1,425,000. The resultant gain is thus $75,000, which is lower than the $90,000 additional depreciation on the entire property. The $75,000 gain then will be used to measure depreciation recapture, rather than the higher additional depreciation of $90,000.

In the above situation, the $90,000 additional depreciation was equal to the sum of $60,000 on the apartment and $30,000 on the substantial improvements. Where property has been in service for a long period and declining-balance depreciation at either 150 per cent or 200 per cent of the straight-line rate has been used, the depreciation since 1963 on the declining-balance method may be less than straight-line depreciation. Thus, the additional depreciation may be negative for some of the older elements. In this situation, elements which show a negative figure are left out in the Step I calculation. However, for Step II, all elements are included and negative additional depreciation on the older elements will offset positive figures on others, and the Step II total will be less than the Step I additional depreciation total.

Step III. The last step is to take the $75,000 gain determined in Step II and allocate it amongst the various elements. The prorata portion of the $75,000 for each element will be multiplied by the applicable percentage for each element. The additional depreciation for the individual element is divided by the additional depreciation for all elements. This fraction is then multiplied by the figure determined in Step II.

Ordinary income on the original apartment building is $36,000. This is the $60,000 additional depreciation divided by the total additional depreciation of $90,000 times the $75,000 figure. The result is then multiplied by the applicable percentage, 72 per cent. The ordinary income on the substantial improvement is $23,000. This is the $30,000 additional depreciation on the substantial improvement divided by the total additional depreciation of $90,000 times the $75,000, with this result multiplied by the applicable percentage, 92 per cent. Total ordinary income on the project is $59,000 under Section 1250, and the remaining $16,000 is Section 1231 gain and, therefore, usually capital gain.

A similar calculation would be made if there were separate units involved and if the total were sold. Thus, if several rental cottages were built and the apartment and the cottages were sold as a package, allocation would have to be made, considering the separate holding periods, additional depreciation, and applicable percentages.

COHN RULE

Under the Cohn rule, which the Internal Revenue Service has made an official rule in Revenue Ruling 62-92, depreciation in the year of sale may be disallowed. In the case of depreciable personal property, the depreciation-recapture rules under Section 1245 discussed above accomplish the same purpose. For the sale of buildings, the application of the Cohn rule may disallow all the depreciation in the year of sale rather than a partial disallowance under the recapture rules of Section 1250. Because not all the courts agree on the imposition of the Cohn rule, it remains to be seen whether it will continue to be applied. Nevertheless, a brief discussion of the development of this rule is useful from the standpoint of observing the development of the attack on the realization of capital gain on the sale or exchange of depreciable property.

Disallowance of Depreciation in Year of Sale

Salvage value is determined at acquisition of property, and it is not usually changed during the useful life of the property even if price levels change. However, an asset should not be depreciated below known salvage. The Internal Revenue Service feels that the sales price determines final salvage value. Thus, if an asset is sold at a gain, depreciation in the year of sale may be disallowed, because an asset should not be depreciated below salvage.

For example, contractor Wentworth purchased a lathe for $6,400 on January 1, 1957. Wentworth estimated the useful life at six years and the salvage value at $400. A $500 deduction for depreciation was taken each year under the straight-line method. Wentworth sold his lathe for $1,500 on December 31, 1961.

The issue is whether the contractor should be allowed any depreciation in 1961. This, of course, is desirable from the taxpayer's standpoint, because the $500 depreciation would be a deduction in determining ordinary income and he would be in an improved position, because any gain would be Section 1231 gain and thus, usually, capital gain. In our example, Wentworth would have a capital gain of $600 (sales price of $1,500 less adjusted basis of $900). He would deduct $500 depreciation in 1961. The Internal Revenue Service conversely argued that there was only a $100 capital gain ($1,500 less adjusted basis of $1,400). The adjusted basis is $500 higher because no depreciation was allowed in 1961, the year of sale. For sales after 1961 of depreciable property other than buildings, the Section 1245 depreciation-recapture rules would convert the gain into ordinary income anyway.

Application to Buildings

The Tax Court upheld the Internal Revenue Service in the disallowance of depreciation in the year of sale in the following situation.

Mr. Rouse was the owner of a number of homes which he held for rental. As the rental business declined, he sold off portions of his holdings. He sold properties at a gain in each case. The Internal Revenue Service did not allow him depreciation in the year of sale.

The Tax Court upheld the disallowance of depreciation in the year of sale. However, the Court did not allow any adjustment of prior years' depreciation, because prior depreciation was reasonable under the facts known at the time.

One Court Rejects Rule

One district court did not impose the Cohn rule. The Motorlease Corporation used the straight-line depreciation method in depreciating its automobiles. There was no problem with the useful lives or the estimated salvage values, as the Internal Revenue Service agreed that they were reasonable. However, depreciation in the year of sale was denied when the automobiles were sold at a gain. The Court's decision not to uphold the Internal Revenue was based on the Regulations, which indicate that salvage value should be determined at acquisition and that there was no change in useful life in the situation.

Future Significance of Rule

For dispositions of depreciable property other than buildings, Section 1245 will convert gain into ordinary income. However, for dispositions of buildings and leaseholds of land and buildings,

Section 1250 may convert only a portion of the gain into ordinary income depending on the additional depreciation and the applicable percentage, as was discussed earlier. Thus, the question is whether the Internal Revenue Service will attempt to disallow the entire depreciation in the year of sale.

For example, assume that an apartment building with an adjusted basis of $50,000 is sold for $100,000, and that $10,000 depreciation is taken in the year of sale. Also assume that the additional depreciation is $50,000 and that the applicable percentage is 50 per cent.

There is a gain of $50,000 ($100,000 less $50,000 adjusted basis). Applying the Section 1250 recapture rules, this would be $25,000 ordinary income. This is the 50 per cent applicable percentage times the $50,000 gain. The $50,000 gain and the additional depreciation are the same here. The other $25,000 is Section 1231 gain and, thus, probably capital gain.

If the Cohn rule is imposed, the $10,000 depreciation in the year of sale would be disallowed. The gain would now be only $40,000 ($100,000 less $60,000 adjusted basis). The taxpayer would have $20,000 ordinary income (50 per cent applicable percentage times gain) and $20,000 capital gain. He has lost a $10,000 depreciation deduction for the year. From the taxpayer's standpoint, he is in a superior position in having a $10,000 depreciation deduction against ordinary income, $25,000 ordinary income, and $25,000 capital gain than if he has $20,000 ordinary income, $20,000 capital gain, and no depreciation deduction.

SUBDIVISIONS

Owners of tracts of land often find it advantageous to subdivide the land and sell it in lots rather than selling it in one entire parcel. The tax problem in this situation is primarily whether the gain or loss on sale is capital gain or ordinary income. This is an area of a great deal of controversy, as is evidenced by the number of court cases on the subject. The big problem is whether the amount of activity involved in subdividing results in the owner's becoming a "dealer" rather than an investor. A dealer, of course, has ordinary income, whereas the investor has capital gain. There are rules, which if followed by an investor subdividing land, will result in capital gain. However, in other situations falling outside these rules, the result depends on the facts of the situation as interpreted by the Internal Revenue Service and the Courts.

Individuals Receiving Capital Gain Under Special Rules

First, we shall examine the special rules which allow individuals who subdivide and sell real property to receive capital-gain treatment. Note that, if these rules are followed, capital gain results. However, this does not mean that other situations will not also yield capital gain.

The rules are as follows: (1) The individual cannot be a real estate dealer in the year that the lots are sold; (2) no substantial improvements that increase the value of the particular lots sold were made by the owner and will not be made as part of the contract of sale with the buyer; (3) the individual must have held the lots for at least five years, except if the property was inherited; (4) the individual cannot have previously held the tract or any lot in the tract primarily for sale to customers in the ordinary course of trade or business; (5) during the same taxable year in which the sale occurs, no other real property can be held for sale to customers in the ordinary course of trade or business, whether or not the individual is a real estate dealer.

Before 1954, any sale of lots from a tract of land which was subdivided was considered to be a sale to customers in the ordinary course of a trade or business. This rule held whether or not the party was a real estate dealer. If the rules indicated above would otherwise allow capital-gains treatment except for the fact that under previous law the taxpayer would be considered as having held the property for sale to customers in the ordinary course of trade or business, he can still get capital-gain treatment.

For example, M. B. Brownley in 1951 subdivided a tract of land that he had held for several years as an investment, and also sold two lots from the tract. Mr. Brownley was considered to have sold the lots in the ordinary course of trade or business under the pre-1954 law because he subdivided the land. He was taxed at ordinary income rates even though he was not a dealer. During 1964 Mr. Brownley sold three more lots and he met all of the requirements discussed above. He is not denied capital-gain treatment because under prior law back in 1951 he was considered to be a dealer.

Substantial Improvements

Recall that one of the requirements of the special rules is that no substantial improvements which increased the value of the lots sold may have been made. Thus, we have the problem of determining what the meaning of "substantial improvements" is for this purpose. To be a substantial improvement, the improvement must be substantial in character and, in addition, increase the value of the particular lot or parcel sold.

10 per cent increase not substantial. A 10 per cent increase in the value of a lot is not considered to be a substantial increase. However, if the increase is in excess of 10 per cent, then it is up to the taxpayer to show that the increase is not substantial. All relevant factors will be considered in the determination.

Usually substantial improvements. Shopping centers are an improvement which would normally be considered to constitute a substantial improvement. Commercial or residential buildings would be likely also to fall into this category. Hard-surface roads and sewer, water, gas, electric, and utility services would also usually be considered substantial improvements.

Not substantial improvements. Minimum all-weather access roads, including gravel roads when required by the climate, are not considered substantial in character. Temporary structures for field offices, as well as clearing operations, such as filling, draining, and leveling, are not considered to be substantial improvements.

Property Held at Least 10 Years

When property is held for 10 years or more, otherwise substantial improvements may not be considered to be substantial improvements if certain conditions are satisfied. If the property was inherited, it must have been inherited more than 10 years before the sale. If the owner has a holding period which includes the holding period of a predecessor owner, then improvements made by the predecessor owner are considered to have been made by the current owner.

For example, Samuel Green, Sr. gives property which he has held for three years to Samuel Green, Jr. Sam, Sr. made substantial improvements on the property while he held the property. Samuel Green, Jr. holds the property for eight years and does not make any substantial improvements. Because the son's holding period includes that of the father's, the son is considered to have made the substantial improvements.

The conditions to be met to cause otherwise substantial improvements not to be considered substantial are as follows: (1) The improvements consist of sewage or drainage facilities, installation of water, hard-surface or other roads, and curbs and gutters; (2) the lots sold would not have brought the prevailing local price for similar sites without the improvement; (3) the taxpayer elects not to adjust the basis of the lots sold or any other property owned by him for the costs of such improvement attributable to such lot and elects not to deduct the cost of the improvement as an expense.

For example, C. W. Jones had held property for 12 years on the east side of Lake Tahoma. He pays for the paving expenses to put a road through the property. By putting in the road, he is able to get the prevailing local price for similar sites which he could not have gotten without the road. C. W. cannot add the paving cost to his property, and he cannot deduct it as an expense. However, because he has met all the rules, the road will not be considered a substantial improvement.

Acquired by Foreclosure of Lien

Property may be acquired by foreclosure of a lien which secured the payment of a debt to the one acquiring the property. In this case, otherwise substantial improvements will not be considered substantial if: (1) the improvement consists of hard-surface and other roads, curbs, gutters, or the installation of water, sewage, or drainage facilities, and (2) the lot sold was held for 10 years or more. The same rule applies to adjacent property if 80 per cent or more of the property which the taxpayer holds was acquired by foreclosure.

Who Made Improvements?

The substantial-improvement rule considers who made the improvements. An improvement is considered to have been made by the taxpayer if it was made by members of his family. And members of the family for this purpose include whole or half-brothers and sisters, husband or wife, ancestors, and lineal descendents. Improvements made by the following are considered to have been made by the taxpayer: (1) A corporation in which the taxpayer owns directly or indirectly 50 per cent or more of the corporation's voting stock; (2) a partnership of which the taxpayer is a member at the time the improvements were made; (3) a lessee, if the improvement is treated as rental income to the lessee or lessor; and (4) a federal, state, or local government or political subdivision thereof. The latter is considered only if the improvement constitutes an addition to the basis of the property to the taxpayer, such as a special assessment for paving a street.

Tract of Real Property

Because we are discussing the subdivision of a "tract of real property," we must consider its meaning in this context. A tract of real property is a single piece of real property. If there are two or more contiguous pieces of real property, they are considered as a single tract. This is true even if they have been acquired over a period of time and whether they are owned separately, jointly, as a partner, or under any combination of such forms of ownership. The division of two or more pieces of property by a road, street, or stream does not prevent the property from being considered contiguous.

Corporate Taxpayers

The rules discussed above are for individuals. Corporate taxpayers may receive capital-gain treatment of sales of subdivided property if certain requirements are met in addition to those outlined for individuals. These additional rules are as follows: (1) None of the shareholders can be either directly or indirectly a real estate dealer; (2) the property is acquired through foreclosure of a lien securing payment of a debt to the corporation or a debt owed to a creditor who transferred the foreclosure bid to the corporation in exchange for all of its stock and other consideration. Property adjacent is also included if 80 per cent of the property owned by the corporation was acquired by foreclosure.

Gain on Sale of Lots

Assume that all the requirements discussed earlier have been met, so that the taxpayer qualifies under the special rules. How the gain is treated depends on whether more or less than six lots are sold.

Less than six lots sold. Capital gain results if less than six lots or parcels are sold from the same tract. Two or more contiguous lots sold to a single buyer in a single sale are counted as only one parcel.

More than five lots sold. When the sixth lot from the same tract is sold or exchanged, part of the gain is ordinary income and part capital gain. Ordinary income results to the extent that five per cent of the selling price exceeds the expenses incurred in connection with its sale. The balance of any gain is capital gain.

Five per cent of the selling price of all lots sold or exchanged from the tract in the tax year in which the sixth lot is sold or exchanged is considered ordinary income. This is also true for subsequent years. If the first six lots of a single tract are sold in one year, then five per cent of the selling price of each lot sold is considered as ordinary income. Selling expenses are first deducted from the portion of the gain treated as ordinary income, and the remaining expenses, if any, are deducted from the capital-gain portion.

Greenstone, who meets all the requirements of the special rule, subdivides a tract and sells the first three lots in 1965 and the next three lots in 1966. Only the gain realized from the sales in 1966 is subject to the five-per-cent rule. If we change the situation and assume that he sold all six lots in 1965, then the five-per-cent rule would apply to all six lots.

Illustration of five-per-cent rule. To illustrate the five-per-cent rule, we shall assume that subdivider Zeff, who meets all the requirements for special treatment, sells five lots from a single tract in 1965 and in 1966 sells a sixth lot. The problem is to consider how much of Zeff's gain on the sixth lot is capital gain and how much ordinary income. We shall assume that the sixth lot was sold for $20,000, that the basis of the lot was $10,000, and that the expense of sale was $600. The computation is as follows:

Sales price		$20,000
Less: Basis of lot	$10,000	
Expense of sale	600	10,600
Gain from sale of lot		$ 9,400
Five per cent of selling price	$ 1,000	
Less: Expense of sale	600	
Portion of gain that is ordinary income		400
Capital gain		$ 9,000

No sales for five years. When no sales are made for five years, the taxpayer can treat the tract as acquired new on the day after the last sale. Thus, he can start to count from zero again after five years have passed without a sale.

R. W. Jorgensen is a calendar-year individual taxpayer. Jorgensen owns a tract of land which qualifies under the special treatment. This land is subdivided on January 1, 1963. He sells two lots in 1963, two lots in 1964, three lots in 1965, and three lots in 1966. Jorgensen has capital gain on the four lots sold in 1963 and 1964. He has ordinary income up to five per cent of the selling price on all the other sales. No other lots are sold until 1972, when he sells three. He has capital gain on the sale of these three lots because five years have elapsed without a sale.

Loss on Sale of Lots

The preceding rules do not apply to losses. Thus, if land held for investment is subdivided and the lots are sold at a loss, the loss is a capital loss and the five-per-cent rule does not apply.

The foregoing discussion summarizes some of the problems involved in the application of the special rules giving capital gain to subdividers in certain situations. Now we shall proceed to other problems of subdividers.

Allocation of Basis

When land is subdivided, large expenditures are often made for installation of sewage, development of roads, and utility surfaces. In order to be able to determine the gain or loss on a sale of an individual lot, it is necessary to allocate these expenditures to the individual lot. Gain or loss is figured on each separate lot. A subdivider cannot wait to recover his capital before he reports a gain or loss. A number of allocation procedures have been used, including estimated sales prices, assessed valuations, and foot frontage. An example of the sales-price method of allocation is found in Chapter 2.

Conflict Over Nature of Gain

Our discussion of the taxation of subdivisions so far has been concerned with the special rules which allow subdividers capital-gain treatment. However, if the special rules are not met, the subdivider may still get capital gain. Here again we have the dealer-versus-investor arguments that we discussed in the last chapter, and the reader may wish to review that section at this point. Recall that the dealer generally has ordinary income whereas the investor has capital gain. A dealer cannot use the tax-free exchange rules that were discussed in Chapter 3, but an investor may do so. The investor offsets his expenses against the selling price, whereas a dealer can deduct his expenses of making a sale according to the accounting method he is using.

Facts of Particular Situation

Whether a subdivider receives capital-gain treatment or ordinary-income treatment depends on the facts of the particular situation. There are no easy general rules to follow, and there has been much controversy on the subject. We shall give some of the results that courts have come to, in order to give some insight into how the tax treatment is determined. Note that we are assuming that the relief provisions that we discussed on page 124 are not met. For, if they were met, the taxpayer would have capital gain subject to the five-per-cent rule.

Achieved Capital Gain

Allowing the real estate broker to have full control of the subdividing has resulted in capital gain. For example, taxpayer Houghten owned a farm which he wished to sell. In order to achieve the best sales price, it was necessary to subdivide the land and make substantial improvements. The land was turned over to a broker, who was to have full control and make the improvements for a commission. The court ruled that Mr. Houghten had capital gain because he was just liquidating his property in the best manner and that he had given up control and supervision. Similar results have been reached by other courts. Another example is the case of Dr. Voss, who also allowed the real estate broker to have full control of the property. Dr. Voss had purchased 60 acres of land in the 1930's. The broker qualified the land for FHA loans; thus, the taxpayer did not have to advance the money for the improvements. The land was improved, subdivided, and sold, and the taxpayer had capital gain because he was just liquidating his investment in the best manner.

In another case, the Tax Court noted the complete lack of "busyness" on the taxpayer's part in development and sale of the property. This is the case of Dr. Van Drunen, who had invested in some real estate but let the broker handle the development, advertising, sales, and all other matters.

Full Control for the Broker

It seems essential that full control should be given to the broker. If not, the broker may be considered the agent of the taxpayer, and the taxpayer may be considered to be a dealer. Too much activity appears dangerous, as is indicated by the following case.

Mr. Gault had invested in a tract of land and spent large sums improving and subdividing the property. Although he was president of a corporation, he spent two or three hours a week on the real estate, helping to develop it into an exclusive residential area. In fact, he handled all the sales himself. The result was that Mr. Gault was considered a real estate dealer and that he had ordinary income.

Purpose Important

The purpose of the subdividing seems to be important. For example, Mr. Oace purchased 125 acres by a lake in order to acquire a five-acre plot to build a new home. He then subdivided and sold the land he did not need to 46 friends. The result was a $60,000 profit to Mr. Oace which the Internal Revenue Service claimed was ordinary income because so many sales were made in a short time.

The Tax Court ruled that the $60,000 was capital gain because Mr. Oace's main purpose was to purchase the site for a home and that it was financial pressure resulting from the cost of constructing an expensive home which caused him to sell so much so quickly.

Inherited Property

A person who inherits land must be careful in subdividing it so that he is not classified as a dealer and thus subject to ordinary income. One possibility is to give full responsibility to a real estate broker to handle the entire affair, as we have discussed on the preceding page, in which case the result seems to be capital gain.

In one situation a taxpayer inherited a 300-acre family estate but did not wish to sell because the market was at a low level. During 15 years, the taxpayer parceled out and sold 100 unimproved acres to unsolicited purchasers. The balance of the property was then sold. The court agreed that the parceling out of some of the property and taking time on the rest of the property did not make the taxpayer a dealer, and that he had capital gain. Further, it was the only practicable way to liquidate.

Liquidation Argument and Losses

In the discussion above, we have noted how the fact that the investor was subdividing as the best method of liquidating his investment was important in the determination of capital gain. It is interesting to note that this argument works in reverse to cause the taxpayer to have a capital loss rather than an ordinary loss on subdivision.

For example, in one situation the taxpayers were unable to sell an 83-acre estate in total, so they subdivided the estate. They had losses rather than gain on the sale of the lots. They claimed to be selling the lots in the ordinary course of trade or business, which would have yielded an ordinary rather than a capital loss. The Tax Court ruled that they had a capital loss because they were just liquidating an investment.

Gain Computed on Separate Parcels

A subdivider is not permitted to recover cost first and thus not pay tax until his basis is recovered. Rather, he must compute gain on each separate parcel.

Status May Change for Same Taxpayer

A taxpayer may be considered an investor in one year and a dealer in another. For example, a doctor owned approximately 50 acres for 15 years. When he sold some of the lots in 1957, he was treated as an investor because he was a full-time physician and had no prior sales. Also, he had only a few sales in 1957. The next year, he was considered to have sold the property in the ordinary course of trade or business, and the result was ordinary income. The reason was the increased sales, together with development work on the property.

Tax-Free Provisions Not Available to Dealer

Owners of real property held for sale to customers in the ordinary course of business cannot use the tax-free exchange provisions available for real property held for investment or held for use in trade or business. Thus, a subdivider is not able to trade subdivision land for other property on a tax-free basis. The tax-free exchange provisions are discussed in Chapter 3.

Summary of Important Factors

We have noted that, if the investor is subdividing just to liquidate his investment in the best possible manner, he may usually obtain capital gain. A taxpayer can be considered to be an investor in one year and a dealer in another year. Active participation in sales and promotion and frequent and continuous sales are indications that the subdivider is selling property to customers in the ordinary course of business. If the subdivider obtains a license to deal in real estate, this is indicative that he is a dealer. An investor is not likely to advertise, have signs, or have a sales office. Just the number of sales is not the most important factor. If the owner of the subdivision has another full-time occupation and has held the property for a long period of time, this is in his favor for determination that he is an investor and not a dealer.

The dealer-versus-investor problem is not unique to the subdivider. It is also important to the owner of improved property held for investment and to the owner of property used in a trade or business, such as the owner of rental properties. As we noted in the dealer-investor discussion in the previous chapter, it is sometimes possible for a dealer to be treated as an investor for specific properties.

Chapter 6

Depreciation

Property used in trade or business and property held for rental purposes is subject to an allowance for depreciation. A deduction for depreciation is taken along with deductions for operating expenses in arriving at taxable income. Thus, the larger the depreciation deduction, the smaller the taxable income and the smaller the tax. Depreciation is computed on improvements only. Land is not subject to depreciation under the tax law.

IMPORTANCE OF DEPRECIATION

Depreciable Basis Greater Than Equity

An owner of rental property most likely will have an equity in the property which is much less than the depreciable basis of the improvements. This is so because a substantial portion of the funds required for the investment will be supplied by a mortgage on the property. Depreciation is computed on the basis of the improvements and not on the owner's equity.

Importance of Accelerated Depreciation

Certain accelerated depreciation methods, such as the double-declining-balance method and the sum-of-the-years-digits method, may be used to depreciate improvements on property. These methods, which we shall discuss in detail shortly, allow more depreciation in the earlier years and less in the later years than the straight-line depreciation method allows.

Depreciation and Cash Flow

Depreciation, as contrasted with other operating expenses such as utilities and janitorial services, is a deduction for tax purposes which does not cause cash to flow out of the operation.

The combination of the following factors makes it possible for an owner sometimes to build up an equity in property out of funds which are tax-free. These factors are: (1) accelerated depreciation; (2) depreciation is computed on the total basis of the improvements and not on the owner's equity; (3) depreciation does not cause any funds to flow out of the business.

Depreciation, Taxable Income, and Cash Flow

To illustrate these factors, assume that an investor has $100,000, which he invests in an apartment house. The purchase price of the property is $400,000. This is financed with a $100,000 down payment and a first loan of $300,000. Maturity of the loan is 20 years and the interest rate is six per cent. Allocation of purchase price according to assessed valuations yields a $100,000 valuation on the land and $300,000 on the improvements. Because the property is new, the double-declining-balance depreciation method is used. The depreciable life is 40 years.

Net income before interest, depreciation, and taxes for the first year is $33,000. The determination of taxable income for the first year is as follows:

Income before depreciation, interest, and taxes		$33,000
Less:		
Interest	$18,000	
Depreciation	15,000	33,000
Taxable income		none

Note, however, that the cash flow from this enterprise is not zero.

Cash from operations	$33,000
Less:	
Loan payment (principal and interest)	26,000
Net cash flow from investment	$ 7,000

Because the double-declining-balance depreciation method is used to compute depreciation on the $300,000 improvement, there is no taxable income. Nevertheless, the cash flow from operations is sufficient to cover the interest and principal payments and still leave over $7,000. At the same time, the owner has paid off $8,000 of the principal of this mortgage, and his equity has increased accordingly.

Later Sale of Property at a Gain

The deductible depreciation and interest charges will decline each year. Although we cannot predict what will happen to the value of the property as time passes, it may well be that deductible tax depreciation will exceed the actual decline in value of the property. The interplay of high tax depreciation and low or even negative actual decline in market value may place the owner of the property in the position of being able to sell or exchange the property at a gain. Insofar as the property may be sold and income taxed at capital-gain rates, the owner will have converted ordinary income into capital gains. And, generally, capital gains bear a maximum tax rate of 25 per cent. Depreciation has been deducted in arriving at taxable income, which is taxed at the owner's or the enterprise's ordinary-tax rate. Gain is taxed at capital-gain rates, which bear a tax of a maximum of 25 per cent. This procedure is limited to a degree by the Internal Revenue Service, which will disallow depreciation in the year of sale when depreciable assets are sold at a gain. It is also limited by the depreciation-recapture rules, which we discussed in the previous chapter, which act to convert a certain amount of capital gain into ordinary income.

Exchange of Property

The owner also has the opportunity of exchanging the property for another property of like kind under the provisions of Section 1031 of the Internal Revenue Code. In this manner he may defer the potential gain on the property and acquire property of greater value without paying any tax on the difference between the market value of his equity in the property and the taxable basis for his property.

NATURE OF DEPRECIATION

The Internal Revenue Code allows for a reasonable allowance for the exhaustion, wear and tear, and normal obsolescence of property used in a trade or business or held for the production of income. The amount of the annual depreciation deduction may be calculated in any way consistent with recognized trade practices. The straight-line method, the declining-balance method, and the sum-of-the-years digits methods are specifically listed in the 1954 Code.

For example, an investor purchases property for $75,000.

Assume that the allocation between land and improvements is $35,000
to the land and $40,000 to the improvements. The straight-line
depreciation method is used, together with a life of 40 years. The
owner deducts $1,000 a year for depreciation, and each year the
adjusted basis of his property drops $1,000. The adjusted basis
is the figure which enters into the calculation of gain or loss on
sale or exchange of property. Thus, if he sells the property for
$75,000 at the end of five years, he would have a $5,000 gain,
determined as follows:

Selling price			$75,000
Adjusted basis			
Land		$35,000	
Improvements	$40,000		
Depreciation	5,000	35,000	70,000
Gain on sale			$ 5,000

The taxpayer cannot forget to deduct depreciation in one year
and add this amount to a later year. The adjusted basis decreases
by the amount of the allowable depreciation even though the owner
neglects to take it.

WHAT PROPERTY MAY BE DEPRECIATED?

Use of Property

Depreciation is confined to property that has a definitely
limited useful life. Land is considered not to depreciate, and no
allowance for depreciation is allowed for land. Depreciation is
allowed only on property used in the taxpayer's trade or business
or property held for the production of income. The use of property
is the use to which the property is put in the tax year. The right
to deduct depreciation may be affected by a change in use. A depreciation allowance may not be taken for the taxpayer's personal
residence. But if the residence is rented or is abandoned as a
residence and is listed for rental or sale, a deduction is permitted.
When property that was originally acquired for personal use is converted to business or investment use, an allowance for depreciation
is allowed from the time of conversion.

A taxpayer is not allowed a deduction on his personal automobile. However, if the owner uses his automobile partly for
pleasure and partly for investment or business purposes, he may
depreciate a proportionate part of the basis of the automobile.

Life Must Be Limited

Depreciation is allowable for machinery, buildings, and fruit trees with a definite useful life. For example, peach orchards and lemon groves have been depreciated for tax purposes. However, fruit trees may not be subject to depreciation when the age of the trees is indeterminate and the productivity increases with age. Examples are avocado and mango orchards and some citrus groves. Private streets, curbs, and paving are improvements with a limited useful life which are depreciable. Although land is not depreciable, a deduction was allowed for pasture land where the grass was planted and the land would lose its economic usefulness over a period of time. However, the expense of installation of a golf course has been ruled nondepreciable on the theory that the life of the greens is permanent if ordinary care and maintenance are provided.

Depreciation on Farmer's Property

A farmer may claim depreciation on farm buildings except for the farmer's residence. He may depreciate farm machinery and other physical property. The machinery is considered to depreciate even though a crop is not planted.

Depreciation may be deducted on livestock acquired for work and for breeding or dairy purposes. An exception is the case where livestock is included in an inventory to determine profit.

Intangible Property

Intangible property may be depreciated if its use in business or the production of income is definitely limited in duration. These items, however, cannot be depreciated under the declining-balance or the sum-of-the-years-digits methods of depreciation. Leaseholds, patents, and copyrights are examples of intangible property which can be depreciated. Items of intangible property of indefinite duration of usefulness are not depreciable. Examples are good will, trade names, trade-marks, and formulas.

WHO MAY DEDUCT DEPRECIATION

The person who owns and has a capital investment in property ordinarily gets the depreciation allowance. It is the person who suffers an economic loss as a result of the decrease in value of the property who is entitled to the depreciation allowance.

For example, assume that Adams leases a building to Brown, and that Brown has only to maintain the property and make necessary

repairs and replacements. Adams receives the depreciation allowance and Brown does not. However, the lessee (Brown) may
claim a depreciation allowance for any improvements he makes on
the leased property.

Life Tenant and Remainderman

A life tenant receives the depreciation deduction. After the
death of the life tenant, the remainderman gets the deduction. The
amount of the deduction is based on the useful life of the property
and not on the life expectancy of the life tenant. When someone buys
a life estate, he is allowed to recover the amount of his investment
through annual deductions spread over the life expectancy of the
seller. This is true whether or not he is the remainderman.

DETERMINATION OF BASIS FOR DEPRECIATION

The basis for depreciation is the same as the adjusted basis
which is used in determining gain from a sale. Note that the basis
for the depreciation calculation is not cost, but the adjusted basis
for determining gain on a sale.

Assume that on January 1, 1965 Realtor Black bought an
electric sign for $12,000, and that the electric sign has a useful
life of eight years. The basis for the depreciation calculation is
$12,000, and the amount allowable in 1965, using the straight-line
method, is $1,500. Usually, the deduction for each of the seven
succeeding years would be $1,500. However, at the close of 1966
(end of two years) Realtor Black determines that the sign would be
used for 10 more years. The adjusted basis of the machine at the
end of 1966 is $9,000. This is the cost of $12,000 less two years'
depreciation, amounting to $3,000. The deduction for each of the
succeeding 10 years will be $900 under the straight-line method.

Under I.R.C. Section 1031, gain may be deferred when
property of a like kind is exchanged. If Duncan exchanges an apartment house having an adjusted basis of $30,000 for another apart-
ment house having a fair market value of $40,000, the basis of the
property received is $30,000. Thus, Duncan may calculate his de-
preciation on $30,000.

Inherited Property Subject to a Mortgage

If a taxpayer inherits property which is subject to a mortgage,
his basis for the depreciation calculation is the value of the property
when acquired without reduction for the mortgage. This is true even

if he does not assume the mortgage. Later, if he settles the mortgage for less than face value, he must reduce his basis for depreciation by the amount saved. He need not, however, apply a reduction in the mortgage retroactively to depreciation deductions taken in prior years. The basis of the inherited property is, of course, reduced for depreciation from the time that the heir receives the property.

Change in Holding of Property

Property that was originally acquired for personal use may later be converted to income-producing use. The basis for depreciation is the adjusted basis on the date of conversion or the fair market value on the date of conversion, whichever is lower.

Property Held by Formerly Tax-Exempt Taxpayer

A tax-exempt taxpayer may lose his tax-exempt status. The basis for depreciation of property must be reduced for depreciation sustained during the period held by the taxpayer while he was tax-exempt.

ALLOCATION OF LUMP-SUM PURCHASE PRICE

Fair Market Value

When a parcel of improved real estate is bought for a lump sum, the purchase price must be allocated between the land and the building. The building is depreciable, whereas the land is not depreciable. Depreciation allowances are limited to an amount that bears the same proportion to the lump-sum price as the fair market value of the depreciable property at the time of acquisition bears to the fair market value of the entire property at that time. Thus, the taxpayer has to determine the value of the depreciable property and the value of the total property. Usually the value of the total property is equal to the purchase price.

Assume that property worth $45,000 is sold for $45,000. If the value of the building is $30,000, the lump-sum price would be divided two-thirds to the building and the balance of $15,000 to the land.

Let us take another situation and assume that property worth $50,000 is sold for $45,000. The value of the building in this case is $25,000. The lump-sum price is divided one-half, or $22,500, to the building and the balance of $22,500 to the land. The 50 per cent allocation to the depreciable property is determined by dividing the value of the building ($25,000) by the value of the entire property ($50,000).

Objective Evidence

The allocation of the lump-sum purchase price between depreciable and nondepreciable property is helped by objective indications of relative market values. The relative assessed valuations of the county tax assessor may often be used in substantiating the allocation of purchase price.

Assume that Martin purchases a bowling alley building for $80,000. The county tax assessor has placed a value of $4,000 on the land and $16,000 on the improvements. The assessed value of the building ($16,000) is 80 per cent of the total assessed value ($20,000). Thus, Martin applies 80 per cent of the purchase price, or $64,000, to the depreciable building and 20 per cent of the purchase price, or $16,000, to the nondepreciable land.

Allocation in Contract

A buyer and seller may specify in the contract of sale the amount of the purchase price which is allocable to the depreciable improvements and to the nondepreciable land. This allocation may or may not hold up for tax purposes. If the allocation had a substantial effect on both the buyer and seller and was a matter of arm's-length bargaining, then the allocation might hold up. If it is only for the benefit of the purchaser, then it probably will not hold up.

Sampson purchases a store from Randolph for $160,000. Sampson asks Randolph to specify in the contract that $140,000 should be allocated to the store and $20,000 to the land. Because Randolph (the seller) will have a gain taxed at capital-gain rates regardless of the allocation, he doesn't care and agrees to the allocation. When Sampson makes his allocation for tax purposes, he will need more objective evidence for his allocation, because the contractual allocation is not important to Randolph.

Improvements to Be Demolished

When improved property is acquired with the intention of removing the improvements, no depreciation is allowed unless the improvements are used prior to demolition. If the improvements are not used prior to demolition, the entire purchase price is allocated to the land. Costs of removing the improvements are added to the basis of the land. Any salvage received for the improvements is offset against the cost of demolition. If the building is not demolished right away, part of the basis of the property may be allocated to the improvements and depreciated over the period that the improvements are used. However, the amount of the basis that can be allocated to the building may not exceed the present value of the right to receive rentals from the building over the period of its intended use. The present value of this right is determined at the time the improvements are first used for production of income or in a trade or business.

A purchaser of property may buy improved property and remove rather than demolish the improvements. If he removes the improvements, he may allocate a portion of the basis of the total property to the buildings he removes.

TAKING INSUFFICIENT OR EXCESSIVE DEPRECIATION

The basis of property has to be reduced for depreciation of prior years. Different rules apply in the case where a taxpayer has taken more than the allowable depreciation and where he has taken less than the allowable depreciation. Obviously, the taxpayer is not allowed to determine his annual depreciation deduction at will. If he could, he would manipulate his taxable income amongst years on the basis of the relative profitabilities of each year.

Taxpayer Has Taken Insufficient Depreciation

If a taxpayer does not take any depreciation or takes less than the amount allowed, he nevertheless must reduce the basis of his property by the allowable amount. This holds true even if the allowable amount would not have reduced his tax.

For example, Property Managers, Inc. have a copying machine with a life of five years which they are depreciating by the straight-line method. Depreciation each year should be $1,000. However, Property Managers, Inc. have incurred losses in year one and two; therefore, they decided not to take any depreciation on their copying machine. However, even though they did not take any depreciation in the first two years, their basis at the beginning of the third year is $3,000. The original basis of $5,000 has been reduced by the $2,000 allowable depreciation in the first two years.

The effect of this rule is to increase allowable depreciation in later years, so that there is no advantage to a taxpayer in later years for a prior failure to take sufficient depreciation.

Taxpayer Allowed Excessive Depreciation

Sometimes a taxpayer will, through error or otherwise, take excessive depreciation, and this excessive depreciation will be allowed. In this case he must reduce the basis of his property by the amount allowed, which reduces his tax. However, the amount

by which he reduces his basis may not be less than the amount of
depreciation properly allowable. The amount allowed which reduces
his tax is called the "tax-benefit amount allowed."

For example: On 1/1/62, Building Maintenance, Inc. purchased a truck for $8,000. Because the life of the truck was eight
years, and it had no salvage value, allowable depreciation, using
the straight-line method, was $1,000 a year. However, depreciation
was actually taken and allowed as follows:

1962	$1,000
1963	none
1964	none
1965	$3,000

Of the $3,000 depreciation allowed for 1965, assume that
only $2,000 resulted in a tax benefit. The basis of the truck should
be reduced as follows:

	Year	Allowed	Tax Benefit Amount Allowed (Amount Allowed Which Reduced Taxpayer's Tax)	Allowable	Reduction of Basis
(1)	1962	$1,000	......	$1,000	$1,000
(2)	1963	0	......	1,000	1,000
(3)	1964	0	......	1,000	1,000
(4)	1965	3,000	$2,000	1,000	2,000
			Total reduction		$5,000

The basis is reduced to $3,000 ($8,000 less $5,000), and
the remaining basis should be written off at the rate of $750 per
year ($3,000 divided by 4).

Technically, Building Maintenance, Inc. should not be allowed a $3,000 deduction for 1965. Failure to deduct $1,000 allowable depreciation in each of the years 1963 and 1964 does not
entitle them to a greater deduction in a later year. However,
where the excessive depreciation was allowed, basis must be adjusted as shown.

The basis must also be reduced by the amount of depreciation allowable in 1963 and 1964 even though Building Maintenance,
Inc. took no deduction in those years.

IMPORTANCE OF SALVAGE VALUE

Salvage value is the amount realized by the taxpayer when he sells or otherwise disposes of property. Salvage value is determined at the time the taxpayer acquires the property, and once determined, it cannot be changed merely because of change in price levels. If it is necessary to redetermine the useful life of the asset to the taxpayer, he may also redetermine the salvage value based on the facts at that time. The salvage value may also be adjusted at the end of the useful life of the property if there is a substantial difference between estimated and actual salvage.

Some assets are disposed of when there is little or no useful value remaining. On the other hand, in some businesses assets are disposed of when they still have a substantial market value. A taxpayer may use either salvage value or net salvage as long as he is consistent. Net salvage value is salvage value less cost of removal. As we shall see shortly, salvage value must be considered in calculating the straight-line and sum-of-the-years-digits depreciation. However, it is not taken into account when the declining-balance method is used.

If property is depreciated below salvage value, the Internal Revenue Service may disallow the depreciation in the year of sale. If a taxpayer customarily sells property after holding it for only part of its useful life, it may be contended that the useful life to the taxpayer is the time he holds it, and the salvage value will then be the fair market value at the time it is sold.

For personal property other than livestock acquired after October 16, 1962, a taxpayer may ignore salvage value up to 10 per cent of the cost or other basis of the property. This property must have a useful life of at least three years, but the rule applies whether the property is either new or used. Note that this rule concerns personal property and not real property.

Assume that the contracting firm of McCafferty and McCarthy purchases an electric saw for $2,000 for use in their business. Ordinarily, the salvage value of the electric saw at the end of its useful life would be $160. However, if the taxpayers so desire, they may disregard the $160 salvage value, because it is less than 10 per cent of the cost of the saw, and may compute the depreciation deduction on the entire $2,000 cost. If the salvage value had been estimated at, say, $250, then McCafferty and McCarthy could disregard $200 (10 per cent of $2,000 cost), and the depreciation would be computed considering $50 salvage.

ALTERNATIVE DEPRECIATION METHODS

The following depreciation methods are specifically noted in the 1954 Internal Revenue Code: (1) straight-line method, (2) declining-balance method, (3) sum-of-the-years-digits method, (4) any other consistent method. However, the annual depreciation allowance may be figured in any way consistent with recognized trade practice. But the method adopted must be reasonable.

Election of Method

A taxpayer who has not previously filed a return chooses a depreciation method in his first return. If a taxpayer qualifies for the sum-of-the-years-digits method or the declining-balance method at twice the straight-line rate, he merely figures depreciation under the appropriate method for the first tax year in which he acquires the property.

A taxpayer does not have to use the same method for all his depreciable property. However, once he has chosen a method for a particular property, he must consistently use that method for that property unless he meets the necessary requirements for a change of method. Note that a taxpayer may use a different depreciation method for similar property which he acquires later, provided that the new property is set up in a separate account.

Change of Depreciation Method

A taxpayer who is using the double-declining-balance depreciation method may change to the straight-line method without permission. Election must be made by the date for filing the return, including extensions.

For any other change in depreciation method on any property, it is necessary to apply for permission within 90 days after the start of the tax year for which the change is desired. Thus, if a taxpayer wants to change from the straight-line method to another method for calendar year 1965, he must apply by March 31, 1965.

STRAIGHT-LINE DEPRECIATION

Under the straight-line depreciation method, the cost or other basis of the property, less its estimated salvage value, is deducted in equal annual installments over its estimated useful life.

For example, Green Bros., Realtors purchased an electric sign, having a useful life of 10 years, for $5,000; salvage value at the end of ten years is estimated to be $1,000. Thus, the annual depreciation deduction under the straight-line method is $400.

The straight-line method may be used for any depreciable property. Prior to 1954 the straight-line depreciation method was the most common method. However, since 1954 the sum-of-the-years-digits and the double-declining-balance method have been used more and more.

DECLINING-BALANCE DEPRECIATION

The declining-balance method may be used with a rate of depreciation which does not exceed twice the straight-line rate. Under the declining-balance method, the greatest amount of depreciation is taken in the first year of use. Continually decreasing amounts of depreciation are taken in successive years. Salvage value is not considered in calculating the deduction. However, salvage value must be accounted for when assets are retired, and the asset cannot be depreciated below a reasonable salvage value.

Under the declining-balance method, a uniform rate is applied to the unrecovered basis of the property.

For example, on January 1, 1965, Marcus bought a new office machine having a useful life of five years. It cost him $5,000 and its salvage value was $500. Under the declining-balance method at twice the straight-line rate, Marcus is able to use a 40 per cent rate (twice the 20 per cent straight-line rate). (An asset that has a five-year life and is depreciated on a straight-line rate would depreciate 20 per cent per year.) The depreciation allowance for the first year would be $2,000 (40 per cent of $5,000). Note that the rate is applied to the cost unadjusted for salvage. The basis at the end of the first year is $3,000 ($5,000 less $2,000). The allowance for the second year would be $1,200 (40 per cent of $3,000). Note that each year, the rate is applied to the remaining balance and not to the original cost.

Change to Straight-Line Method

If a taxpayer changes from the declining-balance method to the straight-line method, the remaining cost less estimated salvage is recovered over the estimate remaining useful life. Both salvage value and useful life must be redetermined from circumstances existing at the time of change.

For example, assume in our example above that Marcus changes from the declining-balance method to the straight-line method at the end of the second year. At the end of the second year, there is an unrecovered basis of $1,800 ($5,000 cost less depreciation taken of $3,200). A review of the circumstances indicates that there are still three years remaining and that the salvage value at the end of that time will be $500. Marcus will take $433.33 depreciation each year for the next three years. The $1,800 remaining basis less $500 salvage equals $1,300. Divide the $1,300 by three years remaining to arrive at $433.33 for the depreciation allowance.

Property Eligible for Declining-Balance Depreciation

There are certain limitations on property eligible for the declining-balance method at twice the straight-line rate. The property must have a useful life of at least three years. In addition, it must be property constructed, reconstructed, or erected by or for the taxpayer after 1953, or property acquired by the taxpayer after 1954, if he is the original user. Note that the taxpayer must be the original user in order to use the declining-balance method at twice the straight-line rate. Property acquired in a tax-free exchange from an original user is not eligible for declining-balance depreciation.

For example, in 1965 Kanter buys a 25-year-old building and makes additions and alterations to it during the year. Only the cost of the additions and alterations may be depreciated under the declining-balance depreciation method.

As another example, assume that Strickling bought a typewriter from Abbott in 1964. The typewriter was made in 1958. Abbott had previously leased the typewriter to Deed in 1958 before selling it to Strickling in 1964. Strickling cannot use the declining-balance method at twice the straight-line rate. He is not the original user of the typewriter he acquired in 1964.

Fox is able to use the declining-balance depreciation method in the following situation. He bought a new house for his personal residence in 1962. Fox cannot take any depreciation on his personal residence. However, he moves out in 1964 and rents the house. He is able to use the declining-balance method on the converted residence. He is the original owner and he acquired it after 1953.

Nonqualifying Property

The declining-balance method at twice the straight-line rate cannot be used for intangible property, such as patents, copyrights, and leases. This method also cannot be used for property in the hands of a distributee, vendee, transferee, donee, or grantee, unless he is the original user and the property otherwise qualifies.

Property that does not qualify for the declining-balance method at twice the straight-line rate may qualify for the straight-line or the limited declining-balance method. Such property does not qualify for the sum-of-the-years-digits method.

Limited Declining-Balance Depreciation

Our discussion of declining-balance depreciation has so far assumed a rate of twice the straight-line rate. Thus, if the useful life of the asset was five years, the straight-line rate was 20 per cent and the declining-balance rate was 40 per cent. We have noted before, however, that certain property, such as property acquired used, does not qualify for this method.

Property acquired new or used prior to 1954 and property acquired used after 1954 may be depreciated on the declining-balance rate at one and one-half times the straight-line rate.

For example, let us take the office machine that Marcus bought on January 1, 1965. The cost was $5,000, salvage value was $500, and the useful life was five years. The straight-line percentage rate was 20 per cent (5 years). The declining-balance rate at twice the straight-line rate was 40 per cent, and Marcus depreciated his office machine $2,000 the first year. However, if we assume that all the facts are the same except that Marcus bought the office machine used; then he cannot use twice the straight-line rate. He would use 150 per cent of the straight-line rate or 30 per cent, and his first-year depreciation would be $1,500. Note that salvage value is not figured in the deduction. A change to and from limited declining-balance depreciation requires the consent of the Internal Revenue Service.

SUM-OF-THE-YEARS-DIGITS METHOD

The sum-of-the-years-digits method and the declining balance rate at twice the straight-line rate are the two primary methods which yield more depreciation deductions in the earlier years of the life of an asset and less in the later years. The basis for the calculation of the sum-of-the-years-digits depreciation is the cost of the property reduced by the estimated salvage value. Each year, a changing fraction is applied to this basis. The numerator of the fraction is the number of remaining years of the estimated useful life of the property. The denominator is the sum of the numbers representing the years of life of the property.

Note that under the sum-of-the-years-digits method a changing fraction is applied to the same base. Also different from the declining-balance method is the fact that salvage value is considered in the calculation of the sum-of-the-years-digits method.

The following examples illustrate the application of the sum-of-the-years-digits method.

For example, Wolf has an asset with a five-year life. The fraction used in figuring the depreciation allowed for the first year would be 5/15, 5 being the number of remaining years of life and 15 being the sum of 1 + 2 + 3 + 4 + 5. For the second year, the fraction would be 4/15, and so on.

Note: You can get the sum-of-the-years-digits for the denominator of the fraction by using the following simple formula:

$$S = N \left(\frac{N + 1}{2} \right) \quad \text{when:} \quad \begin{array}{l} S = \text{sum of the digits} \\ N = \text{number of years of estimated} \\ \quad \text{useful life.} \end{array}$$

Thus, substituting in the formula, for an asset with five years of estimated useful life, you get

$$S = 5 \left(\frac{5 + 1}{2} \right) = 5 \times 3 = 15.$$

Bernstein acquires new property at a cost of $175. It has an estimated useful life of five years. Its estimated salvage value is $25. The depreciation deduction for each year would be that shown in column (c):

(a) Year	(b) Fraction of Cost Less Salvage	(c) Depreciation Deduction
1	5/15	$ 50
2	4/15	40
3	3/15	30
4	2/15	20
5	1/15	10
Total cost less salvage		$150

Property Eligible for Sum-of-the-Years-Digits Method

The sum-of-the-years-digits method may be used for the same kind of property that qualifies for the declining-balance method at twice the straight-line rate. These requirements are described above. Note particularly that it must be an asset with a useful life of at least three years and that the taxpayer must be the original user.

Change in Useful Life

Sometimes a change in the useful life of the asset will be necessary. The basis for depreciation is the amount of the cost that has not been recovered at the time. The computation is made as if the remaining useful life at the start of the tax year of change were the useful life of a new asset acquired at that time.

For example, on January 1, 1962, Davidson bought a new safe with an estimated life of 10 years. When making his return for 1967, Davidson finds that the asset has a remaining useful life of seven years from January 1, 1967. Depreciation for 1967 is calculated as if 1967 were the first year of life. The useful life of the asset is seven years and the allowance for 1967 is 7/28 of the unrecovered basis adjusted for salvage.

COMPARISON OF DEPRECIATION METHODS

The declining-balance method at twice the straight-line rate and the sum-of-the-years-digits method result in larger depreciation deductions in the earlier years and smaller depreciation deductions in the later years than does the straight-line method.

The differences in methods are illustrated in the following example.

Assume an asset costing $50,000 with no salvage value and an estimated useful life of five years. The straight-line method allows 20 per cent of the original cost each year; the declining-balance method at twice the straight-line rate allows twice that rate (40 per cent), but the higher rate is applied to the declining balance, that is, the unrecovered cost of the asset; the sum-of-the-years-digits method allows a fractional rate of 5/15 the first year, 4/15 the second year, and so forth, the numerator being the number of remaining years of life and the denominator the sum of the years of life.

COMPARISON OF DEPRECIATION METHODS

	Straight Line		Declining Balance			Sum of the Digits		
Year	Annual Deduction 20 Per Cent	Cumulative Amount Recovered	Balance (Unrecovered Cost)	Annual Deduction (40 Per Cent of Balance)	Cumulative Amount Recovered	Rate (Fraction of Cost)	Annual Deduction	Cumulative Amount Recovered
1	$10,000	$10,000	$50,000	$20,000	$20,000	5/15	$16,667	$16,667
2	10,000	20,000	30,000	12,000	32,000	4/15	13,333	30,000
3	10,000	30,000	18,000	7,200	39,200	3/15	10,000	40,000
4	10,000	40,000	10,800	4,320	43,520	2/15	6,667	46,667
5	10,000	50,000	6,480	2,592	46,112	1/15	3,333	50,000

Note that under the double- declining-balance method, if the property is used beyond its estimated useful life, depreciation continues until the property is retired. The asset, however, is not depreciated below salvage.

Sale of Asset Before End of Useful Life

Assume that the taxpayer sells this asset on January 1 of the fourth year for $45,000. His gain under each method would be as follows:

	Straight Line	Declining Balance	Sum of the Digits
Sales price	$45,000	$45,000	$45,000
Unrecovered basis	20,000	10,800	10,000
Gain	$25,000	$34,200	$35,000

Note that the taxpayer has a much larger gain under the declining-balance and the sum-of-the-years-digits methods than under the straight-line method.

If the asset is a building or structure used in trade or business or for the production of income, the gain may be capital gain subject to the depreciation-recapture rules of Section 1250. Assets other than buildings or structures are subject to the more stringent depreciation-recapture provisions which we discussed earlier. Using the alternative methods, the taxpayer in our example has deducted the following amounts against ordinary income in the three years: (1) straight-line, $30,000; (2) declining-balance, $39,200; (3) sum-of-the-years-digits, $40,000.

Working-Capital Advantages of Accelerated Depreciation Methods

The accelerated methods (double-declining-balance and sum-of-the-years-digits) allow for larger deductions in the earlier years than does the straight-line method. This means, everything else being equal, a smaller taxable income and less tax payments. Working capital is increased in the earlier years of the life of the asset through the use of the accelerated methods. Businesses that are growing, therefore, through using an accelerated depreciation method, have more money available for expansion. This is an important advantage to small businesses and farmers, who often are dependent on current earnings for expansion. The mcre rapid recovery of investment in depreciable assets permits them to use current earnings for expansion. Accelerated methods also aid manufacturers and other users of machinery to replace obsolete machinery and equipment with up-to-date facilities. The stimulation of purchase of capital equipment was a prime reason for the allowance of the accelerated methods in the 1954 Internal Revenue Code.

OTHER METHODS OF DEPRECIATION

Any other consistent method of depreciation may be used to calculate the annual depreciation allowance for property which qualifies for the double-declining-balance and sum-of-the-years-digits methods. There is the limitation, however, that the total depreciation allowances at the end of each year cannot exceed, during the first two-thirds of the useful life of the property, the total allowances that would result if the declining-balance method at twice the straight-line rate were used.

Unit-of-Production Method

The unit-of-production method is based on the unit of work done rather than the lapse of time.

For example, Realtor Wolf has a Cadillac which he used entirely for business. The difference between cost and salvage value of the Cadillac is $4,800; it is estimated that during its useful life the automobile will be driven 40,000 miles. During the tax year, it was driven 10,000 miles. The deduction would be $1,200 ($4,800 X 10,000/40,000).

Naturally, the taxpayer would determine which depreciation method would be best considering his particular circumstances.

ADDITIONAL FIRST-YEAR DEPRECIATION ALLOWANCE

In addition to the depreciation deduction computed by the taxpayer's chosen depreciation method, the taxpayer may elect an additional initial deduction equal to 20 per cent of the cost of tangible personal property. Real estate and intangible personal property, such as patents, do not qualify. The extra 20 per cent applies only to $10,000 of investment. Either the full cost, or a fractional part of the cost, of a particular item may be chosen for the additional write-off. The $10,000 limit on which the allowance is computed applies to each taxpayer and not to each business in which he has an interest.

Salvage value is not considered in applying the 20 per cent. However, in applying the normal depreciation deductions using the taxpayer's regular depreciation method, the basis must be reduced by both the additional allowance and the salvage value. An exception is declining-balance depreciation, where salvage value does not enter into the calculation. On a joint return, the 20 per cent is applied to $20,000 of cost.

The calculation of the additional first-year allowance and normal depreciation for the first year is illustrated below:

On 1/1/65, Smith Realty, which uses straight-line depreciation, bought for $10,000 an electric sign having a useful life of 10 years. Salvage value is $500. The initial first-year allowance is $2,000 (20 per cent of $10,000). This reduces the basis for normal depreciation to $8,000. Normal depreciation for the first year is $750 (10 per cent X $7,500 [$8,000 — $500 salvage value]). The total first-year depreciation is $2,750.

Note: The initial deduction is allowed in full regardless of when the property is acquired during the year and may be taken regardless of the depreciation method used.

Qualifying Property

In order to qualify for the additional first-year deduction, the property must meet the following qualifications: (1) be tangible personal property such as machinery or equipment; (2) be acquired after December 31, 1957; and (3) have a useful life of at least six years when acquired. The property can be either new or used when acquired. The taxpayer must make an election on his return.

USEFUL LIFE OF DEPRECIABLE PROPERTY

The estimated useful life which helps determine the depreciation deduction is not the physical life of the asset. Rather, it is the period that the asset is expected to be useful to the taxpayer. Although there are depreciation guidelines to aid the taxpayer, every case is one of fact. Experience with the property under consideration and all other pertinent evidence may be used to support a certain useful life. The general experience of the industry may be used if the taxpayer has not had sufficient experience.

A variety of factors help determine the estimated useful life to the taxpayer. Among these factors are: (1) wear and tear; (2) decay and decline from natural causes; (3) economic changes; (4) inventions; (5) climatic and other local conditions; (6) repair, renewal, and replacement policy. Note that useful life depends on the facts of the case. For example, higher depreciation deductions were allowed on buildings in one locality because of acid fumes from a nearby chemical plant.

Also note that useful life may be shorter than structural life. For example, consider a building designed to pay the real estate taxes plus some slight revenue, with the expectation that later it will be removed and a taller building erected. In one case, such a building was sound enough to last at least another 40 years. Nevertheless, the Tax Court concluded from the evidence that the building had an economic and useful life of not more than 21 years and allowed depreciation calculated on the 21-year life.

Depreciation Guidelines

The useful life of depreciable property should be based on the particular operating conditions and experience in the enterprise concerned. As was noted above, if the experience with the particular asset is inadequate, the general experience in the industry may be used.

The Treasury Department has supplied guides for determination of useful lives. For years Bulletin "F" issued by the Treasury Department in January, 1931 and revised in January, 1942 was the basic guide. Useful lives of several hundred items were included, which taxpayers could use as a guide.

In 1962 the Treasury Department issued Revenue Procedure 62-21, commonly referred to as "depreciation guidelines," with the objective of providing basic reforms in the guideline lives. The Procedure also has the aim of helping in the administration of depreciation for tax purposes.

As contrasted with the old Bulletin "F," with a few exceptions the useful lives are no longer given for detailed items of depreciable property, but rather are given on approximately 75 broad classes of assets. For example, equipment used by the hotel industry, ranging from blankets and spreads to fire-alarm and -prevention equipment, has been grouped under one class and given a class life of 10 years.

The businessman is free to set any useful life he desires for the individual assets as long as they average out to the useful life for the particular class. Most of the guideline lives are by industry. However, a few of the new classes are not by industry but rather cover such generally used items as furniture and fixtures, buildings, and vehicles.

Guideline Lives and Real Estate

A central objective of the depreciation guidelines was to encourage rapid equipment-replacement practices. Whereas guidelíne lives for machinery and equipment average, on the whole, 30 to 40 per cent shorter than those suggested previously, the depreciation policy for buildings and components was not liberalized. This is illustrated in the following exhibit.

EXHIBIT I

| | | Useful Life | |
Type of Building	Bulletin "F" Years	Depreciation Guidelines Years	Per Cent Change
Apartments	40	40	--
Banks	50	50	--
Dwellings	40	45	+12.5
Factories	40	45	+12.5
Farm Buildings	50	25	-50.0
Garages	40	45	+12.5
Grain elevators	50	60	+20.0
Hotels	40	40	--
Loft buildings	50	50	--
Machine shops	40	45	+12.5
Office buildings	40	45	+12.5
Stores	50	50	--
Theaters	33 1/3	40	+20.0
Warehouses	50	60	+20.0
Type of Asset or Industry			
Office furniture, fixtures, machines, and equipment	15	10	-33.3
Cattle, breeding or dairy	8	7	-12.5
Leather and leather products	15	11	-26.7
Rubber products	17	14	-17.6

Useful Lives of Vehicles

In addition to the lives of the various kinds of buildings presented in the above exhibit, the realtor or the real estate investor may be interested in the following lives: (1) automobiles, 3 years; (2) aircraft, 6 years; (3) light, general-purpose trucks (actual unloaded weight less than 13,000 pounds), 4 years; (4) heavy, general-purpose trucks (actual unloaded weight 13,000 pounds or more), 6 years.

Land Improvements

The specified life for land improvements is 20 years. This would include improvements such as paved surfaces, sidewalks, canals, waterways, drainage facilities and sewers, wharves, bridges, all fences except farm fences, landscaping, shrubbery, and similar improvements. The 20-year life also applies to agricultural land improvements not classified as soil and water conservation expenditures under the Internal Revenue Code of 1954.

The 20-year life does not necessarily apply when the land improvements are the major asset of a business. Examples would be cemeteries and golf courses. Here the depreciable life will be determined according to the particular facts and circumstances.

Agricultural Lives

Investors interested in commercial farms and ranches, agricultural and horticultural services, and forestry enterprises will be interested in the following lives (logging and saw milling are excepted): Machinery and equipment used in the above ventures have a 10-year life. This includes machinery and equipment used in the production of crops and livestock and in the on-farm processing of feeds. It included fences but excludes other land improvements.

Guideline lives for farm animals are as follows: (1) cattle, breeding or dairy, 7 years; (2) horses, breeding or work, 10 years; (3) hogs, breeding, 3 years; (4) sheep and goats, breeding, 5 years; (5) animals not included in the above, for example, race horses and fur-bearing animals, will have lives according to the particular facts and circumstances.

The particular facts of the situation are most important. An example is found in trees and vines producing nuts, fruits, and citrus crops. Here is is noted that due consideration shall be given in each producing region to the geographic, climatic, genetic, economic, and other factors which determine depreciable life. Farm buildings have a suggested life of 25 years.

Buildings

The suggested lives of buildings were presented in the exhibit above. Note that these lives include the structural shell of the building and all integral parts thereof. Included are equipment which services normal heating, plumbing, air-conditioning, fire-prevention, and power requirements. Elevators and escalators are also included.

Special-purpose structures which are an integral part of the production process and which normally are replaced at the same time as the equipment which they house are excluded. They would be depreciated by reference to the guidelines for the particular industry. Note that nonindustrial and general-purpose industrial buildings are not considered to be special-purpose structures. Examples are warehouses, storage facilities, general factory buildings, and commercial buildings.

Contract Construction

This classification includes general building, special trade, heavy construction, and marine contractors. The suggested life for general contract construction is 5 years and for marine contract construction is 12 years. Note these are not the lives of the asset constructed; rather, they are the lives of the assets used in the construction.

Recreation, Amusement, and Services

The recreation and amusement group has a life of 10 years. This would include recreation, entertainment, and amusement establishments, such as bowling alleys, billiard and pool establishments, theaters, concert halls, and amusement parks. Not included would be facilities which are mainly specialized land improvements or structures. For example, golf courses, swimming pools, tennis courts, sport stadia, and race tracks would be determined according to the particular facts and circumstances.

The service group, which includes services offered by hotels and motels, has a life of 10 years. Note that this is the group life for assets used in the performance of these services and does not include the life of the hotel or motel itself. The suggested life for a hotel is 40 years.

Reserve-Ratio Test

The reserve-ratio test is a technical procedure which is intended to establish objectively if the retirement and replacement practices for assets are consistent with the useful lives of those assets. Presumably, the taxpayer may use this test to determine whether his chosen lives are reasonable. Note that, in any event, the taxpayer is permitted to justify his depreciation based upon the particular facts and circumstances in his case, and that the lives chosen may be shorter than the Guideline lives if they can be justified. Alternatively, longer useful lives than those given by the

Guideline may be used if they are consistent with the taxpayer's retirement and replacement practices. If a business actually retains assets for longer than the lives set up in the Guidelines, the Treasury could force the use of a longer life in figuring depreciation.

AGREEMENTS ON USEFUL LIFE

In order to avoid later question as to the depreciable lives of property, the taxpayer may enter into written agreements with the Revenue Service as to the useful life, proper depreciation rate, and treatment of salvage of any property. Form 2271 is employed for this purpose. The agreement is binding on both parties. If either the taxpayer or the Internal Revenue later desires to change the agreement, they must present facts and circumstances which were not considered in making the original agreement.

Application for agreement is made in quadruplicate and must contain the following information for each property to be covered: (1) character and location of property; (2) original cost or other basis and date of acquisition; (3) adjustments to the basis, including depreciation accumulated to the first tax year to be covered by the agreement; (4) estimated remaining useful life and estimated salvage value; (5) method and rate of depreciation; (6) any other facts needed to estimate the useful life and salvage value. If the application is approved, the Revenue Service issues Form 2271 and a copy of the agreement must be filed for the first tax year affected. Before making the agreement, the Revenue Service may examine the taxpayer's previous returns and may even make a physical examination of the property involved.

INCREASED USE OF PROPERTY

Accelerated use of certain property may support a greater depreciation deduction than in a year of normal use. A taxpayer cannot just change his deduction because he has different amounts of income and it would be to his advantage. Changes in the amount deducted from year to year have to be based on facts concerning the use of the property. The taxpayer must be prepared to prove that the useful life of the property was shortened. A decrease in the estimated useful life of the property because of conditions other than wear and tear may be justified by obsolescence, as will be explained in the following section.

OBSOLESCENCE

In determining depreciation, an allowance for normal obsolescence is included. Obsolescence takes into account the effect on useful life of such factors as technological improvements, progress in the arts, reasonably foreseeable economic changes, shifting of business centers, and prohibitory laws. These are the factors which, apart from physical wear and tear, actually diminish the value of the property or shorten its useful life.

After the original determination of useful life, the taxpayer may be able to show that the estimated useful life will be shortened by obsolescence greater than that originally considered in determining the useful life. In this case, a change to a shorter life will be allowed. This is illustrated by the following example.

If McMartin Construction bought a machine having an estimated useful life of 10 years for $5,200 and the salvage value at the end of that period is $200, the annual depreciation deduction under the straight-line method would be $5,000 divided by 10, or $500. At the end of five years, when the depreciated value is $2,500, the existence of a new invention (not considered in originally determining the useful life) makes it clear that the machine will be economically useless at the end of two more years, even though it may still be capable of operation. In that case, the remaining $2,500 may be spread over the two years, resulting in an annual deduction for depreciation, including obsolescence, of $1,250.

A taxpayer must be able to show that obsolescence has operated. A mere opinion that an asset will become obsolete is not enough. The reader should refer to our discussion of losses for the determination of deductible losses in the case of demolition or when the owner's improvements become completely valueless.

INVESTMENT CREDIT

An investment credit of seven per cent of the cost of qualifying equipment was provided in the Revenue Act of 1962. The objective of the law was to stimulate the economy by encouraging businessmen to invest in productive facilities. It is important to note that buildings and their structural components are not eligible for the investment credit. Nevertheless, investors, brokers, contractors, and others interested in real estate will benefit from the investment credit on purchases of qualifying equipment other than buildings or their structural components.

Buildings, for this purpose, are considered to be a structure or edifice enclosing a space within its walls and usually covered by a roof. A building is the basic structure of an improvement to land whose purpose is, for example, the following: provision of working, office, display, or sales space and the provision of shelter or housing. The basic structure of an office building, warehouse, factory, theater, gymnasium, or clubhouse is not eligible for the investment credit.

Chapter 7

Postponing Tax Payments

Income from certain sales of property which involve payments beyond the year of sale may be reported under special methods which make the gain taxable over a period of years rather than in the year of sale.

ADVANTAGES OF POSTPONING PAYMENTS

The ability to spread tax payments over the future rather than paying all in the year of sale is an obvious help to the liquidity position of the seller. This is particularly true because the payments from the buyer are deferred in time, and if a seller could not report his gain over a period of time, tax payments might otherwise exceed the early receipts from the purchaser of the property.

Postponement of tax has the obvious advantage of providing the taxpayer with the use of the money that would otherwise go out in tax payments. For example, if a taxpayer can pay tax of $1,000 five years from now rather than now, he may invest this money and earn a return on it for five years.

Depending on his particular situation, the taxpayer may actually save through an election to pay tax on the installment method. This would be true, for example, if his taxable income would be less in the future, so that the effective tax on the gain would be less. A taxpayer may, for example, have other income in the year of sale which makes the gain on the sale of property subject to the maximum capital-gain rates. However, he may expect his other income to drop in that future period, so that he will take his gain into income at less than the maximum capital-gain rates.

Postponement of tax may be achieved through the installment-sale method and, in certain cases, the deferred-payment sales method, provided, of course, that the requirements for the use of these methods are met.

INSTALLMENT SALES

Income is reported proportionately as collections are made under the installment-sale method. The installment-sale method may be used for sales of real property when there is no payment in the year of sale or where payments in the year of sale do not exceed 30 per cent of selling price. Careful attention must be given to the special meaning of "selling price" and "payment in year of sale," which are explained below. Otherwise, the 30 per cent limitation may be violated and the taxpayer would be deprived of the use of the installment-sale method.

The installment-sale method of reporting may be used in certain circumstances for casual sales of personal property and for installment sales by dealers in personal property. We shall not be concerned with sales by dealers in personal property in this book.

Sales at a Loss Not Eligible

Real estate may be sold at a loss with payments to be received over a period of time in the future. A taxpayer may not use the installment method for reporting loss. He must, subject to capital-loss limitations, deduct the loss in the year of sale.

Installment Method is Elective

The taxpayer has the alternative of reporting profit either in the year of sale or on the installment method, provided that he meets the requirements necessary to use the method. Note that, if a taxpayer is able to use the installment method but elects not to use it, he generally may not later amend his tax return after the due date to change to the installment method.

Amended Returns

It seems that an amended return may be filed, however, under the following situations: (1) the method first used fails to reflect income correctly, or (2) the sale was not reported and the omission was not due to the taxpayer's negligence or fraud.

There is some question whether an amended return may be filed even in these situations. The Regulations require that the details be reported and the installment method be reflected in the return for the year of sale.

For example, Mrs. Ackerman sold some property in December, 1958. Her capital gain was $9,600, but she was not paid anything until 1959. She first reported the sale and elected the installment method on her 1959 return. The Internal Revenue claimed that the entire $9,600 was taxable in 1958, and their position was sustained by the District Court. The Court found the regulation explicit and reasonable, even though the taxpayer did not receive any money in 1958.

Need to plan. The election to use the installment method must be made in a timely filed tax return for the year of sale. This is true even though the seller does not receive any payments in the year of sale. Thus, the decision to use the installment method should be made prior to the time the terms of the contract of sale are determined. Later we shall discuss the composition of the "payments in year of sale." The transaction should be planned prior to the contract of sale so that the payments in the year of sale do not exceed 30 per cent of the selling price.

Kinds of Sales That Are Eligible

We have noted above that sales at a loss are not eligible for the use of the installment method. Taxpayers who normally use either the cash or the accrual method of accounting may use the installment method for reporting particular sales if the requirements are met.

Election for Each Sale

Gains from one sale may be reported on the installment method and gains from other sales may be reported according to the taxpayer's usual accounting method. Note that the election is available for each sale.

For example, assume that the North River Development Company subdivides a parcel of land and sells the lots. North River Development may make a separate election for each one of the lots as to whether they will use the installment method of reporting or use their normal method of accounting.

Type of Installment Contract

It is not necessary that an installment contract be of a particular kind to qualify for the benefits of reporting. A seller may, for example, retain title for security reasons or, alternatively, may immediately convey title to the property. A seller may execute a conveyance and take back a note for the purchase price or may use an executory land contract. Both of these would satisfy the requirement of the installment method of reporting.

No Payments in Year of Sale

A sale may be treated as an installment sale even though no payments are made in the year of sale. However, to qualify such a sale under the installment method of accounting, there must be at least two payments some time after the year of sale.

Must Be Payee or Mortgagee

If a buyer gives a note or a first or second trust deed or mortgage for the balance of the selling price, then the seller must be the payee or mortgagee if the transaction is to qualify. The installment method may not be used if the buyer gives his note, mortgage, or deed of trust to another party in order to finance the purchase and this other party pays the seller the proceeds.

For example, Martin and Mary Williams purchased a home from Elmer Whiting. To finance the purchase, the Williamses give a deed of trust or mortgage to a bank, and the bank pays these funds to Elmer Whiting. The installment method of reporting may not be used.

Note that a third party can be trustee under a deed of trust without preventing the use of the installment method.

Calculation of Gain

A real estate sale is on the installment plan if there is no payment in the year of sale or if payments in the year of sale do not exceed 30 per cent of the selling price. The amount of gain that must be accounted for is the difference between the selling price and the adjusted basis of the property sold. The proportion of each year's payment that is considered gain is the total profit divided by the contract price. This is illustrated by the following example.

In 1964 Witherspoon sold real property having an adjusted basis of $60,000 for $100,000, payable as follows: cash, $30,000; mortgage for $70,000, payable by the buyer in semiannual installments of $10,000 each, the first to be paid on 4/1/65. The profit was $40,000 ($100,000 selling price less $60,000 basis), which will be accounted for as the $100,000 due on the contract is paid. Accordingly, 40 per cent ($40,000 profit divided by $100,000 con-

1964 payments	$ 30,000	of which	$12,000	is recognized gain
1965 payments	20,000	of which	8,000	is recognized gain
1966 payments	20,000	of which	8,000	is recognized gain
1967 payments	20,000	of which	8,000	is recognized gain
1968 payments	10,000	of which	4,000	is recognized gain
Total payments	$100,000	of which	$40,000	is recognized gain

tract price) of each payment is recognized gain.

Note, in the following example, that the percentage of each payment that is recognized gain is determined by dividing the total profit by the contract price. The contract price does not include the mortgage debt that the buyer assumes. The mortgage debt is included in the selling price.

Hyman owned real property encumbered by a mortgage of $20,000. In 1964 Hyman sold his property, which had an adjusted basis of $60,000, for $100,000, payable as follows: cash, $30,000; first mortgage assumed, $20,000; second mortgage for $50,000 payable by the buyer in semiannual installments of $10,000 each, the first to be paid 4/1/65. The profit was $40,000 ($100,000 selling price less $60,000 basis), which will be accounted for as the $80,000 due on the contract is paid. Accordingly, 50 per cent ($40,000 profit divided by $80,000 contract price) of each payment is recognized gain.

Payments in the Year of Sale

These are all payments, other than evidences of indebtedness of the buyer, which are made during the tax year in which the sale is made. They include payments made on liabilities of the seller, such as liens on his property, interest, taxes, and other charges assumed by the buyer. Note particularly that evidences of indebtedness of the buyer are not included in payments in the year of sale. Amounts received by the seller, from the disposal of the buyer's notes, given as part of the purchase price, and which are due and payable in later years, are not considered as payments in the year of sale.

Payments such as option payments or "good faith" payments made in a year prior to the year of sale are included, if under the contract they become part of the down payment when the sale becomes effective. Commissions and selling expenses are not deducted in figuring payments in the year of sale. These commissions and selling expenses are handled differently for dealers and for investors. This is described on page 160.

Mortgages Not Included

Mortgages given by the buyer are not included in payments in the year of sale. Similarly, an existing mortgage on the property is not included. However, as will be explained below, if the existing mortgage exceeds the basis, the excess is part of the payments in the year of sale, whether the buyer assumes the mortgage or merely takes the property subject to the mortgage. If the buyer actually pays off the seller's mortgage at the time of sale, instead of assuming it, then the amount of the mortgage must be included in the payments in the year of sale and must also be included in the contract price.

Sale of Several Assets in Package

If a seller sells several assets in a single sale to one buyer, he must determine whether the down payment received on any class of the assets exceeds 30 per cent of the selling price allocated to that class (assuming that the taxpayer is not a dealer in personal property). The down payment is allocated to the several classes of assets in proportion to their respective selling prices. If a state law or regulation requires a minimum down payment upon the sale of a particular asset, the state law or regulation takes precedence over allocation by respective selling prices. Only the sale of that class of assets with respect to which the down payment does not exceed 30 per cent of their selling price may be reported on the installment method.

Planning Payments in Year of Sale

The transaction should be planned so that less than 30 per cent of the selling price is received in the year of sale. It would not be desirable, for example, to include in the contract a requirement that the seller retain control of escrowed funds, or a requirement that the seller be entitled to the balance of the sales price on demand.

A provision in the sales contract that the seller is not to receive more than 30 per cent of the selling price in the year of sale is not sufficient protection if in fact he receives more than 30 per cent. A taxpayer may, however, escrow the down payment or part of it so that he will not receive it until a taxable year subsequent to the year of sale. It has been held that a part of the buyer's consideration placed in escrow in the year of sale is not part of the initial payment. As was noted above, the seller should not have control over the escrowed funds.

Selling Price

The determination of selling price is important because the amount of total gain on the transaction is determined by subtracting the adjusted basis of the property from the selling price. It is also important in respect to the requirement that payments in the year of sale cannot exceed 30 per cent of selling price.

Items included. The selling price, for installment-sale purposes, is the entire cost of the property to the buyer. Thus, it would include cash and the fair market value of other property conveyed to the seller and the amount of any notes or other evidences of indebtedness of the buyer. It would also include debts assumed or paid by the buyer. Note that the selling price would include not only notes and mortgages, but liabilities of the seller, such as liens, accrued interest, and taxes assumed or paid by the buyer. If there is an existing mortgage on the property, it also is included as part of the selling price. This is true whether the buyer assumes the mortgage or merely takes the property subject to the mortgage. Commissions and selling expense are not deducted in figuring the selling price. Obligations of the buyer are included at face value. However, obligations of third parties are included at their fair market value. The effect of third-party obligations on the installment method of reporting profits are discussed below.

Contract Price

Contract price is important because it is the contract price and not the selling price which is divided into the total profit on the transaction to determine the proportion of each year's payment to be returned as profit. The contract price generally is the amount to be received by the seller. It is the seller's equity in the property. If no debts are involved in the transaction, the contract price would be equal to the selling price. The contract price is also equal to the selling price in the situation in which the selling price is payable partially in cash and partially on time, secured by a purchase-money mortgage from the buyer to the seller.

Contract price when mortgage involved. Generally, if a mortgage is assumed by the buyer of the property, then the contract price is equal to the sale price minus the amount of the loan. The exception is the case discussed below, in which the mortgage is greater than the seller's adjusted basis for the property. For example, Biancalana sells real property to Martin. The selling price is $100,000, and the property is encumbered by a mortgage of $20,000 which buyer Martin assumes. The selling price is $100,000 and the contract price is $80,000. Note that the contract price is the amount of Biancalana's equity in the property. It is also the amount that he will collect from Martin. If Martin paid off the mortgage on the property at the time of sale instead of assuming it, the amount of the mortgage would be added to the contract price, and the contract price would then equal the selling price.

Mortgage in Excess of Basis

A taxpayer's adjusted basis for his property is his cost plus additions for capital improvements less deductions for such things as allowable depreciation, casualty loss, and so forth. In some situations, a taxpayer will sell property in which the mortgage on the property is greater than his adjusted basis for the property.

Excess part of payments in year of sale are part of contract price. If the mortgage assumed by the buyer is greater than the seller's adjusted basis for his property, the excess is included both in the contract price and in the payments received in the year of sale. In effect, the seller has recovered his entire basis plus an additional amount equal to the excess of the mortgage over his basis in the property.

For example, assume that Swenson purchased property for $10,000 in 1950. As a result of appreciation in property values, Swenson was later able to place a mortgage of $15,000 on the property. In 1964 Swenson sold the property to Dougherty for $80,000. Dougherty paid $10,000 cash, assumed the existing mortgage of $15,000, and negotiated an additional new mortgage of $55,000. The contract price is computed as follows:

Cash	$10,000
New mortgage	55,000
Excess of assumed mortgage ($15,000)	
over seller's basis ($10,000)	5,000
	$70,000

Payments in the year of sale are:

Cash	$10,000
Excess of assumed mortgage ($15,000)	
over seller's basis ($10,000)	5,000
	$15,000

Thus, the amount of the excess of the assumed mortgage over the seller's basis is considered as a constructive payment to the seller in the year of sale. This is true whether the buyer assumes the

mortgage or merely takes the property subject to the mortgage.
If the mortgage is in excess of basis, there is the danger that the
payments in the year of sale will exceed 30 per cent and, as a result,
the seller will not be able to report his gain on the installment basis.

For example, Cinders sells Greenacre to Johnson for
$100,000. The terms are $10,000 cash plus the stipulation that
Johnson is to assume a $90,000 mortgage on the property. The
basis of Greenacre to Cinders is $60,000. Cinders is unable to
use the installment reporting method. Cinders is considered to
have received $40,000 in the year of sale, consisting of the $10,000
cash plus $30,000, the excess of the mortgage ($90,000) over basis
($60,000). Thus, a total of 40 per cent of the selling price has been
received and the installment method cannot be used.

For another example, Blumberg has a $25,000 basis for a
building that he owns. There is a $30,000 mortgage on the building.
Blumberg sells the building to Dickens for $100,000. Terms are
$30,000 cash, Dickens' note for $40,000, plus the assumption of
the $30,000 mortgage by Dickens.

In the above situation, the installment method cannot be used
because the payments in the year of sale consist of $30,000 cash
plus $5,000, the excess of the mortgage ($30,000) over basis
($25,000). Thus, Blumberg is considered to have received 35 per
cent ($35,000) of the selling price ($100,000) in the year of sale.

Effect of Third-Party Obligations

We have noted that notes or other obligations of the buyer
are included at face value in computing selling price and payments
received in the year of sale. Notes or other obligations of third
parties, however, which are received from the buyer are included
at their fair market value.

Payments received on third-party obligations. Payments
received from the buyer on his obligations are payments on the
installment sale and qualify for treatment under the installment
method. If the third-party obligations are included in the installment-sale computation at market value which is less than face
value, then a portion of the payments received on these obligations
must be reported as ordinary income received.

Assume that Simpson sells to Butterworth real estate which
Simpson has used for production of income, and that it is a capital
asset in his hands. The transaction meets all the qualifications,
and Simpson decides to elect the installment method to report his
gain. As part of the transaction, Butterworth assigns to Simpson
a $6,000 note which was owed to him by Caplan. The fair market

value of Caplan's note at the time of sale was $3,000, and this was the amount used in the computation of the installment sale.

Subsequent to the year of sale, the profit included in payments received from the buyer Butterworth will be reported as capital gain. However, the payments received on the third-party note from Caplan do not qualify as installment payments, and 50 per cent of these payments will be included as ordinary income. Recall that Simpson included only 50 per cent of the face value of Caplan's note in his computation of gain on the installment sale.

Imputed Interest on Installment Sales

An appropriate part of installment payments will be treated as interest both to the seller and to the buyer if there is no interest rate or if the interest rate is unreasonably low. There are certain exceptions, which we shall note below. This section is part of the 1964 Revenue Law.

Calculation of interest. The interest is calculated by determining the present value of payments that are deferred for more than six months. The imputed interest will be determined at the "going" rate as determined by the Regulations. The Committee Report seems to indicate five per cent under current conditions. No additional interest will be figured, however, if the interest rate in the contract is within one per cent of the Regulations' rate of interest.

For example, assume that Haas sells Hacker land with an adjusted basis of $10,000 for $16,000. The terms are $4,000 payable within three months and the balance in four annual installments of $3,000 commencing a year after sale. No interest is provided in the contract.

Prior to the 1964 Revenue Law, Haas would have had a $6,000 capital gain. He has sold land for $16,000 which is a capital asset and which has an adjusted basis of $10,000 in his hands. Hacker's basis for the land is his cost of $16,000, and he did not receive an interest deduction.

Under the new law, an interest element is imputed. Because the $4,000 is to be paid within six months of sale, no interest is imputed for it. We shall assume that the imputed interest on the balance of the installment payments of $12,000 amounts to $1,500. Therefore, Haas has capital gain of $4,500. This is the selling price of $16,000 less $10,000 cost and less $1,500 ordinary interest income. If Haas is on the cash basis, he will have $375 interest income as each one of the $3,000 installments is received.

Under the new law, Hacker's basis for the purchase is

$14,500, and, if he is on the cash basis, he deducts $375 interest
as each one of the installments is paid. Note that the imputed interest is prorated equally over the installments. In a contract where
the interest was stated, the interest would most likely be based on
the declining balance.

Sale at a loss. Interest is imputed even though the sale is
made at a loss. In fact, the imputation of the interest could con-
ceivably make the transaction a loss transaction.

In the foregoing example, if Haas, the seller, had a basis
for the property of $16,000, then he would have had a capital loss
of $1,500, equal to the amount of the imputed interest. He would,
of course, have ordinary income in the amount of the interest as well.

Contingent payments. When some of the payments are contingent, for example, as to amount or timing, then the interest element is determined separately from the noncontingent payments.

Assume, in our above example, that in addition to the payments noted above, Hacker also had to pay five per cent of profits
over a specified period. Any payments based on profits would be
discounted back to the contract date and the excess of any payment
over the discounted amount is interest. The $16,000 fixed amount
would be handled as noted above.

When section does not apply. The following constitute exceptions to the application of the rule, and interest will not be imputed: (1) if the sale price is $3,000 or less; (2) if no payment is
deferred by the contract for more than a year; (3) if certain sales
of patents under Section 1235, I.R.C., are involved; (4) if all the
gain would be taxed as ordinary income to the seller, for example,
when the property is neither a capital asset nor a Section 1231 asset;
(5) if any of the payments made were carrying charges, which under
the present law are viewed as interest. This provision relates to
the buyer. Note, under Section 163 (b) I.R.C., that in general a
six per cent deduction is allowed to the buyer on installment purchases of personal property if the carrying charges are separately
stated; (6) if the property is sold in return for annuity payments.

Effective dates. These provisions apply to payments made
after December 31, 1963 resulting on account of sales or exchanges
that occurred after June 30, 1963. The rules do not apply if a
binding written contract or option was entered into before July 1,
1963.

Implications for installment reporting. Recall that the 30
per cent test in respect to payments in the year of sale must be met
before the installment sales method of reporting income can be used.
Care must be taken so that the imputation of interest does not result

in the payments in the year of sale being greater than 30 per cent of the selling price, because part of the selling price is considered to be interest.

Capital Gain or Ordinary Income

Whether the gain on an installment sale is ordinary income or capital gain depends on the purpose for which the asset is held. The use of the installment method of reporting gain does not change the status of the gain as capital gain or ordinary income. Thus, if there is a capital gain on an asset of $10,000 to be taken into account at $1,000 a year for the next ten years under the installment method, this $1,000 would enter into the tax computation each year as a capital gain. If real estate is a capital asset in the hands of the taxpayer, or if it qualifies as a Section 1231 asset (see the chapter on capital gains), then the profit under the installment method will be a capital gain each year.

Relevant Tax Rates

The depreciation-recapture rules may cause some income to be ordinary income rather than capital gain. This is not affected by the method of reporting. The tax rates of the year when the gain is reportable are the rates used, and not the rates of the year of sale. This may influence a taxpayer in deciding whether to elect the installment method. He should project as well as he can his future income position compared with his current tax position in making the election decision.

Required Information

It is essential to show the computation of the gross profit from sales on the installment plan in the tax return for the year of sale or in an attached statement. Computation of the reported income for any year in which payments are received on installment sales should be shown in the year that the gain is reportable. Separate computations must be made for each sale, but they may be shown in a single statement.

Commissions and Selling Expenses

Commissions and selling expenses are not deducted in determining either selling price, payments made in the year of sale, or contract price. Dealers in real estate may deduct the commissions as a business expense. Others must offset commissions and selling expenses against the selling price to determine the profit from the transaction.

Note, in the following example, that these expenses affect the profit realized on the sale but do not affect selling price, payments in the year of sale, or contract price.

Tenahaw (not a dealer) owned real property encumbered by a mortgage of $25,000. In 1964 he sold this property, which had an adjusted basis of $65,000, for $100,000, payable as follows: cash, $30,000; first mortgage assumed, $25,000; second mortgage for $45,000, payable in semiannual installments of $5,000 each, the first to be paid in 1965. Commissions on the sale were $5,000, the abstract of title, $75, and the recording fees, $25.

Selling price		$100,000
Selling expenses:		
Commission paid	$ 5,000	
Abstract of title	75	
Recording fees	25	5,100
Selling price less offsets		$ 94,900
Adjusted basis		65,000
Total profit to be realized on sale		$ 29,900
"Purchase price" to buyer	$100,000	
First mortgage assumed by buyer	25,000	
"Total contract price"		$ 75,000
"Payments in the year of sale"		$ 30,000

The $29,900 profit will be accounted for as the $75,000 on the contract is paid, and 299/750 of each payment will be reported as profit.

A dealer would show the expenses as a business expense and therefore receives benefit of these expenses in the year of sale. The investor alternatively recovers the expenses over the life of the installment contract. Note that, if the property is a capital asset in the investor's hands, he would be reporting his gain as capital gain, whereas the dealer must report his gain as ordinary income.

DEFERRED-PAYMENT SALES

If the requirements of the installment-sale method are not met, it may be possible to use the deferred-payment sales method. Under this method, no gain is reported by the seller until the payments received by him equal the cost or other basis for the property transferred.

It is important to have evidence that the fair market value of the notes is less than the face value of the buyer's obligation or that they are subject to some contingency. Otherwise, if the note is worth face value, then the gain may be taxed in the year of sale.

After a seller has recovered his entire basis for the property, all of the remaining payments are taxable.

Obligations of Buyer Considered Realized to Extent of Fair Market Value

The gain or loss realized at the time of sale is the difference between the sale price, which includes the purchaser's obligations at their fair market value minus the costs of making the sale, and the adjusted basis of the property. Negotiable notes, mortgages, and land contracts which the seller receives are examples of obligations which are to be included at their fair market value in the computation of the amount realized from the sale of the property. Fair market value generally represents the amount which an owner, who is not under necessity of selling, is willing to take and which another person, who is not under a necessity of buying, is willing to pay.

The operation of the deferred-payment method is illustrated by the following example. Milton Brown owned real property encumbered by a mortgage of $20,000. In 1964, he sold this property, which had an adjusted basis of $60,000, for $100,000, payable as follows: cash, $35,000; first mortgage assumed, $20,000; second mortgage for $45,000 payable by the buyer in five annual installments of $9,000 each, the first to be paid in 1965. The fair market value of the second mortgage note was 66 2/3 per cent of face value, or $30,000. Because the payments in the year of sale ($35,000) exceeded 30 per cent of the selling price, the gain on the sale may not be reported on the installment basis. The entire gain ($40,000) may be reported in the year of sale (1964), or it may be spread over a period of years, as follows:

Proceeds realized:		
Cash		$35,000
First mortgage (assumed by purchaser and therefore valued at par)		20,000
Second mortgage	$45,000	
Discount on second mortgage (33 1/3 per cent)	15,000	30,000
		$85,000
Adjusted basis		60,000
Recognized gain reported in 1964		$25,000

The balance of the recognized gain ($15,000) will be reported as the five annual installments are paid:

	1965	1966	1967	1968	1969
Collected	$9,000	$9,000	$9,000	$9,000	$9,000
Less 66 2/3 per cent already reported	6,000	6,000	6,000	6,000	6,000
Recognized gain to be reported	$3,000	$3,000	$3,000	$3,000	$3,000

Note that the buyer's obligations are included at fair market value. In the next example they are not included at all. In the above example, the taxpayer is considered to have received an equivalent amount of his basis equal to the fair market value of his notes. Payment on the notes will be part return of principal and part income.

Buyer's Obligations Have No Fair Market Value

In the above example, the second mortgage of the buyer had a fair market value of $30,000. Now let us assume the same facts as above, except that the second-mortgage notes have no fair market value. The order of the payment is as shown in the table at the top of page 173. The adjusted basis is $60,000. The cash ($35,000), first mortgage ($20,000), and $5,000 of the first annual installment (total, $60,000) are a return of capital. $4,000 of the first annual installment and all of the subsequent installments are recognized

Cash	$ 35,000
First mortgage (assumed by purchaser and therefore valued at par)	20,000
First annual installment	9,000
Second annual installment	9,000
Third annual installment	9,000
Fourth annual installment	9,000
Fifth annual installment	9,000
Total	$100,000

gain when received. If all the installments are paid when due, the taxpayer will report recognized gain as follows: return for 1965, $4,000; 1966, $9,000; 1967, $9,000; 1968, $9,000; 1969, $9,000 (total, $40,000).

Casual Sales of Personal Property Not on Installment Plan

If the selling price exceeds $1,000, cash-basis taxpayers may use the deferred-payment sales method for casual sales of personal property. Accrual-basis taxpayers cannot use the deferred-payment plan for reporting casual sales of personal property.

Character of Gain From Deferred-Payment Sales

Here the gain on the sale of the property and gain on the collection on the note must be separated. If the asset is a capital asset in the hands of the taxpayer, the gain on the sale of the property is a capital gain. If the property is a Section 1231 asset, the benefits of Section 1231 apply.

The gain to be reported on a note received at the time of sale depends on whether the note had a fair market value at the time of sale. If the note had no fair market value, the gain on its collection is reported in the same way as the gain on the original sale of the property. Thus, it is desirable for the taxpayer who has sold a capital asset at a capital gain to have a buyer's obligation that does not have an ascertainable fair market value, because amounts received after the collection of the basis of the note will also be capital gains.

If the note had a fair market value at the time of sale, the amount collected in later years is allocated between the return of principal and ordinary income. The amount of return of principal is the fair market value of the note when received. This amount was taken into account in the determination of the gain from the property. This is illustrated by the following example.

Gerhardt sold property (a capital asset) in 1956 and received as part of the sales price a note for $10,000. The fair market value of the note at the time of sale was $3,000 and this value was part of the proceeds used in figuring a capital gain from such sale. When the face amount of the note was collected in 1964, $3,000 of such collection was a return of principal and the balance of $7,000 was ordinary income.

Qualifications for Deferred-Payment Method

In order to use the deferred-payment method, the seller must receive payments in two or more taxable years, and the gain must not become immediately reportable. Gain is deferred to the extent that the seller is not considered to have received full consideration for the property. As was noted before, negotiable notes, mortgages, and land contracts are examples of obligations included at their fair market value in computing the amount realized.

Lack of market value. The taxpayer must prove that the buyer's obligations have a market value significantly less than their face value. Fair market value will be affected by the buyer's credit

as well as by the terms and negotiability of the notes. Possible
indications of little or no market value are the following: (a) notes
are not sold after much effort; (b) notes are restricted by contingencies; (c) notes are unsecured and are not negotiable; (d) notes
are subject to a prepayment clause at a discount value. The regulations consider that it is only in rare and exceptional situations
that property does not have a fair market value.

 Buyer of discount mortgages. Assume the situation of John
Moneywell, who speculates in mortgages. He purchases first and
second mortgages at 70 per cent of face. He receives principal
and interest payments on these mortgages. The interest is, of
course, taxable as ordinary income.

 In the case of the first mortgages, Moneywell usually sold
them to a bank before maturity. There was little doubt that they
were readily salable for as much as Moneywell paid for them. Thus,
each installment of principal is considered to be 70 per cent return
of capital and 30 per cent taxable income.

 The second mortgages constituted a different situation. They
were speculative, and Moneywell did not know how much he was
likely to collect. In this case, the installments on principal were
not taxed at all until Moneywell recovered his entire cost. After
that, the installments were fully taxable. This treatment is based
on the doubt that Moneywell will recover face value.

Advantages and Disadvantages of Deferred-Payment Method

 Whereas under the installment-sale method a portion of each
payment is taxable as gain, under the deferred-payment method,
where the notes received have no ascertainable fair market value,
collections are not taxed until cost is recovered. Unlike the installment method, there is no restriction upon the amount of the
total payment that can be received in the year of sale.

 A disadvantage of the deferred-payment method is the problem of proving that the notes of the buyer do not have a fair market
value at the date of sale or that they have a fair market value significantly less than face value. Obviously, if they have a fair market
value equal to face value, then the taxpayer is considered to have
received his entire consideration in the year of sale. Also, in the
case of the deferred-payment method, a possible spreading of income advantage is lost, relative to the installment method, to the
extent that gain is bunched in later years.

DISPOSITION OF INSTALLMENT OBLIGATIONS

 In either a sale reported on the installment method or in a

deferred-payment sale not on the installment plan, a taxpayer may dispose of the note, mortgage, or other installment obligation prior to complete collection. Gain or loss will usually result when an installment obligation is disposed of by the seller.

Determination of Gain or Loss on Disposition by Sale or Exchange

If the installment obligations are disposed of by sale or exchange, the gain or loss is measured by the difference between the adjusted basis of the obligations and the amount realized. The adjusted basis of the obligations is the excess of the unpaid balance of the obligation over the income which would be reportable on such unpaid balance were the obligation paid in full. This is equal to the unrecovered cost of the obligations. For capital-gain or -loss purposes, the holding period depends on how long the property was held before its sale.

The following example illustrates the determination of gain on disposition of installment obligations. In 1964 Harley sold for $100,000 real property which he had purchased in 1951 and which had an adjusted basis of $60,000. Payment was to be made as follows: cash, $30,000; mortgage for $70,000, payable by the buyer in semiannual installments of $10,000 each, the first to be paid on 4/1/65. The profit was $40,000, which will be accounted for as the $100,000 due on the contract is paid. Accordingly, 40 per cent of each payment will be reported as profit.

	Face Value	Recognized Gain (40 per cent)	Return of Capital or Basis (60 per cent)
1964 payment	$ 30,000	$12,000	$18,000
1965 payments	20,000	8,000	12,000
1966 payments	20,000	8,000	12,000
1967 payments	20,000	8,000	12,000
1968 payments	10,000	4,000	6,000
Total	$100,000	$40,000	$60,000

Assume that, before any payment is made in 1966, Harley assigns the 1966, 1967, and 1968 notes that he still has (the face value is $50,000), receiving $35,000 for them. The basis of the notes is the unrecovered cost of $30,000 ($12,000 + 12,000 + 6,000). Because the notes were sold for $35,000, the recognized gain is $5,000.

NEW RULE FOR REPOSSESSIONS

For tax years beginning after September 2, 1964 losses are not recognized on certain repossessions, and gain is taxed to a limited extent. If a proper election is made these new rules may apply to a limited degree to repossessions occurring in tax years beginning after December 31, 1957.

When Rules Apply

The new rules apply if: (1) the real property is sold and the seller accepts obligations of the purchaser that is secured by the real estate in return, and (2) the seller reacquires the same property in partial or full satisfaction of the indebtedness arising from the sale.

If the repossession is not in satisfaction of the purchaser's indebtedness, the rules do not apply. This would happen if the seller repurchased the property by paying the buyer consideration in addition to the discharge of the indebtedness, unless the repurchase and payment were provided for in the original contract of sale.

Uniform Method

These new rules provide a uniform method of reporting repossessions. Note that the application of these rules does not consider whether the original sale was reported on the installment basis or the deferred-payment method, whether the title passed to the purchaser or not, or whether the initial sale was at a gain or loss.

Losses and Bad Debts

The new rules provide that losses on repossession are not recognized and are not deductible. Also no deduction is allowed for a worthless or partially worthless debt as a result of a repossession.

Computation Under General Rule

The gain on repossession is the excess of (1) the amount of money and fair market value of other property received over (2) the amount of gain returned as income for periods prior to the repossession. In (1) above, obligations of the purchaser are not included. In (2) gain returned as income in any portion of the tax year of reacquisition is included. There is a limitation on the amount of taxable gain. This limitation is discussed on page 181.

Example: Assume Bacci owned a house and sold it on January 2, 1964, for $25,000. Bacci, a calendar-year taxpayer, accepted a $5,000 down payment plus a $20,000 5 per cent mortgage secured by the property. Smith, the buyer, agreed to pay the mortgage at the rate of $4,000 annually, starting on January 2, 1965.

Bacci had an adjusted basis for the property of $20,000 and

elected to report the transaction on the installment basis. The gross profit percentage is 20 per cent ($5,000 profit divided by $25,000 selling price). In 1964, Bacci included $1,000 in his income (20 per cent of $5,000 down payment) and in 1965 he reported a profit of $800 (20 per cent of the $4,000 annual installment).

Smith defaulted on his payments in 1966 and Bacci repossessed the property. Gain on repossession is computed as follows:

Amount of money received ($5,000 plus $4,000)	$9,000
Amount of gain taxed ($1,000 plus $800)	1,800
Gain (see limitation below)	$7,200

Limit on Gain

The amount of gain determined above is limited as follows: The taxable amount is limited to the excess of the original sales price over the adjusted basis less certain reductions. The adjusted basis is reduced by the sum of: (1) the gain on the sale already reported as income, and (2) the seller's repossession costs.

Using the facts of the previous example and assuming a $500 repossession cost, the computation of the limit follows:

Original sales price	$25,000	
Adjusted basis of property	20,000	$5,000
Gain returned as income	$ 1,800	
Cost of repossession	500	2,300
Taxable gain on repossession		$2,700

Limitation Does Not Apply

The limit does not apply where the sales price cannot be ascertained at the time of sale. An example is where the selling price is stated as a percentage of the profits to be realized from the development of the property sold. Repossessions occurring in tax years beginning before September 3, 1964 are not subject to this limitation. Unstated interest is eliminated in all computations of limitation on gain.

Classification of Gain

The taxable gain on repossession has the same classification as the gain on the original sale. Thus it may be either capital or ordinary gain.

Election-Tax Years Beginning After December 31, 1957

A seller who made a qualifying repossession in tax years beginning after December 31, 1957, may elect to have a partial application of the new rules provided election is made before September 2, 1965.

Chapter 8

Leasing, and Sales
and Leasebacks

LEASING TO ACQUIRE SERVICES

Leasing is an alternative method of securing the services of real estate. If acquisition of title and potential profit on sale of real estate is not an important objective, then leasing of real estate should be compared with purchase as an alternative way to achieve the use of the asset. For example, later in this chapter we shall consider the tax implications of a sale and leaseback, where the owner of property sells his property and then leases it back. Leasing is somewhat similar to debt financing; the lessee incurs a definite obligation to the owner of the property (lessor), and these obligations must be met just as the payments on debt. It is important in considering leasing not to be overconcerned with tax considerations; financial considerations are usually the dominant considerations.

Characteristics of Leases

Although our main concern is the tax implications, a brief look at some of the characteristics of leases is useful for the sake of perspective. A lease is a contractual arrangement in which the owner of the property (lessor) allows another party (lessee) the use of the services of the property for a specified period of time; title to the property is retained by the lessor. The periodic rental payments are fixed and generally may not be canceled for a definite period of time. Oftentimes the lessee may use the property after the initial period of the lease at a reduced rental; also, the lessee may have an option to purchase the property.

Leasing Real Estate

Leasing arrangements are common in real estate financing. For example, the land on which a hotel or an apartment house is to be built may be leased. Some construction firms will buy land desired by a customer, erect a building to the customer's specifications, and lease it to the customer. Varied properties are leased, from land for supermarkets to minor furniture and fixture items for hotel or motel use. Usually, the length of the lease is related to the useful life of the asset and the needs of the lessee. For example, leases on land and buildings are often written for 20 to 25 years with renewal options available to extend the lease period an additional 30 to 40 years.

CONSIDERATIONS OF THE LANDLORD

There are always two parties to the lease. Both the landlord (lessor) and the lessee must consider the lease to be worthwhile or there will be no lease. In order to execute a sale and leaseback, it is necessary for the seller of the property to find a willing buyer who will in turn lease the property back to him.

Advantages to the Landlord

A lessor will expect to have an income from the property that he leases that will return his investment in the property and also give him a satisfactory profit on his investment. A lessor will attempt to minimize his risk; thus, for example, in a sale or leaseback arrangement, a buyer will more easily be found for a general-purpose structure than for a special-purpose structure. Of course, the buyer on a sale and leaseback will primarily be concerned with the income-producing capabilities of the structure and the credit standing of the tenant. The buyer in a sale and leaseback will have the advantage of knowing his tenant, and, because the lease is drawn at the time of sale, he will be able to calculate his return on the investment at the time of the sale and leaseback. Net leases are advantageous to owners who do not wish to worry about maintaining property; under net leases, the tenant pays operating expenses and keeps the property in repair. Tax advantages of owning property have, of course, contributed to the attractiveness of owning and renting real estate as compared with alternative investments.

Landlord's Tax Advantages

If a good purchase has been made, the landlord may look to appreciation in the value of the property. Although the property may be appreciating in value, he is not taxed until the property is disposed of. While he owns the property, he is able to deduct depreciation on his improvements. If there is a mortgage on the property, depreciation is computed on the total basis of the depreciable assets even though the owner's equity in these assets may be much smaller because of borrowing. Generally, subject to the time the property is held, the sale of rental property will yield gain taxable at capital-gain rates rather than ordinary income tax rates. Since the 1964 Revenue Law, certain of the gain may be ordinary income under Section 1250, as was discussed in Chapter 5. Actually, gain may be deferred for a long period of time by exchanging rather than selling investment property under the tax-free exchange provisions which we discussed in Chapter 3. Also, in respect to depreciation, if the property is new, one of the accelerated depreciation methods may be used; this will reduce taxable income and therefore increase cash flow. Most often the arrangement will be such that, after the landlord pays interest and amortization on the mortgage out of the rentals he receives, he will still have a cash return that will give him a reasonable return on his investment.

CONSIDERATIONS OF THE TENANT (LESSEE)

A user of property, subject to a variety of considerations, has the alternatives of purchasing or leasing property. An owner of property, again subject to a variety of tax and nontax considerations, has the alternative of maintaining ownership or selling the property and leasing it back. Sometimes leasing is the only way to get the use of assets; thus, for example, land may have to be leased to get mineral or oil rights. Leasing also is, of course, the only alternative when the use of property is desired for only a short period of time, or where only a portion of the facilities are desired.

Leasing Versus Borrowing

Oftentimes the comparison is made between leasing and purchasing. Better stated, the alternatives are (1) purchase for cash, (2) borrow and purchase, and (3) lease. The latter two alternatives are usually the relevant ones in real estate transactions, because it is only infrequently that a purchaser of real estate would have sufficient cash funds to purchase real estate outright.

Financial Considerations

One of the prime advantages indicated with leasing is that capital is thereby freed for other uses. Thus, for example, a department store need not have its funds tied up in real estate, but instead can use them for financing inventory and receivables. It is important to consider, however, that borrowing also can release funds for other uses. Chain stores may be able to engage in leasing as a means of obtaining funds for new stores. Leasing may be cheaper than having numerous small bond issues every time a new store is opened. Again, there may be borrowing arrangements which will also supply the necessary funds, such as a long-term loan with a take-down arrangement which allows funds to be drawn as needed. Oftentimes the restrictive covenants which often accompany debt financing can be avoided by leasing; for example, many bond indentures put restrictions on officers' salaries and dividend payments.

Some Questionable Advantages

It is often argued that leasing does not restrict credit as much as borrowing does; this argument is often based on the idea that the balance sheet looks more favorable because of the fact that debt shows as a liability, whereas the lease obligation does not. This, of course, assumes that the creditors are not aware of the lease obligations or do not take the leases into account. Another argument that may be questioned is that a lessee can shift risk to the lessor by leasing. For example, if a store turns out to be badly located, a lessee may figure that he can readily leave at the end of the lease. However, it is likely that the landlord will have the lease drawn so that the lessee will have paid for the property plus a profit on his investment by the end of the lease.

Tax Considerations

The crucial item in the desirability of leasing is often the relative cost of leasing versus borrowing. Here is where the tax considerations come in, by affecting the cost of leasing. If land and building are purchased, only the building may be depreciated. However, if the land and building are purchased and then sold and leased back, the total rental payments are deductible. The sacrifice for this is that the lessee foregoes possible appreciation in the value of the land.

Distribution of Tax Payments

Prior to 1954, the basic choice was the deductibility of rental payments versus purchase and deductibility of straight-line depreciation on improvements. Since 1954, accelerated depreciation methods have been allowed which allow a rapid recovery of

investment in property. The consideration of distribution of tax
payments relates to the time value of money. We would rather pay
$100 this year and $200 next year in taxes than $150 each year be-
cause we would have the interest-free use of the $50 for a year.

SALE AND LEASEBACK

A sale and leaseback involves the sale of real estate plus a
simultaneous lease given to the seller; rental payments extending
over the lease term are based upon repayment of the entire sales
price plus an interest return. The early sales and leaseback con-
sisted of a sale of real estate by an owner who at the same time
executed a lease. Chain stores often use the sale-leaseback by
building new stores and then selling them and leasing them back.
Tax considerations have importantly influenced the development of
the sale and leaseback. For example, sometimes a sale and leaseback is executed for land only; the owner maintains title to the
building but sells the land and leases it back. Prior to the transaction, the land did not contribute any tax deductions; after sale
and leaseback, rental payments are fully deductible. The sale and
leaseback is also used on newly constructed property. At the time
of construction, a sale-and-leaseback arrangement is made to be
effective on completion of construction; thus, the only capital requirements for the firm are in the form of short-term construction
financing and land acquisition.

Marketable Investment

Obviously, the advantages of a straight lease to landlord and
tenant also obtain in the case of a sale and leaseback, and they need
not be repeated. Often, in the case of a sale and leaseback, the
tenant will be a particularly good credit risk; this will add value to
the leasehold above the value of the property itself to the owner.
Thus, property with a long-term high-quality tenant may be quite
marketable.

Tax Advantage--Depreciable/Nondepreciable Land

Even though the seller under the sale and leaseback loses
the advantage of annual depreciation deductions and title to the real
estate, as we already have indicated, the seller's entire investment,
including nondepreciable land, is amortized and deductible through
rental payments. Of course, the seller has to be careful that the
rental payments are not so high that all of the advantage goes to the

investor and not the tenant. To take advantage of this situation, a firm, of course, may sell and leaseback both its land and building. However, a firm that does not want to lose depreciation deductions on a high-basis building may rather retain ownership of the building and sell and leaseback the land. To determine whether such a situation is desirable, the alternative results should be projected to determine their relative income tax effects as well as other nontax implications.

Tax Advantage--Sell Low-Basis Property

Because of inflation or because of a good purchase, a firm may have low-basis, appreciated property. Because of the low basis, depreciation deductions will be relatively small. However, the firm desires to maintain the use of the property.

This may be a good situation for a sale and leaseback. Assume the situation of Early Suburban Stores, Inc. The facts of the situation are as follows: Market value of property is $1,000,000; depreciable basis is $400,000; annual depreciation is $10,000; cash is needed for expansion, and Early Suburban calculates that it can achieve a 12 per cent return on funds before taxes or approximately a 6 per cent return after taxes. The property can be sold for a million dollars and leased back for $50,000 a year.

The sale and leaseback will add $22,200 after-tax profit, according to the following calculations made by the controller of Early Suburban Stores, Inc.; a 50 per cent tax rate is used.

```
Gain on sale:  $1,000,000 - $400,000 = $600,000
Capital gains tax:  25 per cent of $600,000 = $150,000
Cash available for expansion:  $1,000,000 - $150,000 = $850,000
Annual increase in after-tax income:
    $850,000 invested at 6 per cent after tax        $51,000
    Less: After-tax rent cost
    50 per cent of $50,000                  $25,000
    After-tax depreciation lost
    50 per cent of $10,000                    5,000         30,000
                                                           $21,000
```

Obviously, the results will be a function of the basis of the property, the selling price of the property, the tax rate, and the required rental payments. Other considerations in leasing should be considered also. We have assumed that none of the capital gain is converted into ordinary income under the depreciation-recapture provisions of Section 1250.

Tax Advantage--Sell High-Basis, Low Market-Value Property

The sale and leaseback also may be advantageous to the owner of property who has high-basis property that has a relatively low market value. The sale of this property will yield cash for expansion. Indirectly, the cash flow will be increased also by the loss, which will offset taxable income. As we note below, sales and leasebacks at a loss are scrutinized quite carefully.

Other Uses of Sale and Leaseback

The sale and leaseback may be used to advantage in a number of special situations. Only the highlights will be indicated, as these are technical areas. For example, property may be transferred to an employee's trust under a trusteed pension plan; the employer receives additional working capital whereas the trust receives current rental income plus the property at the end of the lease period. A gain on sale to an employee's trust would be a capital gain; losses would not be recognized. Again the caution: a variety of technical requirements must be met.

Another use of the sale and leaseback is in the case of a municipality giving property to a firm as an inducement to operate in their area. The basis of the property to the firm is zero, and no depreciation may be taken. However, the firm may sell the property and lease it back, incurring a capital-gain tax but achieving deductible rental expense.

DANGERS AND DRAWBACKS IN SALE AND LEASEBACK

There are important dangers in sale-and-leaseback arrangements which must be considered. We have already mentioned that, if real estate appreciates greatly in value, it is the landlord, not the lessee, who gets the advantage. Alternatively, if an area becomes depressed and the lessee wants to leave, he will be hampered by a long-term rental contract which most likely provides for an expensive cancellation clause. On the sale of appreciated property in connection with a sale and leaseback, there will be a capital-gains tax. It may have been possible to provide additional funds by borrowing on the appreciated property. If the sale is at a loss and the lease is for 30 years or more, the Internal Revenue may deny the deduction. There are a variety of problem areas which will be discussed on page 189.

Lease Over 30 Years

In the case of a sale and leaseback involving a lease of 30 years or more, the Treasury may well attempt to treat the transaction as a tax-free exchange; thus, no loss would be recognized and, if a gain was realized, the gain would be taxed to the extent of the cash received. However, recently there has been an increasing tendency of the courts to hold that an arms'-length sale and leaseback is a taxable transaction.

For example, Downtown Department Stores has property with a basis of $1,000,000 and market value of $750,000. If it sells this property and leases it back for less than 30 years, it will have a deductible loss of $250,000. The rent has to be defensible in comparison with other rents, or the loss may be attacked. If, however, Downtown Department Stores leased the property back for 30 years or more, the Treasury may well contend that there has been a tax-free exchange and that no loss is allowable.

Related Parties

In addition to the possibility of a disallowance of a loss in the case of a sale and leaseback with a lease of over 30 years, particular care has to be taken in the case of sales and leasebacks between related parties. Even if the sales price is reasonable and the rentals are reasonable, a loss between related parties will be disallowed. The reader may wish to refer to Chapter 2 for a discussion on who are "related parties." If the sale results in a gain, the sales price and the rentals must be reasonable in the light of going market values. Particular care has to be taken with respect to related parties. A gain may be treated as ordinary rather than capital gain. If a corporation and a stockholder are involved, the rent may be treated as dividends.

Planning to Avoid Pitfalls

In addition to avoiding transactions between related parties, other things may be done to preserve the transaction as a sale. The sale should be at a reasonable price and the lease should be at an economically defensible rent. For example, a competent real estate appraisal may be helpful in substantiating the sales price. Leases for over 30 years should be avoided. If the lease is to be less than 30 years, there should be no renewal rights; otherwise, the Treasury may add the renewal period to the base period so as to invoke the 30-year rule. An option to repurchase should be avoided, or else there is the possibility that the transaction may be attacked as a loan. Also, the sale and leaseback should have a sound business purpose, or else it may be argued that the transaction was a disguised loan.

Taxed As Unrelated Income for Nonexempt Organizations

Buyers in sale-and-leaseback transactions formerly often were tax-exempt organizations. The combination of their tax-exempt status plus the use of mortgage financing made a sale and leaseback an attractive transaction. However, now general insurance companies and pension funds have replaced charitable organizations as buyers. The reason is that business lease income is included as taxable gross income from an unrelated trade or business for an otherwise tax-exempt organization. A lease is considered a business lease if: (1) the lease is for more than five years; (2) the lease is of real property by a tax-exempt organization; (3) at the close of the tax year of the lessor tax-exempt organization, there is a business-lease debt with respect to the property. Personal property leased in connection with real estate is included. There are some exceptions, such as a lease of premises in a building primarily designed for occupancy and occupied by the organization, and leases entered into primarily for purposes substantially related to the exercise of the charitable or other functions of the organization.

PROBLEMS OF LANDLORD AND TENANTS

Now we shall leave the particular problems of the sale and leaseback and discuss the many tax implications relating to transactions affecting the landlord and tenant prior to the inception of the lease, at the inception of the lease, during the lease, and at the end of the lease. Remember that if there are tax implications for both landlord and tenant, these will affect the negotiations. Therefore, rather than discuss the landlord and tenant separately, we shall discuss the effect on both, under each subject. Thus, for example, we shall consider the taxability of advance rentals to the landlord at the same time that we discuss their tax deductibility to the tenant.

COSTS OF OBTAINING A LEASE

Either party to a lease transaction may incur costs on obtaining the lease. The basic question in this section is whether such costs are deductible currently or are capitalized and deducted over the term of the lease.

Tenant's Costs in Obtainirg a Lease

The tenant (lessee) may be required to pay a sum to acquire a lease for business purposes. Such cost is deducted over the life of the lease; it may not be deducted currently. Whether renewal periods are calculated in the amortization period depends on whether the lease was acquired prior to July 29, 1958. Unless there was reasonable certainty that the lease would be renewed, costs of acquiring leases prior to July 29, 1958 are amortized over the life of the lease without taking the renewal period into account.

If the lease was acquired after July 28, 1958, any renewal period is taken into account in determining the amortization period unless 75 per cent or more of the cost of acquiring the lease is applicable to the remaining period from date of acquisition to the end of the lease excluding renewal options. The rule will not apply if the taxpayer can show at the end of the tax year that is is more likely that the lease will not be renewed rather than renewed.

For example: In 1964 $20,000 is spent to acquire a lease for 20 years; there are two renewal options for five years each. Of the acquisition cost, $14,000 was for the original lease and $6,000 was for the renewal options. The $20,000 must be amortized over the 30 years, which includes the present lease plus the renewal periods. This is so because less than 75 per cent of the $20,000 is attributable to the 20-year remaining life of the present lease.

If $16,000 of the cost of acquiring the lease was applicable to the original lease period without option, then the taxpayer could amortize the entire $20,000 over the 20-year remaining life of the original lease, provided that there was a reasonable certainty that the lease would not be renewed.

Included in a tenant's cost of acquiring a lease would be such costs as a broker's commission for finding the leased property and amounts paid to another party for the lease. If the lease is canceled prior to the end of its term, the remaining balance of the lease costs may be deducted in the year of cancellation. If, however, the lessee purchases the property, then the remaining unamortized balance of lease costs have to be added to the purchase price of the property. Note that the above rules must be followed whether the tenant is on a cash basis or accrual basis of accounting. When a leasehold is sold, excess amortization write-offs may be subject to recapture under Section 1250, as was explained in Chapter 5.

Landlord's Costs in Obtaining a Lease

A landlord (lessor) may incur various expenditures in order to secure a tenant. Brokers' fees, attorneys' fees, alterations to suit tenants, and other expenditures of securing a tenant must be capitalized and cannot be deducted regardless of the method of accounting used by the landlord. These costs will then be amortized over the life of the lease. If a landlord incurred expenditures to get a tenant but was unsuccessful, then he may deduct these expenses in the year incurred or paid, depending on whether he is on the accrual or cash basis of accounting.

If the landlord sells the property, any unamortized costs of getting the lease are added to his basis for the property and affect his gain or loss from sale rather than being a currently deductible expense. If the lease is canceled by the tenant, then the landlord can deduct any unamortized lease costs as a loss in the year of cancellation. If the property is exchanged, the unamortized lease costs are added to the basis of the new property acquired.

ADVANCE RENTALS AND SECURITY DEPOSITS

It is important to a landlord when rents are considered to be taxable income; it is important to the tenant when rent payments are deductible. Security deposits and advance rentals must be distinguished because of different tax consequences.

Security Deposits

A lease may require the lessee to make a security deposit ensuring his performance of the lease terms. Such a deposit is not taxable income to the lessor as long as he holds it as security. It is not deductible by the lessee as long as it is a deposit which must be returned. If a security deposit is forfeited and it is used as an obligation to pay rent, then it is rental income to the landlord and is deductible as an expense by the tenant. Alternatively, if the deposit is used to restore the improvements at the end of the lease, then it would be a nontaxable recovery of damages to property by the landlord; it would, however, be deductible by the lessee.

A security deposit may be held for the term of the lease and then returned to the lessee. In this case, there is neither income to the landlord or an expense to the tenant.

Advance Rentals

A tenant often is required to pay a portion of the rent in advance; thus, for example, he may be required to pay the first and last months' rent in advance. An advance rental is income to the landlord when received, regardless of his accounting method. Thus, a landlord on the accrual method still must report advance rental as income in the year received regardless of the period covered by the return and the time to which the rental payment relates. The tenant has to capitalize the prepayment and take the deduction in the years to which the rents apply.

For example, Philip McCafferty rented a commercial building from Mildred Armstrong in May 1964 for five years. The lease term was from July 1, 1964 to June 30, 1969. The terms of the lease called for an annual rental of $2,400. McCafferty paid the first year's rent on June 1, 1964. When McCafferty files his 1964 income tax return, he may deduct one-half of $2,400, or $1,200; this is the rent applicable to 1964. Note that even though the lessee paid $2,400, he is allowed to deduct only $1,200. The landlord, Mildred Armstrong, must report the $2,400 as income.

Martin Crosley paid the full rental of $50,000 in advance on a rental of a warehouse; this covered five years at $10,000 per year. Crosley must prorate the $50,000 over the life of the lease and deduct $10,000 each year. The landlord must report the $50,000 as income in the year received.

Advance Rentals and Security Deposits--Tax Planning

If a lessee puts up money as either an advance rental or a security deposit, it is not deductible until the period when such amount is applied as rental. Thus, it does not make any difference to him whether it is treated as advance rental or as a security deposit. However, the landlord's position is affected. A security deposit is a useful way for landlords to defer reporting of advance payments.

The lessor may provide in the lease that the deposit is made to secure performance of the lessee's obligations and that the deposit is to be treated as a trust fund by the lessor until the date of release as specified in the lease. Examples of such obligations are the timely payment of rent and the return of premises in good condition. He should not provide in the lease that the deposit will be used as rent for the final period of the lease. It is important that the lessor separate the security deposit from his other funds. Also, the agreement should provide that the lessee should have the right to get back the deposit if the conditions of the deposit are met.

The above is not meant to indicate that it is always advisable for the landlord to have a security deposit rather than an advance rental. For example, the landlord might not like the restrictions on the use of the dsposit. It may be that his income picture is such that he has an offsetting loss or a relatively low income at the time of the advance payments, so that, taxwise, it is beneficial to have the income in the earlier period.

RENT PAYMENTS

The rent paid by the lessee is ordinary income to the lessor when received or accrued, depending on his accounting method. Rent is deductible by the lessee when paid or accrued, depending on his accounting method, provided, of course, that the leased property is used in his trade or business or for the production of income. Naturally, rent for a person's own living quarters is personal and is nondeductible. As was indicated earlier, regardless of the accounting method used, advance rentals are income to the landlord in the year received; the tenant may deduct only the portion of the advance rental which is attributable to the use of the property in the taxable period.

These rules are illustrated in the following example. Note that, if the taxpayer is on the cash basis, rent is taxable when received. Rent is considered to accrue ratably over the period of a lease, unless it is paid in advance, in which case it accrues when received.

Rumph owns an apartment house. Rent for December 1964 and for January 1965 is paid in January 1965. If Rumph reports on the cash basis, the rent is 1965 income. If he reports on the accrual basis, the rent paid for December is 1964 income and that paid for January is 1965 income. But if Rumph rented an apartment for five years in December 1964, and the rent for the whole period was paid to him in advance at that time, it would be 1964 income whether he reports on the cash or the accrual basis.

BONUS TO LESSOR

A lessee may pay the lessor a bonus to obtain a lease, and, alternatively, the lessor may give the tenant or someone else a bonus to secure the tenant. If a lessee pays the lessor a bonus to obtain a lease, it is income to the lessor in the taxable year when received. The lessee must capitalize the payment and deduct it ratably over the life of the lease, regardless of his method of accounting. A payment by the lessee to the lessor for renewal or extension of a lease would be amortized over the remainder of the lease term. If the lessor paid a bonus to get the tenant, this would be amortized over the life of the lease.

RENT IN PROPERTY OR SERVICES

Rent paid in property instead of cash is taxable to the lessor to the extent of the fair market value of such property. For the lessee, it is deductible as rent to the extent of the fair market value of the property, and gain or loss is realized to the lessee on the property so transferred. Payment of rent in services is deductible in the amount of rental agreed, if it is a reasonable, fair rental; however, the value of such services must also be included in the gross income of the tenant performing the services. The value of the services is rental income to the lessor.

AGREEMENT TO RESTORE PROPERTY

The lease may provide that the lessee agrees to restore the property to its original condition at the end of the lease. The tenant may deduct payments for the purpose of restoring the premises. These expenditures would be deductions in the year paid. The obligation to restore should except ordinary wear and tear, or else the landlord may lose his deduction for depreciation on his improvements.

EXCESSIVE RENTS

A limitation may be placed on the deduction for rent if the Internal Revenue can show that the amount is excessive. The limit would be the amount which the lessee would have to pay an outsider for the continued use or possession of the property. Payments of rent to a shareholder or to a family member would likely be scrutinized to see if there was evidence of excessive payments.

LESSEE'S PAYMENTS OF LESSOR'S EXPENSES

The lease may provide that certain charges against the property are to be paid by the lessee. For example, a tenant may be required to pay the lessee's taxes, interest, insurance, or repairs. If a lessee agreed to pay real property taxes on the property, the payment is a deductible payment of rent by the lessee when paid or accrued. The lessor has rental income in an equivalent amount and has a deduction for taxes of the same amount. If the lessee pays interest and principal payments on the lessor's mortgage, they are deductible rent payments by the lessee; they are rent income to the lessor. The lessor has an interest deduction for an equal amount. The above rules apply even though the payments are made to a third party rather than to the lessor.

Sleek Stores, Inc. has a lease with Addison Brown which provides that Sleek Stores shall pay the real property taxes on the property and also disburse the mortgage payments directly to the First Mortgage Company. In 1964 Sleek Stores makes a mortgage payment of $5,000 directly to the First Mortgage Co.; this includes $1,800 interest and $3,200 principal; they also pay real property taxes of $2,500. In addition, they paid $12,000 rent. Addison Brown has rental income of $19,500; this is the mortgage principal and interest payment, the real property tax payment, and the rental payments; he has a deduction of $1,800 interest and $2,500 taxes. Sleek Stores has a deduction for rent of $19,500.

IMPROVEMENTS BY THE LESSOR

There may be improvements on the property prior to the lease, or the lessor may place improvements on the property. Alternatively, the lessee may have improvements constructed. In this section we shall consider the tax implications of improvements by the landlord, and in the next section, improvements by the tenant.

Depreciation of Lessor's Improvements

If there are improvements on the property at the time of the lease, or if the lessor places improvements on the property as a condition of the lease, he may depreciate these improvements. Capital expenditures made by the lessor for the erection of buildings or other improvements subject to depreciation allowances must be recovered as depreciation deductions over the useful life of the improvements without regard to the period of the lease. It appears that the improvement would have to be shown to be valueless at the end of the life of the lease in order to amortize it over the life of the lease rather than depreciate it over the life of the improvements. The lessor has to be careful of any agreements requiring the lessee to restore the property to its original condition. Unless wear and tear are excluded from the agreement, an agreement requiring the lessee to restore the real estate unimpaired and in its original condition may cause the lessor to lose his depreciation deductions. Thus, the terms of the lease should be carefully drawn.

Demolish Improvements to Get Tenant

A landlord may have to demolish the improvements on his property in order to get a specific tenant. The structure to be demolished may not have been completely depreciated. The remaining basis must be deducted over the life of the lease; it cannot be deducted currently.

IMPROVEMENTS BY THE LESSEE

A tenant may make improvements to leased property. Where the lessee improves the property, he may claim the depreciation thereon. The cost of the improvements on property leased for use in trade or business is recoverable through deductions each year over the remaining life of the lease or over the estimated life of the improvements, whichever is shorter.

For example, Pinkins erected a building with an estimated life of 20 years at a cost of $20,000. At that time, the lease had 25 years left to run. Assuming that straight-line depreciation is used, Pinkins will take an annual deduction for depreciation of $1,000 ($20,000 ÷ 20) rather than a deduction based on the total cost of the improvements ($20,000) divided by the number of years remaining of the term of the lease (25), or $800.

Depreciation or Amortization

Note that, if the life of the improvements is equal to or shorter than the remaining period of the lease, the lessee may take an annual deduction for depreciation. In this case, provided that the property qualifies, he is allowed to use the accelerated depreciation methods, such as the sum-of-the-years-digits method or double-declining-balance method. If, however, the life of the improvements is longer than the life of the lease, so that the cost of the improvements are amortized over the life of the lease, then only the straight-line method may be used to amortize the balance.

Renewal Options

Renewal options are important in determining the depreciation or amortization deduction for improvements made by the tenant. If a lessee was under a binding obligation to make improvements prior to July 29, 1958, or for improvements commenced prior to that date, the cost was amortized over the life of the lease without taking the renewal period into account; the exception was the case where the facts showed with reasonable certainty that the lease would be renewed, and in that case the renewal periods were taken into account.

A percentage rule has been established for improvements started after July 28, 1958. Renewal periods are to be taken into account in determining the period over which amortization is allowed, provided that the term of the lease (excluding the renewal period) remaining upon the completion of the improvements is less than 60 per cent of the useful life of the improvements. This rule does not apply if the tenant established that, at the close of the tax year, it is unlikely that the lease will be renewed. If the lease is renewed, or if it is reasonably certain that it will be renewed, then the renewal period will be considered in determining the write-off period. "Excess" amortization write-offs of leasehold improvements may be subject to the depreciation-recapture rules of Section 1250, as was explained in Chapter 5.

The basic rule is illustrated below.

The estimated life of a building constructed by tenant Jeffries on leased property is 35 years. The unexpired term of the lease is 20 years; there is a renewal option for 10 years. Three-fifths of the useful life is 21 years. Because the remaining term of the lease (20 years) is shorter than 21 years, the cost of the building must be written off over 30 years (unexpired term plus renewal term), unless the tenant Jeffries can show that at the close of the tax year the lease will not be renewed.

Note that this is not an absolute rule. For example, the lessee may be able to show that he has no intention of renewing. Alternatively, the Internal Revenue may attempt to indicate that it is reasonably certain that the lease will be renewed and thus add the renewal periods even if the 60 per cent test is met. For example, the Internal Revenue may attempt to use an advantageous rental agreement or suitability of the property for the particular business as evidence that the lessee is likely to renew. Alternatively, the lessee may use evidence that the improvements are not likely to have any value at the end of the lease, or that the option to renew is of questionable value, to argue that he will not renew.

Related Parties

If the tenant and the landlord are "related parties," then the improvements must be amortized over their remaining useful life whether or not there is an option to renew. "Related parties" for this purpose are defined in Section 178 of the Internal Revenue Code. Included are husband or wife, ancestors, and lineal descendants of the taxpayers; brothers and sisters are not included. Included are an individual and a corporation of which 80 per cent or more in value of the outstanding stock is owned directly or indirectly by or for such individual. However, stock owned by a brother or sister is not considered owned by the individual. Included are related corporations and certain beneficiaries, trusts, grantors, and so forth, even if the beneficiary, and so forth, is the brother or sister of the taxpayer. Included are corporations of an affiliated group which are eligible for filing a consolidated return. The rule applies if the lessee and lessor are related persons at any time during the tax year. If parties cease to be related, then for subsequent years (as long as they remain "unrelated") the amortization period may be determined by reference to the percentage rule.

IMPROVEMENTS BY LESSEE--EFFECT ON LESSOR

Improvements made by a tenant that increase the value of the leased property are not income to the landlord unless the improvements are a substitute for rent. Gain or loss is recognized when the property is disposed of. This is illustrated by the following example.

On July 1, 1956 Gettle leased a parcel of land to Dugal for a 10-year term, with an annual rental of $800. The land had cost Gettle $5,000 in 1953. Dugal in 1964 erected a building at a cost of $20,000. The lease expired, and Gettle repossessed the property on June 30, 1966. On the next day Gettle sold the land and building for $30,000. The annual rent was income. But Gettle realized no income from the improvement when it was made in 1964. Nor did he realize income from the improvement when the lease expired on June 30, 1966 and he repossessed the land and the improvement in accordance with the lease terms. But when he sold the land and building for $30,000, his gain on the sale was $25,000 ($30,000 - $5,000).

Prior to 1942 a lessor realized income from an improvement by the lessee when the lease ended; amounts included in income under this rule are added to the basis of the property. However, for 1942 and later, no income is realized, and also no adjustment is made to the basis of the property.

Improvements a Substitute for Rent

If improvements are a substitute for rent, then the landlord realizes income when the improvement is placed on the property; the amount is the fair market value of the property.

For example, in January 1962 Gettle leased another piece of land to Dugal for a period of five years. Under the lease terms, Dugal was not required to pay rent, but in lieu of rent he was to install an irrigation system before the end of the fifth year. Dugal installed the system in the fall of 1966, at which time it had a fair market value of $5,000. Gettle realized $5,000 income in 1966.

If the construction of an improvement is treated as payment of rent, the lessee is able to deduct its cost as rent.

Opportunity for Planning

If a lessee makes improvements on the lessor's property, the lessor does not have income at time of construction or at the end of the lease unless the improvements are a substitute for rents. Thus, at the expiration of the lease, the lessor has improvements on his property which are likely to increase its value; if the property is sold, these improvements will be reflected in the selling price. Gain on sale of a capital asset will be capital gain. Gain on sale of property used in a trade or business will be a Section 1231 gain. If the lessor keeps the property, the improvements by his former lessee will most likely result in higher rentals for a new lessee.

Thus, instead of the lessor making improvements on the property, it may be advisable for the lessor to take a smaller rent in return for the lessee making the improvement. The lessee will not be affected tax-wise, because he is trading a write-off of lease-hold improvements for part of his rental-expense deduction. Obviously, the lease should not indicate that the improvements made by the lessee are considered as rent. There should be a reasonable rent. If there is no rent, or if rental payments are periodically reduced, the Revenue Service may contend that the lessee's improvements are a substitute for rent and constitute taxable income.

CANCELLATION OF LEASE

It may be desirable to cancel a lease prior to its expiration. The party desiring the cancellation may be required to pay a bonus to the other party.

Bonus to Lessor

A tenant may desire to cancel the lease and pay the landlord a bonus. Such a bonus is taxable income to the lessor. The tenant may in the year of payment, even if he is on the accrual basis, deduct the bonus. However, if the bonus is to modify or extend the lease rather than cancelling it, the lessee must deduct his payment over the remaining period of the lease, including any extension period. Amounts received by the landlord for cancellation, amendment, or modification of a lease are considered essentially a substitute for rental payments, and these amounts are ordinary income, not capital gain.

Bonus to Lessee

The landlord may desire to cancel the lease and pay the tenant a bonus. Amounts paid by the landlord for the cancellation of a lease are capital expenditures; these expenditures are recoverable over the remaining term of the canceled lease. If, however, the old lease is canceled so that a new lease can be executed, and it is provided that the cost of cancellation is payable out of the proceeds of the new lease, then the cost of cancellation is recoverable over the period of the new lease on the property.

Bonus From Landlord for Cancellation--Capital Gain to Tenant

A cancellation payment received by a tenant for cancellation of a lease is considered as amounts received in exchange for the lease; usually, capital-gain treatment applies. The same rule applies for payments received by the lessee from the lessor for amendment of a lease or for giving up a restriction in the lease. The theory is that the lease in the hands of the tenant is an asset, and the surrender of the lease is similar to the sale of an asset.

Opportunities for Planning

Because an amount received from a tenant for cancellation, modification, or extension of a lease is taxable income to the landlord in the year of receipt, a large payment may result in a large tax liability. Thus, the landlord must consider this tax liability in determining whether to accept a cancellation payment. If the payment is to modify or extend the lease rather than to cancel it, the landlord may benefit by having the bonus paid over the remaining term rather than in a lump sum. In either event, the lessee must amortize the payment over the term of the lease. The lessor, however, will take it into taxable income in one year if paid in a lump sum or over several years if paid over a period of time.

A tenant, in deciding whether to cancel a lease, would consider that the bonus payment to the lessor is fully deductible in the year paid, as well as the fact that any unamortized balance of leasehold improvements is also deductible. The tax implications of these factors may be enough to effect a decision to cancel a lease in a marginal location.

ASSIGNMENT OF LEASE AND SUBLETTING

As was discussed above, a tenant sometimes gets out of a lease by paying a bonus to the landlord. Alternatively, the tenant may assign his entire interest to someone else or he may sublet the premises.

Assignment of Lease

An assignment of a lease to another party is treated like a sale or exchange. If the lessee holds the property for use in trade or business, the gain is a Section 1231 gain, which is usually a capital gain. If the asset is not used in trade or business, then the gain is capital gain. However, for a lessee who is in the business of selling leases, the gain is ordinary income.

Subletting

Rather than assigning the entire leasehold interest to a third party, the tenant may decide to sublet. Note that the assignment of the leasehold gave a Section 1231 gain. However, rents received from subletting are classified as rents received and are taxable as ordinary income. If leased property is transferred to another party under an arrangement whereby the new party takes over the monthly lease payments and also pays the original lessee an amount for relinquishing use of the property, the transaction is considered a sublease and not the sale of a leasehold. Payments received by the original lessee from the sublessee are ordinary income.

Cost of Acquisition to Purchaser

Assume that a buyer pays a fixed sum to the former tenant and also undertakes the rent obligations of the previous tenant for the balance of a lease. The buyer deducts a proportionate part of the cost of acquiring the lease each year; the deduction is based on the number of years the lease has to run. Any renewal periods must be considered in amortizing the acquisition cost if less than 75 per cent of the cost is for the initial lease period. There is an exception, however, in the case where a tenant can establish that, as of the close of the tax year, it is improbable that the lease will be renewed. These rules are discussed in detail and examples are given in the earlier section of this chapter dealing with costs of acquiring a lease.

Purchase Lease--Part of Cost for Improvements

When a tenant leases improvements, the tenant deducts his rental payments; he also amortizes the cost of obtaining the lease over the lease period. The tenant cannot depreciate the improvements which were placed on the property by someone else. The situation is different, however, when a party is assigned a lease on improved property where the improvements have been made by sum to the lessee for all of his rights plus payments to the lessor of the rent stipulated in the lease. In this case the payment to the lessee may be treated wholly or partially as for the improvements; if considered partially paid for the improvements, the remaining part is considered as paid for the lease.

The division of the cost between improvements and the lease depends on the particular circumstances. Thus, if the rental value of the land has increased substantially since the original lease agreement was made, then part of the price of the assignment would represent acquisition cost of the leasehold.

These rules are illustrated by the following examples.

In 1964, Singer leased unimproved property for 99 years at a fixed rental; he built a commercial building cn the land. The building has an estimated life of 50 years. Singer assigned all of his rights in the lease to White in January of 1965, shortly after the building was completed. White agreed to pay the landlord the rental payments and, in addition, to pay Singer $50,000 for the assignment of the leasehold. White may take a depreciation deduction on the basis of the $50,000 payment; the $50,000 is considered to have been paid for the building, and the building may be depreciated over its life of 50 years. Note that the assignment was made shortly after the lease was entered into, and that it is assumed there was no significant increase in the rental value of the land in the interim between the original lease and the assignment.

Contrast the above example with the following, in which there has been an increase in rental value of the land.

In 1938 Murphy entered into a lease, and in that year had improvements constructed on the property. Murphy used the land and improvements in his business until 1964, when he assigned the lease to Schaeffer. At the time of the assignment, it was determined that the value of the unimproved land had increased $20,000 since the lease was entered into in 1938. Schaeffer agreed to take over the rental payments and also to pay $60,000 to Murphy for the assignment. Of the $60,000 total, $40,000 is allocated to the cost of the improvements and $20,000 to the cost of the lease. Schaeffer amortizes the $20,000 as cost of the lease. He depreciates the $40,000 improvements over the remaining period of the lease or the useful life of the improvements, whichever is shorter.

Abandonment of Leasehold Improvements

A tenant may move from leased property and attempt unsuccessfully to assign or sell the leasehold. If the tenant is attempting to sublet the premises, then he cannot take an abandonment

the lessee and where the agreement requires a payment of a specified
loss on leasehold improvements he constructed. He can, of course,
still take depreciation on the improvements.

For example, Downtown Department Stores decides to move
to a suburban area because of the drop in business in the downtown
area. Downtown Department Stores has eight years remaining in
its lease; 15 years ago it constructed a building on the leased
premises. An attempt is still being made to sublet the premises,
and thus Downtown cannot take an abandonment loss.

Assignment or Sublet--Planning Considerations

A tenant considering the desirability of moving from leased
premises should consider the tax implications of various alternatives.
The tenant may consider assigning the lease or subletting; alternatively, he may be able to pay the owner a bonus to cancel the lease.

The tax results will vary, depending on whether the tenant
will receive more than his rental obligation or less. Assuming that
he can get more than he has to pay to the landlord, an assignment of
all his rights will yield Section 1231 gain if the asset is used in trade
or business and held over six months. Alternatively, subletting
would give ordinary income as the rentals were received. Because
Section 1231 gain generally yields capital gain tax-wise, it is better
to assign rather than sublet if the transaction will yield a gain.
Where the leasehold has increased in value, the landlord may be
willing to pay the tenant a bonus to cancel the lease; in this case,
the tenant has capital gain.

It is important to attend to the legal formalities if an assignment is desired rather than subletting the premises. Otherwise, the
transaction may be challenged as a sublease rather than an assignment.

A tenant may desire to be relieved of a lease obligation where
the rental value of the property has declined. If the property is sublet, the loss is spread over the life of the lease as rentals are received from the sublessee. Similarly, if the lease is assigned and
the original lessee pays the assignee an amount to take over his
lease obligations, this cost must be amortized over the life of the
lease. An immediate loss may be taken, however, if the landlord
will cancel the lease for a specified payment.

LEASE WITH OPTION TO BUY

A lease with option to buy is a combination of sale and lease.
The lease contains an option for the lessee to purchase the real
estate. Assuming that the transaction holds up (we shall discuss

the difficulties shortly) during the term of the lease, the lessor has rental income and the lessee has rental deductions; when the option is exercised, the lessor, now the seller, has proceeds from sale measured by the option price, and the lessee, now the purchaser, has a basis for his property measured by the option price.

Possible Advantages

From the lessee's standpoint, he is able to defer a substantial cash outlay until exercise of option. Also, he has a rent deduction while determining whether or not to buy the property. The lessor may be able to dispose of property in this manner in a more profitable way than through an outright sale.

Manipulation of Terms

A lessee may desire to have increased rental payments and smaller option price. An advantage would accrue to him, because the rental payments would be immediately deductible, whereas the option price becomes his basis for the property which will have to be recovered through depreciation over the life of the property. The lessor may suffer a disadvantage if the property is a capital asset in his hands. This is so because part of his selling price is in effect rental taxed at ordinary rates, whereas the option price, which would be his proceeds for sale of the property, will result in capital gain if the asset is a capital asset or a Section 1231 gain. It is, of course, true that, if the terms of the transaction are sufficiently attractive to the lessor, he will overlook this tax effect.

Lipson has property which he is willing to sell outright or to lease with an option to purchase. Lipson's terms are $25,000 per year plus an option price of $120,000 at the end of eight years. N. W. Brown approaches Lipson and suggests the following terms: (a) rental payments of $30,000 per year; (b) option price of $75,000 at the end of eight years. Brown then is willing to pay $5,000 additional rent for eight years (a total of $40,000) for a reduction of $45,000 in the purchase price at the end of eight years. Brown determines the additional $5,000 deduction as compensation for the earlier payments and also because of the uncertainty of the option price eight years hence. Brown figures that he may take current deductions in full for the rental payments. Lipson doesn't mind, because in effect he is able to spread his gain on sale of real estate over a period of years; also, he can still deduct depreciation. The total advantage of the transaction to Lipson offsets the disadvantage that he is converting some capital gain into ordinary income.

The above transaction may be challenged by the tax authorities if it can be determined that an excess rental payment is being made in exchange for a reduction in option price.

Possible Disallowance

If the agreement is in reality a lease, then the lessee is entitled to deduct rental payments if the property is used in a trade or business. If, however, the lessee is acquiring title, or already has title, then the rents are not deductible. The following different theories have been used in determining whether there was a lease or a sale: (1) The original Tax Court test was to treat a lease with an option to buy as a sale if the rentals were sufficiently large to exceed the depreciation plus the value of the property and thereby give the lessee an equity therein. (2) The Fifth Circuit Court held that the intentions of the parties determined the result. (3) The Revenue Service considers that each case should be decided in the light of its particular facts, but that, without compelling evidence indicating a rental agreement, a transaction will generally be treated as a purchase and sale if one or more of certain specified conditions are present; these are outlined in the following section.

Conditions Generally Resulting in Sale Rather Than a Lease

In the absence of "compelling and persuasive factors to the contrary, an agreement is considered a conditional sales contract rather than a lease if one or more of the following conditions are present:"

1. Portions of the periodic payments are made specifically applicable to an equity to be acquired by the lessee.

2. Title will be acquired upon payment of a stated amount of rentals which the lessee is required to make under the contract.

3. The total amount which the lessee is required to pay for a relatively short period of use constitutes an excessively large proportion of the total sum required to be paid to secure the transfer of the title.

4. The agreed rental payments materially exceed the current fair rental value. This may be indicative that the payments include an element other than compensation for the use of the property.

5. The property may be acquired under a purchase option at a price which is nominal in relation to the value of the property at the time when the option may be exercised, as determined at the time of entering into the original agreement, or which is a relatively small amount when compared with the total payments required to be made.

6. Some portion of the periodic payments is specifically designated as interest or is otherwise readily recognizable as the equivalent of interest.

7. Title will be acquired upon payment of an aggregate amount--that is, the total of the rental payments plus the option price, if any--which approximates the price at which the property could have been purchased at the inception of the agreement plus interest and carrying charges.

Transfer of Title Not Essential

The contract is not prevented from being considered a sale of the property by the fact that an agreement does not provide for the transfer of title, or even if the agreement specifically precludes transfer of title.

For example, an agreement would be treated as a sale if the rents over a relatively short period approximated the price at which the property could have been purchased, and the lessee could use the property for its entire useful life for a relatively nominal payment, even if title did not pass.

Lease Classified as a Purchase--Can Still Get Accelerated Depreciation

If a lease is classified as a purchase, the tenant would capitalize his payments as his basis for the property and he could deduct depreciation on the property. The amounts received by the landlord are considered proceeds realized upon the sale of the property. Accelerated depreciation may be taken on the property by the purchaser.

For example, Blackstone Industries entered into an agreement in 1960 to lease property with an option to buy. The agreement was challenged in 1963 and classified as a sale and purchase rather than a lease. Because the improvements were new in 1960 and the requirements of the accelerated-depreciation method were met, Blackstone Industries depreciates the improvements under the accelerated method beginning in 1960.

Note that normally a taxpayer must choose the accelerated method the first year in which depreciation is available. However, if the lease is treated as a purchase by the Internal Revenue, then a taxpayer can still elect an accelerated method provided the other requirements of the method are met. If a taxpayer mistakenly treats a capital item as a deductible item, he can still get stepped-up depreciation.

Planning in Leases With Options to Buy

Considering the difficulties discussed, it is desirable for the parties to a lease with an option to buy to consider relative market values and rentals for similar properties. They should maintain evidence of these values in case their procedures are challenged.

In addition, it is not desirable to have the agreement provide for transfer of title upon the payment of a nominal amount at the end of the lease term. Rather than just establishing rental payments and an option price, it may be desirable also to include a payment for cancellation of the lease. In this way the tenant can deduct the payment for the cancellation of the lease in the year that he pays it.

For example, B. W. Williams agrees to pay $10,000 a year for the use of real estate provided that at the end of the four years he may purchase the property for $75,000. It is considered that rental payments and the option price are reasonable and can be justified. Williams would be better off tax-wise if he specified $10,000-a-year rental payments plus a lease-cancellation payment of $10,000 and have to capitalize only $65,000; in the first situation, he would have to capitalize the entire $75,000.

Planning--Evaluation of Risk

In the case of a lease which may be challenged, it is desirable to project ahead of time the advantage from a rental deduction versus the tax cost if the deduction is disallowed. If the lease is disallowed and is treated as a sale, the purchaser will have a substantially larger tax liability than if the transaction were a sale from the beginning; this is so because part of the "rentals" are a substitute for deductible interest charges. The interest would have been deductible but the rental payments are disallowed as capital expenditures. In one situation, no part of the lessee's payments were allowed as deduction. However, in another case, the Court allowed part of the payments as interest and, in fact, established the interest rate.

Note that the rules resulting in disallowance of rental payments in the case of leases treated as sales also apply to the leasing of equipment. These considerations are also applicable to sales and leasebacks, in which the original seller and future lessee takes an option to buy the property back from the purchaser.

LEASING LAND ONLY

Many lending institutions will make a mortgage loan for a rental project on leased land provided that the lease is long enough. Particularly in cases of shortage of capital it may be desirable to consider leasing the land and constructing rental units on the leased land. In this way capital is not tied up in the land, and, of course, the lease payments are deductible. The building that is constructed on the land will be depreciable for tax purposes.

Chapter 9

Residences, Cooperatives, and Condominiums

When a person purchases a residence instead of renting, he achieves certain tax advantages. If he itemizes his deductions rather than taking the standard deduction, he is able to deduct mortgage interest and property taxes. If he is unfortunate and has a casualty loss, he is able to deduct the amount of the casualty above $100. When a property owner sells his residence at a gain, he may defer tax on the gain by replacing the property within certain time limits.

The homeowner cannot, however, take a loss on the sale of his residence, and he cannot deduct either repairs or depreciation. However, if he used his home as an office for his business or profession, or if he rents out part or all of his house, then he has an asset used for the production of income. In this case, many expenses are deductible. Interesting problems arise as to values on conversion from personal to business use and in respect to allocation between personal and business expenses when there is both a personal and an income use of the residence.

Many of the tax considerations relevant to an owner of a residence are also relevant to the tenant-shareholder in a cooperative or the condominium purchaser. In the case of a cooperative, the person is a shareholder with a lease on a given apartment. A purchaser of a condominium actually receives a deed to his own apartment. He also has an undivided share in the halls, elevators, heating equipment, and other facilities that are common to the tenants of the condominium.

SALE OF RESIDENCES

Sale of a Residence

First, we shall consider a residence that is not used in any way for the production of income. Generally, gain on the sale of a residence is recognized if the residence is not replaced. A loss on sale of a residence, however, is not deductible. Under a special rule gain on the sale of a residence may be postponed. There is also a special rule for taxpayers over 65 years of age.

Recognized gain on the sale of a residence not used for the production of income and held over six months is a long-term capital gain. A loss is not deductible. For example, Nelson purchases for $20,000 a home which he uses as his personal residence. Five years later, he decides to move to an apartment, and he sells his home for $24,000. Nelson has a $4,000 long-term capital gain. We assume that he does not replace the home under the special rule discussed below.

Assume that Nelson received only $18,000 for his house. He has a $2,000 loss, but this loss is not deductible for tax purposes.

Postponement of Gain

If a taxpayer sells a home that is his principal residence, he may defer the gain if he does one of the following: (1) he purchases a new home and uses it as his principal residence within one year before or after he sells his old residence, or (2) he commences to build a new residence within the year before or after he sells the old residence and uses the new residence as his principal residence within 18 months after he sells his old residence. Members of the Armed Forces may have an extension of time, as will be explained later.

Amount recognized. If the rules indicated above are met, then gain on the transaction is recognized only to the extent that the adjusted sales price of the old residence exceeds the cost of the new residence. Note that, if the adjusted sales price of the old residence is greater than the cost of the new residence, then there will be recognized gain. Recognized gain cannot be larger than realized gain in any case.

Assume that Noble purchased a residence for $20,000 and sold it for $25,000. He replaced his residence in the required time period for $25,000. There is no recognized gain.

Take the same facts as in the previous example except that Noble replaced his residence with one that cost only $24,000. Then there would be a $1,000 recognized gain. This is the excess of the adjusted sales price of the old residence ($25,000) over the cost of the new residence ($24,000). Sales price is reduced by allowable fixing-up expenses to obtain the adjusted sales price.

Noble purchased a house for $20,000 and sold it for $21,000. He then purchased a new house within the time requirements for $19,000. Noble has a recognized gain of $1,000. Although the excess of adjusted selling price ($21,000) over cost of new house ($19,000) is $2,000, gain cannot be greater than his realized gain. His realized gain is the sale price of $21,000 less the cost of the first residence ($20,000), or $1,000.

Rule is mandatory. The rule is mandatory if the conditions are met. Thus, a taxpayer cannot elect to have the gain recognized.

Cooperative apartments. If a taxpayer is a tenant-shareholder in a cooperative apartment and he uses the apartment as his principal residence, this apartment will qualify for the special rule on deferral of gain. The basis will usually be the cost of the stock in the corporation and also includes the taxpayer's allocable share of a mortgage on the apartment building which he is required to pay as a condition of retaining his stock interest.

Calculation of Gain

In order to calculate the amount of realized gain and then the amount of recognized gain, it is important to consider the meaning of the "adjusted selling price" and the "adjusted basis" of the old residence.

Selling price. The amount realized on the old residence is the selling price less selling expenses, such as commissions, "points" incurred in connection with the sale, advertising, legal fees, and so forth. Selling price of the old residence includes the amount of any mortgage or other debt to which the property is subject in the buyer's hands whether or not the buyer assumes such debt. It also includes the face amount of any liabilities of the buyer which are part of the consideration given for the sale.

Fixing-up expenses. These are expenses for work on the old residence to help its sale. Examples of fixing-up expenses are painting and papering. For fixing-up expenses to be deducted in calculating the adjusted sales price, they must meet the following requirements: (1) they are incurred for work performed during a 90-day period prior to the date the contract of sale was entered into, and (2) they are paid for within 30 days after the date of sale, and (3) they are neither allowable as deductions in calculating taxable income nor taken into account in determining gain. Fixing-up expenses do not constitute adjustments to the basis of the old residence. They are neither capital expenditure nor improvements. Fixing-up expenses are considered only in determining the amount of gain on which the tax is postponed. They are not deductible in determining the actual profit on the sale of the old residence. This is probably best illustrated by an example.

Thatcher had an old residence that cost $30,000. On January

10, 1965 he sold it for $42,000. Allowable selling expenses amounted to $2,400. During the 90-day period ending January 10, Thatcher had painting and papering done in the amount of $1,600. He also put in new venetian blinds and a new water heater for $1,000. The work was paid for on February 6, 1965. Note that it was paid for within 30 days from the date of sale. Thatcher found, purchased, and occupied a new home within the required period. The new home cost $37,200.

Gain on old residence. Note that the calculation of the gain does not take into account the fixing-up expenses.

Selling price of old residence	$42,000	
Less: Selling expenses	2,400	
Amount realized		$39,600
Basis of old residence	$30,000	
Improvements (venetian blinds and water heater)	1,000	31,000
Gain on old residence		$ 8,600

Gain currently taxed and gain postponed. Because the fixing-up expenses were made in the proper time period, they are considered in determining the amount of gain postponed.

Amount realized on old residence	$39,600
Less: Fixing-up expenses (painting and wallpaper)	1,600
Adjusted sales price	$38,000
Cost of new residence	37,200
Gain currently taxed	$ 800
Gain on old residence (above)	$ 8,600
Gain currently taxed	800
Gain postponed	$ 7,800

Note that the gain amounts to $8,600 and is not influenced by the fixing-up expenses. These expenses do, however, reduce the amount of the gain currently taxed, because they are subtracted from the amount realized to get to the adjusted sales price, and it is the adjusted sales price that is compared with the cost of the new residence to determine the gain that is currently taxed.

Cost of new residence. This includes only so much of the costs for the acquisition, construction, reconstruction, and improvements as are properly chargeable to the capital account within the allotted time period. This includes the time the period may be extended for persons in the Armed Forces. Thus, the cost of a newly constructed residence is the cost of construction that actually takes place and the land actually acquired within the period that begins one year prior to the date of sale and ends 18 months after the sale of the old residence.

In addition, the cost of the new residence includes debts to which the property purchased is subject at the time of purchase. It is immaterial whether or not they are assumed by the buyer and includes a purchase-money mortgage. Also included is the face amount of liabilities of the taxpayer which are part of the consideration for the purchase and commissions or other purchase expenses. In the case of a cooperative apartment, the cost of a tenant-stockholder's stock includes his ratable share of the cooperative's mortgage.

Acquisition by gift or inheritance. The value of the part of a new residence that is acquired by gift or inheritance is not included in its cost.

Tilden acquired a residence by inheritance and then spent $10,000 in reconstructing this residence. Tilden may include only the $10,000 as cost of this residence for purposes of postponement of tax on gain on the sale of his former residence.

Basis of New Residence

The basis of the new residence after the sale of the old residence must be reduced by the gain not recognized on the sale of the old residence.

Tremain had an adjusted basis of $35,000 for his old residence. He sold this residence for $40,000. Selling expenses were $2,000 and fixing-up expenses were $600. Three months later he purchased a new residence for $36,000. The basis of the new residence is $34,400, as shown below.

Realized gain. This is the amount realized on sale less the adjusted basis of the old residence:

Selling price of old residence	$40,000	
Less: Selling expenses	2,000	
Amount realized		$38,000
Adjusted basis of old residence		35,000
Realized gain		$ 3,000

Adjusted sales price. Here the fixing-up expenses are subtracted:

Amount realized	$38,000	
Fixing-up expenses	600	
Adjusted sales price		$37,400

Recognized gain. This is the gain taxable in the current year:

Adjusted sales price	$37,400	
Cost of new residence	36,000	
Recognized gain		$1,400

Gain postponed:

Gain realized	$3,000	
Gain recognized this year	1,400	
Gain postponed		$1,600

Basis of new residence:

Cost of new residence	$36,000	
Gain postponed	1,600	
Basis of new residence		$34,400

Later improvements during time period. Improvements to the new residence will affect the basis of the new residence and the postponement of gain. To illustrate this, assume the following facts.

January 1, 1965, Thornton purchased a new residence for $20,000
March 1, 1965, Thornton sold his old residence at an adjusted sales price of $30,000. The adjusted basis of the old residence was $10,000.
May 1, 1965, a garage was added to the new residence at a cost of $4,000.

First, let us consider the recognition of gain. During March and April only $10,000 of the $20,000 gain on the sale of the old residence would be recognized. After May 1, 1965 only $6,000 of the $20,000 gain would be recognized. The cost of the new residence is now $24,000. This is the cost of $20,000 plus the cost of the garage of $4,000.

During January and February, the adjusted basis of the new residence is its cost of $20,000, because the new rule does not apply before the old residence is sold. During March and April, the adjusted basis would be $10,000, as the basis of $20,000 is reduced by the $10,000 gain not recognized on the sale of the old residence. Following the completion of the garage, the adjusted basis of the new residence would be $10,000. The basis of $24,000 is now reduced by $14,000, which is the gain not recognized on the sale of the old residence. Note that the gain not recognized on the transaction goes to reduce the basis of the new property.

Basis of residence acquired by gift or inheritance. We noted earlier that the value of a residence that is acquired by inheritance or gift is not included in determining the amount of gain to be recognized on the sale of the old residence. However, it must be included in calculating gain on a later sale of the new residence.

For example, Carver inherited a home having a fair market value of $24,000. Carver decided to make improvements on his new residence that amounted to $28,000. He now sold his old residence for $30,000. The cost of his old residence was $20,000. Before he sold his old residence, he spent $400 for fixing-up expenses for work done and paid for in the required time period.

Carver has a recognized gain on the sale of his old residence of $1,600. This is determined as follows: The adjusted sales price is $29,600 ($30,000 sales price less $400 fixing-up expenses). The gain of $1,600 is the excess of the adjusted sales price of $29,600 over the $28,000 he spent on improvements on his new residence. Note that only the cost of the improvements is considered in determining the gain recognized and the gain postponed. There is $8,400 gain that is postponed. This is the total gain of $10,000 on the old residence (sold for $30,000 and cost $20,000) less the $1,600 gain recognized.

The adjusted basis of the new residence is $43,600. This is the $24,000 fair market value of the new residence at the time of inheritance plus the $28,000 improvements that Carver made less the $8,400 gain that was not recognized on the sale of the old residence.

Trade-In of Residence

If a taxpayer trades in his old residence on a new residence, the transaction is treated like a purchase and sale for the special rule.

For example, Cohen had a basis of $22,000 for his old residence. He purchased a new home that was priced at $60,000. His old home was given as a trade-in at a value of $40,000.

Cohen is considered to have sold his old residence for $40,000, and thus has a gain of $18,000. However, because he replaced it with a new residence that cost more than the adjusted sales price of the old residence, the tax on the gain is postponed. Cohen's basis for his new home is $42,000. This is the $60,000 less the $18,000 gain not recognized on the old residence.

Principal Residence

To qualify under the special rule for nonrecognition of gain, the home that is sold and the home that is acquired must be the taxpayer's principal residence. As was noted earlier, this can apply to a tenant-shareholder in a cooperative. Also, a houseboat or a trailer may be the taxpayer's principal residence if he actually lives in it.

More than one residence. If a taxpayer has more than one residence, this rule applies only in the case of the sale of his principal residence.

For example, Casey has a home in town and a cabin at the beach. He uses the cabin on weekends and during the summer. The town property is Casey's principal residence and the beach property is not.

Chase has a home which he rents out. He resides at another home which he rents. Chase's principal residence is his home that he is living in.

Part personal, part business. If a taxpayer uses part of his residence for living and a part for production of income or in a trade or business, an allocation is made. We shall give an example of this later.

Temporarily rented. Property can still be considered a personal residence if it is temporarily rented out. However, it cannot be considered a personal residence if it is entirely investment property or used for the production of income.

Coleman purchases a new home before he sells the old one. It takes a while to sell the old house, so he temporarily rents out the new house until he can find a buyer for the old one. The property is still considered his new residence for the purpose of this rule.

Retirement home. If a taxpayer invests the proceeds of a sale of his residence in a retirement-home project which furnishes him living quarters, personal care, and so forth, he has not made a satisfactory replacement under this rule unless he acquires a legal interest in the property. Any gain on the sale of the residence is included in income. Note, however, the special rule for taxpayers over 65 to be discussed later.

Time Periods

We noted earlier that there are certain time periods which must be met. It is essential that the taxpayer physically occupy the new residence within the required time period. It is not sufficient to move furniture or other personal belongings into the new home if the residence is not actually occupied.

Residence purchased. If a residence is already constructed, the purchase has to be made within a two-year period that begins one year before the sale of the old residence and ends one year after the sale. Note that the residence also must be physically occupied by the expiration of the time period.

If the new residence has to be reconstructed in whole or in part, a taxpayer is considered to have purchased it rather than constructed it for the time requirements. The purchase of a partly constructed residence which is then completed by the taxpayer is considered a purchase for the time limits. The time limit for construction of a new residence is longer.

Construction of new residence. Construction must commence either prior to the sale of the old residence or not later than one year after the sale. The residence must be occupied not later than 18 months after the sale of the old residence. The construction may be started more than one year before the sale of the old residence. However, in calculating the amount of gain on the old residence on which tax is postponed, only the costs of construction of the new residence for the 30-month period beginning one year earlier and ending 18 months after the sale of the old residence are included.

Carter starts a new residence on January 1, 1962. He sells his old residence on January 1, 1964, two years later. He occupies his still unfinished new residence on June 28, 1965 within the 18-month period. Finally he finished the new residence on December 25, 1965. His costs are $5,000 in 1962, $10,000 in 1963, $10,000 in 1964, $10,000 in 1965 before the expiration of the 18 months, and $5,000 subsequent to that time. Although the total cost is $40,000, only $30,000 can be considered as cost of the new residence for the purpose of postponing gain on the sale of the old one. Only the costs for the 30-month period beginning one year before, and ending 18 months after, the sale of the old residence are included.

Armed Forces. Members of the Armed Forces receive special treatment. The replacement period is suspended during any time that the taxpayer or his spouse serves on extended active duty with the Armed Forces of the United States. The suspension cannot extend for more than four years after the date when a taxpayer sold the residence and applies only where the taxpayer's service in the Armed Forces begins prior to the end of the one year or the 18-month period. "Extended active duty" means that the taxpayer is serving pursuant to a call or order for an indefinite period or for more than 90 days.

Benefits Not Available

There are several situations in which the special rule is not available. For example, a trust does not receive the benefit of the special rule because it is not considered to be a person using property as a principal residence. Also, if the proceeds from the sale of the old residence are reinvested in a new residence and someone else receives title to the new residence, such as a daughter, the special rule does not apply.

New residence sold before old one. If the new residence is sold before the old residence, the special rule for deferral of gain does not apply.

More than one new residence. A taxpayer may purchase more than one new residence during the allowed time limits and occupy them as his principal residence. In this case, only the last of these residences is considered to be a new residence for applying the special rule for deferral of gain. Only one sale or exchange a year can qualify for the special rule.

Coddington sold his old residence on February 15, 1965. He purchased a new residence on March 15, 1965. A month later, on April 15, 1965, he sold the new residence and purchased a second new residence on May 15, 1965.

The gain on the sale of the old residence on February 15, 1965 is not recognized except to the extent to which Coddington's adjusted sales price of the old residence exceeded his cost of buying the second new residence which he purchased on May 15, 1965. Coddington has recognized gain on the sale of the first new residence.

Husband and Wife

In some instances, either the husband or wife may own the old residence, but title to the new residence is in both names as joint tenants. The opposite situation could also exist, where the first house was owned in joint tenancy and the new residence is owned by one of the spouses. In such situations, the gain from the sale of the old residence on which the tax is postponed and the resulting adjustment to the basis of the new residence may be allocated between the husband and wife. In order for this rule to apply, the following two qualifications must be met: (1) both the old and the new residences must be used as the principal residence of both the husband and wife, and (2) both husband and wife must consent to the allocation.

For example, Smith and his wife own, as joint tenants, a home which serves as their principal residence. The home has an

adjusted basis of $10,000 to each of them (total adjusted basis of
$20,000).

The Smiths sell their home at an adjusted sales price of
$40,000. Within a year after the sale, Mrs. Smith spends $40,000
of her own funds to purchase a new principal residence for herself
and her husband. Mrs. Smith takes title in her name only. Now,
if Mr. Smith and Mrs. Smith both consent, the adjusted basis to
the wife of the new residence will be $20,000 and Mr. Smith's gain
of $10,000 on the sale of the old residence will not be recognized.
As a taxpayer herself, Mrs. Smith's $10,000 gain on the sale of
the old residence also will not be recognized.

Let us take as another example Mr. Brown, who individually
owned a home which was the principal residence for his wife and
himself. This residence cost $20,000 and he sold it at an adjusted
sales price of $40,000.

Mr. and Mrs. Brown each contributed $20,000 of their sepa-
rate funds to purchase a new principal residence. They held title
to the new residence as tenants in common. If both spouses consent,
the gain of $20,000 on the sale of the old residence will not be re-
cognized to Mr. Brown. The adjusted basis of Mr. Brown's interest
in the new residence will be $10,000 and the adjusted basis of Mrs.
Brown's interest in the new house will also be $10,000.

Involuntary Conversion

A taxpayer can elect to defer recognition of gain in the case
of an involuntary conversion through seizure, requisition, or condemnation. He may also do so in the case of a sale or exchange
under threat or imminence of such an involuntary conversion. The
special rule for nonrecognition of gain does not apply, however, to
an involuntary conversion from fire, storm, or other casualty.
Gain, however, can be deferred in the case of fire, storm, or
other casualty under the involuntary-conversion rules discussed in
Chapter 3.

Thus, in the case of involuntary conversion through seizure,
requisition, or condemnation, the taxpayer has the choice of deferring gain under the special rule we have been discussing here or
of deferring it under the general involuntary-conversion rules discussed in Chapter 3. The replacement periods allowed under the
two elections are different and should be compared to see which is
the better election. If the taxpayer chooses to elect under the special rule we have been discussing in this chapter, rather than the
general involuntary-conversion rules, he has made an election that
cannot be revoked. He has to attach a statement to his tax return

for the year in which he disposed of the residence which includes a
statement that he is electing to treat the disposition of the old residence as a sale or exchange rather than as an involuntary conversion.
The statement should also indicate the following: (1) the basis of the
old residence; (2) date of disposition; (3) adjusted sales price of the
old residence or the net proceeds from condemnation; (4) purchase
price, purchase date, and date of occupancy of the new residence
provided that it was occupied at the time or before the time the
election is made.

More Than One Postponement

We noted earlier that, if more than one principal residence
was acquired during the replacement period, then only the last one
acquired during the period may be treated as the new residence in
determining the amount of gain on the sale on which tax is postponed.
However, a taxpayer may continue to postpone tax on subsequent
principal residences if he follows the rules discussed earlier.

For example, Hancock in 1956 sold his residence which he
had used as his principal residence since 1948. He purchased a
new residence in 1956 and the tax on the gain was postponed. The
basis of his new 1956 house was reduced by the amount of the gain
postponed. In 1965 Hancock sold his 1956 principal residence and
purchased a new one. He is entitled to postpone the tax again on the
gain that he realized from selling his 1956 home provided he meets
the requirements that we have discussed.

Holding Period

The holding period is important in determining whether recognized gain is short-term or long-term capital gain. If the tax
on any portion of the gain on the sale of the old residence is postponed, then the new residence will be considered to have been held
for the combined period of ownership of both the old and the new
residences.

Reporting Requirements

The reporting requirements depend on whether (1) a replacement is not intended; (2) a replacement is intended and is made by
the time of filing; (3) a replacement is intended but is not made in
time for filing.

No replacement. If the taxpayer does not intend to replace
his residence which he sold, or if the period for replacement has
expired, he reports his gain as a capital gain on his tax return.

Replacement made. If the replacement is made in time and before the filing date, a statement is attached which shows the purchase price, date of purchase, and date of occupancy of the new residence. There is a special form 2119 which may be used. If there is some taxable gain, this is reported as a capital gain.

Replacement not yet made. Replacement may not have been made by the filing date. It still may be possible to replace during the replacement period. If there is an intention to replace, or if the taxpayer is still undecided, it is not necessary to report gain. The sale, not the gain, should be reported. If the replacement is made within the required time period, the District Director should be advised in writing giving the full details.

If it is decided not to replace, or if the replacement period expires, then there will be taxable gain. An amended return must be filed which includes the gain as a taxable gain. Additional tax will bear interest from the due date of the original return until the tax is paid.

Paid tax--replacement made. A taxpayer originally may decide not to replace his residence, and may pay tax on his gain on the sale of his old residence. However, he may later change his mind and replace within the required time limits. In this case he prepares an amended tax return for the year of sale which includes in his taxable income only the amount of tax that is not postponed, and he will be entitled to a refund.

Review Example

When a residence is sold and it is replaced by a new residence under the special rule we have been discussing, it is essential to determine the following: (1) gain realized; (2) gain taxed in the current year, if any; (3) gain postponed; and (4) the basis of the new residence. The following example reviews the rules we have been discussing and also emphasizes the influence on the computation of improvements, repairs, commissions, real estate taxes, and other costs involved in the purchase and sale of a residence.

Assume the following information for John and Mary Todd: Their old residence was sold on June 3, 1965 and they purchased a new principal residence on June 4, 1965.

Old residence sold: (1) original cost, including settlement costs, $16,920; (2) improvements to old residence, including new porch, trees, and fence, $2,080; (3) sales price, $36,900; (4) fixing-up expense done in required time period, $700; (5) balance of mortgage paid, $9,000; (6) penalty for prepayment of old mortgage, $120; (7) real estate taxes for 1/1/65 to 6/3/65 paid to purchaser, $200;

(8) commission paid on sale, $2,000; (9) refund received on insurance, $150.

New residence purchased: (1) purchase price, $30,000; (2) title search and settlement costs, $700; (3) three years' fire insurance paid in advance, $300; (4) mortgage, $15,000; (5) real estate taxes for 1/1/65 to 6/4/65 received from seller, $186.

Gain realized. The first step will be to compute the realized gain. Note that this is not the recognized taxable gain, because part or all of the realized gain will be postponed under the special rule. Note that the balance of the mortgage on the old residence is included in the selling price. The adjusted basis of the old residence includes the original cost plus the improvements. The fixing-up expenses do not enter into the calculation of the realized gain.

Selling price	$36,900
Less: Selling expenses	2,000
Amount realized	$34,900
Less: Basis of old residence	19,000
Gain realized	$15,900

Gain currently taxed. The gain currently taxed is the excess of the adjusted sales price over the cost of the new residence. Note that the fixing-up expenses are deducted from the amount realized to arrive at the adjusted sales price. The cost of the new residence includes the title search and settlement costs as well as the purchase price. The fact that there is a mortgage on the new residence does not affect the calculation, as the cost of the new residence includes the mortgage.

Amount realized	$34,900	
Fixing-up expenses	700	
Adjusted sales price		$34,200
Cost of new residence		30,700
Gain currently taxed		$ 3,500

Gain postponed. The gain postponed is the excess of the gain realized over the gain currently taxed. Here it is $12,400 (gain realized, $15,900, less gain currently taxed, $3,500).

Basis of new residence. This is the cost of the new residence ($30,700) less the gain not currently taxed ($12,400), or $18,300.

Other items. The prepayment penalty on the mortgage on the old residence is deductible as interest if the Todds itemize their deductions. The real estate taxes paid to the purchaser are

also deductible as an itemized deduction, but they are reduced by
the real estate taxes received from the seller. The insurance they
paid on the new residence and the refund they received on the old
residence do not affect their tax in any way.

Installment Sales

The special rule for postponement of gain applies even if
the taxpayer sells his residence on the installment basis. If the
sale qualifies as an installment sale and the original tax return
was timely filed, the part of the gain on which the tax may not be
postponed may be reported on the installment basis. In Chapter
7 we have discussed the essentials of reporting on the installment
basis. Recall that the requirements of the installment basis have
to be carefully met.

Amount of gain. Under the installment basis of reporting,
the amount of recognized gain that is included in income each year
is that portion of the installment payments received during the year
which the total recognized gain bears to the total contract price.
Refer to Chapter 7 for the meaning of "contract price."

For example, Tuttle sells his residence at a contract price
of $50,000. The terms are such that Tuttle may use the installment
method of reporting. The realized gain is $10,000. A portion of
the proceeds are invested in another home, so that $5,000 of the
gain is postponed, leaving $5,000 gain to be taxed.

The gross profit percentage is 10 per cent; this is the $5,000
gain not postponed divided by the $50,000 contract price. Ten per
cent of the payments received each year by Tuttle on the principal
of the note or mortgage are includible in his income. Because the
residence was a capital asset in his hands, the gain will be reported
as capital gain.

Deferred-Payment Sales

A taxpayer may sell his residence on a deferred-payment
sale which does not meet the requirements of the installment plan.
For example, the payments in the year of sale may exceed 30 per
cent of the selling price, and thus the installment method cannot be
used. Recall (Chapter 7) that, on a deferred-payment sale, the
liabilities of the buyer are taken at market value. Thus, if a residence is sold on a deferred-payment plan and the market value of
the liabilities of the buyer are less than their face value, it is necessary to make two calculations. One calculation is made to determine the actual gain which takes the liabilities of the buyers into

account at their fair market value. The second computation is made to determine the amount of gain currently recognized under the special rule for postponement of gain, and this calculation takes the liabilities into account at their face value.

Sixty-Five Years Old or Older

We have noted that the general rule is that if a taxpayer sells his residence at a gain, he has a taxable gain. If he sells it at a loss he does not have a deductible loss. However, under the rule discussed earlier in this chapter, there is a relief provision which allows him to postpone the gain if he invests in a new residence. The 1964 Revenue Law added another relief provision which applies to taxpayers who are 65 years old prior to the date of sale or exchange and who have owned and used the residence as their principal residence for at least five of the eight years before the sale. If the adjusted sales price is $20,000 or less, the entire gain is tax-free. If the adjusted sales price is greater than $20,000, part of the gain is tax-free.

Adjusted Sales Price $20,000 or Less

Recall that the adjusted sales price is the total selling price less selling expenses, such as broker's commissions, and also less fixing-up expenses. If the adjusted sales price is $20,000 or less, there is no taxable gain.

Assume that Thrush purchases a residence for $10,000 12 years ago. He and his wife have used this residence as their principal residence throughout this period. He sells his residence on August 10 of 1965 for $22,500. Thrush was 65 on August 8. He pays commissions of $1,500 and incurs fixing-up expenses amounting to $1,000.

Mr. Thrush has a realized gain of $11,000. This is the $22,500 selling price less the $1,500 commissions less the $10,000 adjusted basis of the residence. There is, however, no taxable gain. The adjusted sales price is $20,000. This is the sales price ($22,500) less the brokers' commissions ($1,500) less the fixing-up expenses ($1,000). Because the adjusted sales price is not greater than $20,000, the entire gain is tax-free.

Adjusted Sales Price Exceeds $20,000

If the adjusted sales price is in excess of $20,000, the gain is tax-free in the proportion that $20,000 bears to the adjusted selling price.

Assume that Wong sells his home for $32,500. He purchased this home seven years ago and has used it continuously as his principal residence. He attained the age of 65 before selling his residence. The residence cost Wong $10,000 and he paid $1,500 in broker's commissions and $1,000 in qualifying fixing-up expenses.

The realized gain is $21,000; this is the sales price ($32,500) less commissions ($1,500) less the basis of the residence ($10,000). The adjusted sales price is $30,000; this is the sales price ($32,500) less commissions ($1,500) less fixing-up expenses ($1,000).

Out of the $21,000 realized gain, only $14,000 is tax-free. This is computed by taking the ratio of $20,000 to the adjusted sales price of $30,000 times the $21,000 realized gain.

Need to elect. An election must be made in order to receive the benefits of this provision. This election may be made or revoked at any time within the statutory period. If the taxpayer is married, an election or revocation must be made by both the spouses.

Note that it is a one-time election. If a prior election is in effect, no part of the gain on a subsequent sale will be tax-free under this relief provision.

Five-Out-of-Eight-Years Rule

We have already noted that, to receive benefits of this provision, the seller must have owned and used the property as his principal residence for at least five out of the eight years immediately preceding the sale. In some cases, a widow or widower will meet the five-out-of-eight-years requirement if the deceased spouse did.

Sixty-Five Years Old

The taxpayer must have attained the age of 65 before the sale. If the taxpayer signs a contract prior to his 65th birthday but does not close the transaction until after his birthday, the sale would most likely be considered as taking place when the deal was closed. If the property is owned jointly and a joint return is filed, the taxpayers receive the benefit of this provision if either is 65 years old or over. A surviving spouse would qualify if the deceased spouse met the holding-period requirements and the use test.

Replacement and Postponement of Portion of Gain Not Tax-Free

Earlier in this chapter we discussed the postponement rules when taxpayers invested the proceeds of a sale of their old principal residence in a new principal residence. There may be a combination of this relief provision and the relief provision for the taxpayer over 65.

Assume that Ikeya, who is over 65, purchased his home 20 years ago for $10,000. Now at the age of 65, he sells it for $32,500. Commissions are $1,500 and qualifying fixing-up expenses are $1,000. His children are grown, so he decides to invest the proceeds in a new smaller home for $13,000.

Before the relief provisions, Ikeya would have a recognized gain of $17,000. The adjusted sales price is $30,000 ($32,500 less $1,500 less $1,000). The excess of the adjusted sales price ($30,000) over the amount reinvested ($13,000) is the taxable amount ($17,000).

Because of the new relief provisions for taxpayers over 65, Ikeya will pay tax on only $3,000 of this gain. Two-thirds of the $21,000 realized gain is tax-free under the relief provisions. This reduces the $17,000 taxable amount by $14,000 to $3,000. Both the fixing-up expenses and the tax-free amount are subtracted in determining the amount that has to be reinvested. Because the figures here are the same as in the previous example, the reader may refer to the previous section for the determination of the $14,000 tax-free amount.

It appears that the tax-free amount in the over-65-year relief provision is a permanent escape as compared with the regular relief provision, which is a postponement. Thus, the $14,000 that is tax-free in our example is permanently tax-free and will not be recovered on a later sale of a new residence.

Involuntary conversions. The relief provision for 65-year-old taxpayers also applies to involuntary conversions. Thus, gains from fire insurance proceeds or from a condemnation award can qualify under this provision. The relief provision for 65-year-old taxpayers can be combined with the relief provision for non-recognization of gain on involuntary conversions. See Chapter 3 for a discussion of these provisions. If part of the gain is tax-free under this new provision, the sales proceeds will be reduced by the tax-free amount to determine the amount to be required to be reinvested.

Cooperatives. Tenant-shareholders of cooperative apartments may also qualify under this provision.

Part residence. If part of the residence is used as a residence and part is used in a trade or business or for the production of income then the relief provision may be used only for the portion that is a residence. Thus, for example, if a doctor used part of his residence for an office, the office part does not qualify. Similarly if a taxpayer rents a two-family house the gain on the rental unit does not qualify.

Sales after 1963. The relief provision applies to sales after 1963 even if the tax year began earlier.

Additions to Basis and Amount Realized

To determine the realized gain on the sale of a house, the adjusted basis of the house is subtracted from the amount realized on the sale. Thus, it is important to the taxpayer to make sure that he has subtracted all allowable amounts from the amount realized and that he had added all allowable amounts to the basis of the residence sold.

Improvements. The cost of improvements may be added to the basis of the house. Recall that improvements in general are expenditures that materially add to the value of the residence or appreciably prolong its life.

Additions to the cost basis of a residence may be made for the following improvements, among others: (1) additions of rooms; (2) completion of rumpus room or attic; (3) new plumbing; (4) new heating system or furnaces; (5) installation of an air-conditioning system; (6) new roof; (7) installation of permanent storm windows; (8) restoration of rundown house; (9) improvements on land, such as a swimming pool or landscaping expenditures.

Original expenditures added to basis. Certain expenditures made when a home is purchased are added to the basis of the residence. These include the following: (1) appraisal fees; (2) late-closing charge; (3) title search and insurance; (4) attorney fees; (5) cost of removing a cloud on title; (6) broker's commissions; (7) survey.

Mortgages. Recall that the amount of any mortgage that is assumed on the purchase of the property is part of the basis of the residence. This is true whether the buyer assumes the mortgage or just takes the house subject to the mortgage.

For example, Fifer pays $8,000 in cash for his residence. He takes title subject to a $32,000 mortgage. Fifer has a basis of $40,000 for his residence.

Effect of casualty. The basis of a residence is reduced by the sum of a deductible casualty loss plus the insurance recovery, if any, for the loss. The basis is increased by any outlays to restore the property.

For example, Ericksen's house is damaged by fire. His basis before the fire was $20,000. Ericksen collects $6,000 from the insurance company and he is entitled to a $2,000 casualty-loss deduction. The basis of Ericksen's residence after the fire is $12,000. Now let us assume that he spends $4,000 to restore the house. His basis then is increased to $16,000.

Amount realized. In determining the amount realized on the sale, all the selling expenses should be subtracted from the sales proceeds. Examples of selling expenses are: (1) mortgage-satisfaction fee; (2) advertising; (3) survey; (4) broker's commissions; (5) federal stamp tax; (6) attorney's fee; (7) title abstract fees.

Effect of mortgage on amount realized. On the sale of a residence, any mortgage assumed by the buyer or paid off by the buyer becomes part of the amount realized.

Evergreen has a residence which he sells for $14,000 cash, and the buyer takes subject to a $28,000 mortgage. Evergreen is considered to have realized $42,000.

The reader may wish to refer to Chapter 2 for a complete discussion of the effect of mortgages on basis.

Repairs. Unless the residence is used for production of income or in a trade or business, repairs are personal expenditures and are not deductible. Repairs are costs that do not lengthen the life of a property or materially increase its value. Examples are painting, new faucets, and appliance repairs. Repairs should be distinguished from improvements, because, even if there is no business or production-of-income use, improvements may be added to the basis of the property, and thus they will reduce gain on sale of the property.

ITEMIZED DEDUCTIONS

The owner of a residence, the tenant-shareholder of a cooperative, and the owner of a condominium all benefit from various itemized deductions related to their residences. This is true even if there is no business use or production-of-income use of the residence. Included are deductions for interest, taxes, and, in certain cases, casualty and medical deductions.

Taxes

The full amount of all state or local taxes paid is deductible. Included would be real estate and personal property taxes, and, in certain cases, mortgage tax. When a house is sold, the deduction for real estate taxes is apportioned between the buyer and seller.

Interest

Any mortgage interest is deductible. This includes payment to a mortgagee for the privilege of prepaying a mortgage. However, amounts paid by the purchaser of a home, in connection with the occupancy of the home for a period prior to the date he assumes an enforcible liability on the mortgage, does not constitute deductible interest, even though the charges are designated as interest on mortgage in the settlement papers. Such charges are considered to be in the nature of rent.

Example of interest and tax deductions. The following example reviews the deductibility of interest and taxes in the case of a personal residence. Marvin and Jeanette Fortuna sold their principal residence on June 3 and bought a new one on June 4.

Marvin and Jeanette made monthly payments to The Loan Co. which included amounts for property taxes, fire insurance, FHA mortgage insurance, and interest and principal payments.

The portions of their monthly taxes that represented taxes on their homes were $208 on the old house and $396 on the new house, or a total of $604 for the year. When they sold their old house, they paid the buyer $200 to cover taxes on the old property. When they bought their new home, they received $186 from the seller to cover taxes on the new home. The Loan Co. actually paid $558 property taxes for them during the year.

The Fortunas have a deduction of $572 for taxes in their itemized deductions. This is the $558 paid by The Loan Co. plus the $200 they paid the buyer of their old property less the $186 they received from the seller of their new property. Note that it is not the amount of the monthly payment that is designated as taxes that is relevant, but it is the amount of the property tax bill paid by The Loan Co. in their behalf that is relevant.

In addition, they have a deduction for interest for the amounts of their monthly payments that represent interest. If there was a prepayment penalty on the mortgage, they may deduct this as interest. The fire insurance premiums and the mortgage insurance premiums are personal nondeductible expenses.

Casualty Losses

Recall that casualty losses are deductible whether the property is used for business, income-producing, or personal purposes. The amount of a deductible casualty loss depends on whether it is a personal or a business casualty loss. A loss on a residence would be a personal casualty loss, and the amount deductible is the lower of the two following amounts: (1) the adjusted basis of the property for determining loss on a sale, and (2) the sustained loss. The sustained loss is the value of the property just before the casualty less its value immediately after the casualty. Whichever of the two figures above applies for measuring the loss has to be reduced by insurance or other recoveries.

First $100 not deductible. As noted before, the 1964 Revenue Law added a provision which makes the first $100 of a personal casualty loss nondeductible.

Fonts has a residence with a basis of $20,000. He sustains a flood loss of $3,000. Fonts has a casualty-loss deduction of $2,900. This is the sustained loss of $3,000 less $100.

The reader may wish to refer to the chapter on casualty losses for a detailed discussion of items that are included.

Medical Expenses

In some cases, certain residence costs will be deductible as medical expenses. The cost of renting an apartment for the exclusive purpose of taking care of an ailing parent in lieu of hospitalization has been ruled deductible. Cost of an air-conditioning unit, less resale and salvage value and operating expenses thereof, that did not become a permanent part of the dwelling and that was used primarily for illness have been held deductible.

If the cost of installing an elevator or making a similar improvement to property otherwise qualifies as a medical expense and does not increase the value of the property, it is deductible as a medical expense. If the improvement does increase the property's value, only the part of the cost that is greater than the increase in value is deductible. Expenditures for new buildings are not deductible as medical expenses even if they are related to medical care.

Contributions

Recall that contributions may be in either money or property. Gifts of property to a qualified organization may be deducted as contributions to the extent of their fair market value at the time of gift. In some cases, a former residence may be the subject of a gift.

Transfer of Appreciated Property in Marital Settlement

A husband has a taxable gain measured by the difference between his basis for appreciated property and its fair market value if he transfers this property to his wife for release of her rights to support and maintenance. Here we are discussing residences. However, this rule would apply to transfers of any kind of appreciated property in such a settlement.

Itemized Deductions and Owning versus Renting

Jack and Evelyn Jones own their residence, which cost them $30,000. It has an assessed valuation of $7,500 and the tax rate is $9 per $100 assessed valuation. Thus, they pay a total of $675 in real estate tax each year. Their interest payment is $1,650 per year. Jack's twin brother Jimmy rents a similar home in which he and his wife Beatrice live.

Let us compare the income tax returns of the two couples, assuming that they do not have any dependents and that each couple gives $100 a year in contributions and pays approximately $175 in deductible gas and sales taxes. Income for each couple after personal exemptions but before the standard deduction or itemized deduction is $12,000 per year.

Whereas Jack and Evelyn pay $1,688 tax, James and Beatrice must pay $2,040 tax. Home ownership for Jack and his spouse results in deductible interest and real estate taxes which, together

	Jack and Evelyn	James and Beatrice
Income before itemized or before standard deduction, but after exemptions	$12,000	$12,000
Standard deduction	--	1,000
Itemized deductions:		
Real estate taxes	675	
Interest	1,650	
Contributions	100	
Sales and gasoline taxes	175	
Taxable income	$ 9,400	$11,000
Tax	$ 1,688	$ 2,040

with his other itemized deductions, give them $352 in tax relative to their brother. James does not itemize any deductions because his standard deduction of $1,000 is larger. Obviously, we have made simplifying assumptions and have not considered the many nontax considerations that could be involved.

RESIDENCE USED FOR BUSINESS
OR PRODUCTION OF INCOME

A residence may be used partially for business. For example, a doctor or dentist may have his office in his residence. A building may also be used partially as a residence and partially for rental purposes. Rooms may be rented in a home, or an apartment-house owner may live in one of his apartments. The tenant-shareholder of a cooperative apartment may rent his apartment to someone else. Tax problems arise as to whether a taxpayer is entitled to deduct a portion of his residential expenses as expenses of trade or business. In addition, it is necessary on sale to allocate the basis between the personal and the business portions. Where a residence is being used for both personal and business or rental use, it is necessary to allocate the expenses of operation.

Classification of Residence

Recall that in Chapter 4 we discussed the importance of the classification of an asset in respect to whether gain or loss is considered ordinary or capital in nature. A personal residence of a taxpayer is a capital asset. If the residence is sold at a gain, the result is a capital gain. A loss on the sale of a personal residence is not deductible. Thus, on a sale of a residence that is partially used in trade or business or in production of income, the portion that is personal is treated as above.

Trade or Business

Sale or exchange of property used in a trade or business is a Section 1231 transaction, and you should recall (Chapter 4) that gains or losses on Section 1231 transactions are netted. If the property is held for more than six months, and if recognized gains on sales of Section 1231 assets are larger than the recognized losses, the net gain is considered to be a gain from the sale or exchange of capital assets and is reported with other capital gains and losses. If there are no other Section 1231 transactions, then the result is a capital gain. When there is a loss on the Section 1231 transactions and the loss is greater than the gains on Sections 1231 transactions, the result is an ordinary loss.

Thus, if a residence is partially used in a trade or business, the sales proceeds are allocated to the personal and business portion. If there is a gain, the gain is a capital gain on the personal portion and the gain on the business portion is a Section 1231 gain. If there are no other Section 1231 transactions, then both gains will be capital gains. If the result is a loss, the loss on the personal portion is nondeductible; the loss on the business portion is a Section 1231 loss, which, if there are no other Section 1231 transactions, is an ordinary loss.

Investment

A person may hold an apartment building for investment and live in one of the apartments. If he sells the apartment building, he must allocate the sales proceeds. We shall assume that the owner merely receives a check from the property managers monthly, and that it is determined that he holds the property for investment and not for use in trade or business. Thus, if he sells the apartment house, he has a capital gain on the rental portion if there is a gain and a capital loss if there is a loss.

Recall (Chapter 4) that there is not a clear-cut distinction between whether property is held for investment or is used in a trade or business. The important factor in determining whether or not there is a trade or business use seems to be the question of the taxpayer's activities in connection with the project. A taxpayer who spends a great deal of his time in the operation and management of rental property would most likely be considered to be engaged in a trade or business.

The distinction is usually more important in the case of a loss than of a gain. In the case of a gain, the result is usually a capital gain in either case, unless there are other Section 1231 transactions. In the case of a loss, however, it is better to have the property classified as used in a trade or business so that there is a Section 1231 loss, which is usually an ordinary loss. If the property is held for investment, a loss is a capital loss and is limited by the restrictions on capital losses. Recall (Chapter 4) that there is a difference of opinion in the courts as to whether the rental of one unit constitutes a trade or business. The Tax Court has ruled that the renting of a single piece of property places the taxpayer in a trade or business. Other courts have rendered a different opinion, and a taxpayer has been limited to a capital loss, because he was not considered to be engaged in a trade or business.

Sale of a Converted Residence

If the residence has been converted strictly to business or production-of-income use, there is a special rule for determination of basis. This special rule would also apply to the business portion of a residence used partially for business or production of income.

Basis for gain. The basis for gain is the adjusted basis at date of sale. For example, Morrison purchased a residence for $40,000 and made improvements on this residence, prior to conversion for rental use, of $10,000. The fair market value at the time of conversion to rental purposes was $44,000. Morrison's depreciation deduction since the date of conversion amounts to $4,000.

Assume that the property is sold for $54,000. Morrison has a gain of $8,000. This is the excess of the proceeds ($54,000) over the adjusted basis of $46,000. The adjusted basis of $46,000 is the cost ($40,000) plus improvements ($10,000) less depreciation ($4,000).

Basis for loss. The basis for loss is different than the basis for gain. In the case of property converted from personal to business use, the basis for determination of loss is the lower of: (1) adjusted cost at date of sale; or (2) the fair market value at date of conversion with post-conversion depreciation subtracted from both.

Assume that Morrison in our previous example received only $34,000 for his converted residence. His loss is $6,000, which is the excess of: the value at conversion ($44,000) minus depreciation since conversion ($4,000) (a net of $40,000) over the sales price of $34,000.

No gain or loss. Because of the above rules for determination of basis, there may be neither gain nor loss realized on the sale of a converted residence.

Assume that Morrison sold the house in our previous example for $46,000. This is just equal to his adjusted basis for gain, so that he has no gain. It is above his adjusted basis for loss of $40,000, so that he has no loss.

If he sold the residence for $40,000, he would not have a loss, because this is equal to his adjusted basis for loss, and he does not have a gain because his adjusted basis for gain is $46,000. In fact, any sales price between $40,000 and $46,000 would yield neither gain nor loss.

Importance of conversion basis. It is important to establish the fair market value at date of conversion if there is likely to be a loss on subsequent sale. Loss in value prior to conversion is non-deductible, whereas loss after conversion is deductible. Thus, it is desirable to have a competent appraisal at date of conversion so that there will be no challenge to the value if a subsequent sale results in a loss.

Postponement of Gain on Property Used Partially as a Residence

If a taxpayer uses part of his property for production of income or for business purposes and the rest as a residence, and he sells the entire property, he may postpone the tax on the gain on the part that is used as a residence. The rules that apply are those that we discussed earlier in this chapter. Allocation is made to determine the portion of gain that may be postponed. Only the part of the sales price that is allocable to the residential portion has to be reinvested in order to have the tax on that part of the gain postponed. It is sometimes helpful to think of the sale as a sale of two properties: one personal and one business.

Example. Assume that Riley owns a four-unit apartment house. Mr. and Mrs. Riley occupy one unit as their principal residence and rent the other three units. The Rileys sell their apartment house and purchase and occupy a new principal residence in the required time period.

The adjusted basis of the apartment is $72,000. This is original cost of $80,000 plus improvements of $4,000 minus depreciation of $12,000. The depreciation of $12,000 is the amount allowable or allowed on the rented three-quarters. No depreciation, of course, is allowed on the personal portion.

The apartment house was sold for a gross price of $100,000 and there was selling expense of $5,600. The Rileys moved into a new residence costing $40,000. A separation of items between the personal portion and the residential portion is made as is shown in the table on page 236.

	Personal Portion	Rental Portion
Selling price	$25,000	$75,000
Selling expense	1,400	4,200
Amount realized (adjusted sales price)	$23,600	$70,800
Basis including improvements	$21,000	$63,000
Depreciation	–	12,000
Adjusted basis	21,000	51,000
Realized gain	$ 2,600	$19,800

The tax is postponed on the gain on the one-quarter of the apartment building which was the Riley's residence, because the adjusted sales price of this one-quarter ($23,600) is less than the cost of the new residence ($40,000). Thus, $2,600 of the gain is not currently taxable. The basis of the new residence, however, is reduced by this amount.

The $19,800 gain on the three-quarters of the apartment building that is rental property is taxed in the year of sale.

Conversion to Business Use

If a taxpayer actually rents his residence or uses his residence as an office, he has converted the relevant portion to a business use. However, there may be a question in some situations. For example, if a taxpayer is transferred to another state and he just offers his home for sale, it would be difficult to show a production of income use. However, if he offers the home for rent, he would be converting it to business use.

Allocation of Expenses

The use of a portion of a residence for business use or for production-of-income use allows the taxpayer to apportion expenses to the business portion and deduct them. The amount allocable to the personal portion, of course, is not deductible.

Operating expenses. If a portion of the residence is rented, amounts of expenses that relate solely to the rental portion are completely deductible. Similarly, if a portion of the house is used as an office, those expenses which relate solely to that office are wholly deductible. Expenses which relate both to the income-production portion and to the personal portion must be allocated on a number-of-rooms basis or a square-footage basis.

If a television set was used in the personal portion of the residence, there would be no deduction on costs of repairs of this set. However, if the television set was solely for the use of a tenant of the rented portion of the residence, a repair bill on this set would be entirely deductible.

Assume that the heating, electricity, and water bills for the year amount to $600, and also that two-thirds of the residence, measured by square feet or per room, is rented. In this case, one-third, or $200, is nondeductible and two-thirds, or $400, is deductible.

Interest and property taxes. Recall that a taxpayer may not itemize his deductions if he chooses the standard deduction. If a portion of his residence is used for the production of income or as an office, he may deduct the allocable portion as a business or production-of-income expense, even if he takes the standard deduction. If he itemizes, he may also take the personal amount.

Rosenthal pays $1,000 in interest and property taxes on a duplex. He lives in one unit and rents the other. Assume that he elects the standard deduction. In this case, he may deduct $500 of the interest and property taxes in computing income from rents and royalties. Because he does not itemize, he may not deduct the other $500.

Let us change the situation and assume that Rosenthal does itemize his deductions. Then $500 of the interest and property taxes is a deduction in arriving at income from rents and royalties, and $500 is deducted as an itemized deduction.

Items of deduction. Expenses directly and soley attributable to the rental portion or business portion, such as the cost of painting, or installing a separate business phone, may be fully deducted. Depreciation and an allocation of general household expenses, such as light, heat, repairs, mortgage interest, and taxes, are also deductible.

Method of allocation. Allocation may be either on a per-room basis or a square-foot basis, whichever reflects actual use. The portion of depreciation, and other costs incurred in maintaining the residence, which is properly attributable to the space used in business is a question of fact. The per-room and per-square-foot methods of allocation are not the only methods which may be used. Any other method which is reasonable under the circumstances will be acceptable.

For example, assume that a professional man uses one room of his eight-room house as an office. If he used the room basis, he can deduct one-eighth of his general household expenses. However, assume that he measures the room and finds that it amounts to 400 square feet of a total of 2,400 square feet of floor space in his home. The use of the per-square-foot method means that his deduction is one-sixth of the operating costs.

Use room as office part time. Assume that a taxpayer uses the rumpus room two hours a night for company work, and that it is used by the family the rest of the time. The Revenue Service suggests a comparison of the average number of hours of use as an office in comparison with the total number of hours in the day. Here only one-twelfth of the expenses attributable to the rumpus room are deductible, and if the rumpus room is one out of six in the home and the per-room method of allocation is used, only one-seventy-second of the general household expenses are deductible. There are six rooms, and he uses one of the six rooms two out of 24 hours a day ($1/6 \times 2/24 = 1/72$). The taxpayer, however, may claim a deduction on the basis of actual hours of usage for business compared with the total hours of usage for business and personal use. For example, if the room were used for four hours a day for business and two hours by the family, then a taxpayer might attempt to claim a deduction for two-thirds of the expenses allocable to the room.

Depreciation

If an entire residence is rented out, depreciation on the entire residence would be deductible. If there is part personal and part business or income-producing use, then there must be an allocation.

Assume that a residence costs $60,000 and has a useful life of 40 years. On the straight-line basis, depreciation would be $1,500 per year. If only one-third of the residence is put to income-producing use, the deduction would be $500 per year, and

the basis would be reduced by $500 per year. Thus, the basis at
the end of the first year would be $59,500. Note that the depre-
ciation on the personal two-thirds is not deductible, and also that
it does not reduce the basis of the residence.

Methods. Either the straight-line method or the 150-per-
cent-declining-balance method may be used if a residence is converted to business use. The declining-balance method at twice the
straight-line rate may also be used, provided that either of the
following requirements are met: (1) it was constructed after 1953
or (2) it was acquired new after 1953 and the first use, whether it
was personal or income-producing, began with the taxpayer.

In a particular situation, the requirements for the declining-
balance method at twice the straight-line rate may not be met.
However, this method may be used for the cost of post-1953 improvements and additions even if it cannot be used on the residence.

For example, a taxpayer buys a house to rent. It is a used
house; thus, he cannot meet the requirements for the declining-
balance rate at twice the straight-line rate on the residence. However, he puts on a new roof. Then he may use this method for depreciating the roof.

Converted residence. If a residence was first used as a
residence and then later put to income-production use, the basis
for depreciation is the lower of the following: (1) adjusted basis
at date of conversion, or (2) fair market value at date of conversion.

For example, Rohrer purchases a residence costing $40,000
and adds a room at the cost of $10,000. His adjusted basis is thus
$50,000. Now he converts the residence to income-producing use
by renting it out. The fair market value of the house is only $44,000.
Because this is less than the adjusted basis at date of conversion,
this is the figure used for computing depreciation.

Let us change the situation and assume that the house is
worth $60,000 at the date of conversion. Then the basis for de-
preciation would be the adjusted basis at date of conversion ($50,000).

Home Used Partly for Business

In certain situations, there is not much question that a portion of a residence is used for production of income or in a trade
or business. Examples would be the rental of a portion of the
residence, and the use of a portion of the residence as an office
by a professional man or an independent contractor. However,
fairly strict requirements must be met in the case of employees.

An employee may deduct a proportionate share of maintenance and depreciation expenses on his home provided that he is
required to provide space and facilities as a condition of employment and provided that he can prove that he uses his home regularly to perform his employment duties.

The theory is that a company will ordinarily provide an
employee with a place to work, so that the cost of an office away
from the company's office is for the employee's personal con-
venience. However, if an employee meets the requirements, he
may get the deduction.

For example, a district sales manager who lives a distance
from the home office of his company and uses a room in his home
as an office would qualify if there were no separate branch office
in his city.

A second office may, however, sometimes qualify. This
assumes that the employee uses a part of his home for business
purposes regularly, not occasionally, and that he works at home
as a condition of his employment.

The facts of the circumstances govern, and in one case a
taxpayer was allowed a deduction for his office at home even though
his employer supplied him with an office on its premises and the
employer did not require him to do the work at home.

Burden of proof. The burden of proof rests upon the taxpayer to establish the following. Records should be maintained to
provide the data necessary to compute the amount of the deduction
in accordance with the allocation rules. Canceled checks, receipts,
and other evidence should be retained.

The factors to be established are: (1) as a condition of employment there is a requirement to provide space and facilities for
performance of some of the employment duties; (2) part of the home
is regularly used for this purpose; (3) the portion of the residence
used for business purposes; (4) extent of such use; (5) pro-rata
portion of depreciation and expenses for maintaining residence
which is properly attributable to such use.

COOPERATIVE APARTMENTS

In a cooperative apartment, a taxpayer is not really an
owner but rather a tenant-shareholder. As we have already mentioned, a tenant-shareholder in a cooperative may deduct interest
and taxes as itemized deductions just as the owner of a residence
may do. He may also benefit from the postponement of tax on gain
on sale of residence if he meets the requirements that we discussed

earlier in this chapter. The over-65-years-old benefits also apply.

Used for Business or Production of Income

A tenant-shareholder of a cooperative apartment may lease his apartment to someone else. Alternatively, he may use his apartment in his trade or business in a way similar to what we have discussed with residences. If there is partial business and partial personal use, the allocation rules for expenses that we have discussed earlier will apply. There are, however, some special considerations involved in computing depreciation.

Depreciation on Cooperative Apartment Stock

Depreciation deductions may be taken for trade or business use or production-of-income use for taxable years beginning after December 31, 1961. The basis for depreciation depends on whether the taxpayer is the original buyer or whether he buys in later.

Original buyer. If the taxpayer is the original buyer, then the cooperative's actual basis for the building is the starting point. For example, assume that Ross purchases a cooperative apartment with the intention of leasing it out. He is the original buyer in a new cooperative.

Ross owns 100 shares of the 1,000 shares outstanding in the cooperative (including treasury stock). The cooperative basis for the building is $400,000 and that for the land is $100,000. Assuming straight-line depreciation and a 50-year life for the building, Ross' depreciation is determined as follows:

Basis of the building to the cooperative	$400,000
Less salvage	40,000
Cooperative's basis for depreciation	$360,000
Depreciation on $360,000 (fifty-year life)	$ 7,200
Deduction for Ross (100/1000 x $7,200)	$ 720

Assuming that the apartment was held for rental or rented for the entire year, Ross will have a depreciation deduction of $720. Note that, for the original buyer, the deduction is the taxpayer's ratio of his shares to the total shares of the cooperative times the cooperative's basis for the building.

Not original buyer. If the taxpayer is not the original buyer, a different basis is computed. This is probably best illustrated by an example.

Assume that Robinson purchases shares in a cooperative on the first of the year. He pays $300 a share for 100 shares of the cooperative. There are a total of 20,000 shares outstanding in the cooperative, including any treasury stock. The basis for depreciation is calculated as follows:

Per share price ($300) times shares outstanding (20,000)	$ 6,000,000
Cooperatives' balance of mortgage principal at time of purchase of shares	4,000,000
Total "as if" basis for land and building	$10,000,000
"Basis" attributable to land	1,000,000
"Basis" allocable to building	$ 9,000,000
Less: Estimated salvage	600,000
Cooperative's "as if" basis for depreciation	$ 8,400,000

Robinson owns a total of 1/200th of the shares of the cooperative. He has 100 shares out of 20,000. Assume that the straight-line method of depreciation is used, and that the remaining useful life of the building at the time of the stock purchase is 30 years. Robinson thus has a depreciation deduction for the year of $1,400. This is $8,400,000 divided by 30 years ($280,000) times 1/200th.

The tenant-shareholder's basis for depreciation, thus, is based on the sum of the fair market value of the shares of the cooperative at the time of purchase plus the principal balance of the mortgage at time of purchase. This result is reduced for salvage on the building and also by the portion attributable to the land.

Conversion from personal use. In the case of a situation in which the taxpayer first used the property as a residence and then later used it for rental purposes or for an office, the basis for depreciation is: (1) basis as computed above; or (2) fair market value at date of conversion, whichever is lower. Fair market value may be computed by taking the original basis as determined above and computing straight-line depreciation for the years of personal use.

For example, assume that Robinson used his apartment for two years and then converted it to business or production-of-income use. Two years' depreciation on the $8,400,000 at $280,000 a year is $560,000, which leaves a balance of $7,840,000 for fair market value. The depreciation deduction for Robinson is still $1,400. This is the $7,840,000 divided by the remaining life of 28 years times 1/200 to get Robinson's share.

Commercial tenants. If part of the cooperative apartment is rented out to a commercial tenant, then the basis for depreciation is reduced accordingly. For example, the first floor of a cooperative may be rented out to a drugstore or similar enterprise. If the floor space occupied by the commercial tenant is one-twentieth of the floor space in the cooperative apartment, then the basis, as we have computed, would be reduced by one-twentieth.

Accelerated depreciation. A taxpayer may use accelerated depreciation rather than straight-line depreciation if the corporation qualifies for its use. Note that the tenant may use accelerated depreciation if the cooperative could use it, even though it does not. In order to qualify, the building had to be constructed after 1953 and the cooperative corporation had to be the first user. It is not necessary, however, that the taxpayer be the first owner of the particular stock. Also, it does not matter what methods are used by the other stockholders.

CONDOMINIUMS

Recall that a condominium purchaser receives a deed to his own apartment. He also receives an undivided share in the halls, elevators, heating equipment, and other facilities which relate to the whole building. A condominium buyer can mortgage his own condominium. Thus, different owners in a particular building may have different mortgages on their condominiums.

The tenant-shareholder in a cooperative does not own his apartment. He owns shares in the cooperative corporation. If a tenant shareholder cannot meet the maintenance charges, he may attempt to sublease the apartment. If he cannot sublease, he may sell his shares and be replaced by a new tenant-shareholder who is approved by the corporation. Because there is no personal liability for the corporation's debts, presumably the tenant-shareholder at worst could surrender his shares and walk away from the apartment.

A condominium owner, however, could not escape his obligations by abandonment. He is liable on his own mortgage and for the common maintenance costs of the building. Decision making for major repairs is probably easier in a cooperative than in a condominium. In a cooperative, it is usually a majority of the shares or directors, whereas in a condominium unanimous consent may be necessary.

Similar Benefits to Homeowners

Condominium owners may deduct mortgage interest and realty taxes in the same manner as homeowners may. The postponement of tax benefits is also available to condominium owners. These are benefits that we discussed earlier in this chapter which allow postponement of gain when a homeowner sells his residence at a gain and reinvests his proceeds in a new residence within the required time period.

Chapter 10

Ownership Forms

ALTERNATIVES IN OWNERSHIP OF REAL PROPERTY

There are a variety of ways that property may be owned. The choice of the form of ownership will be influenced by a variety of factors, and the tax factor is often an important one.

An individual may own property solely in his own name, or he may own it in joint tenancy or in tenancy in common. Alternatively, a partnership or corporation may be formed to own the property. And in some cases, where a corporation owns the property, it will be desirable to elect not to be taxed as a corporation. In this chapter we shall explore the ownership of property in the partnership form. We shall discuss other forms in general first.

Corporate or Individual Ownership

Income from property owned by a corporation is taxed to the corporation at corporate tax rates; these rates currently are 22 per cent of the first $25,000 of corporate income and 48 per cent of the balance. Contrast this with individual tax rates, which currently run from 14 to 70 per cent. In addition, state and corporate tax rates increase the tax burden.

Dividend distributions to a shareholder by a corporation are reported as income even though the corporation paid a tax at the corporate level. The corporation form may be advantageous tax-wise, however, if the object is to accumulate income and reinvest it rather than to distribute it. However, corporate income accumulations of above $100,000 must meet certain requirements or may possibly be subject to an accumulated-earnings penalty tax, as is described in the chapter on corporations. Also, the property owner, in considering the corporate form of ownership, must realize that a sale of his interest in the corporation or the liquidation of the corporation will normally result in an additional capital-gain tax.

Indications for Choice of Corporate Form

Although many factors are involved, the situations discussed below indicate that the corporate form may be desirable. Note that this does not mean that the corporate form is the right one; rather, it means that the projected advantages and disadvantages of the corporate form should be analyzed in comparison with alternative forms of ownership.

If the corporate income tax rate is substantially below the individual's marginal tax rate, it may be desirable for property income to be taxed to the corporation and earnings retained rather than have the property income taxed directly to the individual. This effect will be partially a function of whether the retention of earnings can be justified and the accumulated-earnings tax avoided. If earnings are taxed to the corporation and dividends are not declared, then there is only one immediate tax. Eventually it may be possible to sell the stock or to liquidate the corporation so that earnings are realized at capital-gain rates; the total of corporate tax plus the capital-gains tax may be less, in some cases, than the individual's personal tax rate. In order to forecast the result, it is necessary to project the property earnings and consider the tax effect under the various alternatives. Where an individual shareholder manages the real estate, a salary is allowable as a deduction in arriving at corporate income. In this manner, the salary is taxed only once at the individual level.

If unimproved real estate is involved, then the corporate form may be desirable, because qualification for the benefits of Section 1231 is more easily obtainable. Section 1231 involves capital gains and losses on trade and business property, and is discussed in detail in the chapter on capital gains.

Some corporations can qualify as "small business corporations" under Section 1244 of the Internal Revenue Code. This section allows qualifying corporations to qualify their stock for ordinary loss treatment. Another use of the corporate form would be for an individual who deals in real estate; thus, it is important to have a definite separation of property held for investment purposes from "inventory" property.

Indications for Choice of Individual Form

The situation discussed below may indicate that individual ownership is preferable. Again, a careful analysis of all the factors needs to be made.

The projection of income from a property may indicate that the property will yield a taxable loss for a substantial period of time. If the property is owned by an individual, he will be able to offset part of his other income by this taxable loss.

In the corporation chapters, we discuss the possible pitfalls of a corporation being classified as a personal holding company and thus subject to a penalty tax. We also discuss the accumulated earnings tax which may be imposed in the case of "unreasonable accumulation of earnings." If either of these is a likely prospect for a corporation, then the individual-ownership form may be indicated. Another reason for not incorporating relates to the collapsible corporation rules, which we shall discuss later. These rules generally operate to cause ordinary income rather than capital-gain income.

Corporate Election to Have Income Taxed Directly to Shareholders

Corporations that meet certain requirements may elect to have their income taxed directly to the shareholders. Under this election, the corporate tax is avoided. However, this election is not generally available to the investor in real estate, because the election cannot be made if 20 per cent of the gross receipts are from sources such as rents, interest, and dividends. Details will be discussed later. Note, however, that income derived from the operation of a hotel or motel is not considered as disqualifying rent, even though such income included charges for lodging as well as for personal services.

Dummy Corporation

Sometimes real estate is acquired and title is taken in the name of a "dummy corporation." This may be done to avoid personal liability on mortgages, to conceal ownership, or to avoid liability for damages to persons or property. If a "dummy" is used, the parties involved report the income and deduct the losses themselves. The purpose of the "dummy" is merely to hold title; the "dummy" may be either an individual or a corporation.

Variety of Noncorporate Ownership

If ownership is strictly in the individual, then the question is, how should title be taken? When an individual combines with one or more associates in a real estate venture and the corporate form is decided against, then the determination must be made whether the partnership form is to be used, or whether the corporate form is to be used and an election made to have the income taxed directly to the shareholders. If it is to be a partnership, it

is necessary to determine whether all partners will be general partners or whether a limited parnership will be used. Syndicates often
operate as a limited partnership.

TITLE TO REAL ESTATE FOR INDIVIDUALS

When individuals acquire real estate, they must determine
whether they should hold title to that real estate as tenants by the
entirety, as joint tenants, or as tenants in common. The choice
has important tax implications in respect to income tax, estate tax,
and gift tax.

If two persons own property together with right of survivorship, they are joint tenants. If one passes away, his interest passes
to the survivor. Such property owned by a husband and wife is known
as a "tenancy by the entirety." Joint tenancies are often used in
investments involving family members, because the share of the
deceased passes directly to the surviving tenant.

Income Tax--Joint Tenants

From the standpoint of income tax, the majority of husbands
and wives file joint returns; therefore, joint or separate ownership
of property by married persons is often not too important. Rather,
other considerations, such as estate or gift tax implications, should
govern the choice.

If a husband and wife hold real estate as tenants by the entirety
and they file separate rather than joint returns, then a problem arises
as to how income and loss should be reported. The common-law rule
is that the husband shall receive all the income from the real estate.
However, some states hold that income from real estate is divided
between the husband and wife. The local law controls in the determination of how the income is to be reported.

When property is owned by joint tenants, each joint tenant
reports his proportionate share of gross income from the property.
The gross income is measured by the interest of the tenant in the
property. A joint tenant deducts his proportionate share of the expenses, provided that he pays his share. If one of the joint tenants
pays all the taxes on the real estate or all the mortgage interest,
then he must take the full deduction.

If the real estate is sold, each joint tenant is taxed on his
share of the gain or loss. Usually, joint tenants are presumed to
have equal undivided interests. Thus, gain or loss is divided e-
qually among the tenants.

Income Tax--Tenants in Common

If real estate is held in tenancy in common, then any income or loss from the operation of the real estate is reported according to the respective share of each tenant in common. If one tenant pays more than his proportionate share of expenses, he may deduct only his proportionate share. His proportionate share is measured by his interest in the property. Any excess is considered an advance to the co-owner. On the sale or other disposition of the real estate, the gain or loss is reported according to the respective shares of each tenant.

Whereas each joint tenant is liable personally for all of the expenses incurred on the property, a tenant in common is personally liable for only his proportionate share of the expense. This is reflected in the deductibility of expenses. As we noted above, if one joint tenant pays all the expenses, he may deduct the entire expenses. If a tenant in common pays the entire expenses, he may deduct only his share; the rest is considered an advance to his co-owner.

For example, Wilbur Martin and his son George own property as joint tenants. Wilbur pays $500 in real estate taxes; this is the entire amount of the real estate tax on the property. Wilbur has a deduction of $500 for real estate taxes, and George has none. Now, if we assume that the property was held by father and son, as tenants in common, then Wilbur and George would each have a deduction of $250. George would owe his father $250.

Not a Partnership for Tax Purposes

The above tenancies are not considered to be partnerships. Thus, if property is held in joint tenancy, tenancy in the entirety, or tenancy in common, an information return is not required. Rather, each of the co-owners reports directly on his income tax return his share of income and expenses.

Joint Tenancy--Estate Tax

When an individual dies, his assets are subject to an estate tax, provided that they are above a certain minimum. An important consideration in the choice of tenancy is the effect of the tenancy on the estate tax and the basis of the property to the heirs. The value of the entire property is included in the gross estate of a deceased joint tenant unless the survivor can show that he paid part of the cost of the property. If the survivor proves that he contributed a portion, then the amount representing his contribution is excluded from the gross estate. Property held by the owners as tenants by the entirety is subject to the same rules as property held jointly.

The basis of the property to the heirs is important because this amount will affect future gain or loss on disposition. For depreciable property, it will affect the amount of the depreciation allowance. Under the 1939 Internal Revenue Code, the survivor's tax basis for real estate remained unchanged. However, under the 1954 Internal Revenue Code the survivor has a basis for that portion of the real estate which was included in the decedent's estate at the value at which such property was included in the estate.

For example, assume that William Smythe and his wife Louise took title to their home as tenants by the entirety. William Smythe supplied the entire purchase price of $75,000. On William's death, the entire value of the home will be included in his gross estate. If Louise dies first, nothing will be included in her gross estate, as William can prove that he paid for the property.

Community Property--Estate Tax

Certain states, such as Arizona, California, Idaho, Louisiana Nevada, New Mexico, Texas, and Washington, have community-property laws. The theory of community property is based on the idea that the industry and labor of either or both have created the community estate, and that this estate belongs to both while they are married. It is dissolved, for example, upon the death of either spouse or upon divorce. Community property is included in the estate of a decedent only to the extent of the decedent's interest under the state law.

For example, Bernard and Beatrice Brown live in California. They own real estate which cost $50,000. At the time of their marriage, neither had significant funds and neither received separate property during their marriage. Each is considered to own one-half of the property, and on death half of the value of the community property at date of death or optional valuation date will be included in the decedent's estate. Note that in certain states it is possible for husband and wife to hold property as joint tenants but nevertheless make a community-property agreement so that the property is treated as community property.

Tenancy in Common--Estate Tax

Recall that, under a tenancy in common, each tenant has a fractional interest in the property with the right to use the whole property during his lifetime. The interest of a tenant in common may be bequeathed or devised by him. If a tenant in common dies without a will, the property descends to his heirs at law. Only the fractional interest of the decedent is included in his gross estate if the property was held as a tenant in common.

For example, the three Jenkins brothers inherited the Bar XXXX ranch as tenants in common. Benjamin received a one-half share, Emile received a one-third share, and Lucien received a one-sixth share. When Benjamin dies, one-half of the value of the Bar XXXX ranch will be included in his gross estate.

The new basis to the heirs or devisees is the value used for estate-tax purposes. Again the reader is referred to Chapter 2 for a full discussion of basis of property received from a decedent. Note also that the basis for federal income tax purposes may be different from that for state income tax purposes. Also, the amount included for state inheritance tax purposes may be different than the amount included for estate tax purposes.

Gift Tax Considerations

The term "gift" for gift tax purposes has a much broader meaning than in common usage. Every transfer of money or property, whether made as a sale or otherwise, from one person to another without adequate and full consideration in money or money's worth, is in whole or in part a gift within the meaning of the gift tax law, unless excepted. Gift tax liability generally arises where one joint tenant furnishes the entire cost. One-half of the cost is treated as a gift. In the case of a husband and wife, the creation of a joint tenancy in real property or a tenancy by the entirety does not result in immediate gift tax to the spouse who furnishes the majority of the consideration unless he elects to treat it as a gift at that time. If the one who supplies the funds does not elect to treat it as a gift immediately, there will be a taxable gift if the joint ownership is ended other than by death, unless the spouses divide the proceeds proportionately to their contributions. If a gift is made of a tenancy in common, the treatment is the same as for the gift of any other asset.

In determining the choice of title, both nontax as well as tax aspects should be considered. From a tax standpoint, the implications of federal estate tax, federal gift tax, and state inheritance tax should be considered, as well as the federal income tax implications.

PARTNERSHIPS IN GENERAL

The Internal Revenue Code defines a "partnership" as a common-law partnership, a syndicate, group, pool, joint venture, or any other unincorporated organization that carries on, directly or indirectly, any business, financial operation, or venture, and which is not a trust, estate, or corporation.

Partnerships are of particular interest in real estate because many real estate syndicates operate as limited partnerships. As we shall note later, real estate syndicates operating as limited partnerships may be taxed as corporations if certain factors are present.

A partnership does not pay an income tax. Rather, an information return is filed. The return indicates the amounts that the partners should include in their individual returns. The individual partners are liable for their share of the tax as individuals.

TAXABILITY OF GROUP ENTERPRISES

Groups of investors often join together to invest in real estate. How the organization is taxed depends on whether it more closely resembles a partnership, a corporation, or a trust. The classification is determined by the characteristics of the organization in each case. In our discussion of limited partnerships, we shall consider carefully the attributes of a corporation.

Associations

Associations are generally taxed as corporations. It is not necessary that there be an actual incorporation. An organization is taxed as a corporation if it more closely resembles a corporation than it resembles a trust or partnership.

Syndicates and Pools

A "syndicate" is generally defined as an association of individuals formed to conduct and carry on a particular business transaction. The syndicate is one of the prime ways by which small investors join together to invest in large-scale real estate investments.

A "pool" is an association of persons or a corporation engaged in a particular venture. Generally, all of the investors contribute to a fund placed in the control of a manager because the venture may be too risky or too large for an individual investor. Syndicates and pools may be taxed as partnership or as corporations, depending on which they more closely resemble.

Limited Partnerships

The taxable status of limited partnerships depends on the characteristics they have under the state law where they are created. Limited partnerships will be discussed in detail in the next chapter.

Tenants in Common

Tenants in common who own real estate, rent it out, and divide the profit are not considered to be in business as partners. However, if they actively carry on a trade, business, or venture and divide the profits, they are partners.

For example, Daniel Karr and Philip Quinn own both a farm and an apartment house as tenants in common. The farm is rented to a farmer by the name of Jones, and Daniel and Philip are not considered as partners. However, Daniel and Philip furnish maid service, catered meals, and other services to their tenants in the apartment house. Here they are considered as actively carrying on a business.

Partnership Associations

In several states, there is a distinct business form authorized called a "partnership association." This form is taxed as an association when it is more like a corporation than other types of organizations.

TAXABILITY OF PARTNERSHIP INCOME

The taxable income of a partnership is calculated in the same way as the taxable income of an individual--except that the partnership is not allowed to take certain deductions, and except that some income items are not considered for determination of partnership taxable income.

Deductions Not Allowed to a Partnership

A partnership in calculating its income is not allowed certain deductions. Some of these deductions are separated and are reported by the individual partners on their individual returns.

A partnership may not take the following deductions: (1) standard deduction; (2) deduction for personal exemptions; (3) deduction for foreign taxes; (4) deduction for charitable contributions; (5) net operating loss deduction; (6) deduction for long-term capital gains; (7) deduction for capital loss carryover; (8) certain individual itemized deductions, such as medical expenses, child-care expenses, deductible alimony, and taxes and interest paid to a cooperative housing corporation.

Items Not Figured in Determining Taxable Income

A partnership does not include certain items in calculating its taxable income. These items are segregated on the partnership return and are taken into account by the partners in figuring their individual income tax. They are taken into account whether distributed or not. These items are as follows: (1) short-term capital gains and losses; (2) long-term capital gains and losses; (3) Section 1231 gains or losses relating to certain property used in a trade or business or involuntary conversions; (4) charitable contributions; (5) interest on partially tax-exempt securities; (6) dividends received from certain domestic corporations; (7) taxes paid or accrued to foreign countries or possessions of the United States; (8) other items of income, gain, loss, deduction, or credit, to the extent prescribed by the Revenue Service.

Salaries and Interest Paid to Partners

Reasonable payments to partners for services or for the use of capital are deductible in arriving at taxable income if they are determined without regard to partnership income. Such salaries and interest must be reported as income by the partner in his own return. Note that these payments are not wages or interest for any other purpose. Thus, a partner receiving a salary is not considered an employee of the partnership for the purpose of withholding taxes, deferred compensation plans, or the sickness and accident pay exclusion.

Comparison of Book Income and Taxable Income

In order to illustrate the above, the income statement of the Seaside Hotel bar and restaurant is shown. The SeaSide Hotel is a partnership owned by Wilkins and Whiteside. Note the segregated income items and the deduction items not allowed.

Income statement. The income statement of the Wilkins and Whiteside partnership is as follows:

Sales		$316,418
Less: Cost of goods sold		173,618
Gross margin on sales		$142,800
Dividends received		1,000
Interest (wholly exempt)		3,200
Short-term capital gain		1,600
Long-term capital gain		4,400
Gross profit from operations		$153,000
Deduct:		
Charitable contributions	$ 3,000	
Partners' salaries ($20,000 for		
each partner)	40,000	$ 43,000
Net profit from operations		$110,000
Deduct interest on capital		10,000
Net profit for the year		$100,000

From this income statement, the taxable income of the Wilkins and Whiteside partnership is calculated as follows:
   Segregation.

Profit from income statement		$100,000
Capital gains and losses segregated:		
Gains on short-term transactions	$1,600	
Gains on long-term transactions	4,400	
Subtract net book gain (add back net book		
loss) on capital asset transactions		6,000
		$ 94,000
Income items segregated:		
Interest on wholly exempt obligations	$3,200	
Dividends received from domestic		
corporations	1,000	
Subtract total segregated income items		4,200
		$ 89,800
Deductions not allowed:		
Charitable contributions	$3,000	
Add back total deductions not allowed		3,000
Partnership's taxable income		$ 92,800

Tax Return. The taxable income and the segregated items of the partnership would appear on the return as follows:

Taxable income	$92,800
Net gain from short-term capital asset transactions	1,600
Net gain from long-term capital asset transactions	4,400
Dividends received from domestic corporations	1,000

PARTNERSHIP ITEMS INCLUDED
IN PARTNER'S INDIVIDUAL RETURNS

A partner includes in his own individual tax return his share of the partnership's taxable income or loss. He also includes his share of the other items that are not included in determining partnership income. These items were detailed above. Note that a partner must include in his tax return these items whether they were distributed to him or not, and he must include them even if he is on a cash basis and the partnership is on an accrual basis.

Consider, for example, the Brink and Loomis partnership. Earnings for the calendar year 1965 were $40,000. All taxpayers, as well as the partnership, are on the calendar-year basis. Both Brink and Loomis share equally in the earnings of the partnership. Neither Brink nor Loomis received any money from the partnership during the calendar year. Nevertheless, each must declare $20,000 as income from the partnership on his individual return.

Any item of income, loss, gain, deduction, or credit included in a partner's distributive share has the same character as if it were realized directly by the partner, except for the partnership's taxable income or loss. These are the items that are not included in determining the partnership income, but rather are segregated and picked up separately on the partner's individual return.

Thus, for example, the Brink and Loomis partnership sells depreciable property used in its business at a gain of $8,000. This property is considered to be a Section 1231 asset, and both Brink and Loomis are considered as receiving their share of this gain directly from the sale of the Section 1231 asset. This gain is not figured in determining the partnership taxable income. Rather, it is segregated, and the partners pick up their share of the gain on their tax returns. Some of this gain may be ordinary income under the depreciation-recapture rules.

Chapter 11

Limited Partnerships
and Real Estate Investment Trusts

SYNDICATES

Several parties often combine in order to invest in real estate. Some ventures require more capital than one party is able or willing to invest in one real estate venture. Diversification of risk or management considerations may be the reason why several individuals join together.

A "syndicate" is generally defined as an association of individuals formed to conduct and carry on a particular business transaction. Thus, a syndicate is not a distinct taxable entity. It may be a partnership, a corporation, or a trust. In this chapter we shall be concerned with two forms of organization which are used frequently in real estate investments. These are the limited partnership and the real estate investment trust.

After we have considered the use of limited partnerships and real estate investment trusts in real estate operations, we shall then consider another form of organization. This is the corporation that elects not to be taxed. These corporations, sometimes referred to as Subchapter S corporations, elect not to be taxed at the corporate level. The shareholders pay tax on their share of the income of the corporation in a manner similar to that of partners in a regular partnership. Corporations electing not to be taxed are not useful where rental income is an important source of income, because under such election no more than 20 per cent of the corporation's gross receipts can be from rent and other passive types of income, such as dividends and interest. As we shall see later, certain charges which are normally considered rent are not considered rent for this purpose when significant services are performed, as, for example in a hotel or motel.

LIMITED PARTNERSHIPS

The partnership arrangement allows the enterprise to avoid corporate income taxes. The partners are taxed only on their share of the partnership taxable income. The partnership itself does not pay a tax. The partner benefits from the depreciation to the extent of his interest in the partnership. If there is a taxable loss, this loss may be used to offset other income.

Depending on the characteristics of the enterprise, a limited partnership may be classified as an ordinary partnership or as an association taxable as a corporation. Note that a partnership may be taxed as a corporation if it more closely resembles a corporation than a partnership. The taxable status of limited partnerships depends on the characteristics that they have under the state law where they are created. The danger that a limited partnership will be taxed as a corporation will be discussed shortly.

Advantages of Limited-Partnership Syndicates

Syndicates are most often operated to minimize federal income taxes. Each partner in effect receives a pro-rata share of the tax-deductible depreciation allowance. When the depreciation deduction is greater than the amortization on the mortgage, the excess in a sense shelters part of the earnings from the property. The relationship of the depreciation deduction and mortgage amortization determines the amount of the investor's tax-free return.

Assume that a group of 10 investors join together to purchase a warehouse. Taxable income is computed as follows:

Net income after operating expenses but before depreciation	$200,000
Depreciation	160,000
Taxable income	$ 40,000

Cash available for distribution is determined:

Cash inflow from operations	$200,000
Amortization of mortgage	80,000
	$120,000

Each of the 10 investors would receive cash distributions of $12,000. Of the $12,000, only $4,000 is taxable. Each of the 10 partners reports one-tenth of the $40,000 taxable income of the partnership.

Avoiding decreasing yields. Mortgage payments are often equal annual amounts. As time passes, the amount of amortization of principal increases and the interest portion of the mortgage payment decreases. The result is less interest deductions for tax purposes and higher taxable income.

Where accelerated depreciation has been employed, the longer the property has been in operation, the less the depreciation deductions. And, of course, everything else being equal, the lower the depreciation deduction, the higher the taxable income.

As taxable income increases because of lower depreciation deductions and lower interest deductions, the syndicate may attempt to refinance the mortgage to decrease the amount of the payment that is amortization of principal. Other syndicates may find that it is desirable to sell the property.

Actual loss of value greater than tax depreciation. The concept of a tax-free return is based on the idea that the depreciation deductions for tax purposes are greater than the actual decline in market value of the property. Obviously, if the property turns out to be a poor choice and the loss in market value exceeds the depreciation deductions, then the investor is getting his own capital back.

Disadvantages of Limited-Partnership Syndicates

The danger of being taxed as a corporation, which will be discussed in the next section, is an important one. In addition, the limited partnership does not have the following advantages which may be available in the corporate form or in the real estate investment trust. The latter forms of organization can achieve diversification of risk among a number of holdings. These holdings can be spread out geographically and may include more than one kind of property. Usually a syndicate has only one real estate holding. Professional management available on a continuing basis can more easily be obtained in a large enterprise. When more properties are obtained, high depreciation allowances on one property may be used to offset high taxable income on the other properties. Limited partnerships do not provide for the free transfer of the individual investor's interest, as does a corporation. Also, corporate stock is more likely to be marketable than is an interest in a syndicate.

Problem of Being Taxed as a Corporation

Basically, there are two kinds of partnerships. These are general partnerships, which we discussed in a previous chapter, and limited partnerships. State law usually provides that the limited partners in a limited partnership have limited liability. Thus, the liability of the limited partners is limited to the amount of their capital contributions to the partnership.

As was noted previously, the partnership form is often used in real estate syndicates because it avoids the double taxation of the corporate form and because it passes the depreciation deductions through to the individual investors. In order to improve the functioning of the partnership, it may be desirable to have some of the powers and attributes of the corporate form. Here is the danger; too many corporate characteristics may result in taxation as a corporation. And, if the end result is taxation as a corporation, it would have been better to establish a corporation in the beginning in order to obtain the other advantages of the corporate form. The general rule is that a partnership may be taxed as a corporation if it more closely resembles a corporation than a partnership.

Association problem. According to the Internal Revenue Code, "corporations" are defined to include associations, joint-stock companies, and insurance companies. "Partnerships" include any unincorporated organization which carries on "any business, financial operation, or venture" and which, within the meaning of the Internal Revenue Code, is neither a trust, estate, nor corporation. Thus, it appears for tax purposes that an organized group doing business is either a partnership, an association, or a trust.

The word "association" is not defined by the code. Thus, a problem arises as to whether a partnership is an "association," and thus taxable as a corporation, or an unincorporated organization, in which case it will be taxable as a partnership. For guidance it is necessary to look to the Regulations and to the important cases.

Tests for corporate taxability. The Supreme Court in the landmark case of Morrissey v. Commissioner determined that an alleged trust was in fact an association and thus taxable as a corporation. It was in this case that the Court enunciated the guiding principles generally applicable today; these principles are the basis for the criteria set out in the Regulations.

The Regulations provide that whether a particular organization is to be classified as an association must be determined by taking into account the presence or absence of each of these corporate characteristics. They are as follows:

1. Associates
2. An objective to carry on business and divide the gains therefrom
3. Continuity of life
4. Centralization of management
5. Limited liability
6. Free transferability of interests

The corporate characteristics customarily associated with the other organization involved will be disregarded. Thus, where the other organization involved is a partnership, the following partnership characteristics would be disregarded: (1) associates; (2) an objective to carry on business and divide the gains therefrom. The analysis would center on the four remaining characteristics: (1) continuity of life; (2) centralization of management; (3) limited liability; and (4) free transferability of interests.

Must have more corporate characteristics. All four of the corporate characteristics are not required to be present to establish the corporate resemblance. If the enterprise has fewer than the four corporate characteristics, then the features of similarity and dissimilarity must be weighed to see which form it most closely resembles. If the business more nearly resembles a partnership, it should be taxable as such. If the characteristics are fairly well balanced between corporation and partnership resemblance, other factors may be considered. Both the method of operation of the enterprise and the organization agreement will be examined in determining whether the criteria are present.

Criteria of continuity of life. "Continuity of life" of an organization means that the organization automatically continues independently of changes in its individual membership. In determining whether any member of a partnership has the power of dissolution, it is necessary to examine the partnership agreement and to ascertain the effect of the agreement under local law. If, notwithstanding the provisions of the agreement, any member has the power under local law to dissolve the organization, then the organization lacks continuity of life.

A general partnership subject to a statute corresponding to the Uniform Partnership Act and a limited partnership subject to a statute corresponding to the Uniform Limited Partnership Act which is in force in California specify occasions for dissolution, and thus unlimited life is not present.

Centralized management. According to the Regulations, limited partnerships subject to a statute corresponding to the Uniform Limited Partnership Act generally do not have centralized management, but centralized management ordinarily does exist in such a limited partnership if substantially all of the interests in the partnership are owned by the limited partners. Thus, a large-scale limited partnership might well be considered to have centralized management.

Limited liability. Limited liability, to be corporate in nature, must relate to all of the members of the organization. Thus, generally a limited partnership organized under a statute corresponding to the Limited Partnership Act does not have the characteristics of limited liability, as the general partner's liability is not limited to his contributions to the partnership.

If, however, the general partner has no substantial assets other than his interest in the partnership and is merely a "dummy" acting as the agent of the limited partners, then the limited-liability characteristics would be present. Even if he has no substantial assets other than his interest in the partnership, he still has personal liability if he is not a "dummy." It does not make any difference whether the partners that are personally liable contributed services or capital to the partnership for their interest.

Free transferability of interests. This characteristic exists if each member of those owning substantially all the interests in the organization has the power to substitute another. The power of an individual to transfer his interest must be without the consent of the other parties in the syndicate.

Transferability would not exist if a partner could assign only his right to share in the profits but not his right to participate in the management of the organization. Transferability would not exist if under State law a transfer of an individual's share would result in dissolution of the old organization and formation of a new one.

Planning to avoid the association problem. Based on the criteria set forth above, it is desirable wherever possible to form a limited partnership under the Uniform Limited Partnership Act. Even though it is possible for all partners to have limited liability under the particular local state law, it may still be desirable for one or more partners to have unlimited liability.

Care should be taken when the general partners do not have substantial assets invested in the operation. If there are any transferable interests, they should be those of the limited partners and not the interests of the general partners.

A limited partnership formed under the Uniform Limited Partnership Act will not have continuity and, unless the general partners have no substantial assets and are "dummies," it also will not have limited liability. Thus two, of the four corporate characteristics are absent, and it should be recalled that, in order to be taxed as a corporation, an association must have more corporate characteristics than noncorporate characteristics. If there is danger that the general partners might be considered "dummies," the partnership agreement could be drawn in a manner to limit transferability.

The "Trust" Form for a Syndicate

Except for the special situation of the Real Estate Investment Trust discussed subsequently, the trust is not a particularly desirable form for a syndicate. The "trust" form is one that is particularly susceptible to being taxed as an association.

REAL ESTATE INVESTMENT TRUSTS

The real estate investment trust is a relatively new form of organization for real estate investments. Since 1941, regulated investment companies have had special tax advantages. These are corporations which basically purchase and sell securities and receive interest and dividends and are commonly known as "mutual funds." The basic result of Sections 856-858 of the Internal Revenue Code is to create a new taxable entity, the real estate investment trust, and to give those trusts which qualify tax advantages similar to those presently enjoyed by regulated investment companies.

Taxation of the Real Estate Investment Trust

A qualified real estate investment trust, hereafter referred to as "trust," that distributes 90 per cent or more of its income will not be taxed on that portion of the income that it distributes. Of course, there are other forms of taxable entities, such as partnerships, that are not subject to double taxation. But the advantages of corporate organization, such as centralized management, limited liability, continuity of interest, and transferability of ownership, are available to the trust without the penalty of double taxation.

For example, compare the Magnum Realty Company as a corporation and as a real estate investment trust.

	Corporation	Investment Trust
Income	$800,000	$800,000
Expenses	400,000	400,000
Income before tax	$400,000	$400,000
Corporation tax	200,000	--
Net income	$200,000	$400,000

A 50 per cent tax rate has been assumed in the above example for simplicity. Note that, assuming that its entire income is distributed, the real estate investment trust pays no tax as a business entity. Dividends received by the shareholders of a corporation are taxable to the recipients in their own tax returns. Assuming that the qualifications are met, and that all income is distributed, the income of the trust is taxable only to the recipients.

Taxability of the trust. If a trust distributes all of its ordinary income, there will be no tax at the trust level. If it distributes 90 per cent or more of its ordinary income, the trust will pay tax on the balance of the income retained. The 90 per cent requirement is exclusive of capital gains. If it does not distribute 90 per cent, then it will be taxed at the corporate tax rates of 22 per cent of the first $25,000 and 48 per cent of the balance.

A capital-gain tax of 25 per cent will be paid on the excess of net long-term capital gain over net short-term capital losses if the capital gains are retained by the trust. The trust, however, may distribute the capital gains to the trust beneficiaries and avoid this tax.

Tax differences between the trust and regulated investment companies. Mutual funds can elect to have capital-gain income which is not distributed treated as if it was distributed. In this manner, the shareholder would pay the capital-gain tax even though the mutual fund retained the capital gain. A real estate investment trust cannot do this.

Whereas ordinary dividends of a mutual fund are subject to the dividend exclusion and, prior to 1965, a dividend credit also, distributions of a trust do not receive this benefit. Also, a real estate investment trust cannot pass on a foreign tax credit to its beneficiaries, as can be done by a mutual fund.

Taxation of the beneficiaries of the trust. Distributions received by beneficiaries of a trust may be either ordinary income or capital gains. If a trust has capital gains and distributes them to the beneficiaries, these remain capital gains in the investors' hands and, if they are long-term capital gains, they are subject to a maximum tax rate of 25 per cent. When a beneficiary of the trust receives a capital-gains dividend, it is always a long-term capital gain dividend regardless of the beneficiary's holding period.

Dividends declared and paid after the close of a tax year. Cash-basis taxpayers report dividends in the year in which they receive them. This is true even in the case of the following special election of a real estate investment trust: this allows a trust to treat certain dividends as paid in the prior year for the purposes of determining whether the trust distributed 90 per cent or more of its earnings. The election must be made in the trust's return for the year to which the election applied.

For example, assume that the Hercules Real Estate Investment Trust has taxable income of $200,000 in 1965. During the year 1965 it distributes $176,000. Now assume that the Hercules Trust declares an ordinary dividend of $60,000 on February 10, 1966 and pays it on April 15, 1966. When the Hercules Trust files its 1965 tax return, it may elect to treat $24,000 of the $60,000 as paid during 1965. The remaining $36,000 is treated as dividends paid during 1966.

Note, of course, that the amount subject to the election is limited to the earnings and profits of the year to which the election applies and which were not distributed during that year. Recall that Hercules had $200,000 income in 1965 and distributed only $176,000. Thus, $24,000 paid in 1966 was subject to the election. As would be expected, the $24,000 considered as distributed in 1965 may not be used again in 1966 to determine whether the trust meets the 90 per cent requirement in 1966.

The election for dividends paid after the close of the taxable year also applies to capital gains. Assume that the Hercules Trust had $100,000 net capital gain in excess of net short-term capital loss in 1965. Also assume that, in 1965, $50,000 capital-gains dividends were distributed. If, in 1966, Hercules declares and pays a capital-gain dividend of $20,000, it may elect to treat $70,000 as capital-gain dividends distributed in 1965. This is the $50,000 actually distributed in 1965 and the $20,000 distributed in 1966 applied to 1965. The trust would pay a 25 per cent capital-gains tax for the year 1965 on the difference between the $100,000 capital gains and the $70,000 considered as distributed in 1965. The amount subject to this election is limited to the difference between the actual amount of excess of long-term capital gain over net short-term capital loss minus the amount distributed in that year. Thus, if Hercules paid $60,000 in 1966, it could elect to have only $50,000 treated as paid in 1965. $50,000 of the $100,000 actually was distributed in 1965.

Qualifications--General

Requirements for qualifications as a real estate investment trust are set forth in the Internal Revenue Code and the Regulations. Four basic groups of tests must be met. These are: (1) status requirements; (2) gross income requirements; (3) investment requirements; (4) distribution requirements. For example, the requirement of distribution of 90 per cent of taxable income is a distribution requirement.

If all requirements are met, the trust is taxed only on its undistributed income. Because the real estate investment trust is a relatively new taxable entity, care must be taken that expert professional advice is obtained.

Method of election. A trust makes an election by computing its taxable income as a real estate investment trust in its return for the first taxable year for which it wishes the election to apply. Once made, the election is irrevocable for that and all succeeding taxable years.

Status Requirements

Certain status or structural requirements are requisite to qualification. These requirements relate to ownership of the trust and purpose of the trust.

(a) The beneficial ownership of the members of the trust must be evidenced by transferable shares or transferable certificates of beneficial interest. Note that this requirement means that the certificate of beneficial interest may be very much like a share of common stock. This requirement facilitates the trading of shares of beneficial interest. Recall that a partnership or limited partnership runs the danger of being taxed as a corporation if it has too many attributes of a corporation, and one of these was free transferability of interests.

Ownership. There must be at least 100 or more persons that own the trust for at least 335 days during a tax year of 12 months. "Persons" for this purpose would include individuals, trusts, estates, partnerships, associations, or corporations. The minimum number of 100 shareholders must be met continuously during the life of the trust as well as at the inception of the trust.

No five individuals may own, directly or indirectly, more than 50 per cent in value of the organization's outstanding shares during the last six months of its tax year. In determining the holdings of the five individuals who hold the largest amount of shares, the trust must attribute to them shares held by certain family members and partnerships and corporations in which they own an interest.

Management. Management of the trust must be located in the hands of one or more trustees holding legal title to the property of the organization. These trustees must have exclusive authority over the management of the trust, the conduct of its affairs, and the management and disposition of its property.

Other organizational requirements. The trust must not hold property primarily for sale to customers in the ordinary course of its trade or business. In addition, the trust must possess all the necessary attributes which would, but for the special rules applying to trusts, result in its being taxed as a domestic corporation.

Gross Income Requirements

A trust must meet three tests concerning the source of its income in order to qualify. If it fails to meet any of these gross income tests, its income will be subject to tax as corporate income even though it meets all the other requirements to qualify as a real estate investment trust.

Ninety per cent test. At least 90 per cent of the trust's gross income must be from: (1) dividends; (2) interest; (3) rents from real property; (4) gains on sale of stock, securities, real property, and interests in mortgages on real property; and (5) abatements and refunds of real property taxes.

Seventy-five per cent test. At least 75 per cent of the trust's gross income must be from: (1) rents from real property; (2) interest on obligations secured by mortgages on real property; (3) gain from the sale of real property, including interest in real property and in mortgages on real property, and transferable shares in other qualified real estate investment trusts; (4) dividends or other distributions on transferable shares in other qualified real estate investment trusts; and (5) abatements and refunds of taxes on real property.

In the case of a mortgage which covers both real and other property, the trust must make an apportionment of this interest for purposes of this test.

Thirty per cent test. Gains from stock or securities held less than six months and from sales of real property held less than four years must be less than 30 per cent of the trust's gross income. These are gains not offset by any losses. Condemnations or other involuntary conversions of real property are not included.

Effect of above requirements. The 90 per cent test above limits the amount of income which a trust can get from active activities, such as broker's fees, loan commissions, and services, to 10 per cent. The 75 per cent test requires the trust to earn the majority of its income from real estate investments. Note that income on securities and gains from the sales of securities are not included for the 75 per cent test. The 30 per cent test in effect prevents a large amount of short-term securities trading. This test also means that most real property will be purchased for the purpose of production of income rather than for resale.

Meaning of "rents from real property." Rents from real property were included in both the 90 per cent and the 75 per cent test. This term needs elaboration. The basic idea of the real estate investment trust is that it channels funds into investment and earns income from these investments. This is to be contrasted with earning income from performance of services. Basically, rent meets the 75 and 90 per cent tests when it is payment for the use of property, as contrasted with fees for services performed.

Rents based on profits. Rents do not qualify if they depend in whole or in part on the income or profits derived by any person from the property. They are not disqualified, however, if they depend on a fixed percentage of receipts or sales, because the measure of gross receipts or sales is more a measure of the extent that the property is used rather than a measure of profitability.

For example, rental income from a lease to a department store based on a fixed percentage of sales from different departments might qualify as rents. However, if a trust leased property under an agreement where rental income is based on the tenant's gross receipts and the tenant then subleases the property for a rental based on a percentage of the sublessee's income, the amounts received by the trust would not qualify. This requirement tends to keep the trusts out of the active conduct of business.

Rents where trust owns interest in tenant. Certain rents do not qualify if a trust owns 10 per cent or more interest in the tenant. This would include 10 per cent or more interest in the voting stock or all the outstanding stock of a corporation. It would also include 10 per cent or more interest in the assets or profits in a person other than a corporation.

For example, assume that the Hercules Trust leases a department-store building to a tenant for a yearly rental of $100,000. The lessee, in turn, subleases the building to several subtenants and receives rental income of $500,000. Now assume that Hercules owns 15 per cent of the assets of the furniture department concessionaire, who paid rent of $50,000 to the lessee. Now, Hercules Trust received $100,000 rental income from the lessee. However, $10,000 ($50,000/$500,000) of the rent received does not qualify for purposes of the gross income tests.

Trust operates property or renders services to tenants. Amounts do not qualify as rents if the trust furnished or renders services to the tenants. Rents do not qualify if the trust manages or operates the property other than through an independent contractor from whom the trust itself does not derive or receive any income.

The trustee, however, does not have to delegate his fiduciary duty of managing the trust. The trustee may also conduct such affairs as establishing rental terms, choosing tenants, entering into and renewing leases, dealing with taxes, interest, and insurance relative to the trust property, and making decisions as to capital expenditures and repairs to trust property.

Independent contractor. The independent contractor must be independent. To be independent, the independent contractor cannot own more than 35 per cent of the shares of the trust. If the property manager is a corporation, not more than 35 per cent of its stock can be held by individuals who own 35 per cent or more of the shares of the trust. A real estate investment trust must submit, with its return, the name and address of each independent contractor and the highest percentage of ownership which the contractor had in the trust during the year.

Diversification of Investments

In addition to the status requirements and the requirements as to source of income, a real estate investment trust must also satisfy certain rules as to diversification of its investments. If it does not meet these requirements, it is taxed as a corporation.

Seventy-five per cent investment test. The organization must have 75 per cent or more of the value of its assets invested in one or more of the following: (1) real estate assets, (2) government securities, and (3) cash and cash items. "Cash and cash items" include receivables which arise in the ordinary course of the trust's operations but do not include receivables purchased from another person. Note that this requirement means that a trust cannot invest more than 25 per cent of the assets of the trust in assets such as corporate securities; this is discussed in detail in the next section.

Meaning of "real estate assets." Real estate assets obviously include real property and interests in real property. In addition, this term includes interests in mortgages and deeds of trust on real property and interests in mortgages and deeds of trust on leaseholds of land or improvements thereon.

An interest in real property includes fee ownership and co-ownership of land or improvements and leaseholds of land and improvements. Mineral, oil, or gas royalty interests are not considered interests in real property. Machinery, equipment, and so forth, which are not structural components are not considered "real property"; this is true even though under local law they may be termed fixtures. Shares in other qualified real estate investment trusts are included in "real estate assets" for purposes of the 75 per cent test. However, the trust whose shares are held must qualify as a real estate trust for the full tax year in which falls the close of each quarter for which the computation is made.

Test is applied quarterly. The real estate investment trust must meet the diversification-of-investment requirements at the end of each quarter. If the trust does not meet the investment requirements at the end of a quarter, it has 30 days within which to correct the situation.

Valuation of assets. Market quotations must be used for valuing securities held by the trust when they are readily available. Fair market value as established by the trustees in good faith is used for other securities. For valuation of securities of other qualified real estate investment trusts, the fair market value is not to exceed the market value or the book value of the securities to the issuer, whichever is higher.

Twenty-five per cent investment test. The trust may not have more than 25 per cent of the value of the trust's assets invested in securities other than government securities. This is, of course, the converse to the 75 per cent investment required explained on page 268. In addition, securities of any one corporation are limited to five per cent of the trust's total assets and 10 per cent of the outstanding voting securities of the issuer. Note that, if the trust fails to meet the investment requirements at the close of any quarter during the tax year, it loses its status as a real estate investment trust for the entire year unless it cures the discrepancy within 30 days of the close of the quarter in which it failed to meet the requirements.

Application of investment requirements. The following examples will illustrate the application of the investment-diversification rules.

The Magnum Real Estate Investment Trust in a calendar tax year has the following assets on March 31:

Cash	$ 6,000
Government securities	7,000
Real estate assets	63,000
Common stock of various companies	24,000
	$100,000

Now, if the common stock of the various companies does not exceed with respect to any one issuer 10 per cent of the outstanding voting securities of the issuer or five per cent of the value of the total assets of the trust, Magnum meets the investment requirements for the first quarter.

On June 30, Magnum lists the assets that are shown in the table at the top of page 270.

Let us also assume that Ardmore has only $30,000 of voting stock outstanding. The Magnum Real Estate Investment Trust is in trouble on two counts. The first problem is that the $4,000 invest-

Cash	$ 6,000
Government securities	7,000
Real estate assets	63,000
Common stock of Ardmore Machinery, Inc.	4,000
Common stock of Brookdale Paper Co.	16,000
Other corporate securities	4,000
	$100,000

ment in the Ardmore Machinery, Inc. is more than 10 per cent of the $30,000 voting stock of Ardmore. The second problem is that Magnum has 16 per cent of its assets ($16,000) invested in the common stock of Brookdale Paper Co. Magnum will be taxed as a corporation and not as a real estate investment trust for the entire year unless it corrects both these problems within 30 days after the close of the quarter.

Effect of changes in market value. Because the diversification of a trust's assets is measured by market value, changes in market value affect this diversification. Changes in diversification may be a result of change in market value of securities previously held or of acquisition of new assets. The law is designed not to penalize a trust for changes in market value of securities held at the end of the preceding quarter.

A change in the market value of property held by a real estate investment trust will not, of itself, affect the trust's status. However, if there is an acquisition during a quarter of an asset which partially causes the trust to fail to meet the diversification requirement, then the trust must correct the discrepancy in the same way as if the change were caused solely by the acquisition.

Change in market value only. Hercules Investment Trust, a calendar-year taxpayer, has the following diversification in its assets on March 31:

Cash	$ 150,000
Government securities	110,000
Real estate assets	600,000
Common stock of Clerox Corporation	40,000
Common stock of Delta Corporation	50,000
Common stock of various other corporations	50,000
	$1,000,000

Assume that there are no problems with the $50,000 invested in the stock of various other corporations. During the second quarter, Hercules made no acquisitions of assets, and the value of all assets remained the same except for Clerox, which doubled in value to $80,000.

The total assets of Hercules at the end of the second quarter are $1,040,000, owing to the increase in $40,000 in the value of Clerox stock. Thus, Hercules has more than five per cent of the value of its assets invested in the Clerox Company. Five per cent of $1,040,000 equals $52,000, and the value of the Clerox stock is up to $80,000. Because a change in market value is the only cause of Hercules' failure to meet the investment requirements, it does not have to correct the discrepancy in order to keep its status as a real estate investment trust.

Acquisition of new securities. If failure to meet the investment requirements is caused partially by acquisition and partly by change in market value of securities held, then the discrepancy must be corrected in the same manner as if the change were caused only by acquisition.

On March 31, Gibraltar Trust, a calendar-year taxpayer, has the following assets:

Cash	$ 5,000
Government securities	21,000
Real estate assets	70,000
Common stock of Helio-autos	4,000
	$100,000

At the end of the second quarter, Gibraltar Trust lists the following assets:

Cash	$ 12,000
Government securities	11,000
Real estate assets	70,000
Common stock of Helio-autos	44,000
Common stock of Farmdale Corporation	13,000
	$150,000

The trust no longer meets the 25 per cent limitation, because it now has $57,000 out of $150,000 invested in securities other than government securities. The violation of this limitation is partially a result of: (1) the increase in value of Helio-autos from $4,000 to $44,000, which is solely a change in market value; and (2) the purchase of $13,000 of Farmdale stock. Gibraltar must convert part of its investment in common stock into cash and cash items, government securities, and real estate assets within 30 days or else it will be in violation of the 25 per cent limitation.

Trust as a Partner in a Partnership

A trust can be a partner in a partnership, and as such it is treated the same as any other partner. The trust is considered to own its proportionate share of each of the partnership assets. It is deemed to be entitled to the partnership income attributable to its share.

Record Maintenance Requirements

A trust must keep certain required records; if it does not, it will be taxed as an ordinary corporation. The trust must keep records disclosing the actual owners of its outstanding shares. Permanent records are required which indicate the maximum number of shares of the trust actually or constructively owned by each of the actual owners of any of its stock at any time during the last half of the trust's tax year. This would include the number and face value of securities convertible into stock of the trust. The requirement of keeping records of actual owners is to determine whether a trust is actually a personal holding company.

Written statements from shareholders. The trust must ask certain record shareholders to supply the names of the actual shareholders each year. If the trust has 2,000 or more shareholders of record on any dividend date, it must demand the information as to actual ownership from each record holder of five per cent or more of its shares. The requirement is one per cent or more when there are between 200 and 2,000 shareholders, and one-half per cent or more for 200 or fewer shareholders. The trust's records must include a list of shareholders who fail to comply with the request for this information.

Information required in shareholder's return. If a shareholder of record of a trust, who is not the actual owner, does not submit the information to the trust as explained above, he must submit information with his return to show the actual owner. He may use Form 1087 or a separate statement. This statement gives names, addresses, number of shares owned, and dividends belonging to each actual owner.

Actual owners who have not complied with the trust's demand for information must file detailed statements with their tax returns concerning their ownership of real estate investment trust shares.

Computation of Trust Taxable Income

As was noted before, a trust that meets the requirements and distributes as dividends at least 90 per cent of its real estate investment trust taxable income is taxed only on the trust's undistributed earnings and profits and its undistributed capital gains.

The trust is taxed at corporate tax rates on its real estate investment trust taxable income. This income is computed in the same way as the taxable income of a corporation except for certain adjustments.

Adjustments in determining taxable trust income. The trust's taxable income would be determined as follows:

Net income	$XXX
Less: Excess of net long-term capital gain	
over net short-term capital loss	XX
Ordinary dividends paid to members	XX
Taxable income	$ X

Note that only ordinary dividends, and not capital-gain dividends, are deducted in arriving at the taxable income. A corporate capital-gain tax of 25 per cent of the excess of net long-term capital gains over net short-term capital losses will be applied to undistributed capital gains.

Several other differences between trusts and corporations are as follows: (1) No deduction is allowed for partially tax-exempt interest. (2) No special deductions are permitted with regard to dividends received from certain corporations or with regard to dividends paid on certain preferred stock of public utilities. (3) No net operating loss deduction is allowed. (4) For normal tax purposes, both real estate investment trust taxable income and the dividends-paid deduction are both reduced by the deduction for partially tax-exempt interest.

Depreciation Tax Shelter From Investment Trusts

Let us compare the effect of depreciation in a limited partnership and that in a real estate investment trust. Assume an enterprise with $20,000 income before depreciation and $24,000 depreciation. The enterprise distributes the entire $20,000. If the enterprise is a partnership, the partners would have a $4,000 loss, which they could use to offset other income. Recall that partners each pick up their share of the partnership taxable loss.

In the case of a real estate investment trust in the same situation, the beneficiaries of the trust would have a tax-free distribution of $20,000, but they would not have the $4,000 loss to offset against other income. Losses of a trust are not distributed to its beneficiaries, and the trust is not allowed an operating-loss carryover.

Now assume a situation in which an enterprise has $20,000 income before depreciation and $16,000 depreciation. Assume also that the full $20,000 is distributed. In a partnership, each partner would pick up his share of the $4,000 income of the partnership, and the remaining $16,000 distribution would reduce his basis for his partnership interest. Similarly, in a real estate investment trust, the trust would have only $4,000 taxable income. The beneficiaries of the trust would be taxable on the $4,000, and the remainder of the distribution would serve to reduce their basis for their shares in the trust.

Uses of the Real Estate Investment Trust

Basically, the real estate investment trust allows investors to pool their funds and participate jointly in relatively large and perhaps well-diversified and professionally managed realty investments. The real estate investment trust has many similarities to a closed-end mutual fund, with the exception that its portfolio will be made up predominantly of real estate properties, such as office buildings, apartments, shopping centers, hotels, mortgages, motels, and so forth. A closed-end mutual fund sells its shares by one or successive offerings of shares at a stated price to the public. Then the shares find their own price level in the open market. An open-end mutual fund sells stock continuously to the public at prices based on the pro-rata share value of the assets at the date of sale.

Trust a passive investor. Most large real estate operations are involved in both investing in property and managing property. They provide maintenance and other services as well as retaining earnings for improvement and expansion. Often they sell properties for a profit which is taxable at capital-gain rates. The real estate investment trust, because of the rules for qualification that we have studied, must be a passive investor in real estate. The trust can manage its portfolio of investments; it cannot manage the individual properties. The management of the properties must be furnished by an independent contractor. And the independent contractor cannot own more than a 35 per cent interest in the trust.

A trust is not allowed to hold property primarily for sale to customers in the ordinary course of business. Thus, it cannot be involved in the business of buying and selling properties. The trustees can, of course, acquire and dispose of properties in exercising their fiduciary duties.

Not for a very small group. The real estate investment trust is designed so that small investors may participate in relatively large developments. Recall the qualification that no less than six individuals may directly or indirectly own more than 50 per cent of the trust. Each trust must also have at least 100 owners.

Specialized investment portfolios. Just as there are mutual

funds which specialize in growth stocks, dividend-paying stock, insurance stocks, and so forth, it may be that real estate investment trusts will develop which specialize in particular phases of the real estate market. Just as the mutual funds have done, some real estate investment trusts may have the objective of balancing long-term capital appreciation and current income, whereas some may concentrate entirely on capital appreciation. Some might specialize in particular kinds of real estate investment, such as commercial property or housing projects.

Trusts may develop which have relatively stable income. Here there would be long-term holdings of a variety of types of income-producing properties where depreciation was normalized. Alternatively, a trust could develop a highly leveraged portfolio by maximizing debt financing and/or concentrating on higher-yield properties such as single-purpose units like motels, amusement properties, and shopping centers. The latter portfolio would, of course, be highly speculative.

Not for nonincome-producing property. The trust is not likely to be a good vehicle for nonincome-producing property with a view towards appreciation. Some states have already prohibited trusts' investing in unproductive property, except to a minor degree. For example, the California Administrative Code prohibits investment of more than 10 per cent of the trust assets in nonincome-producing land which will not be improved within one year. In addition, if the property was classified as inventory-type property, the trust would lose its status and be taxed as a corporation.

Often investment in nonincome-producing property produces losses in the first few years. These losses are the result of interest payments and property taxes. Because the trust is a separate taxable entity, the shareholders cannot take these losses as deductions on their own returns. In the case of a limited partnership, the partners can take these deductions on their own returns.

Provided there was no prohibition in the relevant state law, a diversification of nonincome-producing property with income-producing property might be desirable. In this situation, the deductions available on the nonincome-producing property would offset the taxable income from the income-producing property. Although the same thing could be done in a corporation, a trust would have the advantage of paying only one tax when the hoped-for appreciated nonincome-producing land was sold. Recall that the land would have to be held at least four years.

Use for shopping centers and commercial buildings. A promoter might well find the real estate investment trust a helpful device in the development of a shopping center or of a commercial building.

For example, an individual, Stanley Marcus, might purchase an option on a likely shopping-center site. Assume that he then gets a commitment of $1,500,000 on a total land and building value of $2,000,000 from a financial institution.

A real estate investment trust raises the balance of $500,000 by sales of shares of beneficial interest to the public. Marcus transfers his interest to the trust, and the trust constructs the buildings. There is, of course, a $1,500,000 first deed of trust against the property. Marcus will not have an interest in the trust. He may, however, lease the shopping center from the trust and operate the same. Alternatively, the trust may engage Marcus to manage the shopping center. We are, of course, assuming that Marcus is a competent manager, that all the qualifications discussed earlier in this chapter are met, and that there has been competent scrutiny of the applicable state laws and regulations.

SUBCHAPTER "S" CORPORATIONS

Shareholders in a corporation with 10 or fewer shareholders, and which meet certain other requirements, may elect to be taxed directly. The enterprise does not pay a corporate tax. The shareholders pay tax on their share of the income of the enterprise. They are taxed on their share of the profits, whether it is distributed to them or not. The idea behind this election is that the choice of business organization should not be influenced by tax considerations. Thus, a business could be set up as a corporation and have the advantages of a corporation, such as limited liability, but at the same time would not have the problem of double taxation.

Useful Only for Certain Kinds of Real Estate Ventures

This election is not useful for real estate ventures in which rental income is a substantial source of income. The election is terminated if more than 20 per cent of the corporation's gross receipts for a tax year are from rents, royalties, dividends, interest, annuities, and sales or exchanges of stock or securities.

Meaning of "rent." "Rent" does not include payment for the use or occupancy of rooms or other space when significant services are also rendered. For example, charges for rooms in a motel, hotel, boarding house, or motor court would not be considered rent for the 20 per cent limitation. Charges for space in an apartment house which furnished hotel services also would not be considered rent. If significant services are rendered in connection with payments for parking automobiles, for warehousing of goods or use of personal property, then these payments would not be considered rent for the foregoing limitation. Thus, this election might be considered in the foregoing ventures and by builders, contractors, land developers, and other real estate enterprises that do not violate the 20 per cent rental requirement.

Chapter 12

Corporations

CORPORATE OWNERSHIP OF PROPERTY

Individual tax rates range from 14 per cent to 70 per cent. Taxable income from property owned in joint tenancy or tenancy in common or in the partnership form is taxed once at the individual's tax rate. Similarly, income from an electing corporation's and real estate investment trusts is subject to one tax at the individual level, provided, of course, that the qualifications are met. Dividend distributions to a shareholder by a corporation are taxed to the shareholder even though a corporate tax has been paid on the corporation taxable income. Corporate tax rates are currently 22 per cent of the first $25,000 of corporate income and 48 per cent of the balance.

BEST TAX SITUATION
A FUNCTION OF A NUMBER OF VARIABLES

The best ownership form of property, from a tax standpoint, depends on a variety of factors. A corporation may be advantageous tax-wise if the objective is to accumulate income rather than to distribute it. Here, as we shall discuss later, a corporation has to be careful that it does not encounter the accumulated earnings tax, which is imposed sometimes if earnings are accumulated above $100,000. In addition, a shareholder should consider that the sale of stock in a corporation or liquidation of a corporation at a gain will result in an additional capital-gains tax.

However, if the corporate income tax rate is below the individual's marginal tax rate, it is desirable to make a projection to determine whether it is more desirable for property income to be taxed to the corporation and the earnings retained rather than taxed directly to the individual. Where the individual's marginal tax rate is high, it may work out better to incorporate and retain as much earnings as possible, and then to eventually liquidate the corporation at capital-gain rates rather than to have the property in some form of individual ownership. Salaries and interest are deductible expenses in a corporation. Thus, if the owners are the managers, they may deduct reasonable salaries in arriving at corporate income, and, therefore, the salary is taxed only once at the individual level. Similarly, if the owners make loans to the corporation, the interest is deductible for determination of corporate income taxes. In the areas of both salaries and interest, there is a body of rules to prevent excessive compensation and an excess amount of loans. We shall be back to both under the subjects of "reasonable compensation" and "thin incorporation." "Thin incorporation" refers to an excess amount of debt in relation to equity, with both the stock and the debt held by the same parties.

For the elderly or sick, it may be advisable to hold property in the corporate form and leave it to their heirs. Under current law, the stock is taxed in their estate at market value at date of death or optional valuation date. However, subject to the manner of holding title, heirs will have the market value at death as their basis, and the appreciation increment will not be subject to income tax.

Project Particular Situation

Each situation should be projected to see which is the best organization form from a tax standpoint. For example, if all earnings are to be distributed each year, the corporate form will result in a higher tax than a proprietorship or a partnership. Alternatively, if income can be deferred, or if there are advantages in leveling income, the corporate form may result in less taxes.

A corporation may be used in some situations to level income at the shareholder level. Assume that there are large variations in income. Subject to the averaging provisions in the 1964 law, a partner or individual proprietor would find himself in quite high brackets in highly profitable years. A corporation can level income to some extent through the use of a variable dividend policy or through executive bonus plans.

Effect of Character of Income

The character of income to a corporation may differ from that of income to a shareholder. Thus, a corporation may declare a dividend which is taxable as a dividend to the shareholder which is based on tax-exempt interest or capital gain to the corporation. In the case of a partnership or proprietorship, the individual would report his share of tax-exempt interest, dividends, and capital gains and losses as such on his tax return. A capital gain realized by the partnership would be reported as a capital gain by the partner on his individual return.

Corporation Advisable in Special Situations

Certain corporations that are designated as "small business corporations" are allowed ordinary loss treatment on the sale of their stock.

We have already discussed the use of the corporate form for its nontax advantages and, at the same time, electing to be taxed directly at the shareholder level. This, of course, is useful only in certain real estate situations in which rental income is not more than 20 per cent of receipts. In the chapter on capital gains, we discussed the rules on Section 1231 assets. In the case of unimproved real estate, it is sometimes easier to qualify assets "as used in trade or business" under the corporate form. Another specialized use of the corporate form is where an individual holds property for investment purposes and also deals in property. The corporate form is used in this situation to make a clean separation of investment property and inventory property. The purpose, of course, is to get capital gains on the investment property, which is denied to a dealer. This subject is also discussed in the chapter on capital gains.

Large Syndicates Choosing the Corporate Form

In recent years a number of large syndicates or groups of syndicates have changed from the limited-partnership form to the corporate form. If certain requirements are met, the exchange of stock for partnership interests in limited partnerships can be effected tax-free. In situations in which there are substantial depreciation deductions and high interest payments, there may not be much taxable income at the corporate level in the earlier years. Nevertheless, the corporation may be able to make cash distributions based on the difference between cash inflow and cash outflow. If there is no corporate taxable income, the shareholders would reduce their basis for their stock but would not have to pay ordinary income tax. A corporation, thus, may take advantage of a judicial combination of debt and equity. Shareholders would be creditors and debenture holders as well as share owners. Interest on the debentures would be taxable to them but would not be taxed at the corporate level. Distributions to shareholders would be taxed to the shareholders only to the extent that there was corporate taxable income. To the extent that there is no corporate taxable income, these distributions are a tax-free return of capital.

Nontax Advantages for the Large Corporate Syndicate

A public corporation generally owns a variety of properties. These will differ as to type as well as location. This is to be compared with the situation of the limited-partnership syndicate, which is set up usually for only one property. There may be a protection in diversification of properties similar to the protection found in the case of diversification of security portfolios. All the risk is not based on one property.

Another advantage that may accrue in the public corporation is increased marketability of investment. If the stock is publicly traded, it will more likely be easier to sell than an interest in a partnership. There is much more likely to be a satisfactory market in the case of an emergency sale than would be true in the case of the partnership.

There may also be estate and gift tax considerations here. A marketable stock is much easier to value than a partnership interest for estate tax purposes. Also, it may be easier to make gifts to minors under the Uniform Gifts to Minors Act that many states have enacted. Another possibility is that, if the real estate corporation's shares became attractive, the prices of these shares may be pushed up in a favorable market.

Advantages to corporate management. Corporate managers and promoters may achieve a variety of benefits. Some of these accrue also to the shareholder-employees of a close corporation. Because the officers of a corporation are also its employees, they may be able to participate in fringe benefits such as deferred-compensation arrangements, stock option plans, group life insurance, profit-sharing or pension plans, medical and health insurance, employee dining rooms, and so forth. The partners of a partnership are not considered employees and do not get these fringe benefits.

The promoter of a public corporation may be able to control the corporation through the use of more than one class of stock with much less than a majority ownership of all outstanding stock. The raising of equity capital may be easier through the sale of stock in a public corporation than in the case of the sale of a partnership interest. The partnership interest will likely be much more ex-

pensive. The stock can be sold in small units which allow participation by the small investor.

Limited liability of a corporation is of advantage to the promoter of a corporation. Recall that in a partnership all the partners
and in a limited partnership the general partners have unlimited
liability, and, of course, the promoters are usually the general
partners.

In addition to limited liability, the corporation has the advantage of continuation of existence, free transferability of ownership, and centralized management.

Some Problem Areas

We have already mentioned possible problems with an accumulated earnings tax and with excessive debt or salaries. Holding
and investment companies whose income is mainly from dividends,
interest, rent, and royalties and whose gains are mainly from sales
of securities must be careful to avoid the personal holding company
tax. This is a high-penalty tax.

Tax saving used to be achieved through the use of multiple
corporations. That is, each corporation would be subject to a
separate surtax exemption. Given a tax rate of 22 per cent of the
first $25,000 and 48 per cent of the balance, one corporation would
pay $17,500 on $50,000 taxable income whereas two corporations
would pay a total of $11,000 on taxable income of $25,000 each.
The difference of $6,500 is, of course, the difference between the
22 per cent and 48 per cent on $25,000. There is now a body of
rules to prevent the use of multiple corporations for the purpose of
avoiding income taxes, as we shall see later. Another problem is
with so-called "collapsible corporations"; these are corporations
which are used to convert ordinary income into capital gains. We
shall discuss collapsible corporations in a later section and we shall
also go back to personal holding companies and multiple corporations.

Disposition of Business Interests

If the owner of a sole proprietorship sells his business, he
is considered to sell the individual assets. Thus, ordinary income
and capital gain are generally recognized, depending on the nature
of the assets involved. For example, any gain attributable to inventory would be ordinary income. In the case of a sale of a partnership interest, any gain due to substantially appreciated inventory
and receivables is taxed at ordinary income rates. Alternatively,
a corporation may liquidate at capital-gain rates if it is done properly and if the "collapsible"-corporation rules do not come into effect.

MEANING OF "CORPORATION" FOR TAX PURPOSES

For income tax purposes, the term "corporation" is not limited to the usual conception of a corporation. As was discussed in the section on limited partnerships, an organization may be treated as a corporation if it more nearly resembles a corporation than a partnership or a trust. The corporate characteristics are as follows: (1) associates; (2) purpose to conduct a business and distribute its profits; (3) continuity of life on the death or withdrawal of a member; (4) centralized management; (5) limited liability; and (6) free transferability of interest in the organization. For a complete discussion of how an unincorporated association may be taxed as a corporation, see the section on limited partnerships. Recall that it is the combination of these characteristics in a particular situation that affects the determination of taxability of the organization, and that other factors can affect the determination.

Thus, for federal income tax purposes, the term "corporation" includes associations, joint stock companies, insurance companies, and trusts and partnerships that actually operate as associations or corporations.

THE CORPORATION INCOME TAX

A corporation is subject to two taxes. These are a normal tax and a surtax. The normal tax is a percentage of taxable income and the surtax is a percentage of taxable income above $25,000. For taxable years beginning in 1965 and later, the normal tax is 22 per cent and the surtax is 26 per cent. A "48 per cent corporate income tax" is often referred to. This means that, for all taxable income over $25,000, the corporation pays 48 per cent income tax. The corporation income tax is reduced by the investment credit and by taxes paid to foreign countries or possessions of the United States. Taxable income is gross income less deductions.

FORMING A CORPORATION

Let us assume that it has been decided to operate in the corporate form. The situation may be a new business or it may be the incorporation of a previously existing business that had been operating as a sole proprietorship or a partnership. Where money is exchanged for the capital stock of the corporation, there is no gain or loss realized by the shareholder or the corporation. The stock received has a basis to the shareholder equal to the amount of money transferred to the corporation.

The contribution of the property to a corporation may be tax-free under certain conditions. Alternatively, the transfer of property to the corporation may result in a taxable gain or loss. In addition to the question of the immediate tax, whether the contribution is tax-free or not influences the basis of the property to the corporation for purposes of computing gain or loss on future sale or exchange and for depreciation. Where property is mortgaged in excess of its adjusted basis, tax consequences must be considered before contributing it to a corporation, as is discussed below.

Under certain conditions where more than one corporation is involved, transfers to a corporation by an individual after June 12, 1963 can result in a disallowance of the surtax exemption. This matter is discussed in detail in the next chapter.

Tax-Free Transaction

It is entirely possible for a sole proprietorship or a partnership to incorporate and have the transfer of property to the corporation be a tax-free transaction. When property is transferred to a corporation by one or more persons solely in exchange for stock or securities in such corporation, and such person or persons immediately after the exchange are in control of the corporation, no gain or loss is recognized.

Control. For the above purposes, "control" means: (a) ownership of at least 80 per cent of the voting stock and (b) ownership of 80 per cent of all other classes of stock of the corporation.

Bertha Smith and Dagmar Wilson purchased land several years ago for a purchase price of $50,000. Because of growth in land value, the property had a fair market value of $100,000 at the time they incorporated. Bertha and Dagmar transferred their property to a corporation in exchange for all of its authorized capital stock. In this case there is no gain recognized to either the individuals or the corporation.

Now let us change the situation and assume that Bertha and Dagmar contributed their property in exchange for 70 per cent of all the authorized stock of a new corporation. Assume that the 70 per cent of the stock had a fair market value of $100,000. The remainder of the stock went to builder and developer George Arnold, who contributed a proportionate fair market value of property. Because Bertha and Dagmar have not met the control requirements, this is a taxable transaction and they have a taxable gain of $50,000 on the transfer. A taxpayer in certain circumstances may desire to have a taxable transfer if the result is a capital gain to him and a stepped-up basis to the corporation. (See our investor-dealer discussion in the chapter on capital gains.)

Basis of property and stock. When property is transferred
to a corporation in exchange for stock, the basis of the property to
the corporation must be determined as well as the basis of the stock
to the shareholders.

Thus, in our first example, where Bertha and Dagmar transferred land to a corporation and met the control requirements to
make the transaction tax-free, their basis for the stock is the same
as their previous basis for the land ($50,000). Recall that it was
worth $100,000 when they contributed it to the corporation. The
corporation's basis for the property is also $50,000.

Basis to shareholder. The rule for determination of basis
to the shareholder is as follows: the basis of the stock received in
a nontaxable transfer of property to a corporation is the same as
that of the property exchanged, less the money and fair market
value of other property received, and increased by any gain recognized on the exchange. If any other property is received, the basis
is its fair market value. In the above example, there was no money
or other property received by Bertha and Dagmar in addition to the
stock.

For example, Smith transfers property to AAA Corporation
in exchange for more than 80 per cent of the corporation's stock, so
that the tax-free requirements are met. Smith had a basis of
$100,000 for the property. On the exchange, Smith received stock
from the corporation with a fair market value of $98,000 and cash
in the amount of $7,500. The result is that he has a recognized
gain of $5,500. This is the $98,000 plus the $7,500 received less
the $100,000 basis of the property contributed. Smith has a basis
for his stock in the AAA Corporation of $98,000; this is the $100,000
basis of his former property less the $7,500 cash received plus the
$5,500 gain recognized on the exchange. The reader may wish to
refer to Chapter 3, where there is a detailed discussion of the effect
of "boot" on otherwise nontaxable exchanges. Losses are not recognized.

Basis of property to corporation. The basis of the property
to the corporation is the transferor's basis increased by any gain
recognized to the transferor when property is acquired by a corporation on or after June 22, 1954 in a tax-free transfer to a corporation controlled by the transferor or as paid-in capital or as a
contribution to capital.

The reasoning behind the rules for determination of basis
is, of course, that any appreciation in value of property should not
go untaxed. For example, recall that Bertha and Dagmar contributed property which cost them $50,000 and was now worth $100,000
to a corporation which they controlled in a tax-free transaction. If

the corporation would get a basis of $100,000, the increase in value from $50,000 to $100,000 would go untaxed. Instead, the corporation takes the same basis as the transferor plus any gain recognized to the transferor on the exchange.

Effect of Services Rendered

Our foregoing discussion covers the exchange of property for stock of a controlled corporation in a tax-free transaction. The term "property" does not include either services rendered or services to be rendered to the corporation issuing the stock. If stock is received for services, it is taxable income to the recipient.

For example, Builder Knowlton transfers property worth $70,000, and he also renders services valued at $6,000, to a corporation in exchange for stock; the stock has a fair market value of $76,000. Immediately after the transaction, Knowlton owns 83 per cent of the outstanding stock. No gain is recognized on the exchange of the property, as the requirements are met for a tax-free transfer of property. But Knowlton has ordinary income in the amount of $6,000 for services rendered to the corporation.

The effect of services rendered also has to be considered in determining whether or not the rules are met for tax-free incorporation.

For example, assume that Green transfers property with a $15,000 basis and a fair market value of $50,000 to Green Corporation for 75 per cent of its stock. This is a new corporation, and the attorney agrees to take 25 per cent of the stock in exchange for his services in preparing the bylaws and corporation charter and generally setting up the corporation. The result would be that the tax-free provisions are not met because services are not considered property. The attorney did not transfer property, and Green does not have the required 80 per cent ownership in Green Corporation stock. Thus, Green would be taxed on a $35,000 gain. The attorney would be taxed on the value of stock received for services rendered.

Disproportionate Transfers

The transfer of property to a corporation may be by more than one person. It is not necessary that the amount of stock received by each of the contributors be in proportion or even substantially in proportion to his interest in the property prior to the exchange.

Obviously, if the interest in the property contributed is disproportionate to the stock received, there must be some reason, and the law attempts to tax the transaction according to the true nature of the transaction. There may be, for example, an element of compensation for services or a gift involved.

Assume that John Brown and his son Robert organize a corporation with 2,000 shares of common stock. John transfers property worth $1,600 in exchange for 400 shares of common stock. Son Robert transfers property worth $4,000 to the corporation in exchange for 1,600 shares of stock. No gain or loss is recognized, because the tax-free transfer requirements are met. If the fact of the situation is that father made a gift to his son, then the gift tax law must be considered. Observe that father's stock cost him four dollars a share in property value ($1,600 for 400 shares), whereas son Robert's stock only cost $2.50 a share ($4,000 for 1,600 shares).

A similar situation could arise where the disproportion in the amount of stock received was in fact the payment of compensation by one party to another. For example, assume that John and Robert were unrelated, but that Robert had performed services for the corporation, and that the disproportion was really disguised compensation.

Effect of Assumption of a Liability

If a corporation acquires property subject to a liability or assumes a liability against the property, the exchange can still be tax-free.

When a liability is assumed by the controlled corporation or the property is taken by the corporation subject to a liability, gain is not recognized, but the liability is treated as money received by the contributor and is subtracted in figuring his basis.

For example, Daniel transfers property to a controlled corporation in a tax-free exchange. The property had an adjusted basis of $200,000 in Daniel's hands and was subject to a mortgage of $50,000. He receives in exchange stock of the corporation worth $300,000 because the property has appreciated in value. No gain or loss is recognized on the exchange, but the basis of the stock to Daniel is $150,000. This is determined by subtracting the amount of the liability of $50,000 from the basis ($200,000) of the property transferred. The liability is treated as money received.

A special problem arises in the case of liabilities in excess of the basis of the property, which is discussed in the next section. Also, if the purpose is to avoid taxes, or if the transaction is not for a real business purpose, the total liability assumed or acquired is considered as money received by the person transferring the property and is taxed as "boot" received.

Liability in Excess of Basis

Because of appreciation in property values, it is not uncommon for a corporation to receive property subject to a mortgage which is greater than the adjusted basis of the property to the taxpayer. When a taxpayer transfers property to a controlled corporation which assumes a liability in excess of the basis of the property, the excess is taxable gain (to the taxpayer.)

Gains from Depreciable Property

If there is a gain from disposition of depreciable property, all or part of it may have to be reported as ordinary income and not capital gain, regardless of how long the taxpayer has held the property. There is a special rule which states that gain from sales or exchanges of depreciable property, made directly or indirectly, between an individual and his controlled corporation must be treated as ordinary income. The same rule applies to sales or exchanges between husband and wife.

Problem of Depreciated Property Mortgaged in Excess of Basis

Assume that Bland owns an apartment house worth $600,000, and that he decides he needs cash for other purposes. Although his adjusted basis is only $200,000, he mortgages it for $500,000 based on its current market value. Bland transfers the apartment house to a corporation in exchange for all its stock. The result is an ordinary income tax to Bland based on $300,000 rather than a tax-free exchange.

The gain of $300,000 is the excess of the $500,000 mortgage over the $200,000 basis, which is taxable as explained above. Because the property was depreciable, the gain is ordinary income rather than capital-gain income. The above problem could also arise if unsecured debt and depreciable property were transferred to a controlled corporation and the unsecured debt exceeded the basis of the assets.

The moral of the above story is, of course, that careful consideration must be given to tax considerations on the transfer of any property to a controlled corporation.

Taxable Incorporation

If the requirements for a tax-free transfer are not met, the transfer of property to a corporation will be taxable. When the transaction results in a gain, the result is a tax to the transferor, but the controlled corporation has a higher basis for future gain or loss on sale or exchange or for computation of depreciation. Recall, however, the special rules which treat gains from sales or exchanges of depreciable property between an individual and his controlled corpo ration as ordinary income and not capital gain.

A deduction for loss is not allowed if a sale is made, directly or indirectly, between an individual and a corporation of which more than 50 per cent in value of the outstanding stock is owned, directly or indirectly, by or for such individual.

DIVIDENDS

The primary way for shareholders to receive assets from a corporation is by the corporation declaring and paying dividends. Most often dividends are in the form of cash; sometimes they are in the form of property, services, or accommodations.

Dividends are distributions made by a corporation to its shareholders: (1) out of earnings and profits accumulated after February 28, 1913 or (2) out of the earnings and profits of the tax year. Such dividends are taxable income to the shareholders. Distributions that are not made out of earnings are not taxable to the shareholder. Such distributions reduce the basis of the share- holders' stock and are not taxable unless his basis has been re- duced to zero.

Constructive Dividends

Sometimes transactions which are not called dividends are treated as constructive dividends. We have already discussed these situations when we discussed deductions in determining corporate income. Some common situations are excessive salaries to share- holder-officers, excessive rent to shareholders, and dividends dis- guised as loans. Dividends, of course, are not deductible; thus, the usual scheme is to attempt to give the corporation a deduction by disguising the distribution as a deductible item, such as salaries or rent. In the case of loans to the shareholders that never get repaid, the attempt is to avoid the dividend tax at the shareholder level.

The following situations also have resulted in taxable divi- dends to the shareholders: (a) Securities were purchased by share- holders from a corporation at less than their fair market value; (b) A shareholder that owed the corporation was released from his debt; (c) Property was transferred by a corporation to its share- holders for less than fair market value; (d) Property was sold to a corporation for more than its fair market value. If a corporation holds all the incidents of ownership of a life insurance policy and has paid all the premiums, the proceeds paid to a shareholder may be taxed as a dividend.

Stock Dividends

A distribution by a corporation to its shareholders in its own stock is called a "stock dividend." A stock dividend is often declared when the corporation wishes to retain cash but has sufficient earnings and profits on which to base a dividend. For example, a corporation may wish to retain its cash for expansion. The stock dividend results in a transfer from retained earnings to capital stock and paid-in surplus, thus indicating that an amount equivalent to the stock dividend is to be retained as permanent capital.

Taxability. Stock dividends are generally not taxable. Two exceptions to this rule are as follows: (1) If the stock dividend is paid in order to discharge preference dividends for the distributing corporation's current or preceding tax year; and (2) If any shareholder may elect to take money or other property instead of the stock dividend.

Effect of stock dividend on basis. After receipt of a nontaxable stock dividend, the basis per share of the stock held is determined by dividing the previous basis of the old shares by the total number of shares held after the stock dividend.

For example, Johnson owned 200 shares of the Beverly Corporation's common stock, which he purchased in 1964 for $4,000 ($20 per share). In 1967 the Beverly Corporation declared a 20 per cent stock dividend. Johnson now holds 240 shares, because he received 40 shares on the distribution. His basis for gain or loss on future sale is $16.67 per share; this is his $4,000 cost divided by the 240 shares.

The above rule is only for nontaxable stock dividends. When stock dividends are taxable, then allocation is made on the basis of relative fair market values. In a case of nontaxable stock dividends, the date basis of the new shares is the same as the date basis of the old shares. The importance of the date is for determining whether a gain or loss on sale is a long- or short-term capital gain.

In our example above, if Johnson sold some of his shares at a gain three months after receipt of the stock dividend, he would still have a long-term capital gain, because his date basis is the same as that of the old shares which he purchased in 1964.

Corporate Transactions in Own Stock

If a corporation receives money or other property in exchange for its own stock, no gain or loss is recognized to the corporation. This is also true for treasury stock. However, if a corporation receives its own stock in exchange for property other than its own stock, gain or loss may be recognized.

For example, Elmira Corporation owns real estate with a fair market value of $6,000. This real estate has an adjusted basis of $4,500. Elmira Corporation exchanges this real estate for shares of its own stock which has a fair market value of $6,000. The result is a taxable gain of $1,500; this is the $6,000 fair market value less the $4,500 adjusted basis.

A corporation may give its own stock as payment for services and no gain or loss will be recognized. The recipient has taxable income to the extent of the fair market value of the stock received.

Property Dividends

A corporation may pay a dividend in property other than money. In this case the taxable amount of the distribution to the shareholder is the fair market value of the property as of the date of distribution. The corporation's own stock is not considered property for this purpose. (Refer to the section on stock dividends.) If the shareholder assumes a liability of the corporation in connection with the distribution, the amount is reduced by the amount of the liability. The amount would also be reduced by the amount of any liability to which the property was subject immediately before and after the distribution. The basis of the property to the recipient is the fair market value at the date of distribution.

The amount that is a dividend to a shareholder on the receipt of a property dividend is limited to the corporation's earnings and profits.

For example, Beverley Corporation has earnings and profits of $30,000 and distributes property to its shareholders having a basis of $15,000 and a fair market value of $37,500. The dividend is taxable to the shareholder only to the extent of the $30,000 earnings and profits of the Beverley Corporation.

Special rules. There are special rules for property dividends received by corporate taxpayers. Distributions in tax-free reorganization are also specially treated. Also, special provisions apply to DuPont shareholders who received General Motors stock in antitrust distributions.

Effect on Corporation of Property Dividend

The general rule is that a corporation does not realize gain or loss when it distributes property as well as stock or stock rights

to its shareholders. Exceptions to this rule are discussed in the
next section.

For example, Martha Corporation owns securities in the
Beatrice Corporation that cost $50,000. These securities are dis-
tributed to the shareholders, at which time they have a fair market
value of $75,000. Even though the securities had appreciated in
value, there is no gain realized to the corporation.

The above example illustrates the results of a property dividend. However, if a corporation distributes property in satisfaction of a declared <u>dollar</u> amount of dividends, then it has effected
a taxable exchange and it is considered that the declared dollar
amount of the dividend is the amount received by the corporation
in exchange for its property.

For example, Arnold Corporation declares a dividend of
$20,000 to holders of record January 6, payable March 30. Because
of shortage of cash on March 30, Arnold Corporation distributes
property with a fair market value of $20,000 and an adjusted basis
of $15,000 in satisfaction of the dividend. The result is a taxable
gain of $5,000 to Arnold Corporation.

<u>Property dividends resulting in tax to corporation.</u> A corpo-
ration may also realize taxable income on distribution of the following:
(a) property mortgaged in excess of basis; (b) LIFO inventory;
(c) Section 1245 property; and (d) certain installment obligations.

<u>Property subject to a liability.</u> A corporation may distribute
property subject to a liability, or the shareholder may assume a
liability of the corporation in connection with the distribution. If
the liability is greater than the adjusted basis of the property to the
corporation, then gain is recognized to the corporation. The amount
of the gain is the amount of the liability less the adjusted basis of the
distributed property.

For example, Cynthia Corporation pays a property dividend
with property that has an adjusted basis of $40,000 but which is en-
cumbered by a mortgage of $50,000, which the shareholders assume.
Cynthia Corporation has a taxable gain of $10,000. Of course, the
reason for a mortgage greater than basis is appreciation in the value
of the property since acquisition.

If the shareholders do not assume the mortgage but take the
property subject to the mortgage, the taxable gain may not exceed
the fair market value of the property less the adjusted basis.

<u>Section 1245 property.</u> Recall our discussion of depreciation
recapture. If a corporation distributes so-called Section 1245 property as a dividend, it will have Section 1245 income just as if it sold the
property for its fair market value.

REDEMPTION OF STOCK

This section is concerned with redemption of a corporation's own stock other than in partial or complete liquidation. Liquidations will be discussed in the next chapter. A redemption of stock includes the acquisition by a corporation of its own stock for property whether or not the stock is to be canceled, retired, or held as treasury stock. "Property" for this purpose means any property, including money, securities, and indebtedness to the corporation except stock or rights to acquire stock in the corporation.

Exchange or Dividend

The important issue is whether there is an exchange or a dividend. If there is an exchange, then the shareholder is subject to a capital-gains tax. However, if the stock redemption is a disguised dividend, the result is ordinary income.

The following types of redemptions are considered exchanges, and the result is a capital gain or loss to the shareholders rather than dividend income: (1) The redemption is not essentially equivalent to a dividend; (2) A redemption which is substantially disproportionate and the shareholder owns less than 50 per cent of the total voting power after redemption; (3) A complete redemption of all of the stock of the corporation owned by the shareholder; (4) The redemption of stock issued by a railroad pursuant to a reorganization under Section 77 of the Bankruptcy Act.

A redemption is considered to be substantially disproportionate if the percentage of the stockholder's ownership of voting stock after redemption is less than 80 per cent of the percentage owned by him prior to redemption. The percentage is determined by using market values if there is more than one class of common stock. If the redemption is a series of redemptions resulting in a total redemption that is not substantially disproportionate, then the individual redemption will not be considered disproportionate.

Redemptions That Are Dividends

If a corporation has only one class of stock outstanding, a distribution in pro-rata redemption of part of a corporation's stock ordinarily is treated as a dividend. Also, redemption of all of one class of stock ordinarily is considered a dividend if all classes of stock outstanding at the time of the redemption are held in the same proportion. There is an exception in the case of so-called Section 306 stock. Section 306 stock is preferred stock issued as a non-taxable dividend when the issuing corporation has earnings and profits

Distributions to Pay Death Taxes and Expenses

A distribution of property in redemption of stock which has been included in the gross estate of a decedent may qualify as a payment in exchange for the stock under certain conditions. Even though the distribution would have otherwise been treated as a dividend, the resulting gain or loss is a capital gain or loss.

The conditions are as follows: (1) The value of the stock must be included in the decedent's estate for estate tax purposes; (2) The stock must be redeemed after the decedent's death. The time limit is three years and 90 days after the filing of the decedent's estate tax return or, if a petition for redetermination of a deficiency of the estate tax was timely filed, within 60 days after the Tax Court's decision becomes final; (3) The value of the stock must be more than 35 per cent of the decedent's gross estate, or more than 50 per cent of the decedent's taxable estate; (4) The stock must be redeemed for an amount that is not more than the estate and inheritance taxes (including interest) plus the funeral and administration expenses allowable as deductions to the estate. If the amount of the distribution exceeds the allowable taxes and expenses, but all other conditions are satisfied, then the excess amount is treated as a dividend.

Chapter 13

Corporations: Capital Gains
and Special Problems

In the previous chapter we considered the basic ways a corporation is taxed and also discussed some of the tax problems that are met in forming a corporation. We also considered the tax effects on both the corporation and the shareholder when a corporation makes distributions of money or property as a dividend or in redemption of a shareholder's stock in the corporation. The discussion of corporate tax problems will be continued in this chapter as we discuss, first, how capital gains for corporations are treated in a manner different from that applying to individuals. Then we shall proceed to some of the tax problems that the corporation may encounter, as we discuss thin incorporations, collapsible corporations, the accumulated earnings tax, and the personal holding penalty tax. Next, we shall examine some of the tax considerations involved when there are several corporations with majority ownership resting in the same parties. This is the subject of multiple corporations which was affected significantly by the 1964 Revenue Act. After that, we shall consider the rather complicated problems involved when corporations liquidate or reorganize.

CAPITAL GAINS TAXATION FOR CORPORATIONS

Capital gains and losses for corporations are the same as for individuals. This subject has been discussed in detail in Chapter 4. However, a corporation may deduct capital losses and capital-loss carry-overs only to the extent of capital gains. This is the major difference between capital gains and losses for corporations and for individuals. Otherwise, capital gains and losses are treated in the same manner as net long-term gains or losses, and net short-term gains or losses are balanced off to result in a net capital gain or net capital loss for the year.

No Deductions for Net Capital Loss

A corporation cannot deduct any portion of a net capital loss in the year it is sustained. This loss must be carried forward to succeeding years. It may be carried forward and used against any net capital gains in the next five years. If a corporation has net capital losses in more than one year, it must first use the earlier loss before the later loss carry-overs can be applied against capital gains.

For example, assume that the Lincoln Corporation had a net capital loss of $5,000 in 1965. There is no deduction for this loss in the year it is sustained. Contrast this with the situation of an individual, who may deduct up to $1,000 against ordinary income. In 1966 Lincoln Corporation had a $3,000 net capital gain and then in 1967 it had a capital loss of $6,000.

In 1966, $3,000 of the 1965 net capital loss is used to offset the $3,000 net capital gain in that year. This leaves a carry-over of $2,000 capital loss from 1965. The 1965 carry-over may be applied against capital gains through 1970, and it must be used before the 1967 loss can be used. Note that the carry-over is for five years after the year the loss is sustained.

As we noted in Chapter 4, the 1964 Revenue Act removed the five-year limitation on carry-overs for individuals. This rule does not apply to corporations, and corporations can still carry over capital losses for only five years.

THIN INCORPORATION

This term indicates a situation in which the debt in the capital structure greatly exceeds the stock. In such cases, a portion of the debt may be treated as stock for tax purposes. The result, of course, is that the corporation loses its interest deduction in determining the corporate tax. It is analogous to the problem of paying excess salaries to officer-shareholders to avoid the double tax on dividends.

Example of Thin Incorporation

Assume that the Truman Corporation was organized and the shareholders contributed $2,000 for the capital stock. In addition, the shareholders loaned the corporation $50,000 in direct proportion to their shareholdings. At a later date, the shareholders received cash in payment of the principal of the loans plus interest. Such a situation may well be considered a thin incorporation. The result is that the payments of "interest" on the loans would be considered a dividend to the extent that the corporation had retained earnings.

The question of thin incorporation might arise in the original capitalization of the company when there is an excess amount of debt in relation to equity, as explained earlier. As noted in the previous chapter, a problem may also arise when the shareholders borrow money from their closely held corporations. Here there is a danger that the amounts borrowed may be considered dividends.

COLLAPSIBLE CORPORATIONS

Obviously it is often desirable to pay tax at capital-gain rates rather than at ordinary income rates. It is also desirable to pay only one tax rather than a corporate tax and then an ordinary income tax. At one time, a taxpayer could convert ordinary income into capital gain by liquidating a corporation before the corporation sold its assets. The result was that the shareholders paid a capital-gain tax on the distribution in liquidation; they also received a "stepped up" basis for the asset. The corporation paid no tax at all.

For example, assume that the Hamilton Corporation constructed a medical building with the intention of selling it. The Hamilton Corporation was liquidated after construction of the building, and the only tax was a capital-gain tax on the property at the shareholders' level. The shareholders then had fair market value as their basis, so that, if they sold the medical building shortly thereafter, there would probably be no more tax. If, instead of following the above procedure, the corporation had sold the property, then it would have had to pay ordinary income tax on the gain. Dividends to the stockholders would also be taxed.

Under current law, the collapsible-corporation rules would generally prevent capital gain in the above instance. If a taxpayer sells or exchanges "collapsible corporation" stock or receives a distribution in payment for this stock in a partial or complete liquidation, the gain is taxed as ordinary income.

Another way that a taxpayer could formerly achieve capital gain rather than ordinary income was to sell the stock of a corporation to others, who presumably would liquidate it. Thus, if a corporation had appreciated property, presumably this appreciation would be reflected in the selling price of the stock, and the shareholders would achieve their capital gain by selling the stock. The collapsible-corporation rules are also designed to stop this.

Meaning of a "Collapsible Corporation"

A "collapsible corporation" is one formed or used principally (1) to manufacture, construct, or produce property, or (2) to buy property which in the hands of the corporation is held primarily for sale to customers, unrealized receivables, or fees, or certain property described in Section 1231(b) of the Internal Revenue Code held for less than three years, or (3) to hold stock in such a corporation. In addition, the corporation must be formed or used <u>with a view to</u> (1) the sale or exchange of stock by its shareholders (whether in liquidation or otherwise) or a distribution to its shareholders, prior to the realization by the corporation manufacturing, constructing, producing, or purchasing the property, of a substantial part of the taxable income to be derived from such property, and (2) the realization by such shareholders of gain attributable to such property.

The essence of these rather complicated sounding rules is that they are designed to stop transactions which are planned with the objective of realizing capital gain to the owners before the corporation realizes taxable gain.

ACCUMULATED EARNINGS TAX

Corporate earnings are, of course, subject to a corporate income tax. Then, if the corporation declares dividends from corporate earnings, the recipient pays another tax at ordinary income tax rates. Particularly in small corporations, there may be a motivation to retain earnings rather than distribute them as dividends, to avoid the second tax. The shareholders may have enough income from other sources and/or from deductible salaries so that they do not need the cash. The shareholders may feel that they will eventually liquidate the corporation at capital-gain rates, or anticipate selling their stock with gain taxed as capital gain. If the corporation operates for more than three years, the collapsible-corporation rules discussed in the previous section are not a problem. If the stock is to be left in the estate of the owner, it will be subject to an estate tax, but the heirs will have fair market value at date of death as their basis, and thus there will be no tax on the appreciation. Another reason for accumulating earnings is to adjust dividend distributions to years when they have losses from other sources that will offset these dividends.

To prevent the improper accumulation of earnings, there is an accumulated earnings tax. The purpose, of course, is to dis-

courage attempts by stockholders to avoid dividend tax through the
accumulation of earnings. A corporation, however, may accumulate
a portion of its earned surplus to use for possible expansion or for
other bona fide business reasons. It is when a business allows the
surplus to accumulate beyond the reasonable needs of the business
that it may be subject to the accumulated-earnings tax. Accumulations of $100,000 or less are not considered beyond the reasonable
needs of a business.

Penalty Surtax

The accumulated-earnings tax is a penalty surtax that is
imposed on the income of a corporation for any year in which it
accumulates earnings to avoid tax on its shareholders. Note that
it is imposed on the taxable income of the corporation after certain
specified adjustments; it is not imposed on the retained earnings of
the corporation. The tax is in addition to the corporate normal tax
and surtax. A corporation may become liable for the tax when there
are both: (1) accumulation of earnings and (2) purpose of avoiding a
tax on the shareholders.

Purpose to Avoid Income Tax on Shareholders

A corporation may be subject to the accumulated-earnings
tax when it is formed or used to prevent the imposition of income
tax on its shareholders. Thus, it could be a manufacturing, mer-
cantile, or any type of corporation other than a personal holding
company or foreign personal holding company. Determination of
purpose depends on the facts of a particular case. For example,
a corporation might have significant investment in assets having no
reasonable connection with the business, such as government securities or other securities that have nothing to do with the kind of
business in which the corporation is engaged. The extent to which
the corporation has distributed its earnings is important. For example, a corporation may have paid no dividends at all or may have
only an irregular dividend policy with very small amounts of dividends
    Reasonable anticipated needs. The important test is whether
or not the accumulated earnings are beyond the reasonably anticipated needs of the business. Thus, indication that future needs of
the business require accumulation may justify retention as well as
immediate needs may. When there is a definite plan for investment,
the plan does not have to be completed immediately after the close
of the tax year. The accumulated-earnings tax cannot be avoided
when the future use is "uncertain, vague or indefinite." Retention
of earnings to provide against unrealistic contingencies would not

be justified. However, there are certain guides that may be used to justify a reasonable need even though the circumstances in each case govern. Accumulation of earnings to provide for expansion of the business or its plant, or to acquire a new business enterprise through buying its stock or assets, are examples of reasonable needs. The need for working capital or the need to provide for investment in, or loans to a supplier or customers, if necessary to maintain the business of the corporation, are further examples of reasonable needs. Another indication of a reasonable need would be the need to provide for retirement of indebtedness of the corporation.

Burden of proof. The government has to prove that the accumulation is unreasonable if the taxpayer is not notified of a proposed deficiency before a deficiency notice is issued. The burden of proof is also on the government if the taxpayer files a statement of the reasons for the accumulation after he receives a notice of proposed deficiency. This statement has to be filed within 60 days after the notice, with an additional 30 days on request.

The burden of proof is on the taxpayer if he does not file a statement within the proper time or if the grounds in the statement are not supported by the facts. Generally, the taxpayer must prove both that there was no tax-avoidance purpose and that the accumulation was reasonable.

Action to Avoid the Accumulated-Earnings Tax

Because there is no penalty tax if the accumulated earnings of the corporation are reasonable, it is desirable to have definite feasible plans for using the accumulated earnings. Generalized plans for uncertain or vague future requirements are not sufficient to avoid imposition of the tax. Management should have definite plans for expansion of the business or for diversification. They may have plans to acquire new businesses or for the replacement of fixed assets. They may need to retain funds to retire debt or to maintain working capital for a safe liquidity position. It is desirable to have these needs documented in minutes of directors' meetings. Of course, the accumulated-earnings tax may be avoided if sufficient dividends are paid within the year so that the dividends-paid deduction plus the accumulated-earnings credit is equal to the adjusted taxable income.

PERSONAL HOLDING COMPANY PENALTY TAX

The personal holding company tax is a substantial penalty tax which is imposed on the undistributed earnings of closely held corporations with income primarily from passive sources such as dividends, interest, and so forth. Individuals in very high individual tax brackets would incorporate their investments with the idea that the investment income would be taxed to the corporation. Eventually they would liquidate at capital-gain rates or perhaps leave the stock in the corporation to their heirs. The resultant corporate tax plus capital-gains tax would be less than their ordinary income tax rates. Some individuals would incorporate both income-producing rental property and securities so that they could get the corporate dividends-received deduction on the dividend income to the corporation. Prior to the 1964 Internal Revenue Law, rents were not included in personal holding company income if they were more than 50 per cent of gross income. Thus, by having enough rents, it was possible to offset the dividend income, so that the corporation would not be a personal holding company. With an 85 per cent dividend exclusion, only 15 per cent of the dividend income was taxed to the corporation. If a high tax-bracket individual could keep this income in the corporation and eventually get it out at capital-gain rates through liquidation of the corporation, he would likely be better off tax-wise than if he owned the investment as an individual.

Here is an example of the procedure: Harding is in a high tax bracket with a lot of dividend income. He buys income-producing realty which yields more gross income than he receives from dividends. He then contributes both the realty and the securities to a newly formed corporation. This can be a tax-free incorporation, as was explained in the last chapter. At the former corporate tax rates of 30 per cent normal tax and 22 per cent surtax, he was paying only 4.5 per cent or 7.8 per cent on the dividend income. This is calculated by taking the tax rate times 15 per cent, because only 15 per cent of the dividend income is taxed, with an 85 per cent dividend exclusion. He will keep the property at least three years, so that there is no collapsible-corporation problem. Also, he does not have to worry about the first $100,000 accumulated earnings. If the accumulated earnings are above $100,000, he may well justify accumulation, because retention for payment of a mortgage on property would be a reasonable need. Sometime after the three years is up, he may decide to liquidate the corporation. The result is a capital-gains tax. To compare the results: If he owned the stock as an individual, he would have paid ordinary income tax rates on the dividends less the dividend exclusion. In prior years he would have received a 4 per cent dividend credit. By incorporating and later liquidating, he has paid a 25 per cent capital-gains tax, and the corporation has paid a corporate tax of 4.5 per cent or 7.8 per cent, depending on whether the dividends cause income to be above $25,000 or not. Since the passage of the 1964 Internal Revenue Law, the provisions dealing with personal holding companies have been substantially tightened, so that schemes such as mentioned on page 301 have to be very carefully planned.

Rates of Tax

The tax rates are quite severe. For taxable years beginning after December 31, 1963, the rate is 70 per cent of the "undistributed personal holding company income." Prior to this time the rate was 75 per cent on the first $2,000 of the undistributed personal holding company net income and 85 per cent on any amount over $2,000. Although the rate is less, the law is more severe than it used to be, as is explained below.

Definition of a Personal Holding Company

A personal holding company is a corporation meeting the following two requirements: (1) the income of the corporation is mainly personal holding company income, which is income largely from passive sources such as dividends, interest, rents, and so forth, and (2) the corporation is owned by five or fewer individuals. We shall have to explain both of these in detail below. Note that the requirements are applied each year, so that a corporation may be a personal holding company in one year but not in another.

Stock-ownership requirement. Corporations must meet both the income requirement and the stock-ownership requirement to be classified as personal holding companies. Five or fewer individuals must own, directly or indirectly, more than 50 per cent in value of the outstanding stock of the corporation at any time during the last half of the tax year. Some charitable foundations and trusts are considered to be individuals for this purpose.

Most closely held corporations would fall under the stock-ownership test. An individual is considered as owning the stock owned, directly or indirectly, by or for his family or his partner. His family includes only brothers and sisters, spouse, ancestors, and lineal descendants. If an individual owns an option on stock, he is considered to be the owner of the stock. Constructive-ownership rules also apply. If there is a question, the particular situation should be examined in the light of the detailed rules in the Code and the Regulations.

Personal holding company income. In addition to the stock-ownership income requirement described above, a corporation must have adjusted personal holding company income, hereafter referred to as PHC income, which is at least 60 per cent of total adjusted gross income. For taxable years beginning after December 31, 1963,

both gross income and PHC income must be adjusted according to
rules described below. Prior to this time, the requirement was
that 80 per cent or more of the gross income had to be personal
holding company income. Both the old and the new rules will be
discussed, because corporations have the opportunity to go under
the old tests if they liquidate prior to January 1, 1967. From a
real estate standpoint, note particularly that there has been an important change in the handling of rents. From now on we shall talk
of the "old law" as relating to taxable years beginning prior to
January 1, 1964. The "new law" will refer to the requirements
for taxable years beginning after December 31, 1963. Under the
old law, the test was whether PHC income was at least 80 per cent
of total gross income. Under the new law, both gross income and
PHC income are first adjusted, and then the test is whether PHC
income is at least 60 per cent of the total adjusted gross.

Inclusions in PHC income. PHC income includes a variety
of kinds of income, such as dividends, interest, royalties, income
from securities transactions, and so forth, with certain exceptions.
The inclusions will be discussed below with the changes in the new
law indicated.

Dividends, interest, royalties, and annuities. Dividends and
annuities are considered PHC income. Royalties other than mineral,
oil, gas, or copyright royalties, which are given special treatment
as discussed below, are considered PHC income. Under the old law,
interest is considered to be PHC income unless it falls under the definition of rent as described below, or unless it is on reserve funds
deposited under the Merchant Marine Act of 1936. Under the new
law, interest on judgments, tax refunds, and condemnation awards
are excluded from both total gross income and PHC income. In the
case of a dealer, interest on direct United States obligations is excluded from both calculations.

Gains from capital assets and Section 1231 assets. Under the
old law, the excess of gains over losses from the sale or exchange of
stock or securities was PHC income except that regular dealers in
stock or securities were excluded. The new law excludes gains from
both capital and Section 1231 assets from total gross income and PHC
income. Section 1231 assets are defined in detail in the chapter on
capital gains.

Taxable income from estates and trusts. Income from estates
or trusts, and income from the disposition of an interest in an estate
or trust, is PHC income.

Personal-service contracts. Income from personal-service
contracts is PHC income under certain conditions. Amounts received
from the sale or other disposition of personal-service contracts also

are personal holding company income. There are a variety of rules here, including the requirement that the named or designated individual owns, directly or indirectly, 25 per cent or more in value of the outstanding corporate stock some time during the tax year.

Certain payments for use of corporate property. If a stockholder owns directly or indirectly 25 per cent or more in value of the outstanding corporate stock at any time during the tax year, payments by him to the corporation for the use of corporate property is PHC income under certain conditions. For this rule to apply, the corporation must have PHC income for the tax year in excess of 10 per cent of its gross income. Here PHC income is calculated with the inclusion of copyright royalties in full but excluding rent.

Rents under the old law. The change in the handling of rents is probably the most crucial change and is, of course, of particular interest to us. Under the old law, rents were included as PHC income unless they were 50 per cent or more of gross income. Thus, under the old law, a corporation could avoid the PHC tax provided only that gross rents were equal to other PHC income. This was the basis for sheltering dividends, as we explained at the beginning of the section. "Rent" includes payments for the use of, or right to use, property. It also includes interest on debts owed to the corporation to the extent that these debts represent the price for which real property (held primarily for sale to customers in the ordinary course of its trade or business) was sold or exchanged by the corporation. It would not include the payments made by a shareholder for corporate property described in the section above.

Rents under the new law. Now rent has to be reduced by property taxes, interest, rent paid, and depreciation. The gross rent cannot be reduced below zero. Depreciation on tangible personal property usually retained by any lessee for more than three years is not included in the reduction. Rents are reduced by these expenses in both the calculation of adjusted gross income and to determine the portion of rent which is PHC income.

If the following tests are met, rent is not PHC income: (1) The adjusted rent is at least 50 per cent of the total adjusted gross income. (2) If "other PHC income" is larger than 10 per cent of the total gross income reduced by gains, the excess has to be paid out in dividends. The other PHC income does not include rents here, but it does include all copyright royalties and adjusted mineral, oil, and gas royalties, even though under the requisite tests these items are not otherwise PHC income. Payment of dividends includes dividends paid during the year or within two and one-half months after the end of the year, and consent dividends. The first test above is similar to the old law except for the adjustments to both the rent and the adjusted gross income. The second test is new. These rules are illustrated below.

Example of change in handling rents. G. Grant formed a corporation and contributed property which produced gross rents of $60,000 a year, and securities producing dividends of $30,000 a year. He sheltered his dividend income under the old law, because the gross rent was over 50 per cent of the total gross income and thus was not considered PHC income. His only PHC income was the $30,000 dividends, which was less than 80 per cent of the total gross income.

G. Grant is not so happy with the passage of the Internal Revenue Act of 1964. He now owns a corporation that is subject to the PHC tax. Interest, taxes, and depreciation amount to $40,000 on his property. He now has adjusted rent of $20,000 ($60,000 rental income less $40,000 expenses). This is less than 50 per cent of the total adjusted gross income of $50,000, and therefore the rent is PHC income. The total adjusted gross income is the dividend of $30,000 plus the rent of $60,000 less the $40,000 depreciation, and so forth. The PHC income includes the rent of $20,000 and the dividends of $30,000. Thus, in this case the PHC income is equal to the adjusted gross income.

D. E. Lee had a very similar corporation. His property yielded rents of $60,000 less expenses listed above of $40,000, but he had dividends of only $10,000. Here the adjusted rent of $20,000 is above 50 per cent of the adjusted gross income of $30,000; therefore, the rent is not PHC income. However, the dividends of $10,000 are $3,000 more than 10 per cent of the total gross of $70,000 ($60,000 rent plus $10,000 dividends). Thus, the D. E. Lee Corporation will have to pay out at least $3,000 in dividends or else it will be a PHC.

Mineral, oil, and gas royalties. Under the old law, mineral, oil, and gas royalties were not included as PHC income if they were 50 per cent or more of the gross income, and if trade or business expense deductions equaled 15 per cent or more of the gross income. Now they come under rules similar to those for rent above. These royalties are reduced by depletion, property and severance taxes, interest, and rent paid to determine both PHC income and total adjusted gross income. They are not considered PHC income if: (1) the adjusted royalty is 50 per cent or more of the total adjusted gross income; (2) other PHC income is not more than 10 per cent of the total gross income reduced by capital gains; and (3) business and trade deductions are at least 15 per cent of the total adjusted gross income.

Base for Imposition of Tax

The tax rate is based on undistributed personal holding company income. Under the old law, this was taxable income with certain adjustments less the dividends-paid deduction. We shall not go into the adjustments here. Considering the size of the penalty tax, the important thing is not to fall into the personal holding company category. The new law has made certain changes in the tax base with respect to the handling of certain liquidating dividends and to deductions for amounts set aside to pay certain debts arising before 1964. In respect to liquidating dividends to individual shareholders, they will reduce the tax base only to the extent that the PHC so elects by labeling the distribution a dividend. This part of the liquidating distribution is taxable to the shareholder as a dividend rather than as a capital gain.

Opportunity to Liquidate

Although the penalty tax rate is less, the new rules make it much easier to become a personal holding company. Thus, companies that were not personal holding companies in one of the two tax years ending before enactment of the new law, but that would have been had the new law applied, are given the opportunity to liquidate on favorable conditions. If the corporation can liquidate prior to 1966, the old law will be used to test the corporation's liability for PHC tax for 1964 and 1965.

If the corporation liquidates prior to January 1, 1967, under Section 331 (a) (1) of the Internal Revenue Code they will have a capital gain. Alternatively, they may liquidate under modified rules of Section 333 of the Internal Revenue Code. The latter method is often referred to as a "one-month liquidation." The general rules of liquidation will be discussed in a later section. The modification is that the shareholders will not be taxed on appreciation in securities that are distributed in kind if these securities were acquired by the corporation prior to 1963. They will, of course, be subject to a tax when they sell them. If the shareholder held his stock for more than six months, his gain will be taxed as long-term capital gain to the extent that there is retained earnings in the corporation. Any balance of gain is capital gain to the extent that cash, or securities acquired after 1962, is distributed.

A company may be a personal holding company in the year that it liquidates. To escape the PHC tax, it can either pay a dividend before liquidation or else label an appropriate part of the liquidation dividend an ordinary dividend resulting in ordinary income to the shareholders.

For liquidations after 1966, the modified Section 333 rules can still be used if the corporation was subject to debt at the beginning of 1964. Results are similar to the above, except that gain, to the extent of earnings after 1966, is dividend income.

DUMMY REAL ESTATE CORPORATIONS

In the past, real estate was sometimes held in a dummy corporation with bare legal title. One purpose was to provide limited liability. Another reason why the dummy corporation was used was for ease of transferability of ownership. The idea was that the corporation would not be taxed at the corporate level, and that the income would be taxed directly to the shareholders.

For example, Mr. Meeks owned a home in the suburbs. His wife spent a great deal of time abroad, so that he was concerned about transferability of title if he decided to sell the home. He established the Meeks Corporation for the sole purpose of holding title to the property. He paid the taxes and interest on the mortgage as an individual. The result was that the corporation was disregarded for tax purposes, and Meeks could take the deduction for taxes and interest.

The recent trends in court rulings is that the shareholders cannot disregard the corporate entity if the corporation carries on any business at all. If the corporation is not disregarded, there is a tax at both the corporate and the shareholder levels.

For example, Mr. Zephyr and associates took title to a tract of land in the name of Zephyr Corp., a dummy corporation. The purpose was to give the corporation bare legal title and thus facilitate transferability of title if it was decided to sell the land. The land was sold at a substantial profit over a five-year period, and the proceeds were immediately distributed to the shareholders. Zephyr Corp., however, also paid the realty taxes, executed mortgages, and carried on such other activities. The shareholders said that Zephyr Corp. was only a trustee of the property and that the income belonged to the shareholders, that it was taxable only to them, and that no corporation taxes were due. However, the Fifth Circuit Court upheld the Revenue Service in the conclusion that Zephyr Corp. owed taxes on the profit.

AFFILIATED AND RELATED CORPORATIONS

If companies are affiliated, they may file consolidated tax returns. All corporations that have been members of the affiliated group at any time during the tax year have to consent. The consent can be handled just by filing a consolidated return. For taxable years of corporations ending on December 31, 1963 or earlier, there was an additional two per cent surtax imposed on consolidated returns. For taxable years which include January 1, 1964, there is a pro-rating of the additional two per cent tax.

Reasons for Filing a Consolidated Return

Particular circumstances will determine whether it is desirable to file a consolidated return. A corporation cannot deduct a capital loss but must offset it against capital gains. Thus, sometimes it might be worth while to file a consolidated return if one company in the group has a capital loss and another a capital gain. Of course, if a consolidated return was not filed, the corporation with the loss could carry it over for five years. The case of a net operating loss in one of the affiliated corporations may make it desirable to file a consolidated return so that the loss can be offset against a gain in another corporation. This would give immediate use of the loss. The operating loss, of course, could be carried back and carried forward under the provisions we discussed earlier concerning net operating losses.

As we discussed in an earlier section, corporations are allowed an 85 per cent deduction for dividends received from domestic corporations. If corporations file a consolidated return, there is no tax on dividends between these corporations. For taxable years ending after December 31, 1963, there is a 100 per cent dividend-received deduction for dividends between certain related companies, as will be explained below. Affiliated companies, then, will have to make a choice between electing this 100 per cent dividend-received deduction and filing consolidated returns.

Inclusions in an Affiliated Group

The determination of an affiliated group is a function of the stock ownership. The following two conditions result in an affiliated group: (1) at least 80 per cent of all classes of voting stock and at least 80 per cent of each class of nonvoting stock of each includible corporation (except the parent) is owned directly by one or more of the other includible corporations, and (2) the parent corporation must own directly 80 per cent of all classes of the voting stock and at least 80 per cent of each class of nonvoting stock of at least one of the other includible corporations. If stock is limited and preferred as to dividends, it is not included in the above definition. Certain corporations, such as those exempt from tax, certain insurance companies, and real estate investment trusts, are not includible corporations.

Election is Binding

The election to file a consolidated tax return is binding for future years with certain exceptions. These exceptions are: (1) a new member is added to the group, if it was not organized directly or indirectly by any other member of the group; (2) the Revenue Service grants permission for a change; and (3) there is a change in the tax laws or regulations which reduce the advantage of a consolidated return. In the latter case, the Revenue Service usually issues rulings allowing a change to separate returns.

MULTIPLE CORPORATIONS

For small corporations it was most often desirable not to file a consolidated return. Rather, from a tax standpoint it would be desirable to split the corporation into several corporations in order to get additional surtax exemptions.

For example, with the tax rates at 30 per cent of the first $25,000 and 52 per cent of the balance, Company A earns $100,000 before taxes and must pay a corporate tax of $46,500. Company A splits into four corporations instead. Now the corporate tax for each is $7,500, and the total for the four is only $30,000. This is a saving of $16,500, or three times $5,500 (22 per cent of $25,000). As one would expect, splitting corporations for tax-avoidance purposes was attacked by the Treasury. The Revenue Act of 1964 added a variety of provisions which reduce even further the ability to use multiple corporations to achieve additional surtax exemptions. Note, of course, that there may be important business reasons, as distinguished from tax reasons, for having more than one corporation. For example, one project may be much more risky than another, and the owners may wish to insulate another corporation from the more risky venture.

Disallowance of Surtax Exemption

For transfers on June 12, 1963 or earlier, if a corporation transferred property to a newly created or formerly inactive controlled corporation, the controlled corporation could lose its $25,000 surtax exemption and its $100,000 accumulated-earnings credit, unless the taxpayer could prove that the extra exemption and credit were not the main purpose for the transfer. The Internal Revenue Service would allow the exemption and credit in part and allocate it among the corporations.

Control meant the ownership of stock possessing at least 80 per cent of the total combined voting power of all classes of stock entitled to vote, or at least 80 per cent of the total value of shares of all classes of stock of the corporation. Constructive-ownership rules also applied.

Rule tightened. The Revenue Act of 1964 made the above rule apply to transfers of indirect property other than money by corporations after June 12, 1963 as well.

For example, Tahoma Corporation incorporates subsidiary Natoma and acquires all its stock solely for cash. If Natoma then buys property from Tahoma, it may be considered an indirect transfer of property. The result may be a denial of the Natoma Corporation's surtax exemption if tax savings were a major purpose. Note that tax savings only need be a major purpose; they need not be the principal purpose.

The new rules also apply to similar transfers to a controlled corporation by an individual or individuals in certain situations. However, transfers by individuals are not penalized if they control only one corporation.

For example, John Smith controls only the Watusee Corporation. If he transfers property to it, the Watusee Corporation does not lose its surtax exemption. But if, while he controls Watusee Corporation, he forms the Minnetonka Corporation, transfers of property to Minnetonka Corporation may result in denial of its surtax exemption. Also, if he transfers property to the Watusee Corporation while he continues to control both corporations, he may lose the surtax exemption for Watussee if it is inactive.

Meaning of control for individual transferee. Two requirements must be met for control: (1) The individual and not more than four other individuals must own at least 80 per cent of the stock of each corporation in terms of voting power or value; and (2) They must own more than 50 per cent, taking into account as stock owned by each only his least percentage of ownership in each corporation.

For example, Goldberg owns 90 per cent of Art Corporation and O'Brien (unrelated) owns 10 per cent. They form the Magnificent Corporation, in which Goldberg owns 10 per cent and O'Brien 90 per cent. Both corporations are considered controlled by them under the 80-per-cent rule. Here only 10 per cent of the shareholdings of each in each separate corporation is taken into account. Thus, for this rule, they only own 20 per cent of the shares, and the 50-per-cent test is not met.

In addition to the surtax exemption, the $100,000 minimum

credit for tax on unreasonably retained earnings can also be disallowed under similar conditions.

Allocation of Income, etc., by Revenue Service

Gross income, deductions, credits, or allowances may be apportioned by the Revenue Service between organizations owned or controlled by the same interests if it is determined that this is necessary to prevent tax evasion or to clearly reflect income of the taxpayer.

For example, Martin Corporation, a subsidiary of MacMartin Corporation, rented a building it owned to the MacMartin Corporation. Each year the rent was adjusted so as to result in the lowest possible combined tax for the two. In such a situation, an adjustment to show fair rental value is in order.

Acquisition of Corporation to Avoid Tax

If the main purpose of corporate acquisition is to achieve tax benefits, then deductions, credits, and other allowances may be disallowed. Disallowance applies when: (1) a person or persons gain control of a corporation or (2) a corporation gets property with a carried-over or transferred basis from another corporation not then controlled by the former or its stockholders, and the principal purpose for the acquisition is evasion or avoidance of taxes through the benefit of a deduction credit or allowance that would not otherwise be available. For this purpose, a "person" includes an individual, trust, estate, partnership, association, company, or corporation. "Control" means the ownership of stock with at least 50 per cent of the total combined voting power of all classes of stock entitled to vote or at least 50 per cent of the total value of shares of all classes of stock.

Tax Alternatives for Multiple Corporations

As a result of the Revenue Act of 1964, multiple corporations have several tax alternatives in respect to the surtax exemptions. They may: (1) divide one surtax exemption among them; (2) retain their separate surtax exemptions but elect to pay an additional six per cent tax on the first $25,000 of taxable income. If a corporation has its surtax exemption disallowed as we described in the section on "Disallowance of Surtax Exemption," and it is a member of a group electing multiple surtax exemptions, then the six per cent additional tax does not apply to that corporation.

The result of the six per cent tax is a total tax of 28 per cent on the first $25,000 of income, as contrasted with the normal rate of 22 per cent. Each corporation may accumulate a minimum of $100,000 of earnings before becoming subject to the accumulated-earnings tax.

Corporations included. There are two kinds of controlled groups included. These are: (1) Parent companies and their 80 per cent subsidiaries, and (2) brother-sister corporations. Brother-sister corporations are two or more corporations each at least 80 per cent owned by one individual, estate, or trust. The corporations need not be in the same business.

For example, James Martin owns an apartment house in New York, a plantation in Louisiana, and a savings and loan association in California. These are brother-sister corporations, and the new law could apply.

The parent and 80 per cent-owned subsidiary group includes corporations with a common parent corporation where (1) one or more of the other corporations own at least 80 per cent of the total voting shares or at least 80 per cent of the total value of shares of all classes of stock of each corporation except the stock of the parent corporation, and (2) the parent corporation owns at least 80 per cent of the voting stock or at least 80 per cent of the total value of shares of all classes of stock of at least one of the corporations. In determining the voting power or value of the stock, stock owned directly by the corporations other than the parent in the group is not included. Preferred stock that is nonvoting, treasury stock and, in some cases, stock held by related parties is not included.

For example, Harvard Corporation owns 70 per cent of the voting stock of Vassar Corporation and Smith Corporation. Vassar Corporation owns the remaining voting stock of Smith Corporation, and Smith Corporation owns the remaining voting stock of Vassar Corporation. Because the intercompany holdings are eliminated in determining the 80-per-cent control, the result is that the three corporations are a controlled group. For this calculation, Harvard Corporation is considered to own 100 per cent of the voting stock of the subsidiaries.

In the case of the parent-subsidiary classification, a corporation is considered to own the stock it actually owns or can acquire under option. There are more complicated rules for the brother-sister corporation classification.

December 31 the crucial date. The status of a controlled group is determined annually on December 31. If a corporation meets the requirements on December 31, the rule will apply even though the taxable year of the corporation ends at a later date and the corporation is no longer part of the group. It may not be a member on December 31, but it is still considered a member of the group if it was a member for at least half the days in its taxable year prior to December 31. Conversely, the rule does not apply to a corporation if it was a member on December 31 but was a member for only less than half the days in its taxable year that precede December 31.

Dividing a surtax exemption. As was noted earlier, the related corporations may divide the surtax exemption or may each have a $25,000 exemption but pay a penalty tax of six per cent. If they decide to split the exemption, the amount for each is either $25,000 divided by the number of corporations in the group or $25,000 apportioned according to whatever plan for apportionment they may decide upon.

For example, assume that there are five corporations in a related group. Each may take a surtax exemption of $5,000. Alternatively, they may plan to divide it so that Corporation A gets $10,000, B $5,000, C $3,000, D $2,000, and E $5,000, or in any other way they wish.

The Regulations set forth rules as to statements required to elect to apportion the surtax exemption. The apportionment plan, once chosen, cannot be changed after the filing date unless an election is made to pay the six per cent penalty tax.

Six Per Cent Penalty Tax

The corporations may elect to pay the six per cent penalty tax and each have a $25,000 surtax exemption at any time before the expiration of three years after the date on which the earliest income tax return is filed for a member of the group after December 31, 1963. The Regulations indicate the form of consent required by the members of the group.

For 1965 and later, corporate tax rates are 22 per cent of the first $25,000 and 48 per cent of the balance. Thus, there still may be a tax saving by having separate surtax exemptions and electing to pay the six per cent penalty tax instead of having only one surtax exemption.

One corporation with $50,000 of taxable income would pay $17,500 in corporate taxes (22 per cent of $25,000 plus 48 per cent of the balance). Two related corporations with a total of $50,000 taxable income divided equally between them would pay $14,000 in tax (28 per cent of $25,000 times 2).

In the case of brother-sister corporations, it probably will be more desirable to pay the six per cent penalty tax. In the case of the parent-subsidiary corporations, a determination must be made whether they are better off in filing a consolidated return or in electing the 100 per cent dividends-received deduction discussed below. An election may be terminated as of any December 31. Once terminated, a new election cannot be made prior to the sixth December 31 after the effective date of termination.

Dividends-Received Deduction of 100 Per Cent

In our discussion of the calculation of corporate tax, we noted that there was an 85 per cent dividend deduction for dividends from domestic companies. When dividends are paid by one corporation to another in the same affiliated group, the dividend may be exempt entirely. An affiliated group is one that is entitled to file consolidated returns. These are a parent company and its 80 per cent subsidiaries, as described earlier. Note that brother-sister corporations may not file consolidated returns. The 100 per cent deduction applies only to dividends that are paid out of earnings for taxable years ending after 1963. There must be affiliation through the earnings year and at the time of distribution. The group must elect to have the 100 per cent dividend deduction.

Consequences of election. There are additional requirements to obtain the 100 per cent dividend-received deduction. There may be no election of multiple surtax exemptions in effect either for the earnings year or for the distribution year. That is, the companies cannot elect to each have a $25,000 surtax exemption and pay the six per cent penalty. The whole group has only one $25,000 surtax exemption, just as if they filed a consolidated return. Recall also that an affiliated group that files a consolidated return is not taxable on intercorporate dividends.

The group is allowed only one accumulated-earnings credit of $100,000, and $100,000 annual and $400,000 over-all deduction for exploration expense. There is only $100,000 exemption for estimated tax. An election must be made by the parent, and each subsidiary member must consent on the last day of the parent's taxable year. The election may be terminated by all members filing a termination.

LIQUIDATION OR SALE OF STOCK

The shareholders of a corporation may desire to dispose of its properties. They could, of course, sell the stock of the corporation to others. Alternatively, the corporation could dispose of the properties and then distribute the proceeds to the shareholders.

Another procedure would be to distribute the property to the share-holders, after which the shareholders could sell the property. There are a variety of tax consequences to be concerned with in the discussion of these various methods that follows. When there is appreciated property, the question of double taxation at the corporate level and the shareholder level arises. The question of ordinary income or capital gain is also important. When losses are involved, it may be important from the point of view of whether the corporation or the shareholders have the loss. We shall first review the tax consequences of the sale of stock, so as to compare the tax consequences with those of the various liquidation procedures discussed later.

Sale of Stock

The sale or exchange of capital stock by the shareholders usually results in capital gain or loss. And the shareholders may use the installment method of reporting their capital gains if they meet the necessary requirements. From the seller's standpoint, this is desirable because there are no problems of liquidation and there is no problem of double tax at the corporate and the share-holder level. If property has appreciated in value, the buyer will probably not pay a full price for the stock which recognizes the full appreciation of the property. The reason for this is, of course, that if he later sells the corporate property, there will be a corporate tax, and then, if a dividend is paid, he will pay a tax on the dividend. In addition, the buyer of the stock will have a corporation whose basis for depreciation for the property is low.

For example, Gold invests $50,000 in a new corporation and borrows $160,000 to construct an apartment house. After five years, his balance sheet shows: land, $40,000; building, $160,000 less accumulated depreciation of $20,000; mortgage payable, $120,000; capital stock, $50,000; and retained earnings, $10,000. The land and building, however, have a fair market value of $250,000 and a book value of $140,000 ($160,000 - $20,000). Assuming that the stock price reflects this appreciation, he sells his stock for $130,000 ($250,000 property value less mortgage of $120,000). He then has a capital gain of $80,000 ($130,000 less original capital contribution of $50,000). Actually, the tax consequences to the buyer are such that he probably would not pay this amount for the corporation. In relation to the value of the property, the corporation has a low basis. Future sale of the property will yield a tax to the corporation. To the extent that there is depreciation after 1963, there is a depreciatio recapture element to be considered that may cause some of the gain o sale of the property to be ordinary income rather than capital gain.

The foregoing assumes that the corporation has appreciated property, so that the amount the shareholder receives for the stock will be higher than his basis. If the sale would result in a loss, the shareholder would have a capital loss. However, if the corporation sold the property at a loss, there would be a corporate loss that could perhaps be carried back to taxable years. From the buyer's standpoint, it would be better to buy the stock rather than the property if the property were worth less than the corporation's basis for the property, because he would have a larger amount to depreciate and a higher basis for future gain or loss on sale.

Liquidations

A corporation is considered to be in liquidation when it ceases to be a going concern and when its activities are merely for the purposes of winding up its affairs, paying its debts, and distributing any balance to its shareholders. Amounts distributed in complete or partial liquidation of a corporation are treated as in full or part payment in exchange for the stock. If property is distributed, the shareholders are considered to have received the fair market value of the property. Distributions may be either a complete liquidation of a corporation or a partial liquidation.

Partial liquidation. A partial liquidation is a distribution which results in a contraction of the corporate business. Note that, if the distribution is really a dividend, it is not a partial liquidation. A dividend, of course, is taxed as ordinary income to the extent of the earnings and profits of the corporation. A partial liquidation may be one of a series of distributions in redemption of all the stock of the corporation under a plan of complete liquidation. There is also a partial liquidation if the distribution is not essentially equivalent to a dividend, if the distribution is in redemption of a part of the stock of the corporation under a plan, and if the distribution occurs within the tax year in which the plan is adopted or within the succeeding tax year.

Liquidating Dividends--Taxability

Usually no gain or loss is recognized to a corporation on the distribution of property in kind in a complete or partial liquidation. This is true even though the property may have changed in value since it was acquired. The difference between the basis of the stock and the amount received in liquidation of the stock is a capital gain or loss to the shareholder. There are some exceptions, however, where there is ordinary income.

Shareholder's gain or loss. The shareholder's gain or loss is a capital gain or loss, and it is long- or short-term depending on how long the stock has been held. If the distribution is in installments, gain does not have to be reported until the basis of the stock is recovered. If there is a loss through liquidation, the loss is deducted in the year of the final distribution.

Possibility of ordinary income. Ordinary income can result in liquidation if a corporation is a collapsible corporation. We discussed collapsible corporations earlier in this chapter. If property is inventory to the corporation, there may be a serious problem. However, if the property is a Section 1231 asset and, thus, not inventory, the collapsible rules generally will not apply unless the unrealized inventory appreciation is greater than 15 per cent of the corporation's net worth. Thus, the dealer in real estate whose property is inventory has to carefully consider the collapsible-corporation possibility, but the investor in real estate, where the property generally is not inventory, does not usually have to be concerned.

If the liquidation is preceded or followed by a transfer of the corporate assets to another corporation, the liquidating distribution may be treated as an ordinary dividend. The transaction may be treated as one in which no loss is recognized and in which gain is recognized only to the extent of other property received.

Gain or loss to liquidating corporation. When a corporation distributes property for stock in a partial or complete liquidation, the corporation usually has no gain or loss. Recall, however, the depreciation-recapture rules of the 1962 law for property other than buildings and the depreciation-recapture rules in the 1964 law for real estate. The disposition of such property in a partial or complete liquidation may yield ordinary income to the corporation, as will be explained later.

Twelve-Month Liquidation

The 12-month liquidation, often referred to as a Section 337 liquidation, avoids the problem of a double tax at the corporate and shareholder levels when a corporation sells property and distributes the proceeds to the shareholders. Certain rules have to be followed and certain information filed. If within a 12-month period all the assets of the corporation less those retained to meet claims are distributed in complete liquidation, there is no gain or loss recognized to the corporation (if there is no depreciation-recapture potential) when it sells or exchanges its property within the 12-month period beginning with the adoption of the plan. "Property" does not include stock in trade, inventory, property held primarily for sale to customers, and certain installment obligations. There is an exception, and inventory is considered property if it is sold or exchanged to one person in one transaction. Any assets retained after the expiration of the 12-month period for payment of claims have to be specifically set aside for that purpose. They also must be reasonable in amount.

Lakeview Apartments, Inc. is owned by John and Mary Scranton. John and Mary have the corporation adopt a plan of complete liquidation on February 1. On March 20 the apartment building (the only asset of Lakeview Apartments, Inc.) is sold to Martin Bland for $200,000. There is no mortgage on the apartment building, which has a basis of $100,000 to the corporation. The $200,000 is distributed on July 30 to John and Mary. All of the requirements are met for a 12-month liquidation (Section 337), so there is no tax to the corporation, Lakeview Apartments, Inc. John and Mary pay a capital-gain tax on the difference between their basis for their stock and the amount they receive.

Depreciation recapture. In the above, we have assumed that there is no depreciation-recapture potential under I.R.C. Section 1250. If there was a depreciation-recapture potential, there would be ordinary income tax. Let us assume that there was $20,000 "additional depreciation" on the property since 1963, and that the applicable depreciation-recapture percentage is 75 per cent. The 75 per cent is applied to the $20,000, because this is the lesser of the depreciation and the gain, and $15,000 of the liquidating dividend would be taxed as ordinary income rather than as a capital gain.

Inventory property. Gain or loss is recognized to the corporation on the sale of stock in trade or other inventoriable property unless the property is sold or exchanged in bulk to one person in one transaction. If it is sold in bulk to one person, then there is no gain or loss recognized to the corporation.

Liquidate and Distribute Property to Shareholders

A corporation alternatively may dispose of its property by liquidating and transferring the property to the shareholders. The shareholders then can sell the property. As was noted earlier, there is no tax on the liquidation dividend to the shareholders. The stockholders have a short- or long-term capital gain or loss depending on how long they have held their stock, and the amount is the difference between the fair market value of the property and the basis of their stock. When they sell the property, there is a

gain or loss measured by the difference between the selling price
and the fair market value at the date of distribution. Again, the
collapsible-corporation rules have to be examined. In addition, if
the property is subject to recapture under Section 1245 or Section
1250, part of the income to the stockholders will be ordinary income. If there is any danger that the sale of property may be considered a sale by the corporation rather than by the stockholders,
it would be better to follow the Section 337 liquidation procedure
described in the previous section.

One-Month (Section 333) Liquidation

If certain strict conditions are met, a corporation with appreciated property may liquidate without the shareholders being
taxed on the increase in value of the property that they receive in
the liquidation. As might be expected, the tax is only postponed;
it is not forgiven. Generally, the basis of the property that the
shareholders receive in the liquidation is the same as the basis of
the shareholders' stock surrendered in the liquidation. Certain adjustments will be made to the basis if any money is received or any
gain is taxed on the liquidation. A shareholder will have gain on the
liquidating distribution taxable as ordinary income to the extent of
his ratable share of earnings and profits. Again, the depreciation-
recapture rules of Section 1245 and Section 1250 can cause taxable
income; we shall give an example of this below. And if property on
which the investment credit has been taken is disposed of before the
end of its useful life, there may be a recapture of the investment
credit.

Strict requirements. The requirements of the law must be
carefully followed. The following conditions must be met: (1) Liquidation must be made pursuant to a plan adopted on or after June
22, 1954; (2) Distribution must be in complete redemption or cancellation of all the stock of a domestic corporation (other than a
collapsible corporation); (3) The shareholders must file a written
election within 30 days after the adoption of the plan to accept the
benefits of the plan. This election is filed on Form 964 and an information return is filed on Form 966. In addition to these conditions, the stockholders must be "qualified stockholders."

Qualified stockholders. Corporations are excluded from the
use of this section if they hold 50 per cent or more of the stock entitled to vote on adoption of the liquidation plan. Shareholders other
than corporations, and corporations holding less than 50 per cent of
the shares entitled to vote, are qualified electing shareholders if:
(1) their written election is properly filed and (2) like elections have

been made and filed by owners of stock holding at least 80 per cent of the voting power of all classes of stock owned by shareholders of the same group and entitled to vote on the adoption of the plan of liquidation. This ownership has to exist when the plan is adopted.

Some gain is taxed. There may be some recognized gain on the liquidation distribution. This gain is limited to the greater of the following: (1) the shareholder's ratable share of earnings and profits accumulated after February 28, 1913; or (2) money and market value of stock or securities received that were acquired by the corporation after December 31, 1953. Corporate shareholders report any gain as capital gain. Shareholders other than corporations report the portion of recognized gain that represents earnings and profits accumulated after February 28, 1913 as a dividend. Any additional gain is capital gain.

Basis to stockholders. The basis to the stockholders of the property they receive is the same as the basis of the stock canceled or redeemed less the amount of any money received and plus the amount of gain recognized to them.

Depreciation recapture makes liquidation dangerous. Section 333 liquidations (one-month liquidations) were often quite useful to real estate corporations prior to the 1964 Revenue Act, which introduced depreciation recapture on real estate. Now the depreciation-recapture potential has to be carefully watched to determine the tax consequences of the liquidation. Before depreciation recapture, the one-month liquidation was often desirable for a real estate corporation with property that had appreciated drastically but had rather small earnings and profits. These corporations could liquidate with little or no taxes on either the corporation itself or the recipient shareholders. The following example will illustrate the effect of the transaction.

Assume that John Gold owns the Scranton Arms. This apartment is the only asset of the corporation. John Gold wishes to liquidate the Scranton Arms, which has substantially appreciated in value. The following information is necessary for our example: Adjusted basis of building, $1,200,000; fair market value of building, $2,000,000; corporate earnings and profits, $20,000. Prior to the depreciation-recapture rules, Gold could liquidate Scranton Arms Corporation with very little adverse tax consequences. The corporation would pay no tax on the liquidation. Gold, as the shareholder-recipient, would pay ordinary income tax on the $20,000 that represents his ratable share (in this case, all) of the earnings and profits.

To illustrate the effect of depreciation recapture, we shall assume that there is $400,000 "additional depreciation" and that the applicable percentage of recapture is 60 per cent. The reader may wish to review the discussion of recapture on real estate in an earlier chapter. Because of the recapture provisions, Scranton Arms Corporation is considered to have recapture income of $240,000. This is 60 per cent times the smaller of the $800,000 gain and the $400,000 additional depreciation. Using a 50 per cent tax rate for simplification, the corporation has a tax of $120,000 and now has additional earnings and profits of $120,000.

Gold on liquidation is now taxable at ordinary rates on $140,000. This is the original $20,000 earnings and profits plus the $120,000 additional earnings and profits resulting from the depreciation recapture.

The above example illustrates the importance of projecting the tax consequences of any depreciation-recapture potential existing in the property.

CURRENT INFORMATION AND COMPETENT ADVICE

It has taken many words to expose the reader to many of the implications the federal income tax has for decisions involving real estate. Particularly important is the ability of a decision maker to project the tax consequences of a particular decision before the decision is made and to place the tax aspects and non-tax aspects in proper perspective.

As time passes after the final draft of this book there will be new Treasury Regulations, new Revenue Rulings, new Tax Court and Federal Court decisions which will affect the law. It is hoped this text will make the reader aware of the implications of the tax law on real estate operations. It is up to the reader to make sure that he has the most current information and has secured competent advice where necessary.

Assignment Material

CHAPTER 2

Questions

1. What is the difference between a sale and an exchange? What is the tax significance of this distinction?
2. In many instances, a gain may be taxable whereas a loss is not deductible. When are losses deductible?
3. What is the basis of property acquired by inheritance, bequest, or devise?
4. Frequently real property is transferred from one spouse's name to the names of the husband and wife as joint tenants. Under what conditions will this transfer escape gift tax liability?
5. What is the basis of property received as a gift: (a) prior to January 1, 1921? (b) after January 1, 1921?
6. If a businessman decides to demolish an old business building in order to construct a new building, what happens to the book value of the old building for income tax purposes?

Problems

1. Arnold Schafer's boat has an adjusted basis of $12,000. He uses it only for his own recreation. When he sells it for $9,500 at the end of this season, how much of the loss will be recognized? Explain.
2. On January 2, 1964, Steve Saxe bought an apartment house for $65,000. One year later he built additional garages for the house at a cost of $5,000. During 1965, he also spent $2,000 remodeling the apartment house lobby and $3,000 for a new roof. All these items were chargeable to capital account. Assuming that he deducted $1,100 for depreciation in 1964 and $1,240 in 1965, what is the adjusted basis of the apartment house on January 2, 1966?
3. In 1962 William Russell bought a tavern for $30,000. A few months after the purchase, he remodeled the building at a cost of $7,000. In April 1966, he sold the building for $38,000. Depreciation on the property during Russell's ownership was $7,500. What was his recognized gain or loss?
4. On January 1, 1963, Clifford Sutton bought an office building for $40,000. He agreed to assume $2,500 in back taxes. On January 1, 1966, he sold the building for $45,000. During the time he held the building, Sutton paid a maintenance man $3,000 a year to look after it. When he sold the property, he paid $250 for advertising it. Instead of deducting the salary paid the maintenance man and the advertising expense, he charged them to capital account. Assuming that he took $500 yearly depreciation, what is the recognized gain or loss on the sale?
5. (a) In 1960 Streepey bought some building lots for $12,000 cash. In 1962 he put an $8,000 mortgage on the property. In 1966 he exchanged the lots

for other building lots, owned by Strand, valued at $8,000. In addition, he received $2,000 cash, and Strand took Streepey's original lots subject to the $8,000 mortgage. There was no mortgage on the lots that Streepey received. What is Streepey's recognized gain or loss? (b) What would your answer be if, instead of cash, the transferee had given Streepey a negotiable, interest-bearing, promissory note for $2,000? The transferee is solvent and has always paid his debts.

6. Late in 1951, Harold Swanson bought an unimproved plot of land for $70,000. An annual property tax of $1,900 was paid during each of the years 1952 to 1966, inclusive, and during each of these years Swanson spent $200 advertising the property. No deduction was taken for either the taxes or the advertising expense. Swanson elected to capitalize the tax and filed the proper statements with his return. In 1966 Swanson sold the property for $100,000. Figure the recognized gain or loss.

7. (a) What is the basis (unadjusted) of property acquired before March 1, 1913? (b) What is the recognized gain or loss in each case below?

Cost	3-1-13 Value	Selling Price	Recognized Gain	Recognized Loss
$10,000	$15,000	$20,000	$....	$....
10,000	5,000	3,000	....	....
10,000	30,000	20,000	....	....
10,000	3,000	5,000	....	....
10,000	5,000	20,000	....	....
10,000	15,000	5,000	....	....

8. Snyder's father died on June 1, 1962, leaving him by specific bequest certain personal property which had been purchased for $38,000 and which had a fair market value of $30,000 at the time of the father's death.

He also received under the residuary clause in the will personal property which cost his father $90,000 but which was appraised in the estate at $56,000, its actual value on the date of the father's death. This property had a fair market value of $54,000 when distributed to Snyder.

On August 17, 1965 Snyder sold the property received by specific bequest for $24,000 and that received by residuary bequest for $60,000. State the basis for determining, and the amount of, recognized gain or loss. Assume that the executor made no election as to valuation of the estate.

9. Kermit Oliver inherited his grandfather's home that had been built in 1956 for $35,000. When Oliver's grandfather died on March 1, 1965, the home was worth $40,000. It was not, however, until September 2, 1965 that the will was probated and Oliver received the property, now worth $43,000 owing to a sudden rise in real estate values. The executor made no election as to valuation of the estate. On November 2, 1965 Oliver sold the home for $45,000. What is (a) the basis of the home for determining gain or loss on the sale; (b) the amount of recognized gain or loss on the sale?

10. On January 1, 1962 Mr. and Mrs. Pfeifer bought an apartment building for $160,000 and held it as joint tenants by the entirety. Each paid one-half ($80,000) of the purchase price. Mr. and Mrs. Pfeifer filed joint income tax returns for 1962, 1963, and 1964, taking $4,000 depreciation on the building each year. Under state law Mrs. Pfeifer was entitled to one-half the income from the property. On January 1, 1965, Mr. Pfeifer died. The fair market value of the apartment was $200,000. One-half this value

($100,000) was included in his estate. What was the adjusted basis of the property in the hands of widow Pfeifer on January 1, 1965?

11. On January 1, 1958, MacDonald bought an apartment building for $40,000. On January 1, 1963, MacDonald gave the building to his daughter. On that date the property had a fair market value of $37,000. He paid $900 gift tax on the transfer. On January 1, 1966, the daughter sold the building for $36,000. Assume an annual depreciation allowance of $1,000. What was her recognized gain or loss?

12. Arnold Parks bought a hotel for $150,000 on January 1, 1962. Parks gave the property, having a fair market value of $140,000, to his son on April 1, 1964. Parks paid $15,000 gift tax on the gift. One year later, the son sold the hotel for $143,000. Annual depreciation was $4,000. What was the son's recognized gain or loss?

13. On March 1, 1910, Collins bought an apartment house for $120,000, of which $20,000 was allocable to the land. On March 1, 1913, the fair market value of the property was $138,000, of which $28,000 was allocable to the land. On March 1, 1965, Collins sold the property for $84,000, of which $40,000 was allocable to the land. What was his recognized gain or loss, assuming depreciation of $2,000 a year during the entire period that the property was owned?

CHAPTER 3

Questions

1. What exchanges are considered nontaxable?
2. What does the term "boot" refer to?
3. If a mortgage is part of an exchange, how is it handled?
4. What is an "involuntary conversion"?
5. Garold Raff uses a condemnation award to replace the condemned property with similar property. What general rules cover this replacement?

Problems

1. Tom Clark, an outboard motor dealer, entered into the following transactions during the tax year. State whether any gain would be recognized in each case, giving reasons for your conclusion. (a) A motor which Clark held in stock was exchanged for a larger model to be used for the same purpose. (b) A motor which Clark used in his fishing-guide business was exchanged for a newer model to be used for the same purpose. (c) A motor and boat used in his business was exchanged for a sailboat to be used for pleasure only.

2. State whether gain or loss should be recognized on the following exchanges. Give your reasons. (a) A city residence used as a home is exchanged for unimproved investment acreage suitable for subdividing into lots. (b) A gasoline tractor in farm service is replaced by a Diesel tractor to be used for the same purpose. (c) United States Treasury bonds are exchanged for a Palm Beach winter home. (d) A vacant business building lot is exchanged for a 99-year leasehold. (e) Furnaces from the stock of a dealer are exchanged for air-conditioning units placed in stock for sale.

3. William Green, a builder, wanted to buy a wooded tract of land to build a housing development. The land was owned by Steve Travis and valued at $20,000. Travis refused Green's offer of $25,000. He did, however,

offer to exchange the tract for $3,000 and a parking lot that Green owned
The paved parking lot had a fair market value of $16,000. Green accept
and they exchanged the properties. What, if any, was the recognized ga
or loss to Green?

4. Savage, who is a printer, bought a printing press for $10,000. When the
   press was delivered, he discovered that it was too large for his shop. He
   immediately exchanged it for a smaller press having a fair market value
   of $8,000, receiving also $700 cash and a municipal bond valued at $1,00
   What, if any, is the recognized gain or loss on the transaction?

5. (a) Machinery having an adjusted basis of $15,000 was exchanged by the
   taxpayer for similar machinery having a fair market value of $16,000.
   What, if any, was the recognized gain? (b) Assume the same facts as i
   (a), except that, in addition to giving machinery having an adjusted basis
   of $15,000, the taxpayer also gave $2,000 in cash. What, if any, was th
   recognized gain or loss? (c) Assume the same facts as in (a), except
   that, in addition to receiving other machinery valued at $16,000, the tax
   payer also received $2,000 in cash. What, if any, was the recognized
   gain? (d) The taxpayer exchanged machinery having an adjusted basis o
   $15,000 for similar machinery valued at $10,000. He also received
   $2,000 as "boot." What, if any was the recognized loss?

6. Alan Rifcind owns a printing company. On November 30, 1964 he decide
   to install a new printing press to replace an old one. The old press cost
   him $6,500 in December, 1962. The adjusted basis for this press on
   November 30, 1964 is $4,500. The new press will cost $10,500. It has
   a useful life of five years. What will be the recognized gain or loss, and
   what will be the basis of the new printing press in each of the following
   transactions on November 30, 1964? (a) Rifcind exchanges the old pres
   for the new one, giving in addition $7,000 cash (the trade-in allowance
   being $3,500). (b) Rifcind sells the old press for $3,500, and then buys
   the new one for $10,500. (c) Rifcind sells the old press for $5,900 and
   then buys the new press for $10,500. (d) Rifcind exchanges the old pres
   for the new one, giving in addition $5,500 cash (the trade-in allowance
   being $5,000).

7. Fletcher owns a machine bought on December 1, 1960 for $15,000 and
   having an adjusted basis on December 1, 1964 of $3,000. He proposes t
   trade in the old machine for a new one. The new machine will be of a lil
   kind and will be used for the same purpose. It will have a useful life of
   four years. Its purchase price is $12,000. How will Fletcher's income
   be affected, and what will be the basis of the new machine: (a) If Fletch
   on December 1, 1964, sells the old machine to the dealer for $2,000 and
   immediately buys the new one for $12,000? (b) If Fletcher, on Decembe
   1, 1964, exchanges the old machine for the new one, giving in addition
   $10,000 in cash (the trade-in allowance being $2,000)? (c) If Fletcher,
   on December 1, 1964, sells the old machine to the dealer for $5,000 and
   immediately buys the new one for $12,000? (d) If Fletcher, on Decemb
   1, 1964, exchanges the old machine for the new one, giving in addition
   $7,000 in cash (the trade-in allowance for the old machine being $5,000)

8. (a) Smith exchanged a machine used in his business having an adjusted
   basis of $2,000, for a similar machine valued at $2,500, plus $100 in
   cash. What, if any, was the recognized gain? What was the basis of the
   machine received? (b) Black exchanged a machine used in his business

having an adjusted basis of $2,000, for a similar machine valued at $1,500 plus $100 in cash. What, if any, was the recognized loss? What was the basis of the machine received?

9. Rylands exchanged an apartment house with an adjusted basis of $200,000 and a value of $300,000, plus stock in General Motors Corporation with a basis of $120,000 and a value of $100,000, for an apartment house worth $400,000. What is the basis of the apartment house received on this exchange?

10. John Marbury was the owner of a small factory building. Its adjusted basis was $17,000 and it was encumbered by an $8,000 mortgage. Marbury transferred it to Tom Madison in exchange for another factory building having a fair market value of $20,000 and $500 in cash. Madison took the building subject to the mortgage. (a) What, if any, gain or loss will be recognized to Marbury as a result of this transaction? (b) If Madison assumed the mortgage instead of taking the building subject to it, would your answer be different? Explain.

11. In 1964 a manufacturer read in the newspaper that the county government had voted to condemn the property on which his factory was located. He plans to immediately construct a new factory in a different location, and to borrow the money to pay for it. The old factory will not be torn down until 1965, and he will not receive the condemnation proceeds until 1966. Under these conditions, if he so elects, can he obtain the benefits of non-recognition of gain on conversion of the old factory under the involuntary-conversion provisions? Why?

12. Frederick Lincoln owned a motel which had an adjusted basis of $400,000. A hurricane completely destroyed the property. Insurance proceeds amounted to $450,000. Lincoln applied the provisions for nonrecognition of gain upon involuntary conversion. What gain, if any, is recognized if: (a) Lincoln invested the $450,000 insurance proceeds in a new motel? (b) Lincoln invested $420,000 in a new motel?

13. Tom Sewell owned a building which on January 1, 1964 had an adjusted cost basis of $275,000. On that date the building was completely destroyed by fire. Insurance proceeds amounted to $325,000. Sewell elected to apply the provisions for nonrecognition of gain upon involuntary conversion. What gain, if any, is recognized if: (a) Sewell invested the $325,000 in a new building? (b) Sewell invested $295,000 of the proceeds in a new building?

14. Shelton owned a warehouse that had an adjusted basis of $100,000. It was destroyed by fire. The insurance proceeds were $80,000. If Shelton bought another warehouse for $110,000 within one year of the fire, what, if any, would be his recognized loss?

CHAPTER 4

Questions

1. Dennis Martin, an electric cable manufacturer, owns the following property. State whether or not each item is a capital asset, and explain. (a) a factory for the manufacture of cable; (b) Martin's residence in Miami Beach, Florida; (c) ten shares of General Motors stock; (d) an apartment house in Miami Beach, Florida; (e) a truck used to deliver electric cable.

2. What classifications of use of real estate are important for income tax purposes?
3. How is the amount received for an option to purchase real estate treated if the option is exercised? If the option is not exercised?
4. Which of the following are capital assets when selling a sole proprietorship: (a) buildings; (b) good will; (c) leaseholds; (d) inventories; (e) notes receivable (for sale of inventory).
5. William Austin sells property to his son at a gain of $1,000. He had held the property two years. How will this gain be treated for tax purposes? What if the property was sold at a loss of $1,000?
6. Give three examples of transactions not normally thought of as sales or exchanges, which may result in capital gains.
7. When does the holding period for real property begin? When does the holding period begin for a new building?
8. Describe how the long-term capital-gain deduction is arrived at when there is a net long-term capital gain and a net short-term capital loss.

Problems

1. James Monsen owns an apartment house which cost him $50,000 in 1960. In 1965 he sells the building for $80,000. Monsen also runs a drugstore. He sold Section 1231 assets at a net loss of $20,000 in 1965. Assume no other capital transactions. (a) Assuming that Monsen's apartment house was classified as an investment, what is the nature of the gains and losses which would result from the above transactions? (b) Assuming that the apartment house was classified as used in trade or business, what kind of gains and losses would Monsen have?
2. Richard Johnson had two vacant lots which he purchased in 1962 for a price of $6,000 each. In 1965 he sold one of the lots for $15,000 and exchanged the other for another lot with a fair market value of $15,000. What effect would these transactions have on Johnson's 1965 income tax, assuming that: (a) He is considered an investor? (b) He is considered a dealer?
3. Elmer Williams feels that land that is for sale might go up greatly in value because of a proposal by a large firm to build a factory nearby. The property now has a price of $180,000. Mr. Williams decides to purchase an option to buy for one year at that price. The option costs $5,000. At the end of the year, the large firm decides to build the factory, and the property rises in value to $250,000. Elmer decides that he does not want the land. He could borrow the $180,000 to exercise the option at a local bank at six per cent plus a $1,000 fee for taking out the loan. Also, he could sell the option for $69,000. Assume a 50 per cent tax rate for income from this transaction and a 25 per cent rate for capital gains. Which course of action should Elmer take? (Assume that he will sell the property after six months.)
4. Builder Manuel Jones had the following transactions in securities during the year:

Stock	Bought	Sold
Adams Company	9/ 2/61 for $2,500	2/20/65 for $3,500
Baker Company	7/21/65 for $1,500	12/18/65 for $2,800
Carl Company	5/29/58 for $3,500	8/15/65 for $3,000
Denver Company	2/21/65 for $2,600	5/18/65 for $2,300
Edwards Company	11/28/64 for $5,500	2/15/65 for $6,000

(a) Figure the net short-term capital gain or loss in 1965. (b) Figure the net long-term capital gain or loss in 1965. (c) Figure the net gain or loss from the sale of capital assets. (d) Figure the amount of the gain or loss entered as income on the return.

Note: The term "taxable income" as used in this problem refers to taxable income without deduction for exemptions.

5. (a) Amsterdam's income from salary and taxable interest was $20,000. His capital-asset transactions resulted in a net short-term capital gain of $1,200 and a net long-term capital loss of $7,000. His deductions from adjusted gross income to arrive at taxable income amounted to $2,500. What was Amsterdam's taxable income? (b) Blackwell's income from salary and taxable interest was $20,000. His capital-asset transactions resulted in a net short-term capital gain of $1,500 and a net long-term capital gain of $4,000. His deductions from adjusted gross income to arrive at taxable income amounted to $2,500. What was Blackwell's taxable income?

6. State whether the following underlined statements are true or false. Explain briefly. (a) Davis had a net capital loss of $1,500 in 1964 and other income of $7,500. Davis can deduct $1,000 of the net capital loss from other income in 1964. (b) Youngheart Outboards, a local dealer, bought 200 outboard motors on July 15, 1963, for $10,000. On March 20, 1964 the company sold the motors to a boat-rental company for $15,000. Youngheart Outboards had a long-term capital gain of $5,000 in 1964. (c) On April 14, 1964, Lang sold for $2,250 capital assets for which it had paid $1,500. On October 15, 1964 the company sold for $3,000 capital assets for which it had paid $4,500. Lang will show a net capital gain of $750 and a net capital loss of $1,500 on its 1964 return. (d) In 1964 Younger had a net capital loss of $10,000. Younger will offset this loss against net capital gains of $2,000 in 1961, $2,500 in 1962, and $5,500 in 1963.

7. Figure the long-term capital-gain deduction in each of the following:

(a)	Net long-term capital gain or loss	$4,000 Gain
	Net short-term capital gain or loss	None
(b)	Net long-term capital gain or loss	$3,000 Gain
	Net short-term capital gain or loss	1,000 Loss
(c)	Net long-term capital gain or loss	$3,000 Gain
	Net short-term capital gain or loss	1,000 Gain
(d)	Net long-term capital gain or loss	None
	Net short-term capital gain or loss	$3,000 Gain

8. Superior Building Maintenance (a proprietorship) was involved in the following transactions during 1965:

Jan. 1--Sold for $2,900 a tow truck that was bought two years before. At the time of sale, it had an adjusted basis of $2,500.

Jan. 9--Bought for $6,000 a plot of land on which to store cars.

May 29--Sold 500 shares of stock in Superior Waxers, Inc. for $4,000. It bought this stock as an investment on November 29, 1964 for $5,000.

June 17--Sold for $2,000 some office machinery that it had bought three years before for $5,400. Depreciation on the machinery to the date of sale amounted to $2,600.

July 10--Sold for $7,500 the land purchased on Jan. 9.

Sept. 20--Sold for $2,900 an old building it had used for storing auto parts. It cost $5,200 seven years ago, and depreciation to the date of sale amounted to $1,500.

Nov. 3--Sold 10 shares of Broom Manufacturing Corp. stock it had bought on Feb. 13, 1964 for $150. The selling price, less expenses, was $200. Also, during the year taxpayer sold $40,000 worth of used cars that had all been purchased before June 1964 for $25,000.

What is Superior Building Maintenance's net capital gain or loss for the taxable year ending December 31, 1965?

CHAPTER 5

Questions

1. What tax "loophole" is Section 1245 of the Revenue Law of 1962, Section 1250 of the Revenue Law of 1964, and the Cohn Rule of the Internal Revenue Service concerned with?

2. Some transactions which normally do not give rise to taxable income may do so because of the depreciation-recapture rules. Name the transactions which may change.

3. In general, how is depreciation recapture applied to real estate under Section 1250 of the 1964 Revenue Law?

4. When calculating the recapture on the leasehold, what limitation is placed on the write-off period? Assume a lease of 30 years with a renewal option. What is the write-off period if: (a) the option is for 15 years? (b) the option is for 20 years? (c) the option is for 25 years?

5. What test is applied to see whether improvements are substantial and thus subject to recapture?

6. What was the purpose of the Cohn Rule, and what is the future significance of this Rule?

7. Name the special rules which allow individuals who subdivide and sell real property capital-gains treatment.

8. What are the steps that an individual can take to improve his chances of achieving capital gains on subdivided property?

Problems

1. Richard Venning on January 1, 1962 bought a truck to use in his business. He depreciated the cost of the truck, $5,000, using a five-year life and the double-declining-balance method. On December 31, 1964 Richard sold the truck for $4,000. (Ignore any possible application of the Cohn Rule.) Calculate the gain or loss on sale, and indicate the nature of the gain or loss (capital or ordinary).

2. On June 30, 1964 Michael Cork gave his younger brother the car he had used in his business for the past two years. At the date of the gift, the car had a market value of $2,000 and an adjusted basis of $1,000. Michael had bought the car originally for $3,500 and used it only for business purposes during the two years he had owned it. His brother kept the car a year before selling it for $1,500. Because he used the car for business purposes, Michael's brother took $200 depreciation in 1964. (a) What is the treatment of the gain on the sale in 1965? (b) How should the depreciation on the car in 1965 be handled?

3. William White gives to charity a building with a tax basis of $20,000.

The depreciation taken on the building since 1961 up to the date of the gift is $5,000. The building has a market value of $30,000 at the time of the contribution. What deduction is White allowed?

4. Sawyer buys an office building for $205,000 on June 30, 1964 and sells it on December 31, 1967 for $200,000. He had depreciated the building on a 40 years' useful-life basis, using the sum-of-the-years-digits method and assuming no salvage value. Calculate the gain on the sale and indicate whether it is capital or ordinary in nature.

5. Randy Edwards opened a new motel on January 1, 1964. Two and a half years later, in order to meet his competition, he had a swimming pool built. This addition qualified as a "substantial improvement." On December 31, 1969 Edwards sold the motel. At this point he had taken $40,000 additional depreciation on the buildings and $5,000 additional depreciation on the swimming pool. What will the depreciation recapture be: (a) if the gain on the sale is $50,000? (b) If the gain on the sale is $40,000?

6. In the following case, compare the tax situation of John Ellingson for the year 1967 (Show your calculations.): (a) ignoring the Cohn Rule; (b) applying the Cohn Rule. Ellingson built some rental apartments for $100,000. He started operation January 1, 1964. For tax purposes, he depreciated the buildings each year on the double-declining-balance method, assuming a 20-year life. He sold the building for $110,000, on December 28, 1967, and took a full year's depreciation.

7. Mr. Tempres, a lawyer, in 1959 bought a tract of land in the suburbs as an investment. On March 4, 1965 he decided to subdivide the tract and sell it in lots. He was able to sell five lots in 1965 for $1,000 a lot. His basis for each lot was $800. During the time he held the tract, he made no improvements that would substantially increase the value of the particular lots sold, although he did have the underbrush cleared off the property. Mr. Tempres never engaged in real estate operations as a dealer in real estate. (a) How will these transactions affect Tempres' income for 1965? (b) If Mr. Tempres sold six lots in 1965, instead of five, how would the transactions be taxed?

CHAPTER 6

Questions

1. For tax purposes, what is depreciation, and how is it calculated?
2. What is the basis for depreciation?
3. When a taxpayer takes insufficient depreciation or excessive depreciation, how does it affect his tax records?
4. Can a taxpayer change his depreciation methods?
5. What property qualifies for additional first-year depreciation?
6. What requirements must be met in order to use the double-declining-balance method?
7. What is meant by the expression "useful life"?

Problems

1. On January 1, 1965 Williams got a 35-year lease of land owned by Kennan. In January of the next year, Williams built a business building on the property for $50,000. The terms of his lease provided that any improve-

ments placed on the land would become the property of the landlord when the lease ended. He asks you if he can take a deduction on it, and to what extent. (Kennan and Williams are not "related" persons.)

2. State whether the following persons are entitled to a deduction for depreciation and, if so, to what extent (assume that straight-line depreciation is used, and that there is no salvage value): (a) A physician bought an automobile in 1964, paying $3,000 for it. The auto had an estimated life of five years. It is used partly for pleasure and partly in making professional calls. (b) A taxpayer owns a two-family house. He rents the first floor and occupies the second floor. (c) A dentist and his family live on the second and third floors of a house that he owns. He used the entire first floor as an office. (d) Taxpayer bought a piece of land in 1912 for $40,000. The fair market value on March 1, 1913 was $50,000. The value on January 1, 1964 was $35,000. (e) In 1958, a manufacturer of ladies' leather handbags bought stocks of leather, which, owing to changed conditions (styles, and so forth) and shop wear, were not made up into bags. It is estimated that the goods will be worth only one-third their cost at the end of 1964.

3. (a) Jones is a manufacturer of food products. On November 1, 1962, he bought, for $80,000, a five-story residence with 26 rooms. When Jones bought the property, he expected to rent it. He offered it for rent through a real estate agency, improved the heating system, and placed in charge a caretaker who kept it clean, made general repairs, and showed it to prospective tenants. Rental offers were received, but none was satisfactory, and on January 1, 1964, the house was still unoccupied. A reasonable allowance for the depreciation of the building during 1964 was $1,600. Wages paid to the caretaker amounted to $900. Were these amounts deductible in Jones's return for 1964? (b) Black is the auditor of the Holmes Co. On September 1, 1958, he moved into a house in the suburbs which he had just bought for $25,000. On December 22, 1962, Black gave up the house and took an apartment in town. He immediately put the house in the hands of a real estate agent, who showed it to prospective tenants. Rental offers were received but none was satisfactory, and on January 1, 1964, the house was still unoccupied. A reasonable allowance for the depreciation of the building during 1963 was $750. Maintenance expenses during that year amounted to $200. Black also paid real estate taxes of $600 on the property. Were these amounts deductible in Black's return for 1963?

4. When Mr. Clark died in 1961, he left an apartment house to his sister for her life and then to her daughter, Claire. On January 1, 1965, the adjusted basis of the building was $50,000 and the estimated remaining useful life 20 years. On that date the sister's life expectancy was 10 years. What depreciation may be taken on the property, and by whom? Assume that straight-line depreciation is used and that the property has no salvage value.

5. On January 1, 1955, Johnson bought the Elmwood Apartments for $40,000. On January 1, 1957, Johnson gave the property to his son, Ned. On April 1, 1957, Ned exchanged the Elmwood Apartments for the Driftwood Apartments. On January 1, 1964, Ned gave the Driftwood Apartments to his son, Phil, who sold the property on January 1, 1965 for $50,000. Assume

an annual depreciation allowance of $1,000 for both buildings and that no
gift tax had been paid on the transfers. What was the recognized gain to
Phil?

6. A small warehouse was bought on January 1, 1961 for $12,000. The use-
ful life of the warehouse is 10 years. It has no salvage value. The taxpayer took $1,200 depreciation in each of the years 1961 and 1962, but he
failed to claim any depreciation for 1963. In 1964 he claims and is allowed $2,400. Of the $2,400 deducted in 1964, assume that only $1,800
resulted in a tax benefit. What will be the adjusted basis of the property
on January 1, 1965, and to what depreciation deduction will the taxpayer
be entitled for 1965 under the straight-line method?

7. (a) In 1964, the Gordon Construction Corp. built a large apartment house
for $100,000 and leased it to the Tower Rental Company for 80 years. The
Tower Co. rented the house to various tenants for terms from of two to
ten years. Assuming straight-line depreciation and no salvage value, to
what depreciation deduction, if any, is the Tower Company entitled?
(b) On July 1, 1963, Phil Tevis died, leaving an office building to his
son, Seymour, for life and then to Seymour's son, Eric. On January 2,
1964, Seymour sold his life interest to Dave Everly for $70,000. On that
date, the building had an adjusted basis of $125,000, a salvage value of
$5,000, and a useful life of 30 years. On January 2, Seymour's life ex-
pectancy was 20 years. Assuming straight-line depreciation, what is
Everly's deduction for depreciation for the year?

8. What deduction, if any, may be or could have been taken annually for depreciation in the following cases? Figure the deduction in each case.
Assume straight-line depreciation and no salvage value unless otherwise
stated. (a) A completed construction of a factory on January 1, 1965.
The cost was $50,000 and the estimated life 50 years. (b) B bought a
warehouse for $50,000. On the date of purchase, it had a remaining esti-
mated useful life of 10 years and a salvage value of $1,000. Five years
later he made improvements costing $10,000 that extended the life of the
warehouse five years without increasing the salvage value. (c) C, on
August 1, 1964, bought for $100,000 a patent which was issued on August
1, 1957. (d) E completed construction of a building on June 1, 1957, at
a cost of $70,000. Its estimated life was 50 years. On June 1, 1962,
half the building burned down; the other half, after repairs, remained in
use. The value of the building was reduced one-half as a result of the fire.

9. On January 1, 1961, David Cohen bought a new machine for his factory.
At that time the useful life of the machine was determined to be 15 years.
However, at the beginning of 1965, when the machine was four years old,
it became apparent that the machine could be used for 16 more years. On
January 1, 1965, the unrecovered cost of the machine was $1,200. If
Cohen used the liberalized declining-balance method of depreciation, what
deduction can he take for depreciation on the machine for 1965?

10. On January 1, 1965, the Kiley Corporation bought a new machine for
$80,000. The machine had a useful life of eight years and a salvage value
of $8,000. The corporation depreciated the machine using the liberalized
declining-balance method. Also on January 1, 1965, the corporation
bought a new truck for $9,000. Salvage value was $1,000 and the truck
had a useful life of nine years. The corporation uses the sum-of-the-years

digits method of depreciation. Assuming that Kiley Corporation does not elect the additional first-year depreciation on either asset, to what depreciation deduction is it entitled?

11. On January 1, 1965, Dave Henderson bought for $1,500 a new machine for his factory. The machine had a useful life of 20 years and no salvage value. Assume that Henderson did not elect the additional first-year depreciation allowance. Compare the depreciation allowances for the first five years under the straight-line method, the declining-balance method, and the general rule of the sum-of-the-years-digits method.

CHAPTER 7

Questions

1. What is the installment sales method of reporting? Under what circumstances may a taxpayer not elect to use the installment sales method?
2. What amounts are part of the "payments in the year of sale" of an installment sale?
3. What problem may be created if property with a mortgage in excess of the basis of the property is sold in an installment sale?
4. If repossession of property sold under an installment sales contract becomes necessary, what gain or loss is recognized, and what is the basis of the repossessed property?
5. Lack of market value of a buyer's obligations is necessary for the seller to use the deferred-payment method of reporting income. What are possible indications that an obligation has little market value?

Problems

1. In 1964, Clem Hayes, an architect, sold some stock to a friend for $3,000 The stock had been bought in 1961 for $10,000. Hayes received $500 this year (1964), the balance to be paid in five annual installments. Hayes wants to elect the installment method of reporting the transaction. What is the amount of loss to be reported in 1964?
2. Tab Hendricks bought his home in 1961 for $21,000 and sold it on September 21, 1964 for $26,000. Its adjusted basis at the time of sale was $22,000. He received $5,000 at the time of the sale and the balance on January 1, 1965. May he report the gain from this sale on the installment basis? Explain.
3. On January 2, 1964, Jeff Taylor, who is in the business of renting real estate, sold an apartment house for $134,000. Taylor paid $9,000 in commissions and other selling expenses. Scott had bought the building in 1960 for $100,000. From 1960 through 1963, he took $25,000 depreciation deductions on it. The terms of the sale were: cash, $38,000; first mortgage assumed, $54,000; second mortgage for $42,000, payable in seven annual installments of $6,000 each, starting with January 2, 196 Taylor wants to report the sale on the installment plan. (a) What is Taylor's recognized gain in 1964? (b) What will be his recognized gain in 1965?
4. (a) Under what conditions may the sale of personal property by a person other than a dealer be reported on the installment basis? (b) On October 1, 1964, Monroe sold for $60,000 shares of stock in a cooperative apartment house. The shares had been bought on March 1, 1962 for $54,000.

Monroe received $9,000 in cash, stock having a fair market value of
$6,000, and two notes of the buyer, each of which had a face value of
$22,500 and a fair market value when received of $15,000. The first
note was due on October 1, 1965, the second on October 1, 1966. How
should the profit on this transaction be reported, assuming that Adams
uses the installment method? (c) On April 1, 1964, Jefferson, on the
cash basis, sold for $60,000 shares of stock in a cooperative apartment
house. The shares had been bought on March 1, 1961 for $54,000.
Jefferson received $15,000 in cash, bonds having a fair market value of
$7,500, and two notes of the buyer each of which had a face value of
$18,750 and a fair market value when received of $16,500. The first
note was due on April 1, 1965, the second on April 1, 1966. What part,
if any, of the profit on the sale could be deferred beyond 1964? (d) What
would be your answer to (c) if the notes had no fair market value?

5. (a) On October 1, 1963, Drews sold on the installment plan a building that
   he bought on July 1, 1957 for $40,000. The selling price was $70,000,
   as follows: cash, $18,000; first mortgage assumed, $20,000; notes for
   $32,000, payable at the rate of $3,200 semiannually, first payment due
   April 1, 1964. What was Drews' recognized gain for 1963? For 1964?
   (b) The buyer paid $6,400 on the notes in 1964 but did not meet the April
   1, 1964 installment. Drews, who learned that the buyer's notes he still
   held were absolutely worthless, foreclosed and bid in the property for
   $38,000 (first mortgage assumed, $20,000; cancellation of buyer's se-
   cond-mortgage notes to the extent of $18,000). At that time, the fair
   market value of the property was $40,000. Figure the recognized gain
   or loss to Drews.

6. (a) In 1964, Underhill sold for $50,000 several adjoining lots, which he
   had bought in 1957 for $20,000. He received $20,000 in cash and the balance in unsecured notes of $3,000 each, payable one note each year
   starting in 1966 until the total should be paid. The notes had a fair market value when received of $15,000. What part, if any, of the profit on
   the sale could be deferred beyond 1964? Assume that the real estate was
   a capital asset in Underhill's hands. (b) What would your answer be if
   the notes had no fair market value when received?

7. (a) On September 1, 1964, Stahl sold for $40,000 shares of stock in a
   cooperative apartment house. The shares had been bought on February
   1, 1961 for $30,000. Stahl received $6,000 in cash, bonds having a fair
   market value of $4,000, and two notes of the buyer, each of which had a
   face value of $15,000 and a fair market value, when received, of $10,000.
   The first note was due in 1965; the second, in 1966. How should the profit
   on this transaction be reported, assuming that Stahl uses the installment
   method? (b) On March 1, 1964, Somes, who reports on the cash basis,
   sold for $40,000 shares of stock in a cooperative apartment house. The
   shares had been bought on February 1, 1961 for $30,000. Somes re-
   ceived $6,000 in cash, bonds having a fair market value of $8,000, and
   two notes of the buyer, each of which had a face value of $13,000 and a
   fair market value when received of $10,000. The first note was due in
   1965; the second, in 1966. What part, if any, of the profit on the sale
   could be deferred beyond 1964? (c) What would your answer be to (b)
   if the notes had no fair market value?

CHAPTER 8

Questions

1. What tax advantages are often available to owners of property held for lease?
2. What steps can be taken to help avoid the Internal Revenue calling a sale a tax-free exchange with a sale-and-leaseback transaction?
3. Why is it important to distinguish between advance payments and security deposits?
4. Why should agreements for the tenant to restore property at the end of the lease not include ordinary wear and tear?
5. If a building is demolished to obtain a tenant, when is the remaining basis of the building deductible?
6. When is a bonus to a tenant for a lease cancellation deductible by the landlord? What is the usual income tax treatment of the bonus for the lessee (tenant)?
7. What are the dangers of leases with options to buy?

Problems

1. Butterwirth Market owns property with a depreciable base of $7,000,000. Their annual depreciation deduction is $30,000 per year. A local real estate firm offers to buy the property from Butterwirth for $2,000,000 and lease it back to them for $100,000 per year. Butterwirth's vice-president of finance estimates that the proceeds from this sale can be invested in expansion to yield a rate of return after taxes of eight per cent. Assume a 52 per cent tax rate for ordinary income and a 25 per cent rate for capital gains. Should the offer be accepted? Show your calculations.
2. William Johnson entered a lease agreement in 1964 with the Estes Realty Company which called for a payment of $250,000 for the use of a building for 15 years plus a renewal option for an additional 10 years. $170,000 of the $250,000 was for the original period and $80,000 was for the renewal option. (a) Over what period must the lease be amortized? (b) What conditions would change the answer in (a)? (c) What would the period for amortization be if $200,000 was for the original lease and $50,000 was for the renewal option?
3. On January 3, 1964, Avis leased a large lot from Alan Devlin for 50 years. On this he intended to erect a small apartment house. Avis agreed to pay an annual rent of $2,400. Under the terms of the lease, he paid five years' rent ($12,000) in advance. To what deduction for rent is Avis entitled in his 1964 return?
4. Paul Harvey leases a building from Don Foss. The lease agreement calls for annual rent payments of $8,000 with an advance payment of five years' rent. (a) What is Harvey's rent deduction for the first year of the lease? (b) What is Foss's rental income for the first year?
5. Joseph Quietwater leases land from Donald Collins. The agreement provides that Quietwater will pay property taxes relating to the land of $1,500. The rental payments are $5,000. What are the amounts of deductions and income for Quietwater and Collins from this transaction?
6. On March 1, 1962, Keith Winslow bought a piece of land with an old vacant office building on it for $70,000 ($50,000 allocable to the land and $20,000 to the building). When he made the purchase, Winslow intended to tear

down the old office building and replace it with a new apartment building, but financial difficulties forced him to postpone this idea. In the meantime, he leased the old building on April 1, 1962 for two years at an annual rent of $2,000. On April 1, 1964, at the end of the lease, Winslow went ahead with his original plans and demolished the building at a cost of $5,000 and built his apartment house. The new building was completed on December 31, 1964 at a cost of $150,000. The right to receive the $4,000 rent as of April 1, 1962 was valued at $3,400. (a) What deductions, if any, can Winslow take in 1964? (b) What is the basis of the property (land and building) after construction of the new building?

7. Edward Silver is the owner of two pieces of real property. On January 2, 1962 he leased Lot A to a finance company for a term of 25 years. The company agreed to pay a yearly rental of $5,000, and to erect on the leased ground a small office building costing $40,000. The building was completed on January 3, 1964. Straight-line depreciation on the building, based on its estimated life of 20 years, is $2,000. To what deduction is the finance company entitled for 1964?

8. (a) In 1959 Avery West bought a parcel of vacant property for $25,000. On January 1, 1960, he leased it to Dilworth Real Estate Corporation for five years. The rent is $2,000 a year. Dilworth Real Estate immediately built a warehouse on the property at a cost of $10,000. The lease provides that improvements made by the lessee on the leased property become the property of West. When the lease ended on December 31, 1964, the fair market value of the land and the building was $52,000 (land, $40,000; building, $12,000). How much should West include in his gross income in 1964 as the result of the transaction? (b) Would your answer to (a) be different if the lease had provided that the tenant had a choice either to pay the annual rent or build a $10,000 building?

9. Smith leases property from Jones. The lease agreement has 10 years remaining and calls for straight annual rental payments of $10,000 per year. Smith no longer needs the leasehold. He has a choice of assigning his right or subletting to Brown. The assignment would call for a $40,000 payment to Smith, and Brown would pay Jones the annual rental payments of $10,000. If it was sublet, Smith would receive $15,000 per year and he would pay Jones. Which alternative is best for Smith? Assume a 25 per cent capital-gain tax and a 50 per cent rate for ordinary income.

CHAPTER 9

Questions

1. What are "fixing-up" expenses, and how do they affect income taxes?
2. How is the special rule concerning residences applied when the taxpayer has more than one residence?
3. When a homeowner purchases more than one new residence within the year, how is the special rule applied?
4. If at the end of the tax year no replacement of a residence sold during the year has been made and a year has not passed since the sale, what are the reporting requirements?
5. How much of a casualty loss on a residence can be deducted?
6. Of what importance is it that a piece of property be business property rather than investment property?

7. How does the tax law view members of a cooperative apartment? What are the tax consequences of this position?

Problems

1. Peter Smith bought a home in 1946 for $20,000. On March 15, 1965 he sold it for $40,000. During the 90-day period prior to the sale, fixing-up repairs amounting to $1,500 were done. Selling expenses were $2,000. Smith purchased a new home costing $35,000 on December 1, 1965. How is the gain on the sale of the old residence handled?

2. In addition to the data given in Problem 1, assume that Peter Smith had built a skylight in his roof in 1950 at a cost of $3,000. How is the gain on the sale of the residence handled? What is the basis of the new residence?

3. Blanchard was living in a residence which he had purchased in 1960 for $25,000 when he inherited another residence. Blanchard sold his current residence and moved into the inherited home. Using the following data, what gain, if any is taxable, and what is the tax basis of the new residence (Ignore any time requirements.)

Sales price of old home	$40,000
Market value of new home	25,000
Cost base of new home on the books of the deceased	17,000
Improvements to new home	30,000
Fixing-up expenses on old home	1,000
Selling expenses on old home	2,000

4. The following details refer to a switch in residences during 1966 by Lee and Jane Atwood. Using this information, determine the following: (a) Gain realized; (b) Gain taxed in current year, if any; (c) Gain postponed; (d) The basis of the new residence.

Old residence sold on March 10, 1966:

Original cost	$17,950
Improvements (swimming pool)	3,500
Sales price	31,000
Mortgage paid off with sales proceeds	9,000
Penalty for prepayment on mortgage	250
Fixing-up expenses	300
Refund on insurance	200
Moving expenses	800
Commission paid on sale	1,800
Real estate taxes for 1/1/66 to 3/9/66 paid to purchaser	110

New residence purchased on April 18, 1966:

Purchase price	$26,000
New fence built (5/1/66)	500
Painting rooms in new house	1,000
Title search	500
Fire insurance	300
Mortgage on new residence	10,000
Real estate taxes for 1/1/66 to 4/17/66 received from seller	150

5. On February 15, 1964, Ken Young sells his residence for $40,000. He had paid $20,000 for the home. Fixing-up expenses were $1,500. Selling expenses were $2,000. Three months later, Young purchased a new home

costing $35,000. Assuming that the sales contract on the old residence
qualified for the installment-sales treatment and that Young received
$10,000 in 1964, how much of the gain is taxable at the end of 1964?

6. Robert Dunn, age 67, sells his home for $40,000. He has lived in this
home for the past 10 years with his wife Mary. They now plan to retire
and rent a cottage in Pleasant Hills. The old home had cost Dunn $23,000.
Selling costs were $1,500 and fixing-up expenses were $800. How much
of the gain on the sale of the old residence is taxable?

7. (a) On January 2, 1961, Everest purchased a residence for $9,000, of
which $6,000 was allocable to the building. At that time the building had
an estimated life of 30 years. The property was used as his personal
residence until January 30, 1964, at which time the house and lot were
sold for $12,500. Assume that no other residence was purchased within
one year before or after the sale. How does the sale affect Everest's return for 1963? (b) If Everest sold the property on January 30, 1964, and
the amount realized was $6,000, how would the sale affect his return for
1964? (c) Same as (b), except that Everest rented one-half his residence
to a boarder.

8. Steve Chapman purchased a residence for $70,000. He later converted
the residence to rental property. At the time of this conversion, the
property had a market value of $65,000. Since the conversion, depre-
ciation of $6,000 has been taken. If the property is sold for $63,000,
what is the gain or loss?

9. (a) Using the data in Problem 8 and assuming that, when the residence
was converted to rental property, it had an expected life of 20 years, what
would be the yearly depreciation deduction allowed, using the straight-
line method? (b) What would your answer be if the market value had been
$75,000? (c) What would your answer be if the cost of the residence had
been $60,000?

10. A cooperative owns a building costing $2,000,000, with no salvage value,
expected to last until December 31, 1985. There is a $500,000 mortgage
on the building. The cooperative has 10,000 shares issued (including
treasury stock). Jim Christiansen buys 100 shares for $25,000 on January
1, 1966. What depreciation deduction can Christiansen take for 1966
(using the straight-line method)?

CHAPTER 10

Questions

1. What is the difference between the personal liability of a joint tenant and
that of a tenant in common? How is this difference reflected in the deductibility of expenses paid by one tenant which exceeded his pro-rata share?

2. Which of the following are not included by a partnership in calculating its
net income? (a) Short-term capital gains; (b) Salaries paid to partners
for services (determined without regard to income); (c) Salaries paid to
employees; (d) Taxes paid to foreign governments; (e) Charitable contributions; (f) Interest on a note to a bank; and (g) Depreciation on store
fixtures.

Problems

1. Collins and Segram own property as joint tenants. During the year, Collins pays all the expenses related to the property ($1,000). (a) What are

Collins' and Segram's allowable deductions? (b) What would be their allowable deductions if they were tenants in common?

2. Jo Alden, his brother Phil, and their respective wives inherited a farm worth $390,000 as tenants in common. Each received an equal share of the profits from the farm. Jo's wife owned adjoining land worth $210,000. It was agreed to farm this land on the same profit-sharing basis. Jo and Phil each gave Jo's wife $70,000 to transfer title to Jo, Phil, herself, and Phil's wife as joint tenants with right of survivorship. When Jo died, the farm was valued at $430,000 and the adjoining land was valued at $270,000 What amount should be included in Jo's gross estate for these properties, if the executor adopts those values for estate tax purposes?

3. Clay and Luke are business partners. According to the partnership agreement, Clay is to share 60 per cent of the net profit or loss of the partnership and Luke, 40 per cent. In 1964, Clay gave $500 to the Red Cross and Luke gave $200 to the Community Chest. Also, $309 was donated to the Heart Fund in the name of the partnership. Clay received a salary of $6,000 from the partnership and Luke, $5,000. Clay had a personal medical expense deduction for the year of $400. Luke paid real estate taxes on his residence amounting to $500. Both partners are single and have no dependents. The partnership books showed a gross profit of $20,000 for the year. The partnership and the partners all report on a calendar-year basis. Assuming that there are no other deductions, either to the partnership or to the partners, for 1964, (a) What is the partnership taxable income? (b) What is each partner's taxable income? (c) If there had been net partnership loss for the year, would the partnership have to file a return? Explain.

4. During the year, the partnership of Collins and Brass had income of $26,000 and gains of $15,000 on Section 1231 assets. Collins had a personal long-term capital loss of $10,000. The partnership agreement provided that profits were to be divided equally, but it was decided to amend the agreement in such a way that Collins would be allocated all the gain from the Section 1231 assets and Brass would be allocated an additional portion of the profits such that the total income and gain combined of each of the partners would be equal. What amounts of income and gain would be reported on each partner's return?

CHAPTER 11

Questions

1. What are the factors that are considered in determining whether an organization is or is not a corporation?
2. What steps should be taken if it is desired to form a limited partnership and not a corporation?
3. Four basic groups of tests must be met in order for a trust to qualify as a real estate investment trust. What are they?
4. What restrictions are placed upon the types of income that a real estate investment trust can receive?

Problems

1. The Real Estate Investment Trust started operations in 1964. The following dates relate to the first three years of operations.

	Income		Dividends	
	Capital Gains	Operating	Capital Gains	Operating
1964	--	$ 50,000	--	$20,000
1965	$40,000	100,000	$20,000	50,000
1966	10,000	90,000	5,000	80,000

Assuming that the proper elections are made, what is the <u>maximum</u> amount that Real can claim for each type of dividend in 1964 and 1965? Is Real a qualified real estate investment trust in 1964 and 1965?

2. Assume that Brooks Real Estate Investment Trust had the following assets at the end of its quarter ending in March:

Cash	$ 12,000
Government securities	8,000
Real estate assets	60,000
Common stock of Signet Milk Company	8,000
Common stock of Opheim Dust Company	12,000
Total assets	$100,000

Signet Milk Company has $80,000 of voting stock outstanding. Opheim Dust Company has $60,000 of voting stock outstanding. What must Brooks do if it wishes to be taxed as a real estate investment corporation?

CHAPTER 12

Questions

1. What tax factors should be considered in order to determine the best ownership form of property? What non-tax factors are involved in selecting the best ownership form?
2. What are the characteristics which result in an enterprise being taxed as a corporation?

Problems

1. John Jones and Gary Robinson decide to form a corporation. The corporation is authorized to issue 1,000 shares. John Jones contributes land and a building to the corporation for 450 shares. The land cost John Jones $50,000 and has a market value of $80,000. The building cost $40,000 and has a market value of $100,000. Gary Robinson contributes equipment which cost him $15,000 and which has a market value of $20,000, and he received 50 shares in exchange. (a) Is there a taxable gain or loss to either man? (b) What is the basis of each man's stock? (c) What is the basis of the contributed assets to the corporation?
2. Frank Curcio forms a corporation, exchanging some land for all its common stock. The land cost $20,000, has a fair market value of $100,000, and is mortgaged for $50,000. The mortgage is assumed by the corporation. Is there a taxable gain to Frank Curcio? What is the basis of his stock? What is the basis of the land to the corporation?

CHAPTER 13

Questions

1. Compare the way a corporation handles capital gains with the way an individual treats them.
2. Consolidated tax returns can be advantageous to a group of related corporations. What relationship must exist before consolidated tax returns can

be filed? Is the election to file a consolidated return binding?

3. The Wharton Corporation plans to liquidate completely, and it has a purchaser for its assets, which have appreciated in value over the corporation's cost basis. However, if the corporation sells the assets, it will
normally have to pay a tax on any gain. Then, when the proceeds of the
sale are distributed to the stockholders, the stockholders will have to pay
a capital-gains tax on the difference between the amount of the proceeds
and the basis of their stock. How can the corporation avoid such double
taxation?

Problems

1. (a) All the shares of the Ellsworth Co., Inc. are owned by John Ellsworth
and his brother Henry. During the year, the gross income of Ellsworth
Co., Inc. was as follows:

Gross profit from sales	$50,000
Dividends	70,000
Interest	60,000
Rents (race track)	40,000
Expenses on rental property	20,000

Is the Ellsworth Co., Inc. a personal holding company? Explain. (b) All
the shares of the Savage Co., Inc. are owned by James Savage and his
sister Mary. During the year, the gross income of Savage Co., Inc. was
as follows:

Gross profit from sales	$ 30,000
Dividends	70,000
Interest	60,000
Rents (race track)	150,000
Expenses on rental property	70,000

Is the Savage Co., Inc. a personal holding company? Explain. (c) All
the shares of the Epstein Co., Inc. are owned by Frank Epstein and his
son Stanley. During the year, the gross income of Epstein Co., Inc. was
as follows:

Gross profit from sales	$90,000
Dividends	45,000
Interest	44,000
Rents (race track)	46,000
Expenses on rental property	25,000

Is the Epstein Co., Inc. a personal holding company? Explain.

2. Belair Corporation, owned by Robert Christionsen, owns four pieces of
rental property. Since 1963 there has been $30,000 "additional depre-
ciation" taken on this property. On June 30, 1965, Christionsen decides
to liquidate the corporation under Section 337. The rental properties are
sold for $100,000. There are no other assets or liabilities. Christionsen's
stock has a basis of $40,000. Using a 75 per cent recapture rate, deter-
mine what his taxable gain will be.

3. Assume the same details as in Problem 2 except that a "one-month (Section 333)" liquidation is adopted instead of a "Section 337" liquidation. At
the time of liquidation, Belair Corporation had retained earnings of
$20,000 and a book value for the property of $50,000. What will be the
result of this liquidation? (Assume a 50 per cent corporate tax rate.)

Index